Springer Texts in Business and Economics

Springer Texts in Business and Economics (STBE) delivers high-quality instructional content for undergraduates and graduates in all areas of Business/Management Science and Economics. The series is comprised of self-contained books with a broad and comprehensive coverage that are suitable for class as well as for individual self-study. All texts are authored by established experts in their fields and offer a solid methodological background, often accompanied by problems and exercises.

Yuji Aruka

Evolutionary Economics

Springer

Yuji Aruka
Kyoto University of Advanced Science
Kyoto, Japan

ISSN 2192-4333 ISSN 2192-4341 (electronic)
Springer Texts in Business and Economics
ISBN 978-981-97-1381-3 ISBN 978-981-97-1382-0 (eBook)
https://doi.org/10.1007/978-981-97-1382-0

This Springer imprint is published by the registered company Springer Nature Singapore Pte Ltd.
The registered company address is: 152 Beach Road, #21-01/04 Gateway East, Singapore 189721, Singapore

Paper in this product is recyclable.

Preface

The economics I have studied have always offered implicit information about the economic system. First, I was given a truly vague understanding of the market economic system and market transactions. In general equilibrium theory textbooks, exchange is treated as barter, but the question of whether barter is possible in a huge system was not even addressed. Traditional elementary economics is totally indifferent to the historical and social evolution of the environment, be it in relation to market systems or market transactions. Traditional elementary economics, whether related to market systems or market transactions, is completely indifferent to the historical and social evolution of the environment. Perhaps this type of economist espouses the idea of adiabatic approximation to justify the molecular theory of households and firms.

In particular, modern economics uphold the absolute belief that rational economic optimisation can be justified without specifying the external, social and geopolitical environment in detail. Even more curiously, traditional economics does not need to examine in detail the functions and role of government, even though the government, as an economic actor directly or indirectly controls more than half of the nation's economic activity. Governments also have a strong influence over financial activities through the operation of their huge pension funds and can control banking activities through the central bank. In this light, the familiar picture of the economic system needs to be reconsidered. The main economic activity is not simply carried out by firms and households but by governments and banks, which by far are of vital importance.

Today, the Government is not a night watchdog state. In fact, it is common for public services such as police, prisons, water and sewerage to be privatised. The night watchdog state, similar to primitive, uncivilised societies, is a figment of the imagination. In political science, government is bound by a system of separation of powers and is not run fairly by impartial and selfless politicians and officials. Currently, the government is the largest corporation with the biggest asset. The difference between the government and ordinary business is whether it has the power to tax or not. In this context, the government will be a corporation with the right of taxation. Governments can then arrange and enter into profit-making businesses while collecting taxes. Furthermore, governments can also make financial investments and real investments.

In the second half of the last century, the assumption in economics textbooks was that the elements of the economic system were called economic agents and consisted of households, firms and the government; moreover, markets were assumed to emerge from the interaction of households and firms, either voluntarily or through government regulation. However, the actual growth of the economic system and markets cannot take place without the jurisdiction of the government and the banking system. In particular, the inherent national economy could not operate without the banking institutes being closely associated with the government. Therefore, we regard the government as a corporation.

In this light, the familiar economic system diagram keenly needs to be reconsidered. This book then develops a plan for exiting our economics of a long dome that covers and encircles us.

We note that our evolutionary economics does not target the integrative comprehension of the realistic movements of economic entities. Perhaps we only provide the readers with a useful set of smart tools to detect the underlying building blocks for economic analysis. The integrative analysis may belong to social philosophy. Thus, our textbook is composed of the following parts:

Part I Critical assessments of economics
Part II Evolution of economic ideas
Part III Evolutionary reconstruction of economics
Part IV Elementary stochastic methods for economics

*Finally, the author heartily acknowledges the whole activities of Japan Association for Evolutionary Economics since its founding year of 1997 in Kyoto.

Nishiyama, Kyoto-city, Japan Yuji Aruka, Ph.D.
December 2023

The First Published List

This book contains the published contents previously written by the author himself. The correspondence between the chapters in this publication and previously published papers is given below. Parts of this publication are newly written, while the remainder draws on some or all of the previous articles. A list of first publications is given below for each chapter.

Part I. Critical assessments of economics	
Chapter 1	uses some content of the article titled: "The role of money," JPS Conf. Proc. 40, 011009, 2023
Chapter 2	is a newly written chapter, and also uses Sect. 3/4 of the article titled: "The rise of pure economics under a new form of scholasticism in view of the present socio-economic system, Evolutionary and Institutional Economics Review, Springer Nature, 12(1), pp. 3–29, 2015
Chapter 3	uses Sect. 5/8, ibid.
Chapter 4	uses the article titled: "Interpreting the iterated dilemma games using the presentation like 'cellular automatons'," Evolutionary and Institutional Economics Review, 15, pp. 351–365, 2018
Part II. Evolution of economic ideas	
Chapter 5	uses Sects. 2.1/2.3 of the chapter titled: "Sytemic risks in the evolution of complex social systems." In Aruka Y and Kirman A(eds), Economic Foundations for Social Complexity Science—Theory, Sentiments, and Empirical Laws, Springer Nature, pp. 19–49 (Chap. 2), 2017
Chapter 6	uses Sect. 2.4, ibid.
Chapter 7	uses the chapter titled: "A step forward to the future society," Digital Designs for Money, Markets, and Social Dilemmas, Springer Nature Singapore, pp. 1–31 (Chap. 1), 2020

(continued)

(continued)

Part III. Evolutionary reconstruction of economics	
Chapter 8	uses a multiple some sources. Sections 8.1 and 8.2 corresponds to Sect. 1/2 of the article titled: Hodgson's bibliometric report and the reconstruction plan of economics, Evolutionary and Institutional Economics Review, 15(1), pp. 189–202, 2018; Sect. 8.3 uses Sect. 2 of "Formulating social interactions in utility theory of economics". In Takayasu, H.(ed.), The Application of Econophysics, Springer, Tokyo, pp. 322–329, 2004; Sects. 8.4/8.6 was newly written in English but originally appeared in Japanese, as Sect. 1/2 of 'A microscopic reconstruction in view of evolutionary economics (in Japanese)," Keizai-Ronso (The economic review), Kyoto University Economic Society, 192(2), pp. 1–29, 2018.
Chapter 9	uses Sect. 9.3/9.8 was newly written in English but originally appeared in Japanese, as Sect. 3/4 of "A microscopic reconstruction in view of evolutionary economics (in Japanese)," Keizai-Ronso (The economic review), Kyoto University Economic Society, 192(2), pp.1–29, 2018.
Chapter 10	uses the article titled: "The evolution of the exchange process: from the decentralized to the distributed digital exchange," Evolutionary and Institutional Economics Review, 17(2), pp. 379–398, 2017
Chapter 11	uses the article titled: "Some new perspectives on the inter-country analysis of the world production system," Evolutionary and Institutional Economic Review, 14(2):467–498, 2017.
Part IV. Elementary stochastic methods for economics	
Chapter 12	uses 6.1–6.3 of the chapter titled: The complexities generated by the movement of the market economy, in Aruka Y, Evolutionary Foundations of Economic Science, Springer Japan and New York, pp. 153–159, 2014; also uses 5.3.4–5.4.3 of the chapter titled: The evolution of the market and its growing complexity, ibid.
Chapter 13	uses as Sect. 13.2/13.3 the Sect. 6.4 of the chapter, ibid, pp. 178–193, and also uses the article titled: "An examination of market mechanism with redundancies motivated by Turing's rule selection," Evolutionary and Institutional Economic Review, 16(1), pp. 19–42, 2019 (This paper was prepared solely by Yuji Aruka as the first/corresponding author himself).
Chapter 14	uses the article titled: "On the analytical methods considered essential by Prof. Masanao Aoki in his Japanese textbook." In Aoyama H, Aruka Y, Yoshikawa H. (esd): Complexity, Heterogeneity, and the Methods of Statical. Physics in Economics: Essays in Memory of Msanao Aoki, Springer Nature, 2020, pp. 39–65 (Chap. 3).

Contents

Part II Evolution of Economics

Part I

Critical Assessments of Economics

The Role of Money 1

Abstract

Each person's interest follow from each person's history. The role of money is one of the most important issues in the economy. However, the author's reasons for dealing with it first are rooted not only in economic importance but also personal reasons. An account of these personal reasons will provide a rather unique viewpoint on of the research subject. My paternal ancestor was a samurai positioned "shoinban," a regular member of the military guard of the inner palace of a feudal lord (Ogasawara Family). In the closing days of the Tokugawa shogunate, my great grand father was appointed to serve as a currency handling officer for his lord. He then became familiar with both for mint technology and money transactions. Due to his connection, my grandfather was successfuly employed as an operative officer by the Mint of the new Japanese government (Osaka Mint) at the begining of the new era established in 1868. Later, my grandfather changed his careers to enter the spinning industry, in which he then became an executive of one of the three major companies. This is a major reason why the author was interested in economics and the role of money. Readers will learn that the role of money will be seen deeply some historical dynamism, although this chapter never investigates the detailed history of money in general. This chapter will simply give a concise understanding an essential part of the creation of money during the modern times.

1.1 What You Need to Learn from New Economics?

1.1.1 A Historical View

Historically, the East India Company was a state-owned enterprise. Governments have always played a major economic role in the market. This has not changed at all in modern times, but has even been strengthened. In fact, cabinet ministries in developed countries are registered as joint stock companies on the New York Stock Exchange. Cabinet ministries have already acquired a legal economic function that

Y. Aruka, *Evolutionary Economics*, Springer Texts in Business and Economics,
https://doi.org/10.1007/978-981-97-1382-0_1

allows them to act independently of nation-state decision-making. Today, pension funds and other funds are important sources of mutual funds. Governments play a crucial role in finance as well as in the ordering of goods and services. Textbooks have so far overlooked these important facts.

An examination of the history of the Bank of England shows that the international financial superiority of London and England could not have been realized unless the Government had co-operated with the financial institutions in digesting government bonds.

> **The city of London** takes responsibility for supporting the financial services industry and representing its interests.[1]

In general, the central government has a stake in the central bank, but it is not uncommon for municipalities to also have a stake in banks. The Tokyo Metropolitan Government is also a major investor in TOKYO Kiraboshi Financial Group, Inc. The most prominent example is the City of London Corporation.[2]

Thus, Adam Smith's invisible hand is a philosophical ideal rather than a reality. The author also hopes that the freedom of firms and households to act in their own economic interests will produce the best results. Before making this argument, however, I would like to make the reader aware of what the market has actually been like. What I describe below here is not a substantial ideological challenge to existing theories. It is simply an attempt to point out one of the differences between the economic picture usually taught in introductory economics and the actual economy. What follows is not a major breakthrough in economics but merely a summation of what has already been said on the street for a long time. Fear (2006) then cited the next excerpt form Adam Smith.

> Masters are always and everywhere in a sort of tacit but constant and uniform combination not to raise the wages of workers. . . . Masters. . .sometimes enter into particular combinations to sink the level of wages. . . These are always conducted with the utmost silence and secrecy. . .Wherever there is great property, there is great inequality. Civil government, so far as it is instituted for the security of property, is in reality, instituted for the defence of the rich against the poor, or of those who have some property against those who have none at all...Perfect liberty can never happen if government heeds or is entrusted to the mean rapacity, the monopolizing spirit of merchants and manufacturers who neither are, nor ought to be the rulers of mankind.[3]

First of all, the government is not a neutral and impartial actor, but in fact, in collaboration with banks and other financial institutions, it actively promotes eco-

[1] "History and Heritage". City of London website. Archived from the original on 18 May 2013. Retrieved 13 January 2013. https://www.cityoflondon.gov.uk/things-to-do/history-and-heritage.
[2] See the article of Wikipedia "The City of London Corporation" https://en.wikipedia.org/wiki/City_of_London_Corporation.
[3] Wealth of Nations (1776) excerpt: By Adam Smith: http://www.hartford-hwp.com/archives/25/035.html.

Table 1.1 A bank's balance sheet

				(unit: bln)
Assets			Liability	
	Reserves		Deposit	¥600
	Excess	¥40		
	Required	¥60		
Loans		¥500		
Total		¥600	Total	¥600

nomic activity. The government can accommodate enormous amounts of money through taxation without going through the market. Banks are also institutions that, like governments, are granted privileges that citizens are not allowed to enjoy. Under the double-entry bookkeeping system of the banking industry, when a bank lends money, the bank's 'assets' increase by the amount lent. The more it lends, the more its assets increase. In other words, when banking and double-entry bookkeeping are combined, assets come from the sky. However, if a partial reserve ratio system is implemented by the government, the lending limit is fixed by the reserve ratio. Within this limit, banks will be able to lend funds that they do not own in advance and will be able to demand repayment on their loans. This is the open secret of banking.

The open secret of bank loan under the fractional reserve system

Under the double-entry bookkeeping system of the banking industry, when a bank lends money, the bank's 'assets' increase by the amount lent. The more it lends, the more its assets increase. In other words, when banking and double-entry bookkeeping are combined, assets come from the sky. However, if a partial reserve ratio system is implemented by the government, the lending limit is fixed by the reserve ratio. Within this limit, banks will be able to lend funds that they do not own in advance and will be able to demand repayment on their loans. The open secret of banking may appear in the form of Table 1.1 described below.

It is noted that the balance sheet describes the ex post relationship of the transactions. However, the real transaction takes time. After passage of the several periods, the loan appreciates in its real value. If the borrower is unable to repay the loan, the bank can legally seize the collateral. When Soddy (1934), Nobel laureate in 1921,[4] wrote his book titled Role of Money, he isolated the fact that money creation entails the debtor of its user.

> It appears to do so only because the vendors receiving new money for wealth given up consider themselves paid, whereas they are not paid but owed.

[4] Frederic Soddy was Chemist who was awarded Nobel Prize Chemistry in 1921. In economics field, he is also well known as a pioneering ecological economist.

1.1.1.1 Bankers' Privilege

To what constituent of the national wealth will the part to be appropriated as the asset of the bank correspond?

> Bankers' privilege
>
> As long as the banker holds the right to use it as his or her asset, the banker will have the privilege to occupy the loan in advance has been fulfilled.

We suppose money is a legal tender for the payment of debt. Money is then the debt to the owner for a certain value of marketable property on demand. To put money into sense, the creator of the money would need to receive approval from a socially consenting party. This will be easily understood by citing the work put "gas" in to create a digital currency such as **Ethereum**. Thus, money is not value but the debt held by the money creator to people's wealth. In other words, the government owes the debt to a part of national wealth. This is because ordinary citizens are never a consenting party to the initial exchange, which creates money in the first instance that people failed to see its vital national importance. Thus, money is not value but the debt to people's wealth. In short, money in this context is an **I. O. U.** (= I owe you), i.e., certificate of loan.

Money can exchange against a part of national wealth. What we want to evoke here is not a criticism of the system. It is simply that when observing the economic system, the trinity of households, corporations and a neutral government is nothing more than a fairy tale.

1.1.2 Banking and Slavery

Consider simple "slavery". As labour is a special commodity and cannot be bartered, money is needed to pay for labour. However, enslaved people do not own anything, including everyday goods, other than their own labour. The slave owner advances the enslaved person a week's wages. The enslaved person therefore repays the interest on the wage borrowed from the master one week after the advance. This practice actually existed historically. In fact, Karl Marx, in his *Theory of Capital*, adopted "the wage payment in advance" hypothesis and observed even in modern factories that profit could be recovered from the wage payment W. If the input costs other than labour should be zero, and if the profit rate is written R, then the cost price P of the product produced by one unit of slave labour is $P = (1 + R)W$. It is important to note that the amount of profit RW is generated simply by using slave labour, i.e., it implies that profit is expressed in terms of wage, not labour.

Something similar occurs in bank loan lending. Under a partial reserve ratio system, banks can lend out more money than they hold and collect it with interest. This can be easily seen in bank bookkeeping, i.e., the bank's balance sheet. Of course, this is never allowed for individuals. Everyone knows this, but the legal basis as to why only banks are allowed to do so is unclear.

Thus far, economics is indifferent to the study of reality in the basic economic environment. Although many agents, whether firms or households, are evolving, we prefer the entities of agents to be fixed over time, not evolving as they normally do in economics. We believe that producer cannot be consumer, or vice versa.

1.2 Money in View of Economic Theory

As Keynes (1925) recognized, there is domestically little importance of gold standard. The gold standard may be internationally convenient if the international trade is taken into account.

Historically, the bankers owed gold to the extent of their clients "deposits plus the outstanding note-issue in circulation." The bankers soon began to lend not gold but their own notes or promises to repay gold that neither they nor their depositors possessed. This was a continued **virtual wealth** emergence. The borrowers could repay their loan by the bankers notes, i.e., note issue in circulation. Otherwise, money would remain inconvertible forever. This fact is easily observed through the circulation of regional or community currency.

1.2.1 Introduction of Money into a Barter Economy

We suppose that money is introduced into a barter economy. We then examine what kind of processes can accept money. We suppose that there is a toy model of "barter transaction among multiple agents like firms and households." Needless to say, nobody can drive an economy without money. We have several ideas. First, we set in from heaven in a barter system (Helicopter money). Second, divert the households deposit. Third, wages are paid to labor in advance by capitalist.[5]

In short, someone must throw some fund into the system to initiate transactions. This procedure is also indispensable when some cryptocurrency is created. The property of money is specified by the method of initial input. Naturally, there will be a difference in the method of repayment and the timing of payment. It is interesting to see the helicopter money case. It matters how it is possible to destroy this money without collecting it.

As we know, we often see the exchange of bills in commercial transactions. The issue of a bill allows a company to appropriate funds for production without having to borrow money, provided that the other party acknowledges that it has achieved a reliable result. Hence, it is seen that banking is not an indispensable means but a special means to appropriate the funds of firms/households. On the other hand, banking works well if it needs a large amount of fund. However, it is commonly admitted that there are **the two types of banking**, i.e., the full reserve banking and the partial/fractional reserve banking. The latter is currently the broadly accepted

[5] In this case, capitalist are refunded with interest from worker.

version. Therefore, in the following, we will argue that money creation results through banking.

1.2.2 The Opinion of the First-Rated Economists on the Banking System

The issuance of banknotes and the establishment of the banking system in the political history of the United States has an epic history that is still unsettled. Instead of discussing politics, as an economist, I present here how arguments in economics depict this history.

Simple questions about the partial reserve ratio system will be raised as follows. An individual's cheque book does not allow him to lend beyond the extent of deposits he or she holds. However, if you are a banker, you can lend out 7–10 times the amount of deposits you hold. This system of allowing banks to lend is known as a partial reserve ratio system. However, this system can lead to banks going bankrupt when the economy deteriorates and they are unable to recover the money they have lent out. However, apart from a few libertarians, it has been taboo to discuss the acceptability of this system.

Going back to 1930, the so-called Chicago plan on the partial reserve ratio had been proposed by the first-rated economists. They actively recommended it to the US president. Among them, Professor Irving Fisher, not Chicago but Yale University, was the outstanding economist in the first half of the last century, as nobody ought to complain of about this appreciation shown here. However, few no longer have known that Fisher was the earnest adherent of the full reserve rate system of banking system.[6] However, he shared the same opinion with the Chicago plan led by University of Chicago's economists.

> The Chicago plan was a monetary and banking reform program suggested in the wake of the Great Depression by a group of University of Chicago economists including Henry Simons, Garfield Cox, Aaron Director, Paul Douglas, Albert G. Hart, Frank Knight, Lloyd Mints and Henry Schultz. Its main provision was to require 100% reserves on deposits subject to check, so that "the creation and destruction of effective money through private lending operations would be impossible". The plan, in other words, envisaged separating the issuing from the lending of money. This, according to its authors, would prevent the money supply from cyclically varying as bank loans were expanded or contracted. In addition, the payment system would become perfectly safe. No great monetary contraction as that of 1929–1933 could ever occur again.[7]

[6] 100% reserve banking is called narrow banking, or sovereign money system.
[7] Cited from Wikipedia article: Chicago plan.

1.2.3 The Chicago Plan and the Full Reserve Rate Banking

Interestingly, the idea of 100% reserves on checking deposits would be advocated by the first rate economists including Irving Fisher of Yale, Lauchlin Currie of Harvard. Notably, they argued in favor of the "narrow banking" proposal. However, the Chicago plan, mainly promoted by those at the University of Chicago, a stronghold of US economics, recommended the full reserve ratio system for banks to the president, although this history has now faded from memory, except for in the minds of some economists.

Irving Fisher rightly and enthusiastically demonstrated the necessity of 100% reserves on checking deposits. However, he was interested in a practically better working of loan creation by banking as well as business cycles. He was the originator of subjective interest theory and therefore did not go deep into the macrofoundations of bank lending.

1.3 Frederick Soddy, Nobel Laureate of Chemistry in 1921 and his Insights on Money

1.3.1 Soddy Compared with Fisher

Compared with Fisher, Professor Frederic Soddy was smarter on this issue. The difference between Fischer and Soddy is identifiable by the different ways in which the economy itself is perceived. Fisher's idea about wealth was rather grounded to subjective justification, in particular, the interest rate was connected to **time preference**.

On the other hand, Soddy had a different view from many economists about the definition of wealth. Wealth belonged to a "flow" concept that is subject to the natural process and, ultimately, to **laws of matter and energy**. Here, there is not real distinction in physical science between animate and inanimate energy. Soddy emphasized in that we escape from "the merely subjective views we derive from our own means of livelihood and bank balance".[8] This was a big difference from Fisher's attitude to economics.

Soddy, as chemist, was surprized to see that Keynse (1919) [and other economists] think that the law of compound interest is the law of increment of wealth rather than that of debts, which offesets it against the Malthusian law of population increase.

> Soddy also criticized traditional monetary policy theories for seemingly ignoring the fact that "real wealth" is derived from using energy to transform physical objects, and that these physical objects are inescapably subject to the laws of entropy, or inevitable decline and disintegration. Gronewold (2009)

[8] We can see the idea of thermodynamic law from the next observation:"The opposite for every minus there is a plus is not true of wealth, because we are dealing with the availability of energy rather than with its total amount, and because of the natural tendency of all available or wealth-forming energy to pass, more or less quickly, into the waste heat of uniform temperature of the surroundings." Soddy (1921).

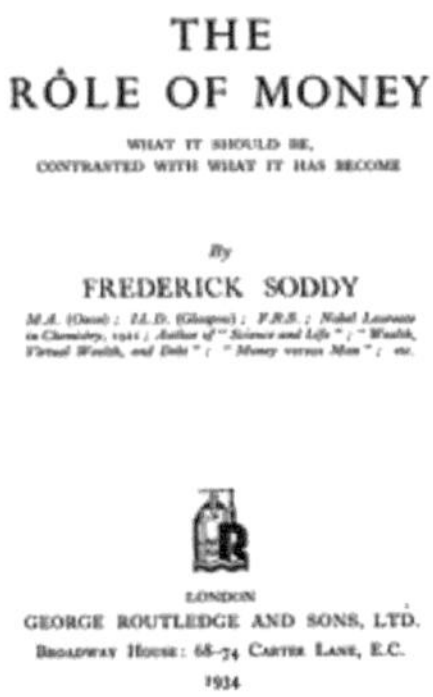
THE
RÔLE OF MONEY
WHAT IT SHOULD BE,
CONTRASTED WITH WHAT IT HAS BECOME
By
FREDERICK SODDY
LONDON
GEORGE ROUTLEDGE AND SONS, LTD.
BROADWAY HOUSE: 68–74 CARTER LANE, E.C.
1934

Fig. 1.1 The Role of Money, and Frederic Soddy

1.3.2 The Role of Money in Soddy's Views

Frederic Soddy (1877–1956), Oxford professor,[9] was an English chemist on radiochemistry who was awarded Nobel Prize in Chemistry in 1921. His research on radioactive elements led to the discovery of alpha and beta decay, etc. He was awarded the Nobel Prize in Chemistry in 1921 for his work on nuclear decay and the theory of isotopes. The Soddy Crater, an eroded lunar impact crater lying on the far side of the Moon, is named after Soddy. He is sometimes known as a pioneer of environmental economics. Interestingly, he was much interested in social issues and, in particular, examined the monetary system in the era of **1913 Federal Reserve Act**. Soddy was critical of this act.

Later in 1934, he compiled a book titled: *The Role of Money* (Soddy, 1934). This book now is easily obtainable from **Amazon Kindle**. Faced with a great reset of the monetary reform, we may find his idea useful to build the banking system back better[10] (Fig. 1.1).

Under the modern exchange system, as Soddy smartly identifies, the community must transfer a part of her wealth for the inconvertible notes. Without barter or a barter-currency, the aggregate of the individuals of the community must give up or nothing and be permanently owed for part of their possessions.

> This is the origin of modern money as nothing for something on the part of the legitimate user; as something for nothing on the part of the issuer, and as something for a promise to pay it back on the part of the borrower, with sufficient security to whom the issuer transferred the acquisition of the something accruing gratis from the issue. Soddy (1934, 49).

Like private banks, central banks use a partial reserve ratio system. Soddy described a profitable operation by the Bank of England.

[9] Also see the article of Allen (1993). This article incorrectly stated that Professor Soddy was a Cambridge professor.

[10] His publications on economics are many. See, for instance, Soddy (1921, 1926).

The Old Lady of Threadneedle Street
It began by the Treasury arranging with the Bank of England and authorising them to issue £15 millions more of their Promise to Pay notes under the 1928 Act. The net profit of this issue, whatever it may have been, was presumably was paid to the Treasury, and to this extent, the taxpayer benefited. Then the Bank of England increased its loans (banking phraseology) by acquiring for itself £32 million of marketable securities from the nation and came into revenue from interest that these securities yielded, paying for them by cheques. Whether or not **the old lady who overdrew her account and sent the banker a cheque for the amount** is an invention, there is not the slightest doubt about this being the normal, natural, and regular method of **the Old Lady of Threadneedle Street**. Soddy (1934, 91)

1.3.3 A Bank's Balance Sheet Under the Fractional Reserve System

We address **the fractional banking system**.

Institution for previlege	A bank creates its own assets simultaneously when it gives loan to the public according to the double-entry book keeping exclusively reserved for bankers. The portion of the bank's lending in excess of the reserve ratio is an asset of the bank, but this asset portion is **a transfer from national income to the bank** if the central banking system is taken account into.
Bank's privilege	Needless to say, banking contributes to accommodating investments. However, banks are automatically privileged to own **the portion** *they did initially not own.*

Under the double-entry bookkeeping system of the banking industry, when a bank lends money, the bank's 'assets' increase by the amount lent. The more it lends, the more its assets increase. In other words, when banking and double-entry book-keeping are combined, assets come from the sky. However, if a partial reserve ratio system is implemented by the government, the lending limit is fixed by the reserve ratio. Within this limit, banks will be able to lend funds that they do not own in advance and will be able to demand repayment on their loans. This is the open secret of banking.

If this part was interpreted with **a transfer from the public**, the portion could be considered **the socially reserved asset** common to the public. This idea will give a new development of finance for public.

The balance sheet describes the *ex post* relationship of the transactions. However, the real transaction takes time. After passage of the several periods, the loan appreciates in its real value. If the borrower is unable to repay the loan, the bank can legally seize the collateral. Thus, Soddy particularly noticed that **money creation entails the debtor of its user.**

In money creation, the debt owed to the citizens by the nation is in goods and services. Hence, Money will not create wealth.[11] In addition, the fact that **the debt owed to the citizens by the nation** is in goods and services and *not in money* does not alter the sign of the transaction. It appears to do so only because the vendors receiving new money for wealth given up consider themselves paid, whereas they are not paid but owed.

1.4 The Birth of the Global Economic Elite

For instance, BigTech or Billionaires, as stated in *Giants* Phillips (2018), cannot behave as if they are not influential at all in the market and the productive activities. Neither can a firm escape from any communication network or supply chain. Much more importantly, given the ICT system, even any manufacturing firm becomes a service provider whose customers must enter its production process in cooperation with the producer. It is quite natural that customers cooperation works as an indispensable input for production. That is, production has *a direct link with consumption via customers' utility*. Thus, the third item is dubious in the actual production system. The details around this structure was described in Aruka (2015). At this stage, we stop our discussion, although we have not referred to **propaganda** such as marketing. This observation will be addressed in a later chapter. It is simply noted that a similar comment to Turing's will be valid to our observations of economics. We need to study to check for the presence or absence of a direct link with consumption via customers' utility. This observation will bring about a decisive branching in economics (Fig. 1.2).

Global power

We will see easily how the global power elite is dominating the national economies. The book titled *The Global Power Elite* Phillips (2018) written by Peter Phillips, a professor of political sociology at Sonoma State University in the USA, identifies the world's top seventeen asset management firms, such as BlackRock and J.P Morgan Chase, each with more than one trillion dollars of investment capital under management, as the 'Giants' of world capitalism. The seventeen firms collectively manage more than $US41.1 trillion in a self-invested network of interlocking capital that spans the globe. Incidentally, compare the amount with the GDP in USA of $20trillion($20,936,600M) in 2020.[12] It is also noted that the figures of personal wealth

[11] It is found in a naive illustration in Soddy (1921) that wealth is a broader concept for him. "I charged economists with confounding debt for wealth. A ham merchant working on what he is pleased to call a 10% basis of profit may buy ten hams for the same sum as he sells nine. He may be pleased to think he has made a profit of one ham, but the certainly has not made a ham."

[12] See https://countryeconomy.com/gdp/usa.

WEALTH OF U.S. BILLIONAIRES GROWS $1.3 TRILLION (44%) IN ONE YEAR March 18, 2020 - March 10, 2021					
First Name	March 10, 2021 Real Time Worth ($ Billions)	Net Worth Mar. 18, 2020 ($ Billions)	Wealth Growth from Mar. 18, 2020 to Mar. 10, 2021 ($ Billions)	% Wealth Growth Mar. 18, 2020 to Mar. 10, 2021	Primary Source
Jeff Bezos	$179.9	$113.0	$66.9	59.2%	Amazon
Elon Musk	$166.2	$24.6	$141.6	575.8%	Tesla, SpaceX
Bill Gates	$125.0	$98.0	$27.0	27.5%	Microsoft
Warren Buffett	$98.5	$67.5	$31.0	45.9%	Berkshire Hathaway
Mark Zuckerberg	$97.1	$54.7	$42.4	77.4%	Facebook
Larry Ellison	$96.8	$59.0	$37.8	64.1%	Oracle
Larry Page	$89.3	$50.9	$38.4	75.5%	Google
Sergey Brin	$86.7	$49.1	$37.6	76.6%	Google
Steve Ballmer	$69.3	$52.7	$16.6	31.5%	Microsoft
Alice Walton	$61.7	$54.4	$7.3	13.4%	Walmart
Jim Walton	$60.1	$54.6	$5.5	10.1%	Walmart
Rob Walton	$59.4	$54.1	$5.3	9.8%	Walmart
Michael Bloomberg	$59.0	$48.0	$11.0	22.9%	Bloomberg LP
MacKenzie Scott	$54.1	$36.0	$18.1	50.2%	Amazon
Daniel Gilbert	$52.6	$6.5	$46.1	709.5%	Quicken Loans
SUBTOTAL	**$1,355.7**	**$823.1**	**$532.6**	**64.7%**	
ALL OTHERS	**$2,888.0**	**$2,124.4**	**$763.6**	**35.9%**	
TOTAL	**$4,243.7**	**$2,947.5**	**$1,296.2**	**44.0%**	

Fig. 1.2 Forbes data analyzed by Americans for Tax Fairness and Institute for Policy Studies, March 10, 2021. *Source* https://docs.google.com/spreadsheets/d/1xaXuqwLh5_dPargCNLGFibX5RCdKaLGuIBNleXQl1P8/edit#gid=1259834744

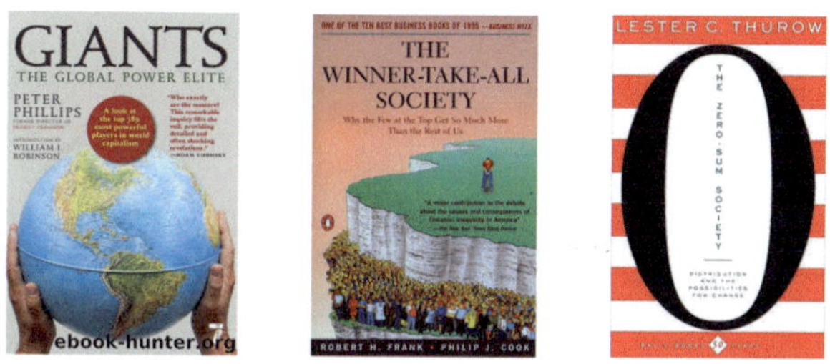

Fig. 1.3 Phillips (2018), Frank and Cook (1996), Thurow (1980)

only refer to the direct ownership. But it is much more important to estimate that a direct ownership will generate a longer link of indirect ownerships. A procurement of a majority of the share holding implies that 51% dominates the remaining 49%. If the company takes over another company, an indirect ownership will be extended to the taken over company. Thus the domination of billionaires will be much more appreciated (Fig. 1.3).

If you should read the following two books, you would understand well to track back the economic history of forming **Giants**. The two books are titled *The Zero-Sum Society: Distribution and the possibilities for change* Thurow (1980) who was MIT professor of economics, and *The Winner-Take-All Society: Why the few at the top get so much more than the rest of us* Frank and Cook (1996). Robert Frank is Cornell professor of economics.

1.5 A New Suggestion Toward a New Monetary System

1.5.1 Asymmetric Revenue Generation by Banks

Even in the modern times, the essential problem of the banking system, as Soddy insightfully observed, is not only changed but also worsened. Dr. Ron Paul, MD (Father), a well known politician, described a strange asymmetric attribute of banking profit management at **the von Mieses Institute** Paul (2009). Here, Paul has sharply summarized the main characteristics of the central banking system, particularly, the the Federal Reserve System in the US.

Privatized profits and socialized losses	What the largest banks desire is precisely what we might expect any large corporation to desire: privatized profits and socialized losses. Privatized profits come from successful loan activities, sometimes during economic booms. However, when the boom turns to bust, the losses are absorbed by third parties and do not affect the bottom line. To cover losses requires a supply of money that stretches to meet the bankers' demands.
Loss socialization	The central bank on a whim can reduce the interest rate that it charges members banks for loans. These banks can buy government debt and add that debt as an asset on its balance sheet. The central bank can also reduce the reserve coverage for loans at member banks.

1.5.2 Dark Matter Hidden in the Current Economic System

It may be helpful to summarize a recent blog by IWB titled: *Central Bank Digital Currencies Are the Ultimate Tool of Financial Oppression* in order to understand a current cognitive confusion.[13]

- Our educational systems don't explore how money is created. It is not discussed in schools. The real story is avoided in colleges and universities.
- For example, former Federal Reserve chairman Alan Greenspan once openly admitted that the central bank answers to no one and does not follow orders from the government. They do what they want when they want.[14]

[13] See IWB (2022) the more the details

[14] FED is not audited, but other central banks are audited.

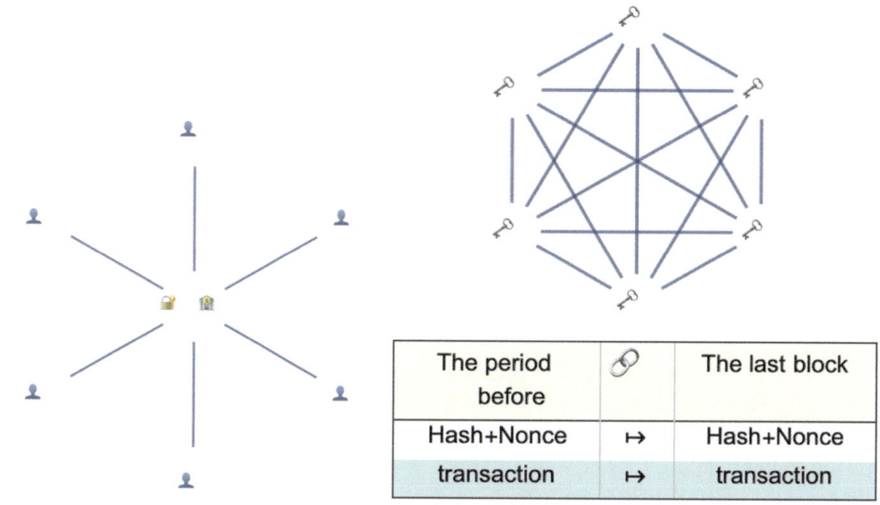

Fig. 1.4 Centralized network and distributive ledger system pf the P2P type

Adding to the above problems, it also exists a mystery around the governing bodies on the monetary system. In fact, many cabinet offices of the advanced country are registered as corporation in the NY stock exchange and so on.[15] Therefore, it is seen that governments are not necessarily bounded by the will of the people. Investment management corporations like BlackRock *mediates* between FED and governments. They are almost unseen, but enourmous, agents.

1.5.3 An Escape from the Binding of the Centralized System

1.5.3.1 The Distributed Ledger System of the P2P Type

In our argument, the distributed ledger system matters. This system is, as usual, a decentralized ledger system, shown in Fig. 1.4. The process is mediated by the mining process using the Hash function, as the table below of the system above. In the former system, the central authority owns the keys of the participants.

Compared with the high frequency transactions (HFTs), the distributed system of the P2P exchange network is slow speed, although its acceleration is currently promoted. The word "slow" may be interpreted as "nonhyperspeed" or "nonmicrosecond". In view of a certain scaling, however, blockchain transactions may be sufficiently speedy, except for the mining speed of Bitcoin.[16]

[15] See the data from US Securities and Exchange Commission Companies for SIC 8888–FOREIGN GOVERNMENTS: https://www.sec.gov/cgi-bin/browse-edgar?action=getcompany&SIC=8888&owner=include&match=&start=0&count=40&hidefilings=0.

[16] See Aruka (2020) for the details of exchange process.

1.5.3.2 Other Problems of Crypto-Currency

It is also noted that blockchain is not a technology only simply for cryptocurrencies. Blockchain also uses a censor technology, e.g., in order to retrieve a defective lot in a factory system of the manufacturing industry. Even if a blockchain technology is to be applied to the financial field, its usage is not limited to cryptocurrency such as Bitcoin or Ethereum. Other usages of blockchain can be found in an attempt to improve the transaction efficiency. On the other hand, If you turn your eyes to finance, you will see two perspectives on the use of blockchain. When talking about blockchain, naturally, we suppose *permissionless* mining process. However, we can establish a *permissioned* mining process. There are actually somewhat hybrid forms for using blockchain, such as **Libra** by FACEBOOK.[17] We note the IBM blockchain applied to the currency exchange, which provides the financial institutions with a better opportunity for trade by means of a world wire network (API): either are transformed into "a stable coin" as the digital asset, which can facilitate a simultaneous exchange between the two. Here, messaging, clearing, and settlement for the desired exchange will be integrated by blockchain technology without falsifying bookkeeping. The latter usage may be classified into a hybrid application of blockchain in a sense that blockchain is incorporated as a sub-system of the currency exchange.

1.5.3.3 Smart Contracts on the Ethereum

In 1993, Nick Szabo described how users could input data or value, then regain from the transfer system as if it were a digital vending machine. **Ethereum** shares the same function as Bitcoin in a sense that **the network** can transfer value from one to another. Different from Bitcoin, Ethereum provides each node with an additional information account, which could function as the distributed ledger for each, while Bitcoin only transfer the value of currency. The advent of Ethereum has given a new development of the market transaction as a whole on the new stage of ICT evolution.

1.6 Concluding Remarks

The monetary exchange and its ledger system will soon undergo significant innovations, synchronizing with the new stage of communication backed by the pervasive nature of quantum computing. It is evident that the distributed ledger system will resolve many entanglements happening on money creation. The dream of economic exchange system will be instant exchange. The closer to this ideal, the smaller the problems may be.

The 2022nd Nobel Prize in Physics was awarded to the following three individuals: John Clauser, Alain Aspect and Anton Zeilinger. "They equally split the 2022 Nobel Prize in Physics "for experiments with entangled photons, establishing the violation of Bell in equalities and pioneering quantum information science." These three scholars fully verified Bell's inequality to negate the hidden-variable theories

[17] The name Libra is due to be changed after 2023.

and quantum mechanics. Thus "[t]he universe is not locally real, and the physics Nobel Prize winners proved it." Garisto (2022) This news will reassure observers of a positive development of quantum finance.

Exercises

1.1 Survey roughly the history of economic doctrines, sometimes called the principles of political economy on the issue of money.

1.2 Consider the establishment of modern industry and the role of money.

1.3 In the case of the law of compound interest, what part of national wealth corresponds to that represented by compound interest?

1.4 Prepare a numerical example of the balance sheet with the bank reserve ratio as k. Reserves funds may be chosen a positive value at will.

1.5 To what constituent of the national wealth will the part to be appropriated as the asset of the bank correspond?

1.6 This chapter dose not refer to regional and/or community currencies. How can you design them. Hint: Nshibe M :"Good money drives out bad" among diversifying e-moneys: cryptocurrency, stablecoin, and digital community currency, in Aruka Y(ed.) Digital Designs for Money, Market, and Social Dilemmas (Chapter 2: 35–73), Springer Nature, 2022.

1.7 This chapter does not present the theory of international trade. How do you think of the monetary exchange only with paper money not guaranteed by gold in the case of the domestic economy?

1.8 Summarize roughly the difference between the two books: Thurow's *The Zero-Sum Society* and Frank's *The Winner-Take-All Society*.

1.9 You will learn the statistical law process of the Rich-get-richer process in a later chapter. Before you study it, how do you think of the evolutionary implementation of the Rich-get-richer process in an advanced countries.

1.10 Blockchain technology has become the preferred way to achieve distributed ledgers. *Wolfram Mathmatica*, for instance, provides a nice set of library titled "Working with Bitcoin Blockchains." Use one of a built-in function to get the number of blocks of Bitcoins in *Wolfram Mathmatica*.

References

Allen, R. W. (1993). Irving fisher and the 100 percent reserve proposal. *Journal of Law and Economics,36*(2), 703–717.

Aruka, Y. (2015). The rise of pure economics under a new form of scholasticism in view of the present socio-economic system. *Evolutionary and Institutional Economic Review, 13*(1), 3–29.

Aruka, Y. (2020). The evolution of the exchange process: From the decentralized to the distributed digital exchange. *Evolutionary and Institutional Economic Review, 17*(2), 379–398.

Cartels, F. J., & Competition. (2006). *Neither markets nor hierarchies.*

Frank, R., & Cook, P. (1996). *The Winner-Take-All Society: Why the few at the top get so much more than the rest of us*. Penguin Books.

Garisto, D. (2022). The universe is not locally real, and the physics nobel prize winners proved it: Elegant experiments with entangled light have laid bare a profound mystery at the heart of reality. *Scientific American*, October 6 2022.

Gronewold, N. (2009). Does economics violate the laws of physics? *Scientific American*. (October 23 2009).

IWB. (2022). Central Bank Digital Currencies Are the Ultimate Tool of Financial Oppression.

Keynse, J. M. (1919). *The economic consequences of the peace*. Macmillan & Co., Limited., London/Internet Archive, 1919/2016.

Keynse, J. M. (1925).The economic consequences of Mr. Churchill. In *Essays in persuasion* (pp. 207–230). Macmillan & Co., Limited, London/Springer link, 1925/2010.

Paul, R. (2009). Chapter 2: The origin and nature of the FED . In *End the fed*. Hatchette Book Group/Grand Central Publishing, 2009/2010.

Phillips, P. (2018). *Giants: The global power elite*. Seven Stories Press, NY.

Soddy, F. (1921). Cartesian economics: The bearing of physical science upon state stewardship. Wegbereiter einer naturwissenschaftlichen okonomie: Mit der deutschen Fassung seiner Schrift Cartesian Economics (German Edition).

Soddy, F. (1926). *Wealth, virtual wealth and debt: The solution of the economic paradox*. George Allen & Unwin, 1926, Second edition (2021), Amazon Kindle, 1926.

Soddy, F. (2015). *The role of money* (2nd edn.). George Routledge & Sons Ltd., London at Internet Archive.org. (Amazon Kindle, 1934).

Thurow, L. (1980). *The zero-sum society: Distribution and the possibilities for change*. Basic Books, Boston, 1980/2001.

A Critical Assessment of Pure Economics

2

Abstract

In their path-breaking and highly cited work, Frank et al. (J Econ Perspect 7(2):159–171, 1993), demonstrates that the more economists study, the more self-interested they become. In other words, cooperation will be reduced. In the real world, there are rare to achieve cooperation rather than compromise. The epoch-defining maker of the modern principles of political economy, Adam Smith focused his life's work on self-interest as well as sympathy. Our interest will be rather why economics was confined to the intersection of exposure to the self-interest model with self-interest behavior. We at first start by learning the method to study science.

2.1 Isn't Our Planet A Perfect Ball?

Newtonian physics is generally recognized to have broken the dark age's worldview. However, its arrival rather coincided with the divine grand idea. The Newtonian approach aims at describing a pure world simila to the one imagined by Euclidian geometry. According to this approach, we need another additional analytical method to transform the divine world into its real world forms . Almost-modern economists of the era preferred this philosophical approach. On the other hand, Joseph-Louis Lagrange (1736–1813) adopted an alternative method. Lagrangian dynamics assumes from the beginning that centrifugal force is an indispensable component. Thus, this method can immediately depict the real observation that our planetary surface is skewed almost everywhere. The **geoid** is a good example. The earth does not seem smoothly spherical, and the sea surface does not seem plain even if the waves are calm. In this chapter, we learn how we learn the real world.

In the 21st century, we are still surrounded by alternative views of the construction of the world. One view sides with the Newtonian insight. We have long been taught that a traditional mathematical formulation of modern economics was developed in 1870s by inheriting the Newtonian spirit of the system, even though Newton's

Y. Aruka, *Evolutionary Economics*, Springer Texts in Business and Economics,
https://doi.org/10.1007/978-981-97-1382-0_2

Principia Newton (1687) never contained any mathematical equation at all.[1] It is rather interesting for us to know that Lagrange completed the mathematical formulation of Newtonian system by developing his analytical mechanics. Here, we should understand that he has done more than just a formulation. His analytical mechanics prepared the way for us to use the new step of integrating statics and dynamics. In our elementary teachings, however, statics and dynamics have been separated. In Lagrange (1788), we learn that the power that changes the motion of a body and the static force that does not change it are treated equally. Newton never acknowledged **centrifugal force** at all when a rotational motion is referred. Rotational motion is regarded simply as a balance between the acceleration and attraction needed for rotation. This balance generates the principle of the parallelogram but not the principle of leverage.

In contrast, we can naturally assume the existence of **centrifugal force**, which was discovered by Christiaan Huygens in 1659 without using the idea of acceleration.[2] Lagrange thus successfully formulated the principle of **virtual work**. Work is defined as the amount obtained by the product of the force by the working distance; if the force and the direction of movement are the same, it represents the work given to the system, and if it is the opposite, it represents the work that the system must consume. A weight w_1 is hung at a distance to the right d_1 and a weight w_2 is hung at a distance to the left d_2 on a horizontal balance with a fulcrum. If the balance move towards clockwise by a minute angle θ, the system will obtain the work of $w_1 d_1 \theta$ on the right hand side, and will lose the work of $w_2 d_2 \theta$. If the former work is positive, the balance will be directed more clockwise. The principle of leverage will hold if both works are equal. This is geometrically called the principle of Archimedes if the virtual work isn't defined at all. In contrast, Lagrange introduced the virtual work at the beginning of the inference.

According to Nishimura (2017, 65),[3] the key is the idea of kinetic energy, i.e., *force vives*, and its conservation. In other words, Lagrange argued that the mass of system was connected by using a physical pendulum with a rigid body on which several mass points are fixed. In contrast, Newton dealt with a Kepler-type planetary system as source of data for his inference. We wish to demonstrate that the introduction of **centrifugal force**, in keeping with Lagrange's observations, can rotate a physical pendulum. Lagrange never added something *impure* to the system. As Nishimura

[1] Issac Newton (1643–1726/27) defined force as the product of mass and acceleration, and mass as the product of density and volume. However, he did not give the definition of density in Newton (1687). Mathematically speaking, his system was not necessarily complete. The later spread of Leibnizian denotations reinforced the Newton's system. Lagrange (1788) formulated the mechanical principles as simple results of the variational calculus.

[2] In 1659, Huygens derived geometrically the now standard formulae in classical mechanics for the centripetal force and centrifugal force in his work *De vi centrifuga* (Concerning the centrifugal force), which was published in 1703. See Wikipedia article https://en.wikipedia.org/wiki/Christiaan_Huygens.

[3] Hajime Nishimura is Professor emeritus, University of Tokyo who was working at Dept. Engineering as physical engineer.

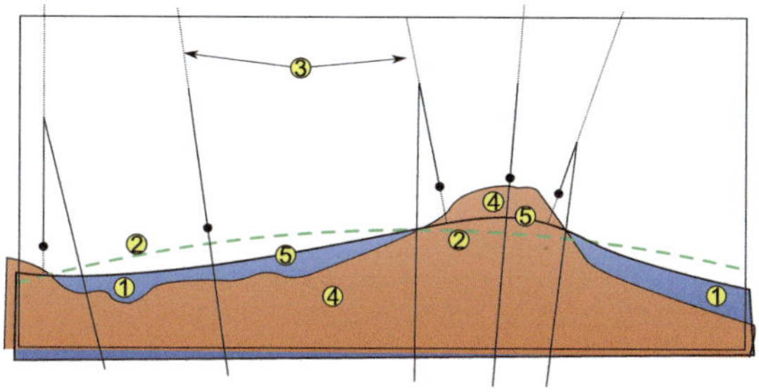

Fig. 2.1 ① Ocean, ② Reference ellipsoid, ③ Local plumb line, ④ Continent, ⑤ Geoid *Source* https://en.wikipedia.org/wiki/Geoid

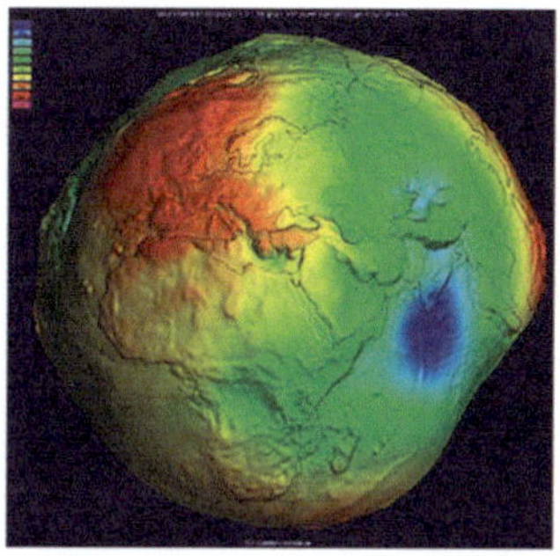

Fig. 2.2 Geoid undulation in false color, shaded relief and vertical exaggeration (10000 scale factor) *Source* https://en.wikipedia.org/wiki/Geoid

emphasized, Lagrange dealt with the connected mass of the system on a rigid body to develop his analytical mechanics, which is not inconsistent with the Newtonian model. Note that ocean's seabed is not only plane like ⑤ in Fig. 2.1. Continent but also unequal like ④ in Fig. 2.1. Given the presence of a centrifugal force, our planet is not a perfect ball due to gravity, as in Fig. 2.2. At the starting point, we can learn a realistic observation.

We regard gravity as the combined force of the attraction and the centrifugal force of the earth. We summarised the reason why the sea surface is influenced by gravity, that is, how the **geoid** is described, as shown in Fig. 2.1.

The nature of gravity 1	Gravitational acceleration increases as one approaches the North Pole and the South Pole, and decreases as one approaches the equator.
The nature of gravity 2	The higher the altitude, the smaller the gravitational acceleration.
The nature of gravity 3	Gravitational acceleration increases when there are heavy objects underground.

Gravitational acceleration depends on the mass of underground objects. The surface that results from extending land at the average height of sea level is called a **geoid**. The height (③) from the geoid (⑤) to the ground surface is the height of the land, which is called **elevation**. In other words, the geoid is the standard for determining altitude (0m). Therefore, the following conclusions can be drawn from the above properties.

Fig. 2.3 Wittgenstein's ladder and his grave at the Ascension Parish Burial Ground in Cambridge *Source* https://en.wikipedia.org/wiki/Wittgenstein

Proposition 1	If there is no difference in the weight of objects underground, the average sea level will be horizontal.
Proposition 2	If there is a heavy object underground, the average sea level will be attracted by gravity and become uneven. Even if the surface of the earth is flat, the average elevation at sea level (geoid ⑤) is uneven due to invisible underground objects (④)
Corollary	Gravity measurement is indispensable for measuring height.

We do not need to compare economics with physics. We do not have almost any observably established fact such as physics in economics. Thus, we do not need to compare economics with physics in details. We simply note that a different style of inference will give rise a to a different interpretation affecting systems that range in scale from the particle to the quantum. This will be revealed when we argue the so-called Copenhagen problem around Schrödinger's imaginary experiment on cat. In his book, Schrödinger (1985, 49) stated physics needed "metaphysics" to *evolve* its grand idea.

Claims about the luminous room

Metaphysics is a front base (outpost) created in the enemy's territory in battle. It will be crushed by the enemy if the main corps front does not come forward, and conversely it will be unnecessary if the main corps front advances ahead of it. However, metaphysics is indispensable for the front to move forward (Fig. 2.3).

This context resembles Wittgenstein's ladder, which appeared in Proposition 6.5.4 of his Tractaus Logico-Philosopicus (Wittgenstein 1922).[4]

> My propositions serve as elucidations in the following way: anyone who understands me eventually recognizes them as nonsensical, when he has used them–as steps–to climb beyond them. (He must, so to speak, throw away the ladder after he has climbed up it.)

[4] Other philosophers before Wittgenstein, including Zhuang Zhou, Schopenhauer and Fritz Mauthner, had used a similar metaphor. See https://en.wikipedia.org/wiki/Wittgenstein's_ladder.

2.2 A Thought Experiment in Cambridge Quintet

We argued above that we needed some metaphysics to identify our problems. We just happen to have a good guide written at the end of the last century. John L.Casti wrote a science story titled: The Cambridge Quintet Casti (1998).[5]

> Imagine, if you will, one stormy summer evening in 1949, as novelist and scientist C. P. Snow, Britain's distinguished wartime science advisor and author of The Two Cultures, invites four singular guests to a sumptuous seven-course dinner at his alma mater, Christ's College, Cambridge, to discuss one of the emerging scientific issues of the day: Can we build a machine that could duplicate human cognitive processes? The distinguished guest list for Snow's dinner consists of physicist Erwin Schrodinger, inventor of wave mechanics; Ludwig Wittgenstein, the famous twentieth-century philosopher of language, who posited two completely contradictory theories of human thought in his lifetime; population geneticist/science popularizer J.B.S. Haldane; and Alan Turing, the mathematician/codebreaker who formulated the computing scheme that foreshadowed the logical structure of all modern computers. Capturing not only their unique personalities but also their particular stands on this fascinating issue, Casti dramatically shows what each of these great men might have argued about artificial intelligence, had they actually gathered for dinner that midsummer evening.

We should learn the difference between a logical inference and a scientific inference. Casti suggests how both inferences could be different by likening the following two similar inferences Wittgenstein's one and Schrödinger's one. According to Casti, we will examine the following statement by a person who is supposed to be Wittgenstein:

Wittgenstein's claim about the emoji room

1. A program is purely a system for sorting symbols.
2. There are implications for human mind.
3. Any sorting of symbols cannot generate any implication.
4. A program is not necessary for the generation of the human mind, and the human mind will not be generated by a program.

At first sight, the inference seems formally true. However, this inference will be false if applied to electricity and magnetism. This is an example of how formal logic does not always hold in reality, although this kind of logic is frequently used in our ordinary life.

Claims about the luminous room

1. Electricity and magnetism are forces.
2. The essential property of light is light emission.
3. Force itself is not a component of light and does not produce light.
4. Electricity and magnetism are not components of light and do not produce light.

---

[5] Amazon's summary cited from https://www.amazon.com/Cambridge-Quintet-Scientific-Speculation-Helix/dp/0738201383.

A person who is supposed to be Schrödinger will be able to comment in the following manner. If we were living in the 19th century, we could regard Wittgenstein's inference as an influential refutation to the Maxwell proposition that light and electromagnetic waves are the same thing. According to Maxwell's theory, however, when a person in a dark room raises or lowers the magnet, the electromagnetic waves spread like ripples, making the room brighter.

Another person who is supposed to be Turing further added to this comment . If the frequency of the magnet is too low, it may not be possible to check for the presence or absence of the luminescence phenomenon because only energy waves that cannot be perceived by the human eye are emitted. In short, this kind of inference never contains an explanation of what kind of situation is required for magnetism to emit light or not at all. Moreover, this inference never refers to the property of light.

Now, comparing the above discussions, we try to apply a similar inference to pure economics.

Production and utility

1. Production is a sorting of capital and labor.
2. There exists utility in human mind.
3. Any sorting of capital and labor cannot generate any utility.
4. Production is not necessary for the generation of utility and utility will not be generated by production.

In this inference, the first item states that products are usually produced by using capital and labor. The second item states that utility is distributed in the human mind separately from the productive activity. Hence, production is irrelevant to utility in the human mind. In other words, the firm and the household must be treated independently in economics. Therefore, utility will never be affected by productive activity.

This interpretation just coincides with our traditional economic textbook. According to this interpretation, we can address the production set and consumption set separately. Therefore, our traditional economics immediately derives the supply function from the production set independently of the demand function, which is to be driven from preference set.

The problem in this inference is found in the third item. In the real world, capital and labor cannot stand without any institutional setting, as seen in Fig. 2.2 in the previous chapter.

Finally, we learn the truth of **pure economics** from Frank et al. (1993). This work continues to be highly cited. Frank showed that the study of economics reduces cooperation in a game setting. The idea is that much of the time, cooperation and consideration of other's perspective are irrational in the narrow sense of the word. Thus, learning that cooperation is irrational in some situations is influencing the behavior of the students towards less cooperation, presumably to the negative. According to Frank's observation, we are encouraged to describe the nature of modern economist in the following manner:

1. Exposure to the self-interest model encourages self-interested behavior.
2. Economists were simply more self-interested to begin with. This is a reason why they chose to study economics.

In the next section, we will learn how pure economists try to justify their self-interested model of rationalism.

2.3 Theological Rationalism in Economics

In Chinese and Japanese cultures, the word *economy* implies all about governing a society and saving its people—every single one of them. In Western culture, the word "economy" can be traced back to the Greek word *oikonomia*, which can be split into "oiko" and "nomos", i.e., "home" and "law." Originally, the economy shared the idea of symbiosis.[6] This meaning has thoroughly evaporated since the old doctrine of political economy was superseded by a newly established economics in the latter half of the last century. Thus, a new school biased towards the doctrine of individualistic rationalities became dominant in the economics community.

According to the *Oxford English Dictionary*, "rationalism" is defined as follows:
Philosophy and theology

1. In philosophy, the theory that reason rather than experience is the foundation of certainty in knowledge.
2. In theology, the practice of treating reason as the ultimate authority in religion.

Rationalism then suggests that assumptions are to be trusted as axioms. Empirical verification in such a case may be merely an *ex post* test. To confirm a "miracle", one must perform an empirical test based on rationalism. Once trusted, reason must be the ultimate authority. The same reasoning may be applicable to the rationalism of economics.

In contrast, "scientific rationalism" is defined as follows:

Scientific rationalism
The practice or principle of basing opinions and actions on reason and knowledge.

As the definition shows, science is understood as a theoretical construction based on both reason and knowledge. However, reason cannot be the sole authority in economics. If this is the case, knowledge would lose its role in its theoretical construction.

Adam Smith's economic doctrine belonged to moral philosophy, which was later developed by John Maynard Keynes as moral science. The principles of political economy in this context could be reduced to the principles of human nature. In essence, there are two types of human nature: one is the *other-regarding* nature, and

[6] See Aruka (2015, 21–22) for detailed expositions on this issue.

the other is the *self-regarding* nature. In particular, Smith demonstrated in depth how the idea of "extended sympathy" on others operated on others. In a rather sophisticated context, Keynes preferred to discuss how to predict others' expectation could be formed, as the example of the Keynesian beauty contest showed.[7] The status of each nature was originally equally weighted. This was a natural outcome because the economic system does not hold without a society in which human beings can be social animals. In the period of classical economics, scholars preferred the expression *political economy* to *economy* because the economy could not hold without taxation and toll custom policies, i.e., a political system, which was historically or traditionally inherited from older regimes. After the stage of the classical political economy passed, however, a school that was inclined to overestimate the self-regarding aspect of human nature became the mainstream in this field.[8] In the doctrine of the classical economy before J. S. Mill appeared, the identification of the human nature was rather undifferentiated. After J. S. Mill's arrival, the doctrine was endowed with an evolving nature in a particular direction, itself, from which some implicitly embedded convolutions could be unfolded into an elegant edifice. Thus, the doctrine could continue to develop extensively, in principle, according to how the doctrine changes, its development may follow rules that are similar to theological arguments. In this sense, the established theory of economics may be called another advent of scholasticism. We will suggest later that scholasticism actually was deeply committed to develop a new economics. It must be noted here that the *style* of the established economics was authorized by its own theological set of rules. In his historically noteworthy essay, Axel Leijonhufvud ridiculed this authorisation as the life of an *econ-tribe*.[9]

In short, *scholasticus* does not imply study itself. Rather, it represents the *style* of studies established in the Western Church following the spread of Roman Catholicism since the 11th century. Scholasticus usually did not aim at a complete unification of various ideas and philosophies in debates. Debates, though their domain was strictly limited to the interpretation of the Bible, were indispensable among the sects of this group. Hence, the group was identified with the institutionalized school. The greatest scholar of this school was Thomas Aquinas (1224–1274), who successfully argued human free will was allowed by God by analysing the ideas of contingency and coincidence occurring in each event. In this world, various conflicting/disturbing events often occur. Such an event is called *contingent* in many cases. If there are multiple causes and interactions among those causes, the results cannot be separated by cause. A consequence seemingly resulting from a unique cause sometimes is promoted by the strengthening of other causes and sometimes suppressed. Unexpected results could appear as a result of interacting causes. Aquinas thus formulated *something coincident* as concurrently occurring from interactive causes. In other words, he was interested in multicollinearity, synergetic phenomena, and the like. As Klaus Mainzer

[7] See Sect. 5, Chap. 12 in Keynes (1936) for the part where he makes observation about price fluctuations in equity markets.

[8] Faith in the mainstream of economics (Hodgson, 2012, 48) may be equivalent to reason here.

[9] See Leijonhufvud (1973).

pointed out.[10] Aquinas had a highly intelligent ability to analyze phenomena in a scientific way.

According to Aquinas, then, the following conclusions emerge:

Thomas von Aquinas

1. *Human free will* is to be acknowledged in the sense that humans cannot cope with incessant uncertainties in life if they are not allowed to act at will.
2. The variety of coincidences in the real world can contrast with and then reveal the purity of God.

Notably, coincidences in the real world gave proof for the necessity of God, but human free became justified in the theological world, though it merely gives sufficient conditions. Here, natural law could work relatively independently of *lex aeterna*, i.e., the law of reason of the cosmos. In other words, natural law would give humans the liberty and freedom to act, irrespective of the existence of God. The church then became socially commit ted to secular management and taxation. This motivated the church to argue economic policies. The church not only coexisted with the secular world but also became compatible with its own secular business.

In Aquinas's *Summa Theologica*, each question-and-answer pair was based on his carefully considered plan. Each emerging question must subsequently be answered without contradicting past answers. Here, the thorough application of *rationalism* must be exerted for every answer in the sense of fulfilling the logical rationality. Uniqueness, regardless of how rationalism is employed, is not necessarily secured in each answer. The logical construction also becomes deeply multi-layered. The importance of the answer to the original question must be much greater than it initially appeared if the hierarchy of the logic grows deeper. Many have had a great deal of fun discussing the technical contents. However, the ontological reason for writing, i.e., proof of the existence of God, was becoming alienated as the system of doctrines grew. The distance between the original question and the present debate issues became larger and larger. Ontology was hidden in the background, while epistemology was thriving. That is, *how to study* (epistemology) became preferred to *how to know* (ontology). This is a general rule in our secular world.

2.4 A Historical Encounter Between Scholasticus and Economics

Long before the restoration of Thomism, called neo-Thomism in the 19th century, Thomism was established by the school of Salamanca. The school thrived at the University of Salamanca from the 16th to the 18th century. The period of this school's prosperity coincided with the establishment of hegemony in Spain. The church was

[10] See Mainzer (2007, 28). See also Thomas von Aquin: Summa contra gentiles. Lat./dt. Übers. K. Albers et. Alt., Darmstadt 2. Aufl. 1987, III, 74, 3.

under great pressure from intellectuals looking to answer the pressing questions emerging from the Spanish colonies. These intellectuals were not satisfied with naive answers; they were looking to legitimize their conquest. Thus, the school was expected to play a great role in systematically guaranteeing secular commitments, such as sovereignty to the law of people and international law, to "just war," colonial policies, and to *economics*. In general, the Church would reconcile and adapt to the secular world when the two worlds had an unbearable conflict, such as same-sex marriage or heliocentric theory. This adaptive history has already been explored at length by those engaged in study of the Bible. Without adaptations from the church, therefore, the harmony between reality and the religious world could not have been maintained.

In economics, the school of Salamanca preferred to address private property, money, interest, and value and price. These points of view were all grounded in human free will, which Aquinas had proven.

Usury

The present meaning of *usury* is to charge an extraordinary high rate of interest on a loan, but an older meaning implied charging any amount of interest on a loan.

Until the medieval period, the Catholic Church continued to prohibit any interest charges or restrictions except in cases of necessity caused by natural disasters and the like. Interest charges were historically an object of moral condemnation.[11]

> The church, as well as the first generation of scholastics, was originally reluctant to allow even a small amount of interest. Interestingly, the historical attitude was not so different from the Islamic one, as seen from Yagi (2008) and Tawney (1926).

However, the rise of the Salamanca school drove the church finally to change its policy on interest charges, though high-interest moneylending remained disallowed. This relaxation of strict monetary policy marked a great change in the economic doctrines. Earning a modest interest was then justified and allowed religious powers to grow with monetary power. This policy shift was a large source of the momentum that empowered mercantilism and Western colonialism. We therefore note that Thomism contributed to the rise of a new economy and spiritual capitalism.

Thus, scholasticism recommended the abolition of monopolies because of their violation of human free will while vindicating free competition and allowing currency exchange and low-interest loans. Such apparent effects on economics emerging from Neo-Thomism were explicitly noted by Hayek (1973) and similarly recognized by Schumpeter (1954). They argued for natural law and pointed out that the Austrian theory of economics was much inspired by scholasticism.[12]

[11] "The Second Lateran Council condemned any repayment of a debt with more money than was originally loaned; the Council of Vienne explicitly prohibited usury and declared any legislation tolerant of usury to be heretical; the first scholastics reproved the charging of interest" (Wikipedia, "School of Salamanca": http://en.wikipedia.org/wiki/School_of_Salamanca).

[12] Schumpeter wrote, "So far as our subject is concerned, we may leap over 500 years to the epoch of St. Thomas Aquinas (1225–74), whose Summa Theologica is in the history of thought what

Prior to the Austrian theory, the Salamanca school was able to discuss in part the subjective theory of value against the predominant theory of production costs.[13] Once human free will has been credited, voluntary activity must be recommended even by the Church. However, actual human will is many-sided. Whether it is intrinsically egoistic and/or individualistic or altruistic simply indicates one-sided criticality. Except for within an ideal field penetrated by rationalism, an actual greedy process will never attain competitive equilibrium. As Arthur (1994) described the effect of *lock-in* in a path-dependent process, the process moves to a singular point or a fixed point. We shall also discuss arbitrage opportunities as another lock-in factor for equilibrium formation later.

Salamanca school and the rise of mercantilism

We also provide a historical note on the formation of the mental sources of capitalism. The Salamanca school definitely took into account the harmony between reality and scholasticus. Here, an interesting pragmatic compatibility between the purity of God and the chaos fabricated by secular human greed arises as a theoretical consideration, but it is well known that historically, Weber (1904) found the source of capitalism in Protestantism. In this context, however, we find that another moral source of capitalism was found in Catholicism in the form of scholasticism. The modern Catholic School's Charter is symbolically represented by bonum commune (the common good) and the personalism. Thus, the present form of Catholicism will never have many affinities with the so-called individualism but rather conflict with it. Therefore, we must note that our references on Catholicism are strictly limited to scholastic arguments.

There is called a large difference between the spiritual ideas of Catholicism and the so-called individualism demonstrated in economics. Some attempts are occasionally made to justify the notorious activities of the Jesus Society in establishing the foundation of capitalism; See Kuwabara (2009, 29).

Now we must identify the mainstream of economics with a new form of scholasticism. Realities in general are distorted from the ideal state. Given such a distortion, in the scholastic view, human free will can be exerted in conformity with God's will. The larger the distortion, the more human free will can be justified. However, it requires a lengthier sufficiency proof with additional assumptions and conditions. The proof

---

the South-Western spire of the Cathedral of Chartres is in the history of architecture" (Schumpeter 1954, 74). In contrast, he regarded Aquinas's economics as "strictly Aristotelian." Mueller (2014, Chap. 2) wrote, "the formula of Scholastic economics is Aristotle + Augustine = Aquinas." St. Augustine suggested "the theory of personal gift." However, Schumpeter never appreciated the theory in the context of economics. Hossein (2003, 29) also criticized Schumpeter to de-emphasize the rediscovery of Aristotles writings. Here, however, we will not discuss whether Schumpeter (1954) rightly recognized the essence of neo-Thomism.

[13] "Diego de Covarrubias and Luis de Molina developed a subjective theory of value and prices, which asserted that the usefulness of a good varied from person to person, so just prices would arise from mutual decisions in free commerce, barring the distorting effects of monopoly, fraud, or government intervention" (Wikipedia, "School of Salamanca": http://en.wikipedia.org/wiki/School_of_Salamanca).

of ideal states may then require a more complicated modelling. The resulting fact that the degree of complication may be much greater in modelling is very welcome in the sense that this kind of work, occasionally involving mathematical refinements, could a fortiori provide economics with the proof of ideal states grounded in divine inspiration. The distortion should thus be spiritually purified.

The ideal state of economics is typically called "equilibrium," the ideal state in an economy. In this type of reasoning, the *invisible hand*, by which the greed of interacting humans is interfered with, is equivalent to God's will because the invisible hand achieves its goal in much as the same way as a functional black box. In a certain sense, in the invisible hand, economists must feel something *ubiquitous*, or universally true, although the forces driving the economy towards equilibrium work in the mathematical world rather than in the physical world. In either condition, God or the ideal state must always exist. Such a conviction is common among standard economists, so they are diligent in elaborating how equilibrium could be attained, usually by the limiting process. According to them, human free will must in any event conform to God's will.

It is interesting to ask in which dimension/domain human free will is suppressed or affected. In the usual formulation, the domain where individuals are moving is endowed with at least one path approaching some ideal set. Without presuming such a path, an individual cannot fulfill his will. If and only if such a path is bestowed can any optimal method to realize one's desire be workable, but optimisation would not be feasible in any domain other than the special domain. The case to prove the law of demand in standard economics properly coincides with this one. Compared with the range of the law, even from the theoretical point of view, the range in which the law is not supported is much larger because of the so-called Giffen effect. Empirical studies also support this result. In the present custom of the proof, the range in which the ideal state holds is too narrow, as long as the individual free will is assumed ideally to be independent. This will be detailed more later.

Alternatively, we have another direction in which to generalize this limitation. We usually assume a certain relationship between some set of individualistic preference orderings and their domain. We furthermore suppose that preference orderings are *exchangeable/transferable* among individuals. The among individuals will relax the fixed relationship between individuals and the domain. The domain attributed to an optimal path above will be revived to find another route toward equilibrium, but the rotation of preference ordering will infringe on the ideally individualistic free will. However, the rotation could occur because of various reasons, such as a new social organization or some technological innovation. It may be understandable to suggest the idea of *non-self averaging*.

Summing up, distortions and purification are a necessary pair of concepts to understand the ideas located at the two poles in scholasticism. As human free will becomes completely purified as the reason for rationalism, however, the *experiences* around human nature could considered *degenerate*. Hence, it then holds as an extreme belief that the purified idea of human nature must essentially exist, i.e., virtually dominate in every sphere of the phenomenal world, similar to universal law. The theory, then, is marked by the deprivation of experience.

2.5 The Establishment of Pure Economics, The Idea of Modelling, and The Use of a New Mathematics

At the end of the 19th century, Leon Walras published *Elements of Pure Economics* Walras (1874). The book is a formal declaration of the purification of the economy through *modelling* the economy. Here, we refer to another mental source of economics, namely, *utilitarianism* in the Anglo-Saxon context because John Stuart Mill also addressed pure economics through utilitarianism. This thought was brought up long before the Walrasian fashion was accepted but had not yet been accompanied by a particular analytical tool for modelling.

According to Takizawa (2014), Mill (1844) established the following propositions:

Mill's propositions

1. Economic activities to pursue wealth are purely separable from other social activities.
2. Every phenomenon emerging from multiply composed motivations is completely reduced to each element, respectively.
3. Thus, economics then becomes an *abstract science* comparable to geometry. The method is marked by a certain a priori method. Hence, the results are true merely at an abstract level.

Interestingly, experience here also evaporates. Rather, the abstract is authorized. The propositions of J. S. Mill thus share the same statements as scholasticism. Though the two views were born from different roots, Mill's thought is also reduced to rationalism. Before Walras (1874), however, neither Mill nor the scholastics could reach the idea of modelling for the analysis of economic phenomena.

The idea called *modelling* has become settled in social science in the last century. A model used to analyze a complex reality is. In this context of modelling, the proposition that human motivation is specialized to pursue wealth is a statement that there is no other motivation than the pursuit of wealth. The existence of this motivation is not proved but an assumption itself, whether it is intended theologically or mathematically.

In the thinking of Mill (1844), economics was equivalent to geometry. However, such mathematical reasoning can never internally derive the existence of the pursuit of wealth. The latter is simply assumed from the space outside the modelling framework. Pure motivations of economics that are geometrically or mathematically designed with abstract logics cannot be proved within the modelling framework. In contrast, the purification of motivation may instead contribute to refinement of the modelling. Independently of reality, a mathematical truth holds. This may be the main reason that experience and knowledge are underestimated in economics.

We know that economists who prefer pure economics occasionally employ a special objective function such as utility or an expected utility function or the like. In limiting the domain to a specific one, thus, their use of mathematics tends to be too special in mathematics in general. If this were the case, it might be easy to prepare a *counterproposal*. Given a special objective function, we may simply suggest another objective function. Leaving aside the prejudice of clinging to the sole motivation of pursuit of wealth, which is intrinsically unverifiable, we are free to implement any form of objective function.

As shown above, the use of a special objective function does not necessarily imply the fixation of environments in the domain. In fact, agent commitments in the domain are not necessarily fixed, as suggested before. For instance, preference orderings are supposed to be *exchangeable/rotatable* among individuals. A preference ordering defined in the domain is not always fixed on a particular environment where an ordering stands. Under a given specific function, a rotation of the environment will make a fixed ordering float on the plane. The internal links among the orderings are thus changed from rotation to rotation, so there is another possibility to be discussed.

When such a rotation occurs, the traditional use of mathematics will fail to work. Instead of a traditional one, *tropical geometry* may be recommended.[14] This geometry is constructed by a rule of two new operations, such as one of the following[15]:

Tropical operations

Tropical addition	$a + b =: min\{a, b\}$
Tropical multiplication	$ab =: a + b$

In short, arguments on a tropical hyper-surface finally provide a "dictionary" between combinatorics and algebra. Such a dictionary can be used to analyze the non-Archimedean amoebas of a *piece-wise* linear set. By applying this geometry, for instance, a social complexity choice theory could be constructed.[16] The use of such a new mathematics will liberate the theory of choice from an individualistic binding.

The use of mathematics, however, merely illuminates constructive structures of an imagined entity, separate from the physical or social substances. In other words, mathematics *neutrally* gives a formal statement. Thus, it is interesting to see how a tropical geometry can be applied for two different purposes:

1. Paul Klemperer used a tropical geometry to prove a *product-mix auction* of multiple assets to suppress collusion. This was utilized by the Bank of England to escape the financial crisis of 2007. This method is now regarded as a more efficient way to find a solution for the liquidity supply for banks in toxic asset transactions.
2. Yoshinori Shiozawa also used a tropical geometry in terms of a max-times semi-ring to prove *Ricardian international trade theory* in the general case allowing multiple intermediate goods with multiple countries.

---

[14] The adjective "tropical" was coined by a French mathematician in honor of the Hungarian-born Brazilian mathematician Imre Simon, who pioneered the field (Wikipedia: http://en.wikipedia.org/wiki/Tropical_geometry).

[15] Sometimes, min-plus is substituted with max-plus or min-times.

[16] See, for example, Marengo and Pasquali (2011, 2012).

The first application was dedicated to a practical purpose in the scholastic sense, which sometimes practically contributed to capitalism as described above, while the second application was used for the classical political economy. The latter can revive the old predominant price theory of cost production. In the case of tropical geometry, it would be easy to apply it if we find a piecewise linear environment.[17] A possible application of it is virtually irrespective of the property of things. In short, with the current use of a new mathematics, mathematics can work neutrally. Needless to say, mathematics can do nothing to judge the necessity of ontological economic thought.

Individualistic rationalism in economics must exist as the *supreme authority* for pure economics. As long as this is esteemed, each pure economist must also allow for freedom of will. One may discuss imperfect competition or game theoretic competition. Thus, an interpretation of rationality may change from case to case. The result may bring pure economics a more general list of shapes of rationality. In such an expansion, modern pure economics has successfully internalized the concept of *bounded rationality*. The new approach may acknowledge the realities to be surrounded or disturbed by various stochastic noises, institutional restrictions, and the cognitive limits of human nature. As argued above, the realities are then distorted from the idealistic state. Hence, the gap between the realities and the idealistic state may be regarded as a driving force to make a path toward equilibrium (an ideal state). Traditionally, equilibrium simply referred to equality between supply and demand in economics, but now we have an expanded list of equilibria, from general equilibrium to game theoretic equilibria, including Nash equilibrium. The logical intention to construct a driving force toward equilibrium is similar to the idea of Thomism. The new Thomism actually motivated to construct a new economic theory such as the theory of subjective value. Now, *a new economics of bounded rationality* has appeared in line with Thomism. In this view, the introduction of bounded rationality does not imply the renunciation of rationality. On the contrary, it implies the strengthening of rationality.

Exercises

2.1 Rationalism in theology can ingest "miracle" based on theological axioms. In contrast, how do you think that "scientific rationalism" can verify miracle.

2.2 Individualistic rationalism is an axiom imagined to be valid in pure economics. Leaving away from pure economics, discuss the possibility of individualistic rationalism permeating economic behaviour everywhere like gravity in physics and being fully exerted.

[17] We show an example later.

2.3 Some people become less altruistic after studying economics. By the way, what else motivates people to become less altruistic besides economics?

2.4 People act emotionally without decision-making depending on the situation, whereas economic behaviour is considered to involve decision-making. Is economic decision-making considered to be solely based on self-interested motives? Describe what you frankly think of it.

2.5 We learnt about several specific examples of Wittgenstein's inference in "emoji room" above. Choose a subject of your choice and apply Wittgenstein's inference.

2.6 Fractal dimension is not expressed an integer. For example, the Sierpinski triangle requires three self-similar structures when reduced to $\frac{1}{2}$, so its fractal dimension is expressed as a logarithmic ratio. In short, not all mathematical spaces can be understood by Newtonian mechanics. Try to look for another example alternative to Newtonian mechanics.

2.7 Describe whether you can infer "usury" and its socio-economic results from any kind of human natures or not.

2.8 "Usury" meant charging interest, but over time, usury came to mean "high interest." In case that there is little increment of wealth but a big increment of debt, how do you think that the law of compound rate should be imposed? Hint: Historically, simple interest was the norm in feudal times.

2.9 Piero Sraffa (1898–1983), economist at Cambridge Trinity College, provided us with the idea of "Production of Commodities by Means of Commodities" as a certain ground on which economics should stand. Wittgenstein's later idea was called much influenced by Sraffa. Do you think Sraffa's idea is still valid? Describe your own idea of what the core of the current economic system is.

2.10 Check whether money is an entity. Hint: Apply "money" to the built-in function "Entity" in *Wolfram Mathematica* by using EntityTypeName[Money]. Also see Chap. 4 for "entity."

References

Arthur, W. B. (1994). *Increasing returns and path dependence in the economy*. University of Michigan Press, Ann Arbor. (Japanese edition).

Aruka, Y. (2015). *Evolutionary foundations of economic science: How can scientists study evolving economic doctrines from the last centuries?* (Vol. 1). Springer series: Evolutionary economics and social complexity science. Springer.

Casti, J. L. (1998). *The Cambridge quintet: A work of scientific speculation*. Perseus Books.

Frank, R. H., Gilovich, T., & Regan, D. T. (1993). Does studying economics inhibit cooperation? *Journal of Economic Perspective, 7*(2), 159–171.

Hayek, F. (1973). *Law legislation and liberty, rules and order* (Vol. 1). University of Chicago Press.

Hodgson, G. (2012). *From pleasure machines to moral communities: an evolutionary economics without homo economicus*. Cambridge UP.

Hossein, H. S. (2003). Contributions of medieval Muslim scholars to the history of economics and their impact: A refutation of the Schumpetarian Great Gap. In W. J. Samuels, J. E. Biddle, J. B. Davis (Eds.), *Companion to the history of economic thought. Wiley-Blackwell, Hoboken, NJ, Chapter 3*.

Keynes, J. M. (1936). *The general theory of employment, interest and money (reprinted 2007)*. Macmillan.

Kuwabara, K. (2009). Salamanca school on globalization (in Japanese). Sophia Philosophica (Departmental Bulletin Paper 28-Feb-2009), (pp. 15–29).

Lagrange, J.-L. (1788). *Mécanique analytique* (4th edn.). Gauthier-Villars et fils, Berlin, first published in 1788, 1788/89.

Leijonhufvud, A. (1973). Life among the econ. *Western Economic Journal, 11*(3), 327–337.

Mainzer, K. (2007). Kapitel 7: Zufall in Kultur, Wirtschaft, und Gesselschaft. In *Der kreative Zufall: Wie das Neue in die Welt kommt?* CH Beck.

Marrengo, L., & Pasquali, C. (2011). The construction of choice: A computational voting model. *Journal of Economic Interaction, 6*(1), 139–156.

Marrengo, L., & Pasquali, C. (2012). How to get what you want when you do not know what you want: A model of incentives, organizational structure, and learning. *Organization Science, 23*(5), 1298–1310.

Mein, S. E., Leben, M. W., & (First publication of Schrödinger's autobiography together with a reprint of Meine Weltansicht and an introduction by A. Dick). (1925). Wien, Zsolnay, Hamburg, (1985). Diogenes. *Zurich, 1989*

Mill, J. S. (1844). On the definition of political economy; and on the method of investigation proper to it. In *Collected Works of J. S. Mill (Ed.), Essays on some unsettled questions of political economy* (Vol. 4). Longmans.

Mueller, J. D. (2014). *Redeeming economics: Rediscovering the missing element (Culture of Enterprise)*. Intercollegiate Studies Institute.

Newton, I. (1687). *Philosophiae Naturalis Principia Mathematica (Mathematical principles of natural philosophy)*. London, 1687; Cambridge, 1713; London, 1726 (Pirated versions of the 1713 edition were also published in Amsterdam in 1714 and 1723).

Nishimura, H. (2017). *Jiyu-jin butsuri (Physics for freemen: principles of wave and quantum mechanics)*. Sendai, Japan: Hon-no-Mori.

Schumpeter, J. A. (1954). *History of economic analysis (Edited from a manuscript by Elizabeth Boody Schumpeter)*. Allen & Unwin.

Takizawa, H., & Model-kagaku toshiteno keizaigaku (in Japanese) [Economics as a modeling science and the methodology of J.S. Mill], Chapter 9. In Shiozawa Y, & Aruka Y, (Eds.). (2014). *Keizaigaku wo Saiken suru (in Japanese) [Constructing Economics in view of Evolutionary Economics and Political Economy]*. Chuo University Press.

Tawney, R. H. (1926). *Religion and the rise of capitalism: A historical study*. Harcourt, Brace.

Walras, L. (1874). *Éléments d'économie politique pure, ou théorie de la richesse sociale (Elements of Pure Economics, or the theory of social wealth, transl. W. Jaffé), 1874. (1899, 4th ed.; 1926, rev ed., 1954, Engl. transl.)*. 1874/1899.

Weber, M. (1904). *Die protestantische Ethik und der Geist des Kapitalismus*. Penguin, NY, 1904/2002. (In English: Baehr, P. R., Wells, G. C. (2002) *The protestant ethic and the "Spirit" of capitalism and other writings*).

Wittgenstein, L. (1922). In K. C. Klement (Ed.), *Tractatus Logico-Philosophicus*. University of Massachusetts.

Yagi, K. (Ed.). (2008). *Hi-seiouken no keizaigaku (in Japanese) [Economics in the Non-western area]*. Nippon-Keizai-Hyoron-sha.

Redomaining Equilibrium Economics 3

Abstract

There is a historically famous story that equilibrium could not be attained even if time were taken infinitely. The notion of equilibrium will no longer have the classical strict meaning: equality between supply and demand. The dominance of HFT has actually forced the financial market into a new system where the physical distance from the transaction server at the trader's location becomes a decisive factor to realize a transaction. Outside equilibrium, in contrast, we can observe that arbitrage opportunities will never disappear but rather reinforce themselves. Usually, a successful extra profit earner can then increase the size of his order if he follows the martingale rule. If he is successful, his earnings could double. In this case, his dynamics will have the same form as the *rich-get-richer* process. The dynamic description is depicted as a *fractal* map. The power law distribution will be deduced from it. It seems intuitively natural that the variance of expenditures among the richest is larger than that among average consumer because rich consumers are used to spending more for their particular purposes, such as purchasing ships or airplanes. Given a new society, the law of demand would be alternatively explained by focusing on another property: the variance of an income class increases as its class category rises from the bottom to the top. Here a usual meaning of the microscopic rationality will then be lost. In addition, we will learn various other topics for redomaining equilibrium economics. Interestingly, students studying disciplines other than economics occasionally question why the prisoner's dilemma does not hold in real life. They sometimes have a strong sense of discomfort regarding an occurrence of such a dilemma. In fact, such dilemmas do not necessarily occur in daily life. To be sure, real life incurs irrational conclusions. In many cases, however, better solutions are occasionally found to solve dilemmas. The more the realties are added, the more the boundary condition will be imposed to find a particular solution. Thus, the tree of boundary conditions will grow until the original implication may be lost.

Y. Aruka, *Evolutionary Economics*, Springer Texts in Business and Economics,
https://doi.org/10.1007/978-981-97-1382-0_3

3.1 Examinations of New Analytical Tools and the Ideas of Equilibria

Before discussing the new mode of analytical tools, we refer to the futility of the various debates. Scholasticism historically grew by repeating various debates at different stages, as argued in the preceding section. An effective way of debating is to employ a contraposition and embed it into a given proposition. We illustrate this way of debate by using an example. Suppose, first, advocating self-interest. We then have the option to take into account an other-regarding interest. In the prisoner's dilemma , egoistically maximized self-interest will not secure the best solution in this circumstance. The other-regarding consideration can yield a better outcome.[1] The conditions behind the maximization are then weakened and/or generalized. We have another example, in that the externality of an economy may be internalized into an economy, for instance, in a way suggested by the Coase theorem (Coase, 1960).

We also have the other way around of the argument such that self-interest may suffice to maximize the other-regarding satisfaction. There may be further debate on the necessary and sufficient conditions for self-interest and other-regarding interest, but this type of argument is constructed by a series of logical operations like those in mathematics, irrespective of the property of the substances. Here, everything that is indispensable for a further argument will be provided by the complete set of archives of propositions derived from past debates, as well as the use of them in debates. It looks like sometimes mathematics and sometimes like jurisprudence. Based on the compilation of all the propositions previously established, internal consistency must be maintained. The *econ-tribe*, i.e., scholars in the field of standard economics, must not leave this inner world. However, it will not be feasible for us to assess standard economics unless we leave the established set of propositions. We are then keen to assess new analytical tools

3.1.1 Examinations of New Analytical Tools

Nowadays, we can often use a *genetic algorithm* to make various *automata* on DNA-like series, in which not only a change in choice but also a change in choice rules is implemented, sometimes by reference to environmental information and sometimes by itself. The complexity appearing in this type of automata may be classified as a *light* complexity.[2] because a shorter program is judged as more efficient. This implies a *rationality of algorithm*. It is important to recognize that a rationality of algorithm is required even without a certain individualistic rationality.

[1] See, for example, Bowles and Gintis (2005).

[2] See Aruka (2015, 145) concerning the difference between high and low complexity. Sequences with low complexity are more likely than those with high complexity, as we saw with DNA (Mainzer, 2010, 156).

Leaving aside the universality of the internal world of standard economics, we now discuss a socio-economic system, and can positively deal with the following *methodological characterizations*:

Methodological characterization

1. Incorporation of rules changes and rule dynamics
2. Introduction of unknown agents to formulate mutants
3. Utilization of big data with high frequencies

These methods are not covered by standard economics. If it covered them, the calmness of the internal world would no longer be secured.

We shall also target the following effects as our analytical marks:

Analytical marks

1. Scaling law, power law distributions, and non-self averaging effects
2. Self-organizations and co-ordinations through a heterogeneous interacting agent

The former is often discussed in econophysics and the latter in agent-based modelling.

Both methodological characterizations and analytical marks explore **singularities** in standard economics. On the contrary, standard economics will rather believe in the following manner:

Infinite number of agents
Take time or a sample size as an infinite number. It may be an infinite time or an infinite number of agents, so the stated singularity may be lost as a temporal phenomenon appearing at an intermediate stage.

The idea of an infinite number of agents described above is a ridiculous idea. We sometimes see that an infinite number for a labor force is set 1, and the unemployed rate is distributed in the distance [0, 1]. If this is the case, the number of unemployed will become infinite. Even if we find equilibrium in this case, the realistic relevance of the unemployed will be lost. We therefore dismiss the case of an infinite number of agents.

We then focus on the idea of infinite time. This is a common operation in mathematics, so it deserves examination regarding the purpose or object of the operation taking infinite time.

3.1.2 Redomaining Equilibrium

There is a historically famous story that equilibrium could not be attained even if time were taken infinitely.

In the literature on business cycle theories, there was an everlasting divergence from equilibrium in the case of limit cycles. The nonlinear acceleration principle in an investment function was known to generate this behavior.[3]

The idea was conceived by Jules-Henri Poincaré (1854–1912), a mathematician. In this case, equilibrium exists, but a force toward equilibrium is not workable once the system leaves equilibrium. As chaos theory has demonstrated, however, equilibrium itself will not be secured in a chaotic trajectory. A force toward some attractors will exist but fall into a so-called *black hole*. No workable navigation will be found there. From this point of view, the idea that an equilibrium path exists in any system will be judged extreme. Moreover, we now know that a *non-self-averaging* process never converges to equilibrium (Aoki and Yoshikawa, 2006, 2007).[4]

The classical meaning is lost in equilibrium

> The notion of equilibrium will no longer have the classical strict meaning: equality between supply and demand.

It must also be noted that the notion of equilibrium will no longer have the classical strict meaning: equality between supply and demand. In standard economics, needless to say, Nash equilibrium is definable independently from the classical meaning. The use of equilibrium actually is losing its classical implication, similarly to the meaning of usury. However, we can also regard a *stable distribution* as an equilibrium state according to statistical physics. Equilibrium was originally a concept in physics. In earlier times, the balance between supply and demand was often used in economics. The present use of equilibrium has included those ranging from a game theoretic equilibrium to a statistical distribution. We must recognize the multiple uses of equilibrium.

Take the example of a power law distribution in the case of taking time infinitely. Standard economics often likes to underly the environment supported by the normal/Gaussian distribution. In the long run, self-averaging may sometimes lead to a Gaussian distribution. However, taking time infinitely does not mean that any distribution will become a Gaussian distribution. As recently explored, furthermore, the central limit theorem can be applied to many stable distributions. This is called a *generalized central theorem*.[5] That is to say, infinite time will never eliminate a distribution other than a Gaussian distribution.

---

[3] Goodwin (1950, 1951) as for an acceleration principle. See also Goodwin (1990) on chaotic economic dynamics in the context of Poincaré.

[4] Aoki and Yoshikawa (2006, 2007, 49 November 26).

[5] See Cook (2010). See also Aruka (2015, 167–170): "6.2.1.1 Generalized Central Limit Theorem (GCLT)."

3.1.3 The Dominance of High Frequency Trade (HFT)

The present phase of the financial system is dramatically evolving. In particular, we mark an explicit divergence from human nature for operations of financial activities. The continuous double auction was originally adopted predominantly in modern stock exchanges rather than the classical batch auction. The rule is the principle of time priority, that is to say, the principle of *first come, first served*. In other words, time is the most decisive factor for winning. Since the so-called Lehman shock, high-frequency trading (HFT) has become familiar in the financial market. HFT usually involves a transaction per microsecond. As Aruka (2015) argued in detail, in HFT, the arbitrage opportunities will be successively fabricated when the processing speed at the stock exchange server of usually millisecond base is smaller the speed of high frequent transaction. The gap of the order of magnitude, which is currently around 1, will secure an arbitrage opportunity for algorithm traders.

The dominance of HFT and the phase transition of the market

> The dominance of HFT has actually forced the financial market into a new system where the physical distance from the transaction server at the trader's location becomes a decisive factor to realize a transaction.

The dominance of HFT has actually forced the financial market into a new system where the physical distance from the transaction server at the trader's location becomes a decisive factor to realize a transaction. At this phase transition, the role of a human trader has been greatly diminished, replaced with an algorithm. Thus, with the advent of HFT, the time of algorithm trading arrived. In this type of transaction, reactions at the terminal server must be also prompted. Such hyper-quick reactions require some *machinery* signal processing that is not necessarily based on a traditional programing tool. Human skills must be behind the transactions. Therefore, the role of human nature must be alienated at least from the location of trading. As a result, the room available for human intuition to be workable will decrease. Instead of the human principle, the alternative principle based on algorithm will then be workable. At this stage, the economics of human nature must be examined again.

3.1.4 Alternative Implications of Arbitrage

In the economics of human nature, the role of *arbitrage* is a driving force to equalize the excess surpluses that are unevenly distributed among sectors or competitors. These are the source of arbitrage trading.

In a financial transaction, however, an *indirect* path is often generated to attain a desired asset.

The arbitrage opportunity in the financial market
Suppose that three assets $\{a, b, c\}$ are exchangeable. The *arbitrage opportunity* at the exchange between a and b suggests an opportunity to obtain a larger profit by the indirect path $a \to c \to b$ than by the direct exchange $a \to b$.

Both paths cannot coexist in equilibrium because their coexistence contradicts the definition of equilibrium. Because equilibrium is always assumed to exist, we can dismiss the possibility of *alternative effects* from arbitrage opportunities.

The rich-get-richer process outside equilibrium
Outside equilibrium, in contrast, we can observe that arbitrage opportunities will never disappear but rather reinforce themselves. Usually, a successful extra profit earner can then increase the size of his order if he follows the martingale rule. If he is successful, his earnings could double. In this case, his dynamics will have the same form as the *rich-get-richer* process. The dynamic description is depicted as a *fractal* map. The power law distribution will be deduced.

We know that such a process will never become a Gaussian distribution even if time is taken infinitely. Only a giant can then be born in the market. The self-averaging of either profit or size cannot occur. Even if opportunities are successfully eliminated in the market at a particular time, therefore, new opportunities for arbitrage would emerge repeatedly. An opportunity will be generated again if some higher-frequency order is newly realized at a given processing speed of the exchange server. Once a reinforcement process towards generating arbitrage opportunities begins, the size of the profits earned from a reinforced opportunity may be accelerated. Namely, the self-averaging process of profits would not work.

In the financial market, even if there are no arbitrage opportunities at all, the market can make an arbitrage. Modern algorithm can make it easierIt then seems queer to state that an arbitrage opportunity is utterly irrelevant to a big chance to earn profit in the real market. We also must observe the actual effects of arbitrage opportunities to implement a reinforcement mechanism to create extra profit. In this sense, we cannot find reality in equilibrium theory.

> People have historically looked for a big chance for arbitrage opportunities to generate big profits. In this context, the present hedge funds are not much different from the older colonialist companies such as the East India companies of the Netherlands and Britain. The South Sea Bubble in 1720 in the UK was a result an earnest pursuit of arbitrage opportunities. Arbitrage opportunities are not limited to artificial causes but also include natural disasters. Disasters, whether artificial or natural, are still one of the most attractive opportunities that can accrue big profits.[6] War is the most important opportunity.

There is a simulator booth for visitors at the.[7] Visitors can enjoy the market simulation by referring to the current world news on any event on the GUI display of a terminal. The news is not limited to economic matters but also relevant to institutional, political, social, or natural matters. Visitors are encouraged to play at trading by conjecturing about how the world will develop. That is to say, visitors are expected to implement a comprehensive system of decisions, which must not degenerate into *purely* economic decisions by neglecting other social influences. This

[6] See Klein (2007), an enlightening book.
[7] See the following url: http://www.tse.or.jp/english/about/arrows/visit.html.

conjecture is like societal forecasting.[8] In this context, the actual price movement will be seen as *impure* by pure economists. For further details, see Aruka (2015).[9]

3.2 The Validity of the Law of Demand

The statement that crowd behavior is *impure* for an economic system is understandable if one is a pure economist. However, such a statement deserves further examination if one is interested in a socio-economic system. Before we refer to crowd behavior in the market, it may be advisable to address the fundamental laws of economics. The most traditional law of economics is just the law of demand.[10] As commonly interpreted, for instance, excess demand or increasing demand for a commodity will push the price upward. The reverse is true for most cases if a unique price is valid in the market. In connection with this interpretation, it also matters whether *the law of indifference* will hold or not. In our discussion, the extent to which these laws can be applied matters. Furthermore, vulgar opinions that either the online market or HFT will make market transactions much more competitive are often stated. Can this really be so?

3.2.1 Infringements Upon the Law of Indifference

Mizuno and Watanabe (2010) and Mizuno et al. (2010) analyzed the big data provided by Kakaku.com, the largest online market in Japan. The studies showed that the online market will never secure the law of indifference. That is to say, averaging toward a single price has not occurred in the online market.

> Much more interestingly, *those who follow the demand law are not necessarily the majority.*

Many customers do not react to the lowest price asked by retail stores joining the online market. As a result, prices at a store demanding the highest prices.[11] can also be concurrent with the other prices for a year. In the online market, a store that fails to obtain any customers at all must be urged to leave the market. Hence, a store with the highest price realized a contract at that price.

An infringement of the law of difference

> The law of difference, i.e., *a coexistence of different prices*, is often evident even though the market fulfills all the conditions of perfect competition.[12]

---

[8] See the "FuturICT" project led by Dirk Helbing: http://www.futurict.eu/the-project.

[9] See Aruka (2015), particularly Chapter 4: "Matching Mechanism Differences Between Classical and Financial Markets."

[10] The law of value has often been discussed with a similar meaning as the law of supply and demand in classical political economy.

[11] It is not unusual that the highest price amounts to twice the lowest price.

[12] Kakaku.com provides an environment for perfect competition.

It should be noted that the online market always manages to maintain the circumstances for perfect competition. Compared with other markets, the online market is much better systematically administered to realize the conditions of perfect competition. Nevertheless, the law of indifference does not hold. Thus, we must recognize that *many heterogeneous customers* are widely distributed in the range between the lowest and the highest prices. In short, some irregular behaviors of customers partly reflect the *income effect*. In addition, we will argue that *the strict law of demand*.[13] also does not hold. Either the law of indifference or the strict law of demand may be ineligible to be called a law.

3.2.2 The Extent of the Impact of the Giffen Effect

Students of economics know that the strict law of demand cannot hold without the assumption of *gross substitutes*. Given a gross substitute, by definition, demand always moves in the same direction as the substitute effect. A gross substitute then holds when the income effect is kept *positive*. Equivalently, the Giffen effect will then be removed. It is interesting to estimate how much a gross substitute can dominate on the plane of relative prices. The range was specified in Hildenbrand (1994). Here, we take an example of an economy with two commodities. Figure 3.1 shows that Giffen phenomena are eliminated in the grey parts. In contrast, Giffen phenomena will be observed in the remaining parts. Thus, there remains a large set where irregular demand may occur.

In Fig. 3.1, the shaded range where the law of demand holds.

Both axes are price axes. In Fig. 3.1, p is a price vector of two commodities' prices. F is a demand vector of the two commodities' demand.

To eliminate irregular demand caused by the Giffen effect, Hildenbrand (1994) smartly proved a non-negative income effect by introducing the idea of *heterogeneous income classes* and their different expenditure behaviors.[14]

He focused on the property that

> the variance of an income class increases as its class category rises from the bottom to the top.[15]

[13] The strict law indicates a strictly positive increase in demand as the price decreases. In contrast, the weak law includes a zero increase in reaction in terms of a non-negative increase.

[14] See Hildenbrand (1994). See also Aruka (2015): "2.2.4 The Demand Law as Solved by Hildenbrand (1994)."

[15] It seems intuitively natural that the variance of expenditures among the richest is larger than that among average consumer because rich consumers are used to spending more for their particular purposes, such as purchasing ships or airplanes.

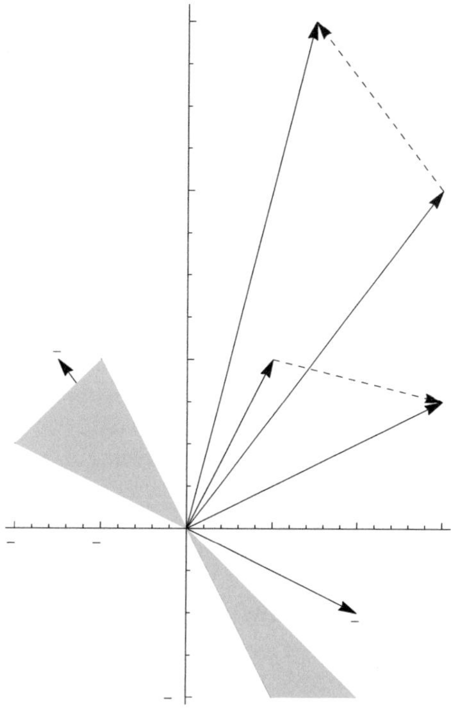

Fig. 3.1 The law of demand driven by the Slutsky equation system

He proved this property theoretically as well as empirically. This was actually one of the most splendid contributions to microeconomics since Pareto-Slutsky's original formula. In this formula, the law of demand was merely derived as one of the supposed mathematical possibilities. We actually require the idea of *heterogeneous consumers* to establish the law of demand. That is to say, even the law of demand, which is fundamental to economics, cannot be secured without a factor such as heterogeneity that is seemingly outside the inner ideal economic environment. Here, we must introduce a *socio-economic* idea such as heterogeneous consumers. Homo economicus, the concept of the consumer, must be defined a priori as homogeneous in economics. Heterogeneity in this case is supposed to be incompatible with homogeneity. On the contrary, the introduction of heterogeneous consumers may convince the standard economists of something *impure*.

3.3 Socio-Economic Factors and the Idea of Reciprocity

In the previous sections, we have discussed the scholastic origin of pure economics. This view will support the idea that there exists ideally an unchanged market system but an incomplete appearance in reality. According to this tradition, there must be pure motivations, such as the pursuit of wealth, to attain an optimal situation, accompanied by filtering such as averaging noises to eliminate distorted realities.

1. First, we do not know whether such errors can really be reduced to white noise or not.
2. Furthermore, the observed phenomena will apparently exceed the supposed range of errors in the case of either the Giffen effect or the law of indifference, as shown in Fig. 3.1.
3. We should not be allowed to identify digressions from the supposed law with a statistically permissible error.

Thus, the traditionally frictionless analysis in standard economics is not valid to confirm realistic laws. Some heterogeneous factors shall be rather relevant in establishing the laws of economics. They are not impure but indispensable to secure empirically derived laws. Thus, it is natural to derive an economic law from socio-economic considerations. An economic system underlies the social system. A social system is not chosen solely by the economic system. Rather, an economic system is constantly *renovated* by the changing social systems.

3.3.1 Technology

We have already discussed heterogeneous customers as a socio-economic factor. We may also regard *technology* as a socio-economic factor.

All economic activities have been completely changed as a result of advances in computational technology. The algorithmic trading derived from these advances accounts for over 70% of the total number of stock exchange transactions. The currency exchange is in the same situation as the stock exchange. Traders in the currency exchange once followed the custom of calling and communicating their own information. This is a typical case in which a direct human decision has become invalid. A final human decision will be respected, of course, but direct decisions depend on algorithmic workability.

1. The economic system is not working only with direct human decisions.
2. Human decisions are too slow to respond to algorithmic reactions. In other words, algorithms coexist with humans.

Even pure economists must thus recognize the fact that the real economic system no longer coincides generally with their suppositions about an ideal world. Roughly speaking, the prototype image of market exchange is that of a vendors' market voluntarily emerging in a local marketplace in the 19th century. This traditional design has been now undermined because of computational innovations .[16]

[16] See Mainzer (2010, 219). See also Aruka (2015, 29): "The smart grid system is managed by the negotiation algorithm, a kind of genetic algorithm, not by humans, as humans cannot operate at machine speed. But negotiation in a game theory situation is different from the negotiation algorithm by AI. Even if standard economics could include optimization in the negotiation process, its algorithm would require a loser, because the idea of optimization is not valid in the landscape of

Algorithmic decisions

> Algorithmic decisions underlie the special technology of computational capability. The design of such a technology directly affects the economic system.

As Brian Arthur suggested, the so-called renovation of financial business has been feasible only because the computer evolved to solve the complicated risk calculation for option dealings.

In the 1960s, putting a proper price on derivatives contracts was an unsolved problem. Among brokers it was something of a black art, which meant that neither investors nor banks in practice could use these with confidence. But in 1973 the economists Fischer Black and Myron Scholes solved the mathematical problem of pricing options, and this established a standard the industry could rely on. Shortly after that, the Chicago Board of Trade created an Options Exchange, and the market for derivatives took off. Arthur (2009, 154)

Technology

> Technology is not a subclass of the economy.

Technology rather essentially designs the economy. A similar approach also is found in a new book written by Brian Arthur: *The Nature of Technology*. The economy arose from its technologies.[17] We can say, then, that "technology" creates itself out of itself.[18]

3.3.2 Why Does the Prisoner's Dilemma Not Hold in Real Life?

Students studying disciplines other than economics occasionally question why the prisoner's dilemma does not hold in real life. They sometimes have a strong sense of discomfort regarding an occurrence of such a dilemma.

> In fact, such dilemmas do not necessarily occur in daily life. To be sure, real life incurs irrational conclusions. In many cases, however, better solutions are occasionally found to solve dilemmas.

---

complex interactions of heterogeneous agents at high speed and/or frequency. The same problem also applies to the stock exchange."

[17] It arose from the productive methods and legal and organizational arrangements that we use to satisfy our needs. It therefore resulted from capturing of phenomena and subsequent combinations (Arthur, 2009, 3).

[18] Early technologies form using existing primitive technologies as components. These new technologies in time become possible components–building blocks–for the construction of further new technologies. Some of these in turn go on to become possible building blocks for the creation of yet newer technologies (Ibid, 21).

Thus, our real-life experiences are anything but absurd, so we will take a brief look at several reasons for this.

> An intuitive reason is that they either know their opponents well or get to know each other through several repetitions of the dilemma game. The rate of defection will naturally decrease if the participants in the game become mutual acquaintances. In an evolutionary game, an increase in the rate of acquaintances in the population will lead to a similar situation with the randomized matching of players. There is often a tendency of an increasing rate of cooperation as a result of increasing *viscosity* among the population of participants.[19]

We will discuss the case that an agent's memory is limited to the last one period. In an extreme case of just two participants, it is easy to see that the custom called "tit for tat" (the **TFT** strategy).[20] is enough to make the situation shift toward a cooperative one. The TFT strategy is provided by the following conditions:

1. The first move is always cooperation *C*
2. Defection *D* is simply adopted as the reaction to the opponent's defection *D*.

Thus, the contestant who employs TFT will never be exploited by the opponent's shift to *D*. This will also hold if both players employ TFT. Hence, a TFT policy could be a better strategy than others for both players. If the opponent used defection in a subsequent game, the contestant could not recover his advantage in the added payoff value without a TFT reaction. Hence, the contestant's TFT move will guarantee a sufficient condition for his expected payoff maximization.

TFT moves have not only been verified theoretically by Folk theorems.[21] but also grounded experimentally in an iterated prisoner's dilemma round-robin tournament contest by arranged Axelrod and Hamilton (1981).[22] As this tournament showed, this theorem is not limited to a two-person game but can also be extended to a randomized matching framework.

3.3.3 The Idea of Reciprocity and a Viscosity Formation

At first, our daily custom seems irrelevant to bounded rationality. A hint to prevent dilemmas is suggested by socio-economic factors. Here, we focus on the idea of reciprocity among either animals or humans living in a society.

---

[19] See, for example, Helbing and Lozano (2010) and Helbing and Rauhut (2011).

[20] TFT, i.e., "tit for tat" is a strategy in which one cooperates on the first move and subsequently echoes (reciprocates) what the other player did on the previous move. The name was given by Anatol Rapoport when Robert Axelod organized the iterated prisoner's dilemma tournament in 1984.

[21] TFT moves on both sides will conform to a cooperative viscosity in a game through some experimental retorts or the incorporation of the "trembling hand." Here, "trembling hand" refers to an intentionally erroneous move.

[22] See Axelrod (1984) for an expanded, detailed version.

Table 3.1 Pavlov's policy in the case of a two-person, two-strategy game with agent memory of the last two periods 2

Agents' move configuration	Combinations			
The contestant's last move	C	C	D	D
The opponent's last move	C	D	C	D
The contestant's next move	C	D	D	C

[a]Changed moves of the contestant are marked in yellow

Society can work well with any social reciprocal relationship, virtually embedding viscosity among individuals, even though the market principle asserts the need for anonymity to maintain fairness. In many cases, humans really need much more viscosity rather than anonymity for their own activities. *A decrease in social viscosity because of a relaxation of reciprocity within a network of individuals may weaken the efficacy of networking in a social organization.* The viscosity of an organization usually changes depending on the memories/histories of the participants involving their own action and the counteractions of their opponents.

As discussed above, TFT trivially reinforces such viscosity.

Beyond Axelrod and Hamilton (1981), Nowak (1993) successfully proved that Pavlov's policy would be the strongest in a generalized case of a greater number of memories than one. This is a good example of a social custom that is formed by such a simple policy but invokes the past memories of the opponent and the contestant, as Pavlov's policy can accommodate a better solution by reinforcing the viscosity of the environment. According to Nowak (1993), the "Pavlov strategy" is defined as follows:

Pavlov strategy

1. Keep your current action when the opponent cooperates.
2. Change your current action when the opponent defects.

Table 3.1 shows Pavlov's policy in the case of a two-person, two-strategy game with agent memory of the last two periods 2.

This policy suggests that the contestant only changes his strategy when the opponent adopts D as the next move. Otherwise, the contestant will never change his policy.[23] The formation of viscosity will be promoted by other factors, such as "kin selection" (Hamilton, 1964). As for "group selection", however, it is interesting to

[23] There exist 16 strategy combinations in the two-person, two-strategy game where an agent's memory reaches the last two periods 2. Pavlov's strategy is one of these 16 strategies. It is known that Pavlov's efficacy can cover a broad range of two-person, two-strategy games with any memory.

learn that lemmings' group suicide was a fabrication. Even Konrad Z. Lorenz, a Nobel laureate, supported an existence of such a group selection.[24] However, "reciprocity" among humans and animals is often observed directly and/or indirectly.

3.3.4 Crowd Behavior

We may furthermore regard crowd behavior as a socio-economic factor. Above, we referred to a simulator booth for visitors at the Tokyo Stock Exchange.

> Many customers in the stock exchange and the commodity markets are inclined to follow the majority choice. They often react collectively to political or social news or natural disasters. If a huge number of news articles were carefully analyzed, we could obtain a prediction of the economic future with high precision. Data mining thus is becoming a new influential tool to forecast future economic conditions.

With this method of observation, it seems extremely difficult to define decisions and change in the current market business only from pure economic factors. Market business is a general indicator of society, and "social elements" cannot be removed from the economic system. One example is crowd behavior. Pure economists are occasionally used to regard a crowd behavior impure or inessential as a key word stated for journal contributions However, crowd behavior always has a serious influence on the economic system. Thus, with the use of agent-based modelling, we can obtain better modelling to replicate an actual market process appropriately by taking crowd behavior as a main variable.[25]

> A psychological factor such as crowd behavior is deeply involved in driving the market.

3.4 A New Scholasticism–A New Synthesis with Bounded Rationality

Here, we will finally examine "a new synthesis with bounded rationality" smartly suggested by Gintis (2009).[26] "While abandoning payoff rationality, Gintis defends a broader concept of rationality, defined as a consistency of behavior" (Hodgson, 2012, 49). On the other hand, Hodgson stated:

> Payoff rationality and self-interest were regarded as articles of faith among mainstream economists from the 1950s to the 1990s, and to question them was enough to lose one's credentials as an economist. Hodgson (2012, 48)

However, Gintis rather intended to relax payoff rationality in order to generalize a broader capability of "payoff rationality and self-interest." In the context of

[24] Lorenz (1965) believed that self-sacrifice exists in nature.
[25] See Hawkins (2011) and Lux (2009).
[26] Gintis (2009).

Thomism, even a pure economic system does not necessarily manifest itself at once. An actual system must be more or less blocked to manifest an ideally individualistic rational system. Some vestiges of payoff rationality remain in an actual stage. We may detect consistency in behavior linked to the original payoff rationality from such a vestige.

Today's economists work mainly around three perspectives:

Three perspectives of today's economists

1. Deterministic perspective with an individualistic dimension.
2. Game-theoretic perspective with an interactive dimension among individuals.
3. Evolutionary perspective with a population dimension.

If all three perspectives were organically joined, the first dimension could serve as the foundation of the grand edifice of the latter two dimensions, which is called a comprehensive socio-anthropological synthesis. The original idea of equilibrium that is well fitted to a deterministic perspective (1) is usually compatible as is with the notion of equilibrium applied to a game-theoretic perspective (2). In the case of multiple equilibria in scenario 2, however, we are induced to embed some equilibrium selection mechanism into the original system. However, the original system may be affected when a particular selection mechanism is introduced. Thus, we are urged to examine how a selection mechanism could be newly constructed by invalidating the original equilibrium.

We take here the example of "correlated equilibria." In a correlated equilibrium, the particular choice of equilibrium relative/correlated to a particular space maters. Thus, such a restriction to make a particular correlation workable must be examined. Some mediator that is external to the original environment will be required to obtain a particular equilibrium.

3.4.1 The Features Specific to Correlated Equilibrium

We first refer to a mathematical architecture for a non-cooperative game. In a linear payoff matrix when a non-cooperative game is defined, the mathematical requirement for a non-cooperative game demands that all players' mixed strategies are assumed to be stochastically independent. Without this stochastic independence, equilibrium cannot be established at all. Hence, Kono (2008a) focused on how the stochastic independence of any strategy could be maintained. A certain normal space for strategies will be pertinently constructed to make players converge to a particular equilibrium strategy where the stochastic independence of any strategy is always secured. Thus, Kono (2008a) introduced a finite set T to support players to stay in a particular equilibrium choice. A set T contains useful independent instructions for players, mediated by a third person, someone other than the players. Given such an information set as well as a neutral mediator, an exogenous equilibrium, i.e., an equilibrium mediated by the third person, will then be realized.

Therefore, we assume the following assumptions and condition:

1. Let T be a finite set of choices for the third person, a mediator, and let $R(T)$ be a set of all T-valued random variables. A T-valued random variable could be interpreted as the mediator's suggestion.
2. For simplicity, the game is a two-person game with Player A and Player B. Suppose that X_A is Player A's strategy and that X_B is Player B's strategy. Let us first formulate a framework for a non-cooperative game with a mediator. First, let us fix $Z \in R(T)$, and let $R_Z(S)$ be the subset of $R(S)$ that satisfies the following condition.

Condition (Kono, 2008a, Condition A): $(X_A, X_B) \in R_Z(S)$ is conditionally independent relative to Z; that is,

$$P(X_A = i, X_B = j|Z = k) = P(X_A = i|Z = k)P(X_B = j|Z = k)$$

holds for all $i \in S_A$, $j \in S_B$, and $k \in T$. Here, $P(\alpha|\beta)$ is a conditional probability of an event $\alpha \in F$ relative to an event $\beta \in F$ defined by $P(\alpha|\beta) = P(\alpha, \beta)/P(\beta)$. When $P(\beta) = 0$, then $P(\alpha|\beta)$ is not defined as or thought to be 0 for convenience.

It is well known that a non-cooperative game often has multiple Nash equilibria. Thus, how to select a particular equilibrium matters. In accordance with Kono (2008a, 2008b, 2011), we will find two different ways to find a particular one. The first one is called an exogenous correlated equilibrium. The other one is an endogenous one. In the first exogenous non-cooperative game, "the third person influences each player's strategy independently, or plays a publicly observable random device." In the endogenous game, on the other hand, "the restriction of the stochastic independence" just drops. Instead of assuming a mediator, possible communications between players would seek an endogenous equilibrium. In short, the difference between the two equilibria depends on whether a strategy profile maintains stochastic independence or not.

Definition 3.1 (*Kono*, 2008a, *Def. 3*) A game Γ is called an exogenous correlated non-cooperative game if and only if any strategy profile $(X_A, X_B) \in R(S)$ in question belongs to the set $R_Z(S)$ where a mediator suggests Z.

Definition 3.2 (*Kono*, 2008a, *Def. 4*) A strategy profile $(X_A, X_B) \in R_Z(S)$ is an equilibrium if and only if

$$\text{(i)}\ E[u_A(X_A^*, X_B^*)] \geq E[u_A(X_A, X_B^*)]$$

holds for all $X_A \in R(SA)$ such that $(X_A, X_B^*) \in R_Z(S)$, and

$$\text{(ii)}\ E[u_B(X_A^*, X_B^*)] \geq E[u_B(X_A^*, X_B)]$$

holds for all $X_B \in R(S_B)$ such that $(X_A^*, X_B) \in R_Z(S)$.

Definition 3.3 (*Kono*, 2008a, *Def. 5*) A game Γ is called an endogenous correlated non-cooperative game if and only if any strategy profile $(X_A, X_B) \in R(S)$ in question has no restriction.

Definition 3.4 (*Kono*, 2008a, *Def. 6*) A strategy profile $(X_A, X_B) \in R(S)$ is an equilibrium if and only if

$$\text{(i)}\ E[u_A(X_A^*, X_B^*)] \geq E[u_A(X_A, X_B^*)]$$

holds for all $X_A \in R(S_A)$, and

$$\text{(ii)}\ E[u_B(X_A^*, X_B^*)] \geq E[u_B(X_A^*, X_B)]$$

holds for all $X_B \in R(S_B)$.

Summing up, the difference between an exogenous and an endogenous correlated game is a reservation of stochastic independence. The former retains it, but the latter does not. Without it, or by dropping stochastic independence, a joint distribution of strategies could not be derived from each marginal distribution. To establish an endogenous correlated equilibrium, we are forced to add to a new parameter r. According to Kono (2011), it then holds that the expected payoff for each player is as follows:

$$\text{(i)}\ E[u_A(X_A^*, X_B^*)] = 1 + r$$
$$\text{(ii)}\ E[u_B(X_A^*, X_B^*)] = 2 - r.$$

In this case, a payoff greater than 1 is guaranteed to each player. However, we cannot resort to any mediator at all as we can in an exogenous equilibrium.

A game between the two great swordsmen
The only thing that players can do is to negotiate to estimate r. However, the negotiation demands that players estimate the same value. Such an expectation is rather suggestive of a game between the two great swordsmen than a rational expectation.

The expectation may be achieved through hard practice to train the estimation skill (Kono, 2011, 9).

3.4.2 The Essence of Bounded Rationality

As shown above, an original equilibrium, i.e., payoff rationality, may not necessarily be manifested automatically without employing a sophisticated device, that is to say, with some bounded conditions. Advocates of the hedonistic principle will positively support the imposition of such bounds to restrict the domain where a particular selection should be achieved.

The original implication may be lost

The more the realties are added, the more the boundary condition will be imposed to find a particular solution. Thus, the tree of boundary conditions will grow until the original implication may be lost.

Here, we will see the limits of theory, or, equivalently, with the same expansion of bounded layers, the concept of rationality may be modified. The original payoff rationality must not be preserved. Decisions may be allowed to be consistent on a contingency plan basis. This is just a demonstration of the quality certification of the egoistic idea of equilibrium, provided that the original idea of equilibrium exists. Hence, we have seen the same procedure as in the logic discussed in Sect. 3.1. Any theoretical device that is intelligently designed gives sufficiency for the necessity of the idea of equilibrium. Here, God is replaced with the idea of equilibrium.

Exercises

3.1 Mention some historical cases where other regarding interests take precedence over one's self interest.

3.2 Describe the difference between high and low complexity.

3.3 Summarize descriptively the classical meaning of equilibrium, and the equilibrium state in statistical physics, and compare the difference and commonality for both ideas.

3.4 How to assess the equilibrium state as a fixed point and the state of orbiting around a fixed point but not reaching an immovable point? Hint: Check the paragraph referring to Jules-Henri Poincaré.

3.5 First, explain Pareto-Slutsky's original formula, and then discover the Giffen effect to infringe the traditional law of demand. Furthermore, examine how narrow the traditional law merely holds by using Fig. 3.1.

3.6 As discussed above, arbitrage opportunities on exchanges are logically eliminated in equilibrium. However, state why indeirect paths are preferred in the currencies market.

3.7 Test the effectiveness of this strategy, using the idea of the TFT strategy in the repeated game. Then explain another solution of the prisoner's dillemma in terms our real-life experiences. Moreover, how do you appreciate the idea of viscosity.

3.8 Make the strategy table of Pavlov's policy in the case of a two-person, two-strategy game with agent memory of only the last period 1 with reference to Table 3.1.

3.9 Crowd behaviour is regarded as psychological behaviour. Try to explain whether crowd behaviour can be interpreted in terms of pay-off rationality or self-interest.

3.10 Explain in your own words the correlated equilibrium of a two-person game and consider whether the equilibrium is attained in the absence of stochastic independence.

References

Aoki, M., & Yoshikawa, H. (2006). *Reconstructing macroeconomics: A perspective from statistical physics and combinatorial stochastic processes*. Cambridge UP.

Aoki, M., & Yoshikawa, H. (2007). Non-self-averaging in macroeconomic models: A criticism of modern micro-founded macroeconomics. Economics Discussion Papers. http://www.economicsejournal.org.

Arthur, W. B. (2009). *The nature of technology*. Free Press.

Aruka, Y. (2015). *Evolutionary foundations of economic science: How can scientists study evolving economic doctrines from the last centuries?* (Vol. 1). Springer series: Evolutionary economics and social complexity science. Springer.

Axelrod, R. (1984). *The evolution of cooperation*. Basic Books.

Axelrod, R., & Hamilton, W. D. (1981). The evolution of cooperation. *Science, 211*, 1390–96.

Bowles, S., & Gintis, H. (2005). Can self-interest explain cooperation? *Evolutionary and Institutional Economics Review, 2*(1), 21–41. October.

Coase, R. H. (1960). The problem of social cost. *Journal of Law and Economics, 3*, 1–44.

Cook, J. D. (2010). Central limit theorems. Wolfram Demonstrations http://www.johndcook.com/central_limit_theorems.html. (linked from Cook. (2010). How the central limit theorem began? http://www.johndcook.com/blog/2010/01/05/how-the-central-limit-theorem-began/.

Gintis, H. (2009). *The bounds of reason: Game theory and the unification of the behavioral sciences*. Princeton.

Goodwin, R. M. (1950). A nonlinear theory of the cycle. *Review of Economic Statistics, 32*, 316–20.

Goodwin, R. M. (1951). The nonlinear accelerator and the persistence of business cycles. *Econometrica, 19*(1), 1–17.

Goodwin, R. M. (1990). *Chaotic economic dynamics*. Clarendon Press.

Hamilton, W. D. (1964). The genetical evolution of social behavior i & ii. *Journal of Theoretical Biology, 7*(1–16), 17–52.

Hawkins, R. (2011). Lending sociodynamics and economic instability. *Physica A, 390*(7), 4355–4369.

Helbing, D., & Lozano, S. (2010). Phase transitions to cooperation in the prisoner's dilemma. *Physical Review E, 8*(5), 057102.

Helbing, D., Yu, W., & Rauhut, H. (2011). Self-organization and emergence in social systems: Modeling the coevolution of social environments and cooperative behavior. *Journal of Mathematical Sociology, 35*(1–3), 177–208.

Hildenbrand, W. (1994). *Market demand*. Princeton University Press.

Hodgson, G. (2012). *From pleasure machines to moral communities: An evolutionary economics without homo economicus*. Cambridge UP.

Klein, N. (2007). *The shock doctrine: The rise of disaster capitalism*. Knopf Canada (A Penguin Random House Company).

Kono, N. (2008). Noncooperative game in cooperation: Reformulation of correlated equilibria. *The Kyoto Economic Review, 77*(2), 107–125.

Kono, N. (2008). Noncooperative game in cooperation: Reformulation of correlated equilibria (II). *The Kyoto Economic Review, 78*(1), 1–18.

Kono, N. (2011). Nash equilibria with negotiations. In M. Aoki, H. Aoyama, Y. Aruka, & H. Yoshikawa (Eds.), *Keizai-kyoshitsu no 50 keywords (in Japanese) [Economics Classroom of 50 keywords]* (pp. 41–48, no. 3). Tokyo-Tosho Publishing.

Lorenz, K. (1965). *Evolution and modification of behavior*. Chicago: University of Chicago Press.

Lux, T. (2009). Rational forecast or social opinion dynamics? Identification of interaction effects in a business climate survey. *Journal of Economic Behavior Organization, 72*, 638–655.

Mainzer, K. (2007). Kapitel 7: Zufall in Kultur, Wirtschaft, und Gesselschaft. In *Der kreative Zufall: Wie das Neue in die Welt kommt?* CH Beck.

Mainzer, K. (2010). *Leben als Maschine?* Mentis: Von der Systembiologie zur Robotik und Knstlichen Intelligenz.

Mizuno, T., & Watanabe, T. (2010). A statistical analysis of product prices in online market. *European Physical Journal, 3B*(76), 501–505.

Mizuno, T., Nirei, M., & Watanabe, T. (2010). Closely competing firms and price adjustment: Some findings from an online marketplace? *Scandinavian Journal of Economics, 112*(4), 673–696.

Nowak and SigmundNowak and Sigmund1993]ch3Nowaksps1993 Nowak, M. A., & Sigmund, K. (1993). A strategy of win-stay, lose-shift that outperforms tit for tat in Prisoner's Dilemma. *Nature, 364*(6432), 56–58. March.

Interpreting the Iterated Dilemma Games by Using the Presentation Like "Cellular Automatons"

4

Abstract

Myopic optimization around scarce resources makes the least use of available information. Such optimization was a winning strategy in the stage when big data was not common but is no longer effective. In reality, winning game differs from the maximizing payoffs. In this article, we focus on an ontological meaning of the game and the time development of the dilemma game. In particular, we are interested in the time development of the dilemma game. After examining the structure of the iterated game, we then introduce the Wolfram simulator by Chandler (Iterated games. http://demonstrations.wolfram.com/IteratedGames/, 2011) to the original form. This is the presentation like "cellular automatons" (**CA-like presentation**) of the iterated game. We furthermore expand his original program to discuss TFT, ESS, Avatamsaka game, and the tagging mechanism. The use of **CA-like presentation** may renovate the traditional implications of the game solution.

4.1 An Ontological Meaning of the Game and the Time Development of the Dilemma Game

4.1.1 An Ontological Meaning of the Game

We often need to *limit* the field for discussion. In this sense, the Complex Adaptive System (**CAS**) is a good example neatly restricted by John Holland . By limiting to **4 properties** and **3 mechanism** of a system under inspection, Holland provide a basic frame of reference to analyze complexities that are mildly restricted.[1]

The complex adaptive system **CAS** is construed on the whole as a constellation of seven basics of four properties and three mechanisms Holland (1995, Chap. 1):

[1] Even in an organism of an adaptive complex system in a sense of Holland, it is difficult to identify self with non-selves. A radar system also has a similar problem to **IFF** (Identification friend or foe).

Y. Aruka, *Evolutionary Economics*, Springer Texts in Business and Economics,
https://doi.org/10.1007/978-981-97-1382-0_4

Aggregation (property)
Nonlinearity (property)
Flow (property)
Diversity (property)
Tagging (mechanism)
Internal models (mechanism)
Building blocks (mechanism)

Any system characterized by the **CAS** mainly exhibits **a perpetual novelty**. The commodity markets is an example of the CAS, because it continually produces a series of new products, or re-labels existing ones and presents them as new.

We do not yet need to analyze complexities in general. As well known, in particular, **genetic algorithm** is a powerful method suited to to this idea. However, it has been noted that such a successful application is vialbe given **another classifier system** as well. To use an alternative, we need more certain basis, like classifier system, cellular automaton, and so on in particular cases respectively. We argue in detail later **interactive cellular automata**(ICA).

It is interesting to learn that the term of **ontology** is used to be employed in **Information Science**. **Wolfram language** contains a new operator called "entity".[2] " **The core meaning** within computer science is [that of] **a model for describing the world** that consists of a set of types, properties, and relationship types."[3] According to this definition, a traditional game like prisoner's dilemma is definitely formulated by a simple set of explicit types, properties, and relationship types. Thus, it is important for us to incorporate a core system like a classifier system. The traditional game was much considerably modified by Axelrod (1981), as well as Nowak and Sigmund (1993) by transforming one-shot game into iterated games inset by **the random matching mechanism**, as seen later. This transformation is clearly in line with the idea of genetic algorithm. Hence, we must analyze the mechanism of evolution of the game will evolve, without imposing something special akin to human rationality on it through rules.

When arguing for a CAS, a biological system is a good example. Human body is an evolving creature that has adapted over time to **various occurrences**. Adaptation dominates our evolutionary process, either locally or globally. It should be noted that individualistic humans behavior cannot be allowed to exist infinitely. Due to their questionable mortality, people who act in this manner are invariably at a risk of harm. Thus we must notice the next proposition.

Proposition 4.1 *Winning game differs from the maximizing payoffs.*

---

[2] Cited from Stephen Wolfram's blog in July 2017: http://blog.stephenwolfram.com/2017/07/the-practical-business-of-ontology-a-tale-from-the-front-lines/.

[3] Cited from Wikipedia article **Ontology(information science)**: https://en.wikipedia.org/wiki/Ontology_(information_science). There is also generally an expectation that the features of the model in an ontology should closely resemble the real world.

4.1.2 The 2-by-2 Game Forms

Before we examine the iterative games, we offer a few observations. As I previously cited elsewhere, coagulation is a good example. Indispensable reaction was never designed as an optimal configuration to maintain human body. The body does not have a universal mechanism for such local reactions as coagulation. Coagulation is indispensable for both lower and higher organisms. However, when coagulation occurs in the latter, such as in the human brain, it can be fatal.[4] This raises the question of whether this kind of **immunoediting paradox** is a Trojan horse. The coagulation system overlaps with the immune system. Coagulation can physically trap invading microbes within blood clots. Moreover, some products from the coagulation system can contribute to the innate immune system through their ability to increase vascular permeability and act as chemotactic agents for phagocytic cells. The process of coagulation and fragmentation can be applied to social modeling and mathematically analyzed within a coagulation fragmentation model.[5]

However, a classical inference confines the game to a narrow set of rationality principles. By resorting to classical inference, thus, we can not arrive at a unique solution. If a broader frame is designed to allow players access to memories of their past moves and strategy scenarios, the case of the memory of the last two periods can help devise 2^{21} by 2^{21}(4.4 trillion) combinations of strategies in a two-player game.

Therefore, we first examine a new game mechanism by using the example of **an iterative**, standard, two-player, two-strategy game. We have to introduce some interactive decisions in the most recent two turns in addition to informational structure. von Stackelberg (1934) was the first to recognize the inference by observing the complex interaction among the participants in a duopolistic market. However, the procedure of examining strategic interactions using massive amounts of data is beyond human capacities. Thus, we need to alter our approach from a mathematically pedantic inference to an agent-based one. Econophysics emerged at the end of 20th century owing to its facility with big data. At the same time, using large amounts of simulated data, agent-based modeling was used for the network analysis of heterogeneous interaction and the examination of sentiments. In the following, we provide a detailed analysis of this iterative game (Table 4.1).

We represent **the total number of situations and nodes** in the strategy tree as follows.[6]

---

[4] See Mainzer Chap. 7 (Mainzer 2007).

[5] Sentiments can be handled by data/text mining. Using this, machine learning is remarkably effective. Machine learning is more beneficial in locating a potential connection. Text mining provides new insight into prediction. In particular, this kind of inference may be robust in scenarios where the traditional method does not work well. Moreover, sensor technology in combination with machine learning is drastically altering our style of daily life, such as driving a car. Industries and industrial policies are also moving toward the intensive utilization of information.

[6] See Wikipedia article **AlphaGo**: https://en.wikipedia.org/wiki/AlphaGo.

Table 4.1 The total number of situations and nodes of the famous traditional games

Game	The total number of situations	The total number of nodes
Othello game	10^{28}	10^{58}
Chess	10^{50}	10^{123}
Go game[Igo]	10^{160}	10^{400}

Table 4.2 The pay-off arrangement of the 2-by-2 game

		Player 2	
		Choice 0	Choice 1
Player 1	Choice 0	p_{11}	p_{12}
	Choice 1	p_{21}	p_{22}

We quickly summarize traditional game theory for readers unfamiliar with economics, and then introduce a program provided by one of Wolfram Demonstration Projects.

We consider the 2-by-2 game, i.e., involving two players and two strategies game. In general, the pay-off matrix of the 2-by-2 game is as follows (Table 4.2).

The payoff is confirmed when the choices of both players are confirmed. Let $i \neq j, i; j = 1, 2$. For simplicity, choice i is denoted by Ci, and the payoff of Player i is represented as $P_i(C_i, C_j)$, which indicates the payoff of Player i when Player 1 employs C_i, Player 2 employs C_j.

If it is the case, it then holds that

$$P_i(C_i, C_i) > P_i(C_j, C_i), \tag{4.1}$$

The strategy set $\{C_i C_i\}$ is called Nash equilibrium. In other words, (14.1), i.e., **Nash equilibrium** is the situation where the payoff is reduced if Player 1 changes strategy from i to j. On the other hand, we impose another condition.

$$P_i(C_i, C_j) > P_i(C_j, C_j) \tag{4.2}$$

If (4.1) and (4.2) are satisfied, the strategy set is called Evolutionary Stable Strategy **ESS**.[7] It should be noted that ESS contains the Nash equilibrium but not vice versa. It is easily verified that the solution of PD games must satisfy the above two conditions due to its special property of executing dominant strategy.

[7] The second Eq. (14.4) can be replaced with the next, weaker condition:

$$P_i(C_i, C_i) = P_i(C_j, C_i), P_i(C_i, C_j) > P_i(C_j, C_j)$$

4.1.3 The Prisoner's Dilemma Game of the Iterated Form

The classic formulation of the prisoner's dilemma (**PD**) was provided by Tucker.[8] This game is called the iterated prisoner's dilemma (**IPD**) .

We assume two independent players. They execute their strategies without exchanging information concerning their activities. We exclude the possibilities of either coalition and negotiation. The players are not allowed to exchange information once engaged into the game. The PD game is based on a scenario involving prisoners who are allied. However, they are arrested and isolated from each other, and each is pressed to give up the other. The original PD game yields its pay-offs in the following manner:

$$p_{21} < p_{11} < p_{22} < p_{12}$$

In the PD game, the pay-offs are allocated by

$$p_{11} = -2, p_{12} = 0, p_{21} = -3, p_{22} = -1$$

Here the negative sign of the payoffs above means "in prison". In this numerical example, either Player 1 or Player 2 is sentenced to 2 years in prison if he/she refuses to talk and set free if he/she cooperates with the authorities. It is interesting to note that an asymmetrical arrangement is allocated on the off-diagonal cells in the PD game, and this asymmetric implementation can lead to a paradoxical result, irrespective of any symmetric cell on the diagonal elements. Hence, while **Choice 0** implies **defection**, **Choice 1** implies **cooperation**. It may be assumed in this article that Choice 0 is **defection** and Choice 1 is **cooperation**.

However, the PD game in real lief seldom provides a unique solution as concluded in traditional economics. The choice is purely based on prioritizing the payoff at the cost of the relationship. The latter problem can be improved by incorporating the idea of **iterated game**. This idea can be generalized by implementing **the random matching mechanism**, as motivated by Nowak and Sigmund (1993).[9]

---

[8] Cited from Wikipedia article **Prisoner's dilemma**: It was originally framed by Merrill Flood and Melvin Dresher working at RAND in 1950. Albert W. Tucker formalized the game with prison sentence rewards and named it" (Poundstone, 1992). https://en.wikipedia.org/wiki/Prisoner's_dilemma.

[9] The uniqueness of the PD solution is questionable if we reconsider our real life. Psychologists immediately reacted to economic interpretation once the dilemma was discussed. In the 1950's, approximately 1000 papers were published on this issue. There may be various solutions that can be implemented as long as players take into account realistic circumstances and communications. In practice, few opportunities arise related to the uniqueness of the prisoner's dilemma. We use the alternative approach to frame the field of random matching by multi-agents. In this framework, the participants can remember the personal histories. The effects of memories on repeated plays may induce the tendency to avoid the worst situation. This field may generate cooperation formation to avoid a series of exchange of defection.

Irrespective of any payoff allocation, the game is repeatable. That is to say that the game will be repeated for some *finite* times. Given its iteration, we can observe a historical path of rounds of the game. The history of rounds of games may suggest a comprehensive/long-run scope for participants to ponder a serial move. Thus, the entity of the game will be newly enhanced by moving from a one-shot game to an iterated version. The iterated game then requires the examination of the more complicated interaction between players' strategies in terms of a *serial* move of strategies over time. Fortunately, we have now sufficiently powerful simulators to inspect the historical paths of the 2-by-2 games provided by of **Iterated Games** of **Wolfram Demonstration Project**.[10] According to this program, the number of historical paths of the 2-by-2 games are set to a maximum of eight. By using the operator **ArrayPlot**, while **Choice 0** is colored with "white", **Choice 1** with "black". This graphical presentation reveals that the system under investigation is akin to a **cellar automaton**. This view essentially provides us an unobstructed view, in contrast to the traditionally restrictive view.

By way of example, Player 1 might start by playing strategy 1 (Choice 1) and continue playing it unless the history of interactions were such that Player 2 (the opposing player) had played strategy 2 (Choice 0) on his/her last two turns. Such strategy management is a well-known part of the iterated game, and is called "trigger strategy". We would not retaliate immediately even if the opponent has defected. At the least, we probe, i.e., check whether the opponent will continue to choose to defect. If the opponent defects in the next round, we *retaliate*. If the opponent retracts defection in the next round, we cooperate again. The roundabout retaliation is called **Tit for Tat(TFT)**. Thus the following theorem was proven in the traditional framework due to by Rubinstein (1979) and others:

Theorem 4.1 (Folk Theorem) ***Trigger strategy*** *plan in* ***an iterated PD game*** *can, on the average, give a greater total expected gain over the duration of the game period than any other trigger strategy, if the discount rate nearly is close to 1.*

The idea of this proof is intuitive. The participating players always try to achieve as large an expected payoff as they can on average all over the game rounds. To that extent, players must be careful to avoid falling into cut-throat competition. In contrast, the affected player catch up with the defector by retaliating mildly, i.e., making moderate loss against the defector. If there is no retaliation at all, the affected player must profit less than the defector. Hence the theorem holds. However, this result could be not always be guaranteed, unless players always control themselves and confine their reactions to their narrow span of the game rounds. In addition, little attention has been paid to the fact that the game field is fixed by narrow assumptions pertaining to rationality. Consequently, the variety of institutional designs may be

[10] See http://demonstrations.wolfram.com/IteratedGames/. This simulator is programmed in Wolfram language by Seth Chandler.

lost in this context. We will subsequently discuss a similar problem also in production theory.

In this article, we are rather interested in accepting any kind of players. Players are allowed to plan any kind of time development of their moves. Winning the game in any kind of environment differs from looking for a special/mathematical environment to make the greatest profit. In the secular world, the interest is commonly winning the game rather than behaving rationally. Thus, we must consider all possible situations generated by the game's environment. This approach is similar to find the locus of the **allele** of a particular location in gene evolution. We will also refer to this issue.

4.2 The Trajectories of Game Tree Dependent on the Memories of Players

4.2.1 The Trajectories of an Iterated PD Game and Their Presentation Like Cellular Automata

We apply the above Wolfram simulator designed by Chandler (2011) to the original form of the PD game to examine the effects of memories, or mutual historical observations, on the strategy moves. The final state of this simulator indicate the vicious circle of the mutual choice of defection, i.e., {Choice 0, Choice 0}. The simulator then tracks back to the last two-period (two-rounds) observations.[11] We call this description the presentation like "cellular automatons", i.e., **CA-like presentation**.

Figure 4.1 exhibits a typical vicious circle of the PD game. As easily seen in Fig. 4.1, at the last one-period, there are the 4 possible combinatorial situations. In this figure, there are

$$\sum_{t=0}^{2} 2^{2t} = 2^0 + 2^2 + 2^4 = 21.$$

The simulator we use defines **the histlength** in the program to calculate the historical length, which can bring 21. The maximum length of this game's history is also set to 8 at most, but this restriction was sufficient to generate numerous possible situations for each player. Hence the total number of situations for a player of this game is

$$2^{21} = 2,097,152.$$

Thus, the simulator can examine 2, 097, 152 possibilities for each player

$$2^{21}2^{21} = 21^{42}$$

[11] The original values were specially assigned in light of the prisoner case. To make the payoffs better fit ordinary scenarios, we use other numerical values for all nonnegative elements fitted to the iterated game. As long as the payoffs allocation fulfills the PD game specification, needless to say, any replacement of payoffs will not give rise any change.

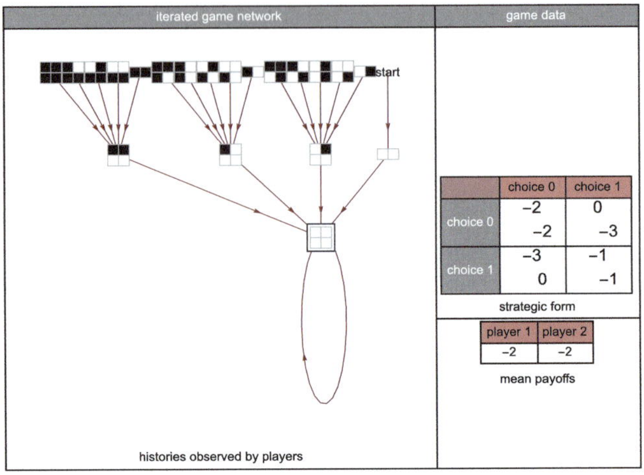

Fig. 4.1 A typical configuration of the PD game initially given

Table 4.3 The strategy profiles at time 1

{(Choice 1, Choice 1), (Choice 1, Choice 0), (Choice 0, Choice 1), (Choice 0, Choice 0)}

Table 4.4 Strategy profiles at time profiles {time 0, time 1}

Time 0	Time 1
(Choice 1, Choice 1)	{(Choice 1, Choice 1), (Choice 1, Choice 0),(Choice 0, Choice 1),(Choice 0, Choice 0) }
(Choice 1, Choice 0)	{(Choice 1, Choice 1), (Choice 1, Choice 0),(Choice 0, Choice 1),(Choice 0, Choice 0) }
(Choice 0, Choice 1)	{(Choice 1, Choice 1), (Choice 1, Choice 0),(Choice 0, Choice 1),(Choice 0, Choice 0) }
(Choice 0, Choice 0)	{(Choice 1, Choice 1), (Choice 1, Choice 0),(Choice 0, Choice 1),(Choice 0, Choice 0) }

Histories that are part of **the steady-state cycle** are shown as framed. There are 2^{42} (about 4.4 trillion) possible combinations of strategies that the players can employ in this game, and that can be selected using the two top sliders of the simulator (Table 4.3).

Given this set, we can furthermore trace back to the previous two-period each of the last one-period situations. This backward reasoning will bring us to the initial past configuration. In this way, we can obtain all the time profiles stated in Table 4.4.

Table 4.5 The strategy choice distribution in the 2-by-2 game

Player 1	Player 2
Choice 0	Choice 0
Choice 0	Choice 1
Choice 1	Choice 0
Choice 1	Choice 1

Table 4.6 Colored plots of the strategy choice distribution in the 2-by-2 game

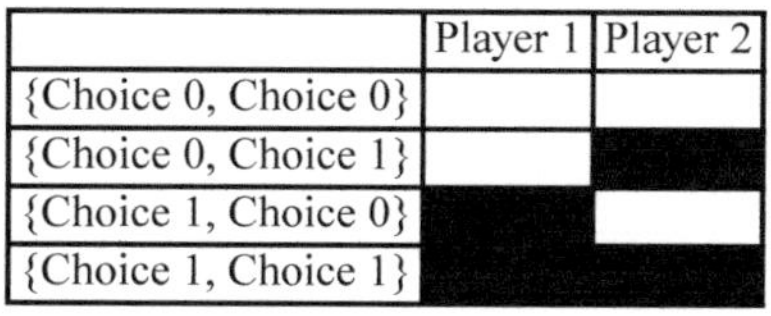

Table 4.7 Historical paths at time 0

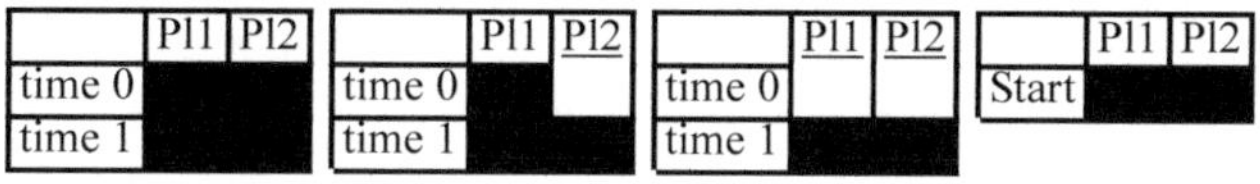

To simplify the presentation, the simulator can represent game decisions using black and white colors, like **cellular automatons**. Tables 4.5 and 4.6 illustrate the correspondence between two different representations (Table 4.7).

4.2.1.1 The TFT Solution by Simulation in IPD

By using the simulator, heuristically, we can discover the so-called **trigger strategy** to support the folk theorem. As shown by the creator of the simulator, the TFT strategy can be implemented by having player 1 use **strategy 1398101** and by having player 2 use **strategy 1973785**. Figure 4.2 depicts the histories observed by the concerned players of these choices of strategy. Even given these strategies, there are three possible histories and two **state cycles**, one of which may yield a vicious cycle as initially discussed in Fig. 4.1. Incidentally, it is noted that the mean payoffs of Fig. 4.2 are clearly greater than those of Fig. 4.1.

4.2.2 Strategies for IPD Reconsidered in Ontological Context

Interest in the iterated prisoner's dilemma (**IPD**) was primarily motivated by Robert Axelrod's unique project summarized in Axelrod and Hamilton (1981) and Axelrod (1984). He designed the n step prisoner's dilemma tournament by using a so-called **random matching mechanism** with the finite period and the finite participants. He

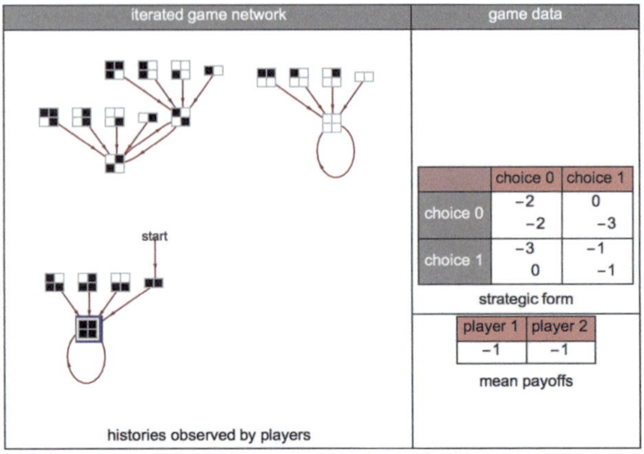

Fig. 4.2 The solution of TFT

also invited computer scientists all over the world to submit their algorithm agents to compete in the IPD tournaments. This was a historic pioneering challenge to control social experiments by aid of artificial intelligence (**AI**). Various computer strategies competed in IPD tournaments to generate an "algorithmic complexity." Interestingly, the various complex strategies, however intelligent, did not achieve success if they are greedy or intolerant types, i.e., of the selfish-type. Axelrod discovered that the longer the tournament period, the more probable a simple program of more altruistic type to win.

The random matching mechanism of the IPD is one where a finite even number of participants randomly encounter on another in pairwise fashion, and are reset for a prescribed number of rounds without any fixed contract with a particular person. This is a kind of **natural selection process**. This mechanism was reformulated in terms of an evolutionary game by Nowak and Sigmund (1993).[12] In this evolutionary game, altruistic strategies achieved greater success, and grew even if they were in a minority if some noise were allowed. This is equivalent to the trigger strategy evolutionary game form. PAVLOV's policy, as stated in Nowak and Sigmund (1993) may be summarize as follows:

1 If the player feels good, he/she will not change her action.
2 If he/she feels uneasy, he/she will change her action.

In the case of profile {time 0, time 1}, the two kinds of strategies might obtain in view of action and reaction, the normal **TFT** strategy, and the anti TFT strategy (**ATFT**). In the latter, the player may cooperate if the opponent defects. Tables 4.8, 4.9, 4.10 describe the historical paths of each case. **The grey cell** repre-

---

[12] It is noted that evolutionary game deals with population dynamics. This implies that the size of each population may be infinite. But when we deal with the dynamics of employed and unemployed, we may allow an infinite number of unemployed.

Table 4.8 TFT case 1 in Pavlov policy

	Pl1	Pl2
time 0		
time 1		

Table 4.9 TFT case 2 in Pavlov policy

	Pl1	Pl2
time 0		
time 1		

Table 4.10 ATFT case 1 in Pavlov policy

	Pl1	Pl2
time 0		
time 1		

Table 4.11 ATFT case 2 in Pavlov policy

	Pl1	Pl2
time 0		
time 1		

sents both choice possibilities, i.e., mixed strategies, of Player 2, if Player 1 observes the game (Table 4.11).

More importantly, the Pavlov policy is verified as successful in other games. We have already shown that it is useful in **Avatamsaka game**, whose payoff is characterized by an infinite number of Nash equilibrium as Akiyama and Aruka (2006) proved the next proposition:

Theorem 4.2 (ESS) *In case of infinitely repeated game,* ***PAVLOV*** *is the* **ESS** *for m (memory size)* ≥ 2. *If the probability of another repetition of the Avatamsaka game is less than one,* ***PAVLOV*** *is the* **ESS** *for any memory size. This result can easily be applied to any dependent game (with any number of players and with any number of strategies). The Pavlovian strategy is the ESS in a dependent game: Keep changing my action until the others benefit me.*

Table 4.12 The number of strategies that lead to the stable state

	Player 1	Player 2
The special assignment	**1398101**	**1973785**

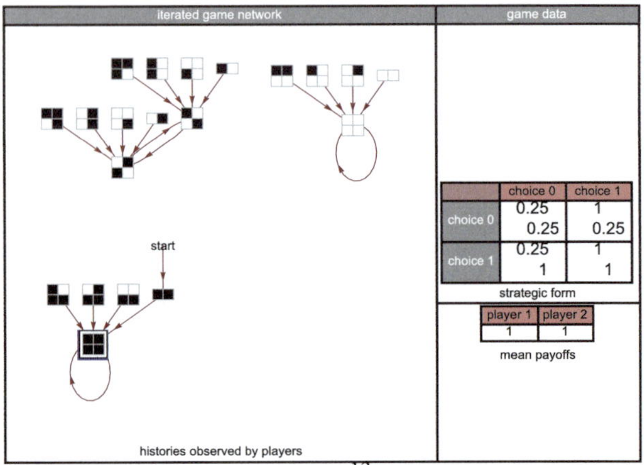

Fig. 4.3 The solution of Avatamsaka's game

Avatamsaka game was proposed by Aruka (2001a).[13] The pay-off matrix is arranged according to the following conditions[14]:

> Each player's payoff completely depends on the others' action, *never* on his/her own action.
> No player has any incentive to change his/her action from the game-theoretical point of view.
> Any combination of mixed strategies is a Nash equilibrium.

In this game, the incentive for immediate maximization of personal profit is removed. Note also that there are infinite Nash equilibria in this game.

4.2.2.1 Stable sate of Avatamsaka game

However, note that we have already known another way to quickly represent the same convergence toward the stable state. Upon careful inspection, it turns out that Fig. 4.2 always holds for any arrangement of payoffs of either Prisoner dilemma game or Avatamsaka game. **The stable state of Avatamsaka game** is obtained by assigning the same strategy numbers as the PD game, i.e., **TFT strategy set** (Table 4.12).

Given this strategy assignment, the Avatamsaka game can reach the stable state as shown in Fig. 4.3. Note that the game data of Fig. 4.3 differ from the data of Fig. 4.2. It is also easy to check that the mean payoff achieves its maximum value at (1, 1).

---

[13] Also see Aruka (2001b) in view of a Polya urn process. As for a non-self averaging, see Aruka and Akiyama (2009).
[14] For a payoff sample of numerical values, see Fig. 4.3.

Table 4.13 The case that Player 1 is judged to be good

	Good-type	Bad-type
	Pl1	Pl2
time 0		
time 1		

Table 4.14 The case that Player 1 is judged to be bad

	Good-type	Bad-type
	Pl1	Pl2
time 0		
time 1		

4.2.3 Tagging Mechanism of the PD Game

Tagging is one of the main mechanisms of **CAS**. To solve the so-called data size problem, we introduce **a tagging mechanism** into the PD game. It may be a useful way for the player to identify an opponent player with a *preferable* partner. There are often recognized **parasites** who never cooperate but earn from other, cooperative players. As the fitness of the society increases, the parasite also is allowed to earns more. Thus, their expulsion from the game is significant. Several recent contributions have been made in this context by Ohtsuki and Iwasa (2004, 2006).[15] They have suggested a tagging mechanism by labeling the reputation tag. They assumed that there existed two types of reputation of good (G-type) and bad (B-type) among the players. We apply the same presentation diagram that we used to this problem.

In Table 4.13, Player 2 is assumed to belong to the bad-type one. This indicates that Player 1 is assigned the tag *good* if he proceeds with Choice 0 (cooperation) against Player 2's Choice 1 (defection), but reacts by means of **the mixed strategy** as gray-colored against the next move of Choice 1 (defection). The latter strategy would be justified in protecting himself/herself from loss. In Table 4.14, Player 1 is assumed *bad*. The table shows that Player 1 always uses the mixed strategy against any reaction of Player 2. This formation of strategies allows players to make profits, as Ohtsuki and Iwasa (2004) and (2006) proved. By resorting to tagging, we have then confirmed **the optimal choices**:

Proposition 4.2 *If a player is tagged as good and encounters an opponent of good type, the optimal choice is always Choice 0 (cooperation). But the next move may be allowed to be the mixed strategy.*

If the players is tagged as bad and encounters an opponent of good type, the optimal choice is always the mixed strategy anytime.

[15] Also see Iwasa and Lee (2013) as for **the punishment mechanism**.

Thus, we can incorporate a tagging mechanism to make easier the fitness to lead to goodness. The identification as good or bad is a kind of **custom**. There are found several variants of this. There are at least two social norms: Kandori and Stern-judging. See Kandori (1992) for the former, and Sugden (1986) and Pacheco et al. (2006) for the latter.

However, a tagging mechanism as a custom is still challenging, because we do not know well either how to give a tag to many players or how to recognize who's who when we encounter. In particular, we newly require **some institution** or **rule** to publicize **the scores of players**. But we do not know smarter selection from the big data pertaining to complex situations and a large number of players.

4.3 Concluding Remarks

Thus far, we have discussed how to find a stable state from an enormous number of states provided by a simple 2-by-2 game. Our findings in the above exercises are mainly based on a heuristic method. We have specified a particular configuration to exhibit the steady states of Figs. 4.2 and 4.3 but discovered from 2^{21} possible states. This derivation was achieved by resort to intuition. A more direct method may be needed to make the simulation efficient. When the number of states are large, it may be challenging for us to formulate an appropriate. Thus, it seems difficult to attain the desired purpose and the evolution of the system, without finding any computable rule. We wish to employ a research policy to apply simulations, but a smarter manner that is the case at present.

Exercises

4.1 You have learnt about the CAS (complex adaptive system) as a set of four properties and three mechanisms. Mention an example or an observed case corresponding to each of them, and then describe what kind of actual systems may be identified with a CAS.

4.2 In the text above, blood coagulation is introduced as a Trojan horsew's effect for biological bodies. Given an imunoediting paradox often found in living creatures, write how organisms adapt to their environment to survive with reference to the CAS definition.

4.3 Make up your own numerical examples of the prisoner's dilemma, with reference to Table 4.5. Also verify its Nash equilibrium property.

4.4 Describe shortly the Tit for Tat (TFT) strategy and the Folk Theorem and examine whether your personal experiences of applying TFT to everyday life is successful or not.

4.5 Examine the numerical example of the Prisoner's Dilemma that you have created yourself to show that the optimal strategy implies the evolutionary stable strategy (ESS) . If possible, use the simulator of the interated game to verify the result. Hint: See refer to the simulator programmed by Seth Chandler. See footnote 9. http://demonstrations.wolfram.com/IteratedGames/.

4.6 Describe how the introduction of iterated games can transform the gaming environment and conclusions.

4.7 Describe how the introduction of repeated games can transform the gaming environment and conclusions. In this framework, show that winning game does not necessarily differs from the maximizing payoffs.

4.8 The Art of War (military text by Sun Tzu, 512 BCE) , even now often actually used, is not shy on the use of deception which runs through many of the suggested stratagems. In this kind of view, examine the next Axelrod' s proposition: "the longer the tournament period, the more probable a simple program of more altruistic type to win."

4.9 Referring to tagging mechanism in Sect. 4.2.3, imagine another instance of tagging in the PD game. Moreover, suggest a tagging in the Avatamsaka game, if possible.

4.10 In the iterated game, we sometimes observe "state cycles" depending on the histories of the choices of strategy. Estimate in what kind of the histories such a cycle will emerge.

References

Akiyama, E., & Aruka, Y. (2006). Evolution of reciprocal cooperation in the Avatamsaka game. In A Namatame, T. Kaizoji, Y. Aruka (Eds.), *The complex networks of economic interactions: Essays in agent-based economics and econophysics* (pp. 307—329). Springer Heidelberg.

Aruka, Y. (2001a). Avatamsaka game structure and experiment on the web. In Y. Aruka (Ed.), *Evolutionary controversies in economics* (pp. 115—132). Springer.

Aruka, Y. (2001b) Avatamsaka game experiment as a nonlinear Polya urn process. In T. Terano, A. Namatame, et al. (Eds.) *New frontiers on artificial intelligence* (pp. 153–161). Springer.

Aruka, Y., & Akiyama, E. (2009). Non-self-averaging of a two-person game with only positive spillover: A new formulation of Avatamsaka's dilemma. *Journal of Economic Interaction and Coordination, 4*(2), 135–161.

Axelrod, R. (1984). *The evolution of cooperation*. Basic Books.

Axelrod, R., & Hamilton, W. D. (1981). The evolution of cooperation. *Science, 211*, 1390–1396. March.

Chandler, S. (2011). Iterated Games. http://demonstrations.wolfram.com/IteratedGames/.

Holland, J. H. (1995). *Hidden order: How adaptation builds complexity*. Basic Books.

Iwasa, Y., & Lee, J. H. (2013). Graduated punishment is efficient in resource management if people are heterogeneous. *Journal of Theoretical Biology, 333*(21), 117–125.

Kandori, M. (1992). Social norms and community enforcement. *The Review of Economic Studies, 59*, 63–80. January.
Mainzer, K. (2007). Kapitel 7: Zufall in Kultur, Wirtschaft, und Gesselschaft. In *Der kreative Zufall: Wie das Neue in die Welt kommt?*. CH Beck.
Nowak, M. A., & Sigmund, K. (1993). A strategy of win-stay, lose-shift that outperforms tit for tat in Prisoner's Dilemma. *Nature, 364*(6432), 56–58. March.
Ohtuski, H., & Iwasa, Y. (2004). How should we define goodness?: Reputation dynamics in indirect reciprocity. *Journal of Theoretical Biology, 231*, 107–120.
Ohtuski, H., & Iwasa, Y. (2006). The leading eight: Social norms that can maintain cooperation by indirect reciprocity. *Journal of Theoretical Biology, 239*, 435–444.
Pacheco, J. M., Santos, F. C., & Chalub, F. C. (2006). A simple, successful norm which promotes cooperation under indirect reciprocity. *PLOS Computational Biology, 2*(12), e178.
Poundstone, W. (1992). *Prisoner's dilemma: John von Neumann, game theory, and the puzzle of the bomb*. Anchor NY.
Rubinstein, A. (1979). Equilibrium in supergames with the overtaking criterion. *Journal of Economic Theory, 21*(1), 1–9.
Sugden, R. (1986). *The economics of rights*. Cooperation and Welfare. Basil Blackwell.
von Stackelberg, H. (1934). *Marktform und Gleichgewichit; (English translation 1952: The theory of the market economy, Oxford University Press, Oxford, UK)*. Wien und Berlin: Springer.

Part II
Evolution of Economics

The Evolution of Molecule System and the Systemic Risks

5

Abstract

Clearly, the biological notion of the multi-cellular organism entailing multi-level evolution in terms of computational complexity is helpful for understanding society. This perspective enables the identification of the institutional factors and integrative character of modern evolving system s. The computational complexity, which is based on algorithms, engenders the possibility of the complex emergence of higher orders of institutions based on cooperation. In the case of the economy, the notion of "Markomata " propounded by Mirowski (J Econ Behav Organ 63(2):209–242, 2007) plays a decisive role. Accordingly, the existence and competition between hierarchical economic institutions also implies problems of computational complexity, again with no definite direction or outcome as a likely result. Evolution itself is a profoundly complex process, and so it is when it happens to economic institutions. Economic institutions must serve as the coordinating device. Conversely, this device will function as a sensor mechanism for sustaining the underlying system. We have witnessed a number of debates centering on the polarity between Keynesian and Hayekian economic theories and on a "command and control" perspective versus an "unregulated market" perspective. A contemporary biologist, David Sloan Wilson, has proposed "e'v'onomics" (Wilson in Stop crying about the size of government. Start caring about who controls it. The Role of the State in the Economy, 2016) that highlights the significance of the multi-cellular organism. A multi-cellular organism is composed of trillions of cells that must be healthy at the cellular and organ levels for the multi-cellular organism to be healthy. In the same way, for a large-scale human society to work well, it must be organized as smaller-scale units that work well and are properly coordinated for the benefit of the whole. Clearly, the biological notion of the multi-cellular organism entailing multi-level evolution in terms of computational complexity is helpful for understanding society.

Y. Aruka, *Evolutionary Economics*, Springer Texts in Business and Economics,
https://doi.org/10.1007/978-981-97-1382-0_5

5.1 Economics of Eigenstates

"Eigenstate" is not a monopolistic discovery. Peiro Sraffa, Cambridge economists who was bon in Italy, has noticed already at least at the end of 1920's the same idea such as "eigenstate" in the sense that the same proportion is held after a transformation of the original state. This idea was published in 1960 in the book form of Sraffa (1960). Sraffa argued the eigenstate where the output ratio is the same as the input ration in the transformation from inputs A to outputs B.[1]

$$Bx = \lambda Ax.$$

He called this state x **standard commodity**. A input vector x is preserved after an eigen-transformation λ as a output vector. In the system of standard commodity, any cost change will be also cancelled out in the output price system.

It is noted that Sraffa's idea of standard commodity is not different from an eigenstate of **quantum state** in the sense that

$$H\psi_o = E\psi_0.$$

Here ψ is a wave function formulated by Schrödinger. It is noted that ψ is preserved after the transformation. We do not need to discuss the wave function of physics here.[2] We simply emphasize that an eigenstate does not represent any causal association such as a functional relationship $f(x)$ from input A to output B.

We already knew that the idea of eigenvector space is a natural extension of eigenstate. Once upon a time, Goodwin (1976), who was hinted by Sraffa (1960), suggested the idea of **general coordinates** to represent a whole situation of the input-output system, although Goodwin did not deal with imaginary roots. Its generalization has been formulated in Aruka (1991), where a price-cost movement equation system on the system (A, B) was decomposed into eigensectors, which can be interpreted as real clusters except for sectors associated with imaginary roots. Imaginary number may capture dynamics of the system, although there is lost a realistic entity in static states.

The eigenstate of economics was originally exemplified as **a constant value measure** on commodity space by Sraffa (1960).[3] The transformation to make the output ratio the same as the input ratio generates an eigenstate. Thus Sraffa's eigenstate is represented as a composite commodity of the eigenvectors to construct its eigenstate. But it is interesting for us to see a similar idea of eigenstate among physics and economics in a sense that outputs after transformation belongs to the same dimension as input. Thus when we argue economics, we will not confine our perspective to a functional approach like **production function** to examine an economic system from scratch.

[1] A, B may be interpreted as matrices of n by n.

[2] ψ is a dimensionless number.

[3] See "Notes on Malthus's Measure of Value" by David Ricardo in 1832. https://www.goodreads.com/book/show/1126247.Notes_on_Malthus_s_Measure_of_Value_.

Incidentally, Schrödinger depicted that the state of a system evolves with time. A closed quantum system then evolves by following a unitary operator, the time evolution operator. As well known, there is preserved either any distance or any inner product in the unitary transformation. However, this idea does not apply to economics, because any matrix of input does not necessarily fulfill a unitary transformation. This point is a decisive difference between physics and economics.

Economic scientists often work apart from pure economists. They usually come from physics, informatics, and systems science backgrounds. Why have economists convinced themselves that the economic system could be an independent system purely separate from other social systems and/or institutions? In contrast, it holds that economic scientists prefer to address the socio-economic system rather than simply the economic system when they discuss economic phenomena.

In the same way that we cannot live without minding our health, we must also be aware of our economic activities. To this end, several analytical tools with multipotency that are applicable to various wider fields are thriving. It may be easier to adopt some of these tools for economic analysis than other. It is not unusual to encounter scientists who are interested in and seeking to cultivate new economic analyses. Here, pure economists should recognize that their prescriptions naturally cannot give other scientists or the public reason to believe their opinions because pure economics may never guarantee a practical result.

Currently the use of algorithms dominates the financial market and other socio-economic systems. How should we re-examine the economics of human nature without referring to artificial intelligence? In the era of algorithm dominance by artificial intelligence, it must be the case that our society no longer holds under the principle of human nature only.

We are nevertheless exposed to the so-called worldwide standardization of economic disciplines. In general, however, any compulsion to follow doctrine would likely be futile in either religion or science.

5.2 Toward the Reconceptualization of a New Analytical Device

While the previous century witnessed consumption of physical goods and services on a massive scale, information utilization on a similar scale, in various contexts, is a feature of the current century. Intensive utilization of information as a result of pervasive information and communications technology (ICT) is a key characteristic of contemporary society. For example, high-frequency trading (HFT) markets and "smart grids" for the allocation of electricity are based on the idea of smart information management at astronomical scales that extend well beyond the scope of our imagination. However, given the scarcity of resources, the achievement of optimal performances is solely contingent on the deployment of human rationality.

The concept of myopic optimization in relation to scarce resources assumes the least use of available information. Evidently, myopic optimization was a winning strategy during a previous developmental stage when access to big data was denied.

However, this strategy no longer seems tenable. The reality has shifted now that quantum computing is no longer a distant possibility. With the implementation of HFT, markets can even operate under essentially traditional rules, while producing a qualitatively different series of fluctuations from those of the past. A political revolution is not necessary; rather, a systemic revamping as suggested, for example, by "Industry 4," automatically entails a "re-domaining" of the socioeconomic system.

AlphaGo's victory

AlphaGo's victory over its human opponent in an Igo game competition in 2015 was a symbolic marker of the overwhelming gains of non-human intelligence over human intelligence. This was apparent given that Igo is the most difficult game in which the strategy tree comprises a total of $10^4$00 nodes. With the advent of a new era coexisting with that of artificial intelligence, it has become imperative to revise our methods of inference within economics and, more widely, within the social sciences. A more realistic consideration will evidently expose us to a domain at an astronomical scale . This can be illustrated using the example of an iterative two player-two strategy game. Even in this game, a classical inference that is confined to a narrow set of rational principles for detecting a solution would not hold for a broader framework that is designed to allow players access to past memories of their moves. Memories relating to the preceding two periods would enable the formulation of possible strategic combinations of the two players to a value of $2^2$1 by $2^2$1(4.4 trillion). Here, we simply introduced interactive decisions made during the preceding two turns associated with the burgeoning information structure.

von Stackelberg (1934) was the first to recognize inference based on the observation of complex interactions among participants in a duopolistic market. However, the procedure for examining the complex deployment of strategic interactions at such a vast scale is beyond our grasp. As this example demonstrates, the time has come to change our analytical approach from mathematically pedantic inference to agent-based inference.

Econophysics has become an established field following its emergence at the end of the last century as a result of the extensive collection of large amounts of data . With the availability of substantial amounts of simulated data, network analysis of heterogeneous interactions is being promoted through agent-based modelling that also enables human sentiments to be analyzed based on data/text mining. This mining reveals just how effective machine-based learning, which is not just limited to humans, actually is. This kind of learning will prove beneficial in discovering potential connections. Text mining will provide new insights for prediction. This kind of inference, in particular, may prove to be robust in an area wherein the traditional method does not work well. In addition, sensor technology, in combination with machine learning, is now, for example, drastically transforming our method of driving a car. Consequently, industries as well as industrial policies are also shifting toward intensive utilization of information.

Summing up

To sum up, we can observe how the method of inference would be transformed as a result of adapting to the societal change that is currently underway. Our traditional method of inference should be revised to become information sensitive, marking a shift from myopic purification which does not entail any heavy commitment to a massive influx of information. The time is ripe for a change of theories as well as the formulation of analytical tools that are oriented toward this shift. Equipped with new insights resulting from considerations that are information sensitive, we aim to develop a new approach for handling the two-sided transformation of ontology and epistemology. This requires us to first attempt to construct the theoretical and ontological foundations of the new approach. Subsequently, empirical and epistemological studies can be conducted to examine sentiments and other movements within financial markets.

5.3 Some Philosophical Designs for Economics

I have previously discussed an alternative pathway for economics at some length (see Aruka, 2015). Elsewhere, we have witnessed a number of debates centering on the polarity between Keynesian and Hayekian economic theories and on a "command and control" perspective versus an "unregulated market" perspective. A contemporary biologist, David Sloan Wilson, has proposed "e'v'onomics" (Wilson, 2016) that highlights the significance of the multi-cellular organism:

> A multi-cellular organism is composed of trillions of cells that must be healthy at the cellular and organ levels for the multi-cellular organism to be healthy. In the same way, for a large-scale human society to work well, it must be organized as smaller-scale units that work well and are properly coordinated for the benefit of the whole. This is a daunting task that has been accomplished largely by unintended cultural group selection in the past, as Hayek was wise to note. But it needs to take place through intentional cultural evolution now more than ever before, realizing that this doesn't mean command and control. I think that Vincent and Elinor Ostrom were reaching in the same direction with their concept of polycentric governance .

Multi-level evolution

> Clearly, the biological notion of the multi-cellular organism entailing multi-level evolution in terms of computational complexity is helpful for understanding society.

This perspective enables the identification of the institutional factors and integrative character of modern evolving systems. The computational complexity, which is based on algorithms, engenders the possibility of the complex emergence of higher orders of institutions based on cooperation.

"Markomata"

> In the case of the economy, the notion of "Markomata " propounded by Mirowski (2007) plays a decisive role. Accordingly, "markets come to bits ." As noted by Rosser (2009): "[t]he existence and competition between hierarchical economic institutions also implies problems of computational complexity, again with no definite direction or outcome [as] a likely result. Evolution itself is a profoundly complex process, and so it is when it happens to economic

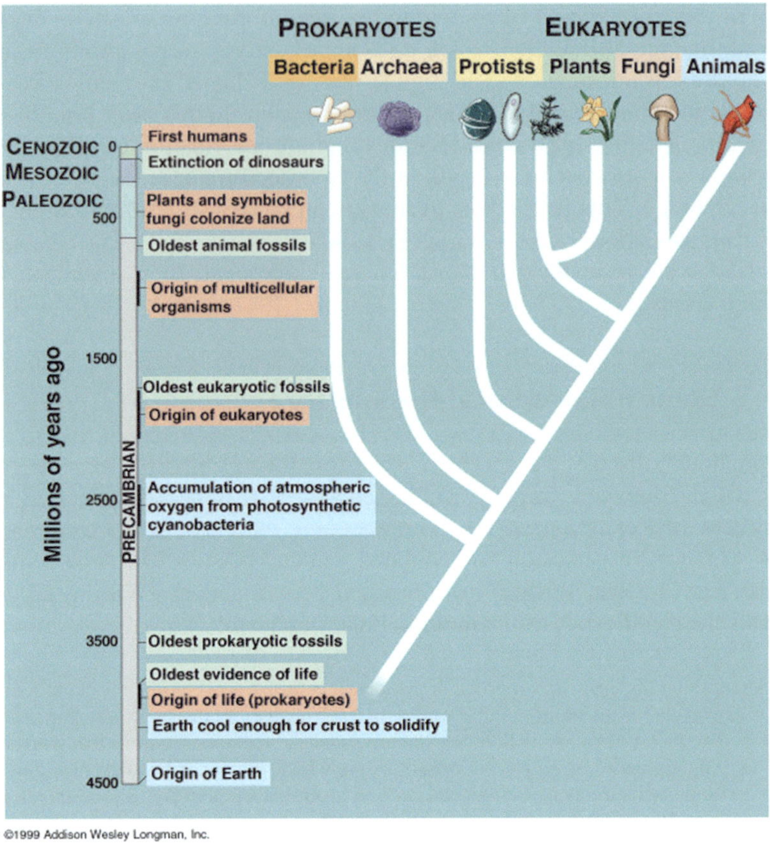

Fig. 5.1 A phylogenetic and symbiogenetic tree of living organisms showing the origins of eukaryotes and prokaryotes (reproduced from an iStock vector image:139422)

institutions." Economic institutions must serve as the coordinating device. Conversely, this device will function as a sensor mechanism for sustaining the underlying system.

Before we proceed further, it would be helpful to broadly illustrate the earth's history by depicting a phylogenetic and symbiogenetic tree of living organisms that shows the origins of eukaryotes and prokaryotes. Figure 5.1 shows the evolutionary process from uni-cellular to multi-cellular systems.

5.3.1 The Characteristic Features of Living Systems

We shall now examine the inner workings of multi-cellular organisms. However, before we do so, we will introduce the application of probability within biology, that is, in relation to living systems. According to the law of large numbers, probability defines the limits of relative frequency. However, as established by Sober (2000), the definition is *circular* as a result of employing another probability that is either objective or hypothetical.

Based on an examination of Karl Popper's propensity theory, Nakajima (2013) has proposed a new application of probability within biology. Briefly, Nakajima (2013) has used "cognizer system" modelling to demonstrate that the characteristic abilities of living systems, namely discriminability and selectivity, enable them to engage with uncertainty. Moreover, these abilities could affect the relative frequencies of the occurrences of events. This influence occurs during different stages extending from the level of a molecule to that of a human being. Nakajima (2013) has, in fact, provided an apt instance to illustrate this:

The molecular structure and chemical properties of proteins affect the probability that they will have encounters with other molecules, which in turn determines the rate of a certain molecular reaction in which proteins act as an enzyme.

Observations do not depend on any specific attributes of influencing factors such as a particular ligand. In the example of dice throwing, the physical conditions accompanying the throw, namely the direction of gravity, the angle of a table surface, and others will affect the frequencies. Consequently, we require the concept of internal probability in relation to the cognizer.

We must first assume that there is a cognizer. The nature of the cognizer may be either an objective material such as a molecule or a living cell, or a person. Let us suppose that the state transition is cognized by the cognizer. As I subsequently demonstrate, the competence of the cognizer may depend on the quality of the analytical device.

The state transition of A comprising a set of the elements $a_1, a_2, \cdots, a_n$ can be described by the following configuration of states:

$$\{a_1, a_2, a_3, a_4, \ldots, a_1, a_2, a_5, a_6\} \tag{5.1}$$

"Cognition" is defined by the following function:

$$f : (a_i, \cdot) \to a_k \tag{5.2}$$

Here, $\cdot$ indicates an unspecified environment. This configuration of states includes a double a_1 and a double a_2, that is, several multiplicities of the same state(s).

Thus, a "focal cognizer " is subsequently subjected to the uncertainty of events. We, therefore, need to focus on how successor a_i will change or converge. This is a cognitive process. In this context, cognition is represented by the motion function. This motion function is constituted by several participating agents, whether material or human.

In the above world constituted by A, we will let a cognizer have the ability to discriminate between e_2 and e_5. Consequently, multiple (one-to-many) correspondences hold between a given cognition $(a_1, \cdot) \to a_2$ and subsequent cognitions, $(a_2, e_2) \to a_3$ and $(a_2, e_5) \to a_4$ for internal cognizers.

5.3.2 Internal Probability

Given the existence of uncertainties, interactions between cognizers and their environments must be significant. Each cognizer interacts with others, and the state changes to a subsequent state as the motion to cognize its environment.

> Internal probability subsequently emerges within the cognizer system.

This is because necessary interactions affect "not only the degree of uncertainty, but [they] also affect the relative frequency of the occurrence of events after repeated trials" (Nakajima, 2013, 72).

It appears to be self-evident that a state A depends on variations of environment $E\{e_1, \ldots, e_n\}$. However, a human or other subject cannot be an omniscient observer with the ability to discriminate between them.

> There appears to be a distinction between a state and an event resulting from a limited ability to discriminate. According to Nakajima (2013, 75) , in relation to internal cognizers,"[e]vents can occur indeterministically even within a deterministic world."

In sum, a cognizer cognizes or discriminates a state a_i over time in the world which all existing cognizers have the ability to constitute. Now, let a state $a \in A$ occur in the environment $e \in E$ where E is composed by a set of variations$e_1, e_2, \ldots, e_n$.Thus, a cognizer's cognition of A is defined . We will subsequently examine how an extremely penetrative monitor could perceive the exact correspondence between A and E.

Discriminability The ability to discriminate simply means distinguishing a specified environment such as e_i or e_k from among different environmental configurations (Nakajima, 2013, 72).

Selectivity Selectivity is simply defined as the choice of one action from among many possibilities that affect a particular outcome. Moreover, the selecting subjects are not limited to humans (Nakajima, 2013, 72).

Thus, we can posit that both properties of selectivity and discriminability influence the degree of uncertainty as well as the relative frequency of the occurrence of events in an iterative cognitive process. Here, we should note that relative frequency exists as an objective fact for an external observer.

A final consideration is that a more developed discriminative ability results in a reduced level of uncertainty for a particular cognizer. In other words, the limited discriminative ability of the cognizer generates uncertainties relating to successive occurrences.

5.3.3 Evolution and Heterogeneous Interactions

The probability of events occurring is often calculated as a measure of their variance. In particular, when we observe the appearance of states and events in the process of self-organization, their variance can be considered a surrogate variable for measuring the degree of their order in the system's configuration. A higher level of cohesion will be formed when the system reflects a lower level of variance. An entity that entails a higher degree of cohesion will include some structural components. In the latter environment , the application of probability is restricted by its structure within which a particular pattern is to be sustained as the result of a nonlinear or heterogeneous interaction.

Taking an example from biology, the cell structure will be formed either through chemical reactions or through mutual interactions among constituent molecules or cells. Consequently, the probability of events occurring is affected by this attributes of living systems. This insight led Nakajima to formulate his internal probability theory in relation to biological or living systems. Predator-prey modelling is in fact cognizer modelling. While a predator endeavors to catch its prey, the prey attempts to flee from the predator. How they move is not a random motion; it is restricted by a structural relationship.

More importantly, the cognizing subjects in this process are not only limited to humans, but also include materials. The material observer behaves as an "internal observer." It is a matter of common knowledge that observations are part of the material interactions between the observer and the objects being observed. Moreover, this kind of interaction appears within biological interactions.

Recent advances within molecular biology aimed at understanding evolution are remarkable. As evidenced by the history of economic thought, during the inception of the discipline, the first step taken to understand the economy had its origins in the conceptualization of blood circulation. One attempt to conceptualize the economy was made by the anatomist, William Harvey (May 1, 1578–June 3, 1657) in his Theory of the circulation of the blood published in 1628. A second attempt was made by another anatomist, William Petty (May 26, 1623–December 16, 1687). Based at Brasenose College, Oxford, Petty developed Political Arithmetic around 1676 and published this work in 1690. In continental Europe, Tableau économique, written by François Quesnay (June 4, 1694–December 16, 1774), a French economist of the Physiocratic school and a physician to the king, who rose to the rank of the first consulting physician, was published in 1758.

5.3.3.1 The Evolutionary Paradox of Coagulation

Coagulation is indispensable for both lower and higher organisms. However, when coagulation occurs in higher organisms like the brain, it can be fatal (Mainzer, 2007). This raises the question of whether this kind of immunoediting paradox is a Trojan horse. The coagulation system in fact overlaps with the immune system. Coagulation can physically trap invading microbes within blood clots. Moreover, some products from the coagulation system can contribute to the innate immune system through their ability to increase vascular permeability and act as chemotactic agents for phagocytic cells. The process of coagulation and fragmentation can be applied to social modelling and mathematically analyzed within a coagulation-fragmentation model. For example, Düring et al. (2017) have developed a stylized model for wealth distribution.

5.3.3.2 Immunoediting

The process of immunoediting refers to the modification of the immunogenicity of a cancer following immuno-surveillance, often giving rise to immunodeficiency. An important point to note is that immuno-competency is lost in the immunocompetent host .

The immune cell is usually capable of distinguishing between normal and abnormal cells. Taking cancer as an example, an antigen could be decomposed into peptides of amino acids. According to the Department of Immunotherapeutics at the University of Tokyo Hospital (2012), the following specific antigens have been identified:

Specific antigens in immunotherapeutics

1. Cancer, testicular antigens (Cancer-Testis antigens): MAGE, XAGE, and NY-ESO-1 proteins that only manifest a cancer cell and do not develop into a normal cell (other than in the testes).
2. Differentiation antigens: gp100, Melan/mart-1, Tyrosinase, PSA, and PAP proteins which only develop into an organization produced by a cancer.
3. Proteins (Mutated proteins): p53, K-ras, N-ras, H-ras, and BCR-ABL according to gene variation.
4. Overexpression proteins (Overexpressed antigens): HER2, MUC-1, PSMA, survivin , and WT-1 proteins that are rare in normal cells and are frequently found in cancer cells.
5. Tumor fetus antigens (Oncofetal antigens): CEA protein, which is the AFP that develops organizationally into a cancer cell of the fetus in the womb.
6. Proteins (Viral proteins) that are derived from a cancer-causing virus such as EBV, HBV, HCV, HPV, and HERV.

The T cell receptor (TCR) on an immune cell, which is specific to an antigen, subsequently reacts to the cancer cell. The antigen counters the antibody in an antigen-antibody reaction. The capacity of the immune system to provide immunity, which is known as immunoediting, functions bilaterally to suppress as well as shape abnormal cells.

According to Dunn et al. (2002), cancer immunoediting is characterized by three phases ("the three Es") which may occur either sequentially or independently. These are: elimination, equilibrium, and escape.

The "three Es" of cancer immunoediting

1. Elimination corresponds to cancer immunosurveillance, wherein immunity functions as an extrinsic tumor suppressor in naive hosts;

2. Equilibrium represents the process whereby the immune system iteratively selects and/or checks the generation of tumor cell variants with increasing capacities to survive an immune system attack;
3. Escape refers to the process wherein an immunologically sculpted tumor expands in an uncontrolled manner within an immunocompetent host. Here, tumor cell variants with dampened immunogenicity grow into clinically apparent cancers.

5.3.3.3 White Blood Cell Evolution

As previously discussed, at the end of the 17th century, the theory of blood circulation was applied in the development of economics. A body of literature has now accumulated focusing on studies of blood at the molecular level. Here we consider the example of white blood. The following description is derived from Abo (2010) and is also depicted in Fig. 5.2. At an early stage in the evolution of white blood cells (WBCs), primitive lymphocytes are generated by primitive macrophages. Within the previously organized immune system , natural killer cells first branch off from primitive macrophages, followed by extrathymic T cells. Thus, the immune system is newly organized with thymus-derived T cells.

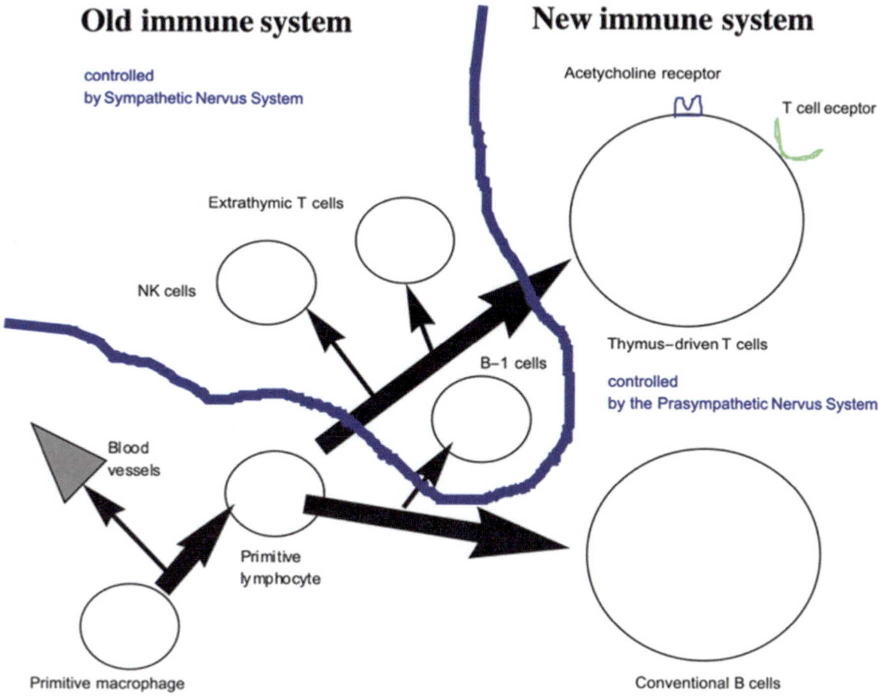

Fig. 5.2 Evolution of a white blood cell (derived from Abo, 2010)

5.3.3.4 Risks to the Defense System

In this chapter, we will demonstrate how a material cognizer initiates a complex action/reaction. It seemingly looks like an action by the use of a systemic device . Accordingly, the cognizer decides on its course of action by applying some sort of structural device, whether intentionally or unintentionally. Even at a biological cellular level, the structure of such a device must itself reflect an advanced level of complexity. Here we examine an instance of a complex interaction generated by the immune system (Fig. 5.3).

5.3.3.5 Co-stimulators

A complicated mechanism exists to activate T cells, which are usually antigen-specific. These cells are activated as a result of being stimulated by a particular antigen that is bound to the TCR. The antigen stimulation constitutes the first signal that is received by the TCR. However, the first signal is not sufficient to activate the T cell, which requires a second signal for its activation. This second signal, which confirms activation, is known as the co-stimulatory factor. If notification by the second signal failed to occur, the TCR would enter an energy state, indicating a state of inactivation. Immune tolerance would consequently occur. In sum, the integration of a signal for antigen stimulation in association with a co-stimulatory molecule around a particular antigen can activate an antigen-specific T cell.

5.3.3.6 Co-inhibitors

A co-inhibitory molecule exists in parallel with a co-stimulatory molecule. This molecule, which is located in the same extracellular region as the co-stimulatory molecule, transmits a signal of restraint to a T cell. The inhibitory signal only operates when it is stimulated by an antigen. This membrane-type receptor is known as an inhibitory molecule.

Neither co-stimulatory nor inhibitory factors can ever influence the TCRs in the absence of antigen-specific T cells. Because of this characteristic, T cells have a considerable immunological advantage in being able to restrict their effects within a specific locale, regardless of whether their action relates to stimulation or inhibition.

The concept of **a checkpoint** may be helpful for handling systemic risks.[4] The immune system defends biological cells. Here, we focus on the surface-level immune system of human cells. The surface-level cancer immune evasion mechanism that mediates between **T cells** and **antigen-presenting cells (APCs)** illustrates this. The basic mechanism comprises stimulation as well as inhibition occurring between T cells and APCs. Stimulation is associated with particular tags. A manifested tag will be targeted. A widely recognized tag is the major histocompatibility complex (MHC). As defined by Wikipedia (2016), this is "the tissue antigen that allows the immune system (more specifically T cells) to bind to, recognize, and tolerate itself (autorecognition)".

[4] See Syljuaasen (2007) for checkpoint adaptation.

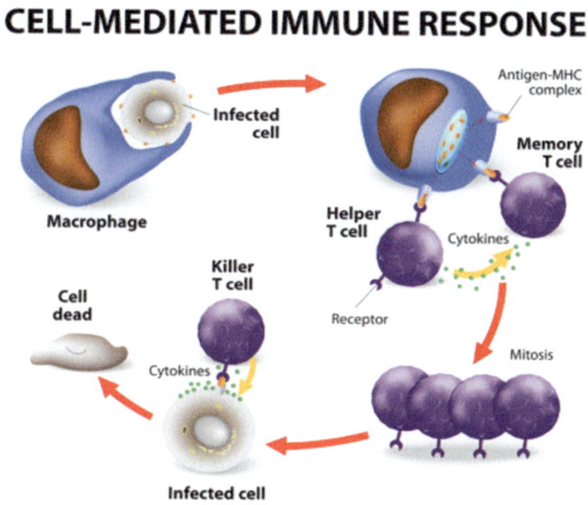

Fig. 5.3 A cell-mediated immune response (reproduced from an iStock vector image: 42359420)

If the tags do not manifest, T cells will lose their target. The relationship associated with inhibitors has been well studied. In this case, a cell's programmed death 1 (PD1) is blocked by a programmed death-ligand 1(PD-L1), which is an inhibitor of the immune system. A number of asymmetrical matchings in which tags between stimulators and inhibitors are absent have been detected. Many blockades (not limited to one) against activation or inactivation are generated simultaneously within these matchings.

Distinct from the motion that occurs between T cells and APCs, another motion occurs in which activation of T cells generates **cytokyne** irrespective of the existence of a particular target. The latter will generally contribute to inflammatory attacks on certain parts.

In sum, the immune system is multi-dimensional in terms of its reactions, entailing sophisticated interactive motions at the bottom. The recent surge of works on agent-based modelling (ABM) or simulation in medicine is notable. These studies include Piras et al. (2011), Fullstone et al. (2015), and Altrock et al. (2015).

5.3.4 A Systemic Risk Generated in the Immune System

Immune cells, both *B* and *T* cells, evolved from macrophagesc. The immune system is the result of biological evolution that has led to the development of the human body as a complex system entailing the immune system among other systems. More importantly, a particular cancer tumor, which represents a systemic risk for the human body, is composed of a collection of heterogeneous cells.

When a reproductive cell mechanism is partially disrupted, but is still capable of reproducing chromosomes within the kernel or nucleus of the cell, an excessive number of chromosomes will proliferate. These chromosomes will then produce newly *degraded* cells, resulting in further degradation.

Immunodeficiency

> Consequently, the concerned tumor may be composed of a collection of heterogeneous variants. The interaction of such factors within a complex system may induce **immunodeficiency** that can be verified.

> It is very interesting to see that immune system will be taken over by the cells of immunodeficiency. This may apply to the market system. Pure rational agents will be replaced with seeming irrational agents.

A single primitive cell may evolve into a more complex one. The antibody-antigen reaction does not necessarily function efficiently. **Immunodeficiency** may be generated as a subset entailing inadequate functioning of either antioxidant or immune stimulators to suppress cancer cells. As you see, we recognize some positive contribution to immunoefficiency from **apotosis**, **necrosis**, **autophagy** and **ferroptosis**.[5] However, some negative contribution due to them will also be noticeable.[6]

5.3.4.1 The Discovery of Autophagy

Professor Yoshinori Ohsumi has been awarded a Nobel Prize in physiology or medicine for his discovery of **autophagy** in 2016. This process is defined as : "a normal process in which a cell destroys proteins and other substances in its cytoplasm (the fluid inside the cell membrane but outside the nucleus), which may lead to cell death. Autophagy may prevent normal cells from developing into cancer cells, but it may also protect cancer cells by destroying anticancer drugs or substances taken up by them."

5.4 Biodigital Convergence Looking at Transhumanism

We never only limited to this kind of flaws in economic thinking. At the end of the last century, the society has moved to be engineered by AI related technology. We just look at another aspect of human being at the current society. Here we take the existence of **Neurorights**. This idea is given Neurorights Foundation.[7] Chile has became the first country to enact **the Nuerorights Law** in 2021. Needless to say, everything is not necessarily certain to be directed towards this new rights. In the present world, we are easy to encounter not only a breakdown of universality of agent but also force to take into account the neurorights, which is different from our traditional civilian rights.

This new stream will be formed in the form of **transhumanism**. At the end of the last century, transhumanism turned into being a main context as a target of the

[5] See process and function on ferrotosis for Xie et al. (2016).

[6] See the homepage of National Cancer Institute (2016).

[7] https://neurorightsfoundation.org.

AI technology became human body.[8] This is not a conspiracy theory but a reality in the translational technological field like **translational medicine**, which has the same name journal from *Science*.

Biodigital convergence

Istvan (2016/17) stated as follows:[9]

We must force our evolution in the present day via our reasoning, inventiveness, and especially our scientific technology." This idea will lead to the idea to grant rights to AI computers and proposing to "upgrade" animals into rational beings. Some research group might challenge to improve human bounded rationality by annexing with a quantum computer server at maximum. This trend, like it or not, cannot fail to influence ideas in economics. In fact, this stream is called **biodigital convergence** looking at transhumanism. It is interesting to learn a challenge titled: "Biocompatible near-infrared quantum dots delivered to the skin by microneedle patches record vaccination" by McHugh et al. (2019).

5.4.1 The Neurorights Foundation

We then have to cross the line soon. Elon Musk's Neuralink has the objective of promoting the widespread use of **BCI** (Brain-Computer Interface) technology.[10] Reading from neurons is problematic enough on its own. Wireless brain-computer interfaces may interact with current or future wireless GSM infrastructures. There is also the potential for hackers and other malicious actors to compromise such networks to obtain and use people's brain data.

BCI: Brain-Computer Interface

- BCIs are devices that can not only read data from neurons, but also write data to them.
- BCIs can rigorously alter perceptions of basic things such as emotions and values, and can alter thresholds for satiety, happiness, anger and disgust. For example, BCIs can change entire behaviours such as appetite and desire suppression, as described in Maslow's hierarchy of needs theory.
- With direct access to the human brain and its contents through digestible nanotechnology, as a despot, control of human behaviour becomes possible in any way.

[8] Julian Huxley was a biologist who popularised the term transhumanism in an influential 1957 essay. Cited from https://en.wikipedia.org/wiki/Transhumanism.

[9] https://www.technocracy.news/oxymoron-christian-transhumanism-is-trending/.

[10] In 2013, during the Obama administration, the Defence Advanced Research Projects Agency DARPA launched the BRAIN Initiative, an acronym for Brain Research Through Advancing Innovative Neurotechnologies. BRAIN is an acronym for Brain Research Through Advancing Innovative Neurotechnologies.

The digital and bio technologies are thus deeply overturning the traditional common sense. **Moral bio-enhancement** (abbreviated MBE), is the use of biomedical technology to morally improve individuals. During the last decade, MBE has become a main issue often argued in the academic journals either ethics or neuroscience.[11] In particular, many advocates of MBE prefer the utilitarian principle to justify the use of it. Those usually apply a kind of straight forward application of the global utilitarian principle. However, the global utilitarianism of MBE involves many serious problems about the goals of medicine, the principle of justice, and the cultural complicity. Furthermore, we also know negative utilitarianism.[12] Life in the state of nature is nasty, brutish, and short. Our pain and pleasure system did not evolve to maximize utility. This point of view will provide us with a grave alarm of the use of utilitarianism. In this chapter, however, we will not deal with the essence of utilitarianism.

Exercises

5.1 In the text above, it was stated that the biological notion of the multi-cellular organism entailing multi-level evolution in terms of computational complexity is helpful for understanding society. Employing an economic example like "market," evaluate whether the evolution from the traditional industrial society to the current digital society was in accordance with this kind of development.

5.2 Mention an economic example of "markomata" by Mirowski (2007) , and to exemplify an economic multi-level evolution.

5.3 Business cycle models are often expressed by a differential equation system, which solution is represented in terms of eigenvectors. Exemplify an economic mode which may be represented by the eigenstates.

5.4 Sraffa's constant value measure was developed in a more general form in Aruka (1991). With reference to Aruka (1991), prepare a numerical example of the Sraffa-Leontief price system of a 3 by 3 input matrix , and then construct a linear differential equation system in the rate of profit r. See Theorem 3 in Aruka (1991).

5.5 Originally, there were various theories of evolution. However, the Darwinian theory of evolution has survived to this day by being valid at the DNA and cellular level. Mention just one interesting new finding of the immune system stated in the text above and then evaluate it.

[11] See, for instance, Kudlek (2022), Kudlek-Smith (2022).

[12] See, for instance, the idea of negative utility: https://nonlinearfunction.org/notes/negative-utility.

5.6 We learnt an immunoediting paradox around blood coagulation in the previous Sect. 4.1.2. We also learnt Immune cells, both *B* and *T* cells, evolved from macrophages in this Sect. 5.3.4. Discuss the idea of optimality in an evolving biological system, describe what an evolutionary paradox is.

5.7 Markov blanket condition (i.e. a statistical boundary precluding direct coupling between internal and external states) is called supporting recently became discussed in relation to the free energy principle. Using Markov blanket, try to explain the reason for the existence of cell membranes.

5.8 Describe the idea of internal probability in terms of Nakajima(2013), and then explain briefly the motion function by using the idea of cognizer/focal cognizer.

5.9 While a predator endeavors to catch its prey, the prey attempts to flee from the predator. This relationship, which is called the predator-prey model, must not be depicted simply by a random matching mechanism. Describe in this modelling why we need the idea of cognizer and their internal probabilities which internal observers can receive.

5.10 Nanotechnology is performing a bio-digital convergence. In economic point of view, evaluate how effect of BCI (Brain-Computer Interface) change the human decision making.

References

Abo, T. (2010). *Dr. Abo's immunology lecture (in Japanese)*. Sanwa-shobo.

Altrock, P. M., Liu, L. L., Michor, F. (2015). Affiliations, the mathematics of cancer: Integrating quantitative models. *Nature Reviews Cancer.*

Aruka, Y. (1991). Generalized goodwin theorems on general coordinates. *Structural Change and Economic Dynamics, 2*(1), 66–91.

Aruka, Y. (2015). *Evolutionary foundations of economic science: How can scientists study evolving economic doctrines from the last centuries?* (Vol. 1) Springer series: Evolutionary economics and social complexity science. Springer.

Duering, B., Georgiou, N., Scalas, E. (2017). Chapter 7: A stylized model for wealth distribution. In *Economic foundations for social complexity science* (pp. 135–157). Springer.

Fullstone, G., Wood, J., Holcombe, M., & Battaglia, G. (2015). Modelling the transport of nanoparticles under blood flow using an agent-based approach. *Scientific Reports, 5*, 10649.

Goodwin, R. (1976). Use of normalized general coordinates in linear value and distribution theory. In K. Polenske, & J. Skolka (Eds.), *Advances in input-output analysis (also reprinted in Goodwin 1983a)*. Macmillan.

Istvan, Z. (2016/17). *Transhumanism and our outdated biology*. Huffpost, Apr 21, 2016. Updated Dec 6, 2017.

Kudlek, K. (2022). On the uneasy alliance between moral bioenhancement and utilitarianism. *Bioethics, 36*(2), 210–2171.

Kudlek, K., & Smith, P. T. (2022). The Kantian promise and peril of moral bioenhancement. *Journal of Applied Philosophy, 39*(3), 487–503.

Mainzer, K. (2007). Kapitel 7: Zufall in Kultur, Wirtschaft, und Gesselschaft. In Der kreative Zufall: Wie das Neue in die Welt kommt? CH Beck.
McHugh, K. J., Jing, L., Jaklenec, A., et al. (2019). Biocompatible near-infrared quantum dots delivered to the skin by microneedle patches record vaccination. *Translational Medicine, 11*(523). (Dec 2019).
Mirowski, P. (2007). Markets come to bits: Evolution computation and markomata in economic science. *Journal of Economic Behavior and Organization, 63*(2), 209–242.
Nakajima, T. (2013). Probability in biology: Overview of a comprehensive theory of probability in living systems. *Progress in Biophysics and Molecular Biology, 113*(1), 67–79.
National Cancer Institute. (2016). Autophagy.
Piras, V., Hayashi, K., Tomita, M., & Selvarajoo, K. (2011). Enhancing apoptosis in trail-resistant cancer cells using fundamental response rules. *Scientific Reports, 1*, 144.
Rosser, B. (2009). *Computational and dynamic complexity in economics*. Handbook on the economic complexity of technological change. Edward Elgar.
Sober, E. (2000). *Philosophy of biology* (2nd edn.). Routledge.
Sraffa, P. (1960). *Production of commodities by means of commodities: Prelude to a critique of economic theory*. Cambridge UP.
Syljuaasen, R. G. (2007). Checkpoint adaptation in human cells. *Oncogene, 26*(40), 5833–39.
von Stackelberg, H. (1934). *Market structure and equilibrium: 1st edition translation into English by D. Bazin*. Springer. (original, 2011).
Wilson, D. S. (2016). Stop crying about the size of government. Start caring about who controls it. The Role of the State in the Economy.
Xie, Y., Hou, W., Song, X., Yu, Y., Huang, J., Sun, X., Kang, R., & Tang, D. (2016). Ferroptosis: Process and function. *Cell Death and Differentiation, 23*, 369–79.

A Measure of Systemic Risk Derived from the Input-Output Table

6

Abstract

We now turn to a consideration of economic matters. In a previous section, we touched on the pioneering contributions of classical political scientists like William Harvey, William Petty, and François Quesnay, all of whom were medical doctors. These individuals conceptualized the economic system in a way that was similar to blood circulation as a kind of node-based network constituted by the circular processing of materials, resources, and services. Quesnay's economic table was the first monumental achievement in this context. Over the course of the 20th century, the forms of this table have changed, as evidenced in Leontief's input-output table and von Neumann-Sraffa's production system. The input-output table has been selected here for empirical reasons.

6.1 The Linear Economic Model

A linear input-output relationship is commonly formulated as follows. Let $m \neq n$ in the number of processes $i = 1, \ldots, m$, and in the number of goods $j = 1, \ldots, n$. The following production process generally occurs:

$$a_i = (a_{i1}, \ldots, a_{im}) \Rightarrow b_i = (b_{i1}, \ldots, b_{im}), i = 1, \ldots, n \tag{6.1}$$

in matrix forms, namely,

$$A \Rightarrow B$$

· Let the number of productive processes i be $m.a_{ij}$, representing the requirement of good j per unit of activity for producing good j, while b_{ij} is the output produced by a unit of activity x_i as follows:

$$a_i x_i = a_{i1} x_i + \cdots + a_{in}, i = 1, \ldots, m \tag{6.2}$$

$$b_i x_i = b_{i1} x_i + \cdots + b_{in}, i = 1, \ldots, m \tag{6.3}$$

Y. Aruka, *Evolutionary Economics*, Springer Texts in Business and Economics,
https://doi.org/10.1007/978-981-97-1382-0_6

The configuration of the activities of the entire system x of a production system is represented by:

$$x = (x_1, \ldots, x_m) \tag{6.4}$$

Consequently, the net producibility in a matrix form is:

$$[B - A]x \geq 0 \tag{6.5}$$

The input-output table holds that when matrices B and A are square, or square or a special case $m = n$. If this occurs, a non-negative eigenvector x^* associated with a maximal eigenvalue λ is guaranteed. Meanwhile, even in a special case, we can find any complex vector, apart from the unique real eigenvector, in the remaining eigenvectors.

6.2 The Location of Eigenvalues in the Complex Plane of the Production System

Drawing on the findings of Brody (1970), Mariolis and Tsoulfidis (2016) have suggested that the eigenvalues of complex numbers could be considered as an index for the degree of capital heterogeneity. Here, we find the existence of a conjugate pair of two different industries except for its sign. Such a pair of industries can mutually influence each other. Aruka (1991) has shown that a price dynamics based on a linear production system may oscillate as a result of its own complex modes, although the dominant mode is influential. It would thus be feasible to make some allowances for the oscillation of values, in spite of the largest eigenvector, if deviations from some golden path occur. In our classification of 13 sectors, the largest real value greatly exceeded those of other real parts of the complex eigenmodes on the real eigenvalue axis, as shown in Fig. 6.1. In the largest real eigenmode, the most influential

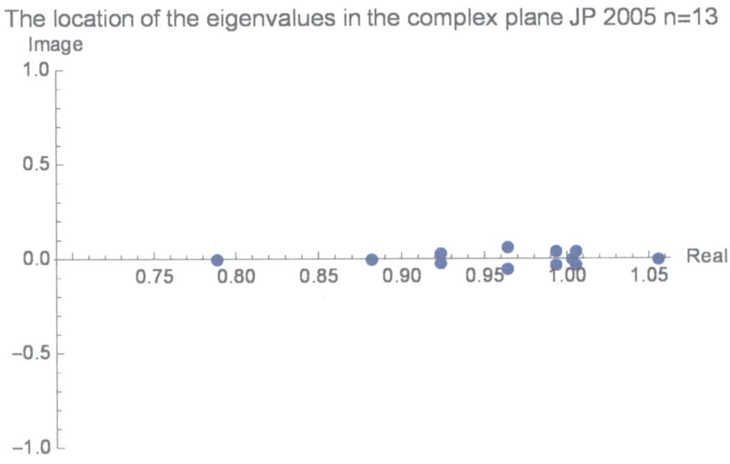

Fig. 6.1 Eigenmodes in 13 sectors in 2005

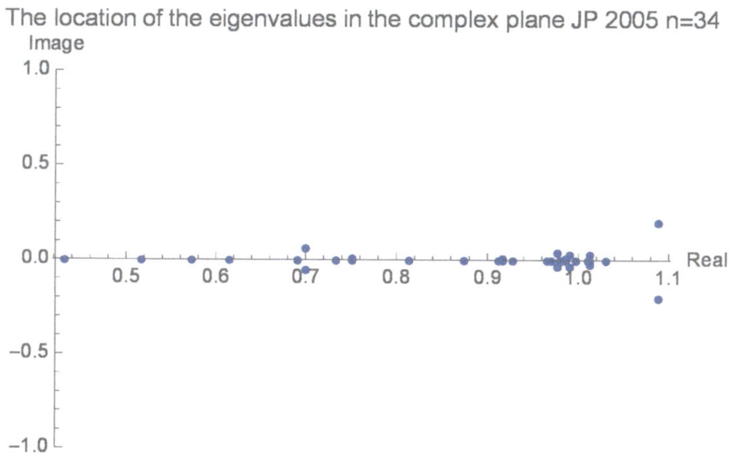

Fig. 6.2 Eigenmodes in 34 sectors in 2005

factor, which was the maximal coefficient, was derived from the service industry (no. 12), followed by that from the transport industry (no. 9). The influential factors in the largest complex modes appear to be the following industries: construction (no. 4), commerce (no. 6), and service (no. 11). These could cause some nonlinear effects, for example, network effects to the production system. As shown in Fig. 6.2, in our classification of 34 sectors, the largest of the real parts of the complex mode exceeded the largest real value. In the complex mode, the most influential dominant factor appeared to be the transport industry (no. 25). This could also result in some nonlinear effects being exerted on the production system. Meanwhile, in the actual mode of real values, metal products (no. 11), the construction industry (no. 19), and business services (no. 31) were evidently influential media/measure.

6.2.1 A New Randomization of the Input-Output Table

Temporarily leaving aside the complex plane, another characterization of the input-output table can be considered in view of correlated sectors of the input output system. The input coefficients with a transformation of subset t^i can be reinterpreted as follows:

$$\{t_1^i, \ldots, t_T^i\} \to n^i \tag{6.6}$$

where t denotes the kinds of inputs and n denotes the kinds of outputs. Applying covariance analysis, we can analyze the correlations between and when $t = n$ in the input-output table.

6.2.1.1 Extraction of Non-random Modes and the Largest Eigenmode

The subsequent procedure, known as Iyetomi's method,[1] entails the following steps:

1. Construct a correlation matrix
2. Check the randomness of this matrix
3. Identify any strong correlations, namely an influential hub group, among the $a_i j$s, evidently of non-random origin.

The largest eigenmode is considered a composite measure of system heterogeneity. The results showed that all of the components of the largest mode followed the same direction. These results for the input-output correlations resemble the market mode in relation to stock price fluctuations. Thus, we could employ the largest dominant mode of input-output correlations to estimate the main evolutionary pathway of the core system.

6.2.2 Remarks on the Extraction of Non-random Modes

It is widely acknowledged that the Hawkins-Simon Condition (Hawkins & Simon 1949) in relation to the input-output table is required to fulfill the net-producible production system. The first point to be noted is that the actual input-output production system must be normally identified with a system producing a net surplus. Hence the largest eigenmode supporting the net-producible system must exist. However, the Hawkins-Simon Condition may need to be imposed each time the matrix is randomized.[2] Each random matrix derived from the input-output table should fulfill the Hawkins-Simon Condition. Accordingly, the area of random distributions will be restricted by the Hawkins-Simon Condition. However, while some random modes may fail to be identified, non-random modes, and especially the largest eigenvector, may be accurately detected. Thus, the results obtained usually cannot be drastically modified.

An alternative perspective is that strict application of the Hawkins-Simon Condition is not required. Our current focus is on the evolutionary change of the production system. In this process, several permutations may occur within a given system without fulfilling the Hawkins-Simon's Condition. While Hildenbrand (1981) elaborated a novel alternative approach, here our focus is on a random network of the production system (Fig. 6.3).

[1] See Iyetomi et al. (2011a, 2011b).

[2] As for a quick but perfect description of random matrices, see https://mathworld.wolfram.com/RandomMatrix.html.

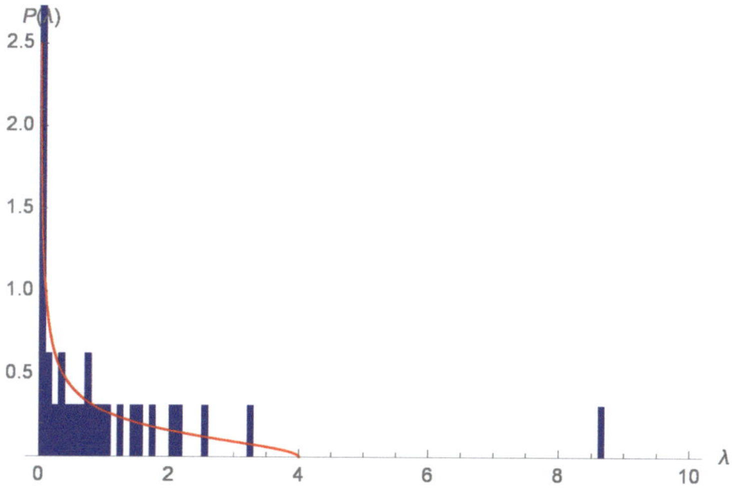

Fig. 6.3 A comparison of the actual modes in the 108 sectors with a random matrix distribution

6.3 Measuring the Difference Between a Weighted Random Graph Model and Real Distributions

We have identified the real system with a sub-system containing non-random modes. It may be useful to elucidate the difference between random and real distribution. There are several ways of representing the characteristics of random distribution. We begin by demonstrating how to generate a weighted random graph model. This model is generated based on the probability $q(w)$ that a weight w (i.e., a number of links) occurs between any pair of vertices as follows: $q(w) = p^w(1 - p^w)$.

An adjacency matrix is a binary matrix where α_{ij} means that vertices are connected, while a weighted adjacency matrix is a matrix where $w_{ij} = n$ means that there are n links between vertices. It then follows that there are three different distributions of the weighted adjacency matrix:

$P_>(w)$ is the cumulative weight distribution. $P_>(k)$ is the cumulative degree distribution where $k_i = \sum_{j=1}^{N} \alpha_{ij}$. $P_>(s)$ is the cumulative strength distribution where $s_i = \sum_{j=1}^{N} w_{ij}$.

Here, w_{ij} was interpreted as a covariance matrix coefficient of the input-output table a_{ij}. Consequently, three different distributions of the randomly generated matrix of 108 nodes were compared with the real distribution of 108 sectors of the covariance matrix of the input-output table in 2011. Based on a comparison of the random and real distributions, and using Iyetomi's method, differences in the degree to which real distribution was influenced by some of the non-random modes discussed above were easily verifie. The results appeared to be natural, because the real system had been shaped not only by histo-compatible adaptation, but also by some intelligent institutional designs. Each w_{ij} was interpreted as an input coefficient a_{ij}. Hence, the sum with respect to each i indicated the demand sum of each industry, i.

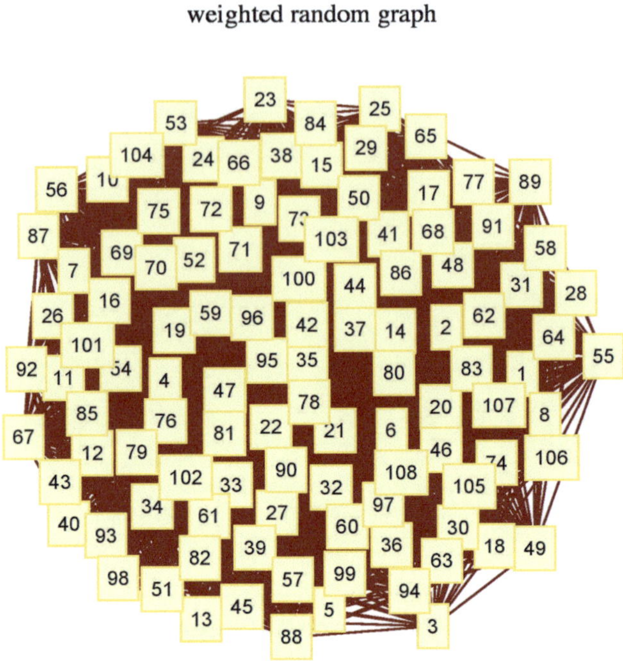

Fig. 6.4 A weighted random graph of 108 nodes with $p = 0.55$. Adapted from Tiziano and Garlschelli (2016)

Figures 6.4, 6.5 and 6.6 were produced based on the application of an extended version of the "Weighted Random Graph" depicted in the Wolfram demonstration project (Tiziano & Garlaschelli, 2016). Strength distribution was subsequently selected. Figure 6.4 shows the formation of random distribution with the probability of the vertices being conjugated set at 55%. The second figure shows the real distribution (Fig. 6.6).

6.4 Alpha Centrality Characterizing the Growth Pathway

We have so far applied Iyetomi's method to examine the non-randomness of the characteristics based on a covariance matrix of the input-output system. We now return to the real input-output matrix. Given the problem of complex numbers, these were classified into industries generating nonlinear effects on the entire system as discussed above (Fig. 6.5).

The definition of the α centrality of the system follows from the input-output system. It is accepted that α centrality depends not only on the adjacency matrix (network connections) $A = [a_{ij}]$, but also on important exogenous influences on node j: e_j. In other words, e_j was incorporated into the overall influence during each round. Applying the input-output matrix, positive surplus or net-output could

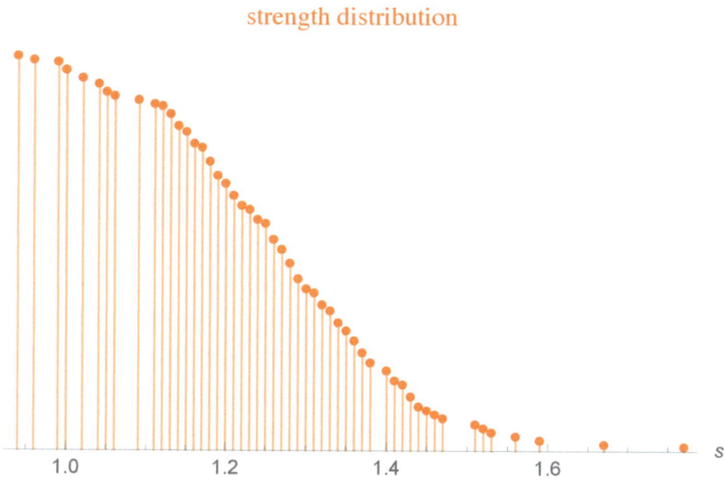

Fig. 6.5 The strength distribution of the weighted random graph

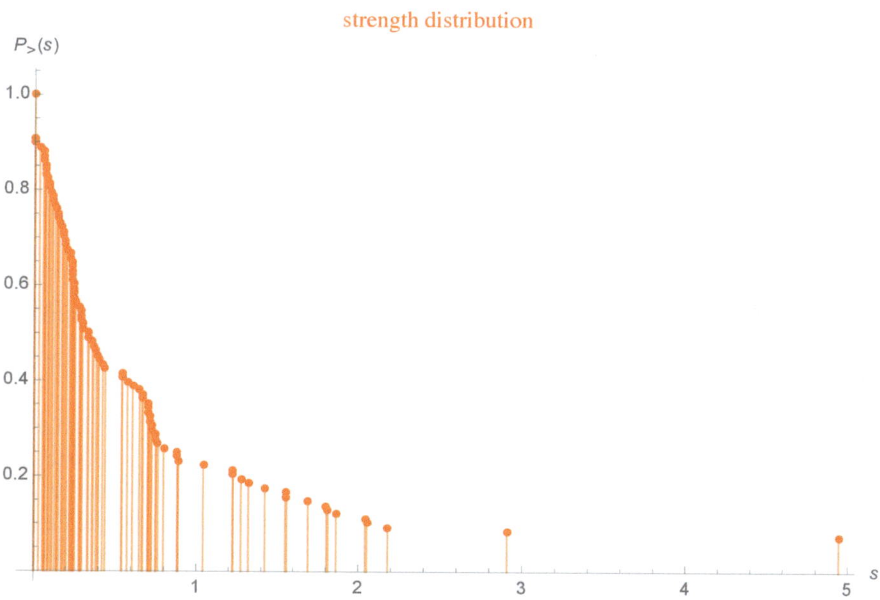

Fig. 6.6 The strength distribution of the real system of 108 sectors in 2011

be generated or the Hawkins-Simon Condition could be met. Given that a non-negative square matrix is non-negatively invertible, it follows that the process will converge during the next state as shown below:

$$x_j = \alpha \sum a_{ij} x_i + e_j \tag{6.7}$$

The solution for this system is:

$$x = (I - \alpha A^T)^{-1} e \tag{6.8}$$

If $\alpha = 0$, there is no adjacency effect in the system, which is only dominated by external influences. Meanwhile, if α is infinitely large, the system will be an eigenvector-centric one.

Alpha centrality will be employed as a measure of spreading risk within the system in the following manner. Based on the adjacency matrix (network connections), each incoming spread received from inward neighbors will be distributed among outward neighbors. The process will then be repeated until convergence is achieved as follows:

$$x_i = (1/\lambda) \sum a_{ij} x_j \tag{6.9}$$

Here, x_i is the extent of influence that node i carries. A^T is the adjacency matrix, and λ is the principal eigenvalue. The λ outward spreads are balanced by inward spreads. This balance is equivalent in meaning to Sraffa standard commodity (Sraffa, 1960). This suggests that input-output analysis and network analysis are the same. The dual forms of quantity and price systems are verifiable. While this kind of equilibrium formation has been discussed elsewhere, our focus, in this chapter, is on the alpha centralities of the world input/output table.

Quantity system

$$x_j = \alpha \sum a_{ij} x_i + e_j \tag{6.10}$$

Price system

$$p_i = \alpha \sum a_{ij} p_j + l_i \tag{6.11}$$

Viewed in relation to these dual forms, alpha centrality indicates the growth factor $\alpha = 1/(1+g)$, where g is defined as the rate of growth. Precisely, g is interpreted as a uniform growth rate across all sectors. Thus, it is clearly relevant to the growth or degeneration of the system. Although the extent of centrality reflects some degree of proportionality to the system, it is only considered as a parameter within network analysis and, therefore, requires redefinition. The value of α is usually set at 1.

In the field of social networks, the concept of alpha centrality is viewed as an amplification factor and/or attenuation parameter. It can be applied as an asymmetric weighted adjacency matrix to the input-output table. Here a_{ij} denotes the amount of good i used for the production of product j. (ω_{ij} denotes the share of product i in relation to the total amount of intermediate inputs employed by industry j). Hence measures of the inward/outward spread of external disturbances are defined as follows:

Outward spread: AMPLIFICATION INDEX (AI)

$$x = (I - \alpha A^T)^{-1} e = (I + \alpha A^T + \alpha^2 [A^T]^2 + \cdots + \alpha^t [A^T]^t + \cdots) e \quad (6.12)$$

Inward spread: VULNERABILITY INDEX (VI)

$$x = (I - \alpha A)^{-1} e = (I + \alpha A + \alpha^2 A^2 + \cdots + \alpha^t A^t + \cdots) e \quad (6.13)$$

6.4.1 The Three Types of Input-Output Table at Producers Prices

Before performing an empirically based calculation of α centrality, it is necessary to select one of the three types of input-output tables that have been officially published by the Statistics Bureau (2016).

The Various Inverse Matrices

1. $[I - A]^{-1}$: The construction of input-output table A is based on the assumption of competitive imports. In this table, domestic and imported products are viewed neutrally and no distinction is drawn between them.

2. $[I - [I - M]A]^{-1}$: Construction of the import coefficient matrix M entails the removal of imported products from the above described competitive table A. This is based on the common ratio of the imported product to the total input among all of the products. All of the export outputs are assumed to be domestic products.

3. $[I - A_D]^{-1}$: Based on the assumption of non-competitive imports, the actually detected ratio of the imported products to the total input of each industry can be calculated. Subsequently, a non-competitive table A_D was constructed according to the extent of our knowledge.

6.4.1.1 Industries Exposed to Systemic Risk in View of VI

By definition, the vulnerability index (VI) in relation to industry represents inward directed ripple effects such that industries from the upper value stream are forced to reduce their downward activities. Based on an explicit consideration of the import factor, the amplitude index VI for the last two cases could be demonstrated. A was replaced with A_D in the case of industries entailing competitive imports and with $[I - M]A$ in the case of industries entailing non-competitive imports, respectively.

The VI Modified by Systemic Risk

1. VI_M was calculated for industries with competitive imports according to the $[I - [I - M]A]^{-1}$ input-output table.

2. VI_D was calculated for industries with non-competitive imports according to the $[I - A_D]^{-1}$ input-output table.

According to the concept of alpha centrality, the industry with the largest index value may be regarded as the industry that is most sensitive to inward directed disturbances, that is, the vulnerability index, (VI). In line with a standard sociological convention, we initially assumed that $\alpha = 1$ and then listed VI values for industries with both competitive and non-competitive imports (Figs. 6.7 and 6.8 and Table 6.1).

Thus, the list identifies industries susceptible to the upper stream of industries around the top ten industries. Notably, the index for non-competitive imports exceeded that of competitive imports in the case of the petroleum refinery industry.

6.4.2 The Nonlinear Effects on the Entire System Based on the Vulnerability Index

The existence of industries generating nonlinear effects on the entire system has already been covered in our discussion of the alpha centrality of the weighted adjacency matrix, that is, the real input-output system. As long as the Hawkins-Simon Condition holds, the real non-negative eigenvalue can always be guaranteed. However, other eigenvalues may contain complex numbers. These can be identified in relation to industries generating nonlinear effects on the entire system. We have,

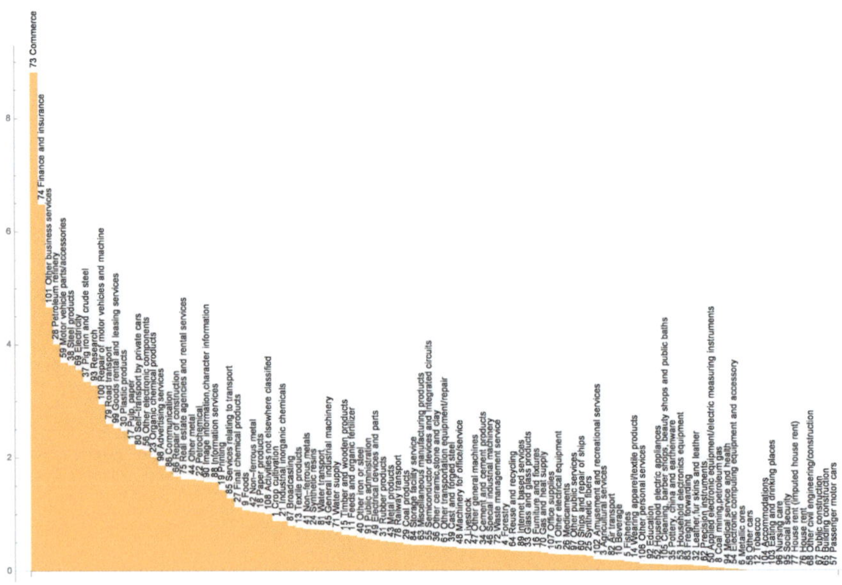

Fig. 6.7 The ranking of VI indices for cases of industries entailing competitive imports

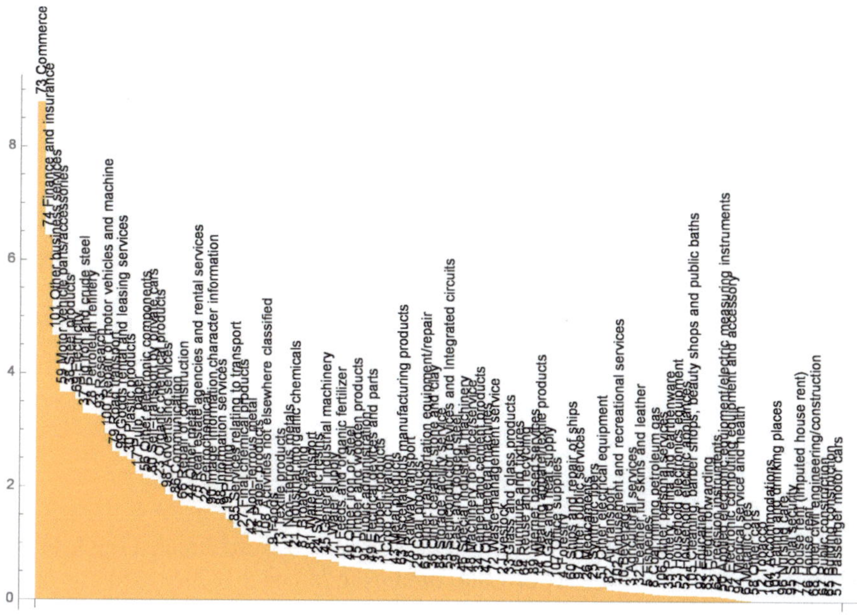

Fig. 6.8 The ranking of VI indices in the case of industries entailing non-competitive imports

Table 6.1 Top ten industries in relation to vulnerability Indices

Ranking	VI_M	VI_D
1	73 commerce	73 commerce
2	74 finance and insurance	74 finance and insurance
3	101 other business services	101 other business services
4	28 petroleum refinery	59 motor vehicle parts/accessories
5	59 motor vehicle parts/accessories	38 steel products
6	38 steel products	69 electricity
7	69 electricity	37 Pig iron and crude steel
8	37 pig iron and crude steel	28 petroleum refinery
9	93 research	93 research
10	100 repair of motor vehicles and machines	100 repair of motor vehicles and machines

therefore, focused on these industries in the ranking results calculated for alpha centrality. Two industries were identified in relation to VI according to whether imports were competitive or non-competitive. Nonlinear effects generated by these industries were as follows (Table 6.2).

Table 6.2 Nonlinear effects

	AI_M	AI_D
1	73 commerce	73 commerce
2	74 finance and insurance	74 finance and insurance

6.4.2.1 Industries Exposed to Systemic Risk in View of AI

By definition, the VI in relation to industry represents outward directed ripple effects such that industries from the lower stream are forced to reduce their downward activities. As in the VI case, by explicitly considering the import factor, the amplitude index (AI) was demonstrated for cases of industries entailing competitive and non-competitive imports, respectively.

6.4.3 Industries Exposed to Systemic Risk in View of AI

By definition, the AI in relation to industry represents outward directed ripple effects such that industries from the lower value stream are forced to reduce their downward activities according to the calculation shown below:

$$x = (I - \alpha A^T)^{-1}e = (I + \alpha A^T + \alpha^2(A^T)^2 + \cdots + \alpha^t(A^T)^t + \cdots)e \quad (6.14)$$

A was replaced with A^T in the case of competitive imports and with $[I - M]A^T$ in the case of non-competitive imports, respectively.

As in the case of VI, the AI was demonstrated for industries entailing competitive and non-competitive imports, respectively. The industry with the highest index value AI was considered the industry most sensitive to outward directed disturbances, that is, AI. In line with the sociological convention, we first assumed that $\alpha = 1$ and subsequently listed AI values for industries with both competitive and non-competitive imports.

Thus, we distinguished industries that were influential to the lower stream of industries around the top 10 industries in the list. It is noteworthy that entries in both cases were almost common but several cases (Table 6.3).

6.4.4 The Nonlinear Effects on the Entire System Based on the Amplitude Index

Relative to the VI indices, there are many industries that can possibly cause some nonlinear effects to the entire system. These could be identified in the ranking results calculated for alpha centrality. In view of AI, there were 13 industries in the category of competitive imports and 17 industries in the category of non-competitive imports as represented in Table 6.4. These industries could generate nonlinear effects.

Table 6.3 Top ten industries in relation to amplitude indices

Ranking	VI_M	VI_D
1	57 passenger motor cars	57 passenger motor cars
2	58 other cars	58 other cars
3	107 office supplies	108 activities not classified elsewhere
4	108 activities not classified elsewhere	107 office supplies
5	59 motor vehicle parts/accessories	59 motor vehicle parts/accessories
6	23 organic chemical products	48 machinery for offices/services
7	60 ships and repair of ships	24 synthetic resins
8	24 synthetic resins	23 organic chemical products
9	48 machinery for offices/services	2 livestock
10	2 livestock	30 Plastic products

Table 6.4 Top 13/17 industries in relation to amplitude indices to cause nonlinear effects

Ranking	VI_M	VI_D
22	Petrochemicals	5 Fisheries
28	Petroleum refinery	20 Chemical fertilizers
29	Coal products	22 Petrochemicals
37	Pig iron and crude steel	28 Petroleum refinery
38	Steel products	29 Coal products
39	Cast and forged steel	37 Pig iron and crude steel
40	Other types of iron or steel	38 Steel products
43	Metal products	39 Cast and forged steel
44	Other metals	40 Other types of iron or steel
47	Other general machines	43 Metal products
79	Road transport	44 Other metals
80	Self-transport by private cars	47 Other general machines
81	Water transport	60 Ships and repair of ships
		64 Reuse and recycling
		79 Road transport
		80 Self-transport by private cars
		81 Water transport

6.5 Conclusion

In this section, we have explored some philosophical designs for developing economics around systemic risks viewed in terms of their internal probability. This concept of probability is based on observations of living systems. An important point to note is that cognizing subjects are not limited to humans, but also extend to materials. The material observer behaves as an "internal observer." Further, material interactions between the observer and the objects being observed must generate a complex process. Based on this conception, we aimed to develop an understanding of how systemic risks could be recognized in this kind of interaction. In line with this objective, we examined this in relation to immunology and immunoediting that occurs on the surface level of the immune system. Our exploration revealed the importance of checkpoints such as nodes within a networked structure that is formed based on the above complex interactions, enabling us to better understand systemic risks. Last, we focused on the network node or link of the input-output system of the economic system, and introduced network-related concepts such as alpha centrality, successfully identifying a measure of risk in Japan's current economic system (Figs. 6.9 and 6.10).

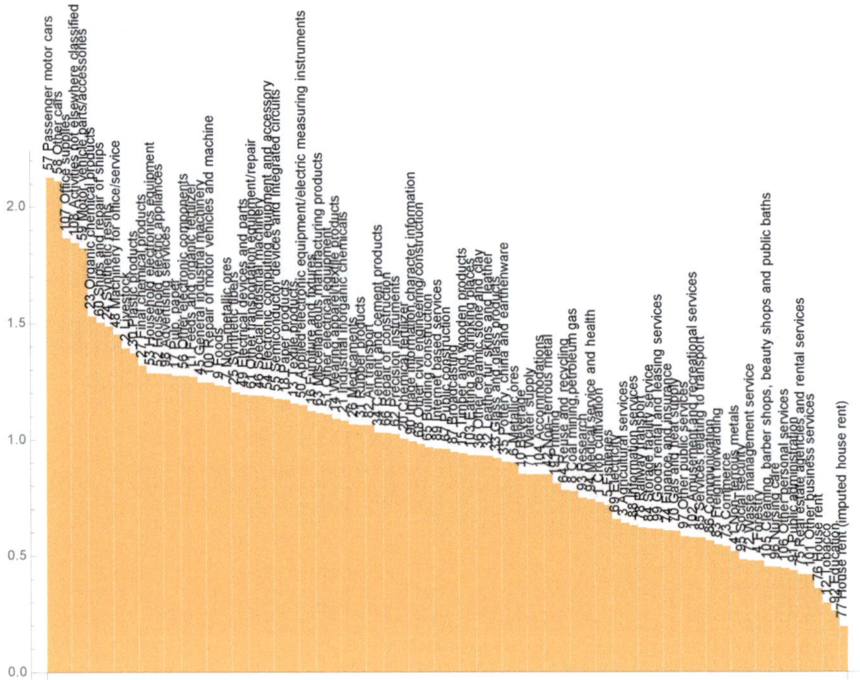

Fig. 6.9 The ranking of AI indices for industries characterized by competitive imports

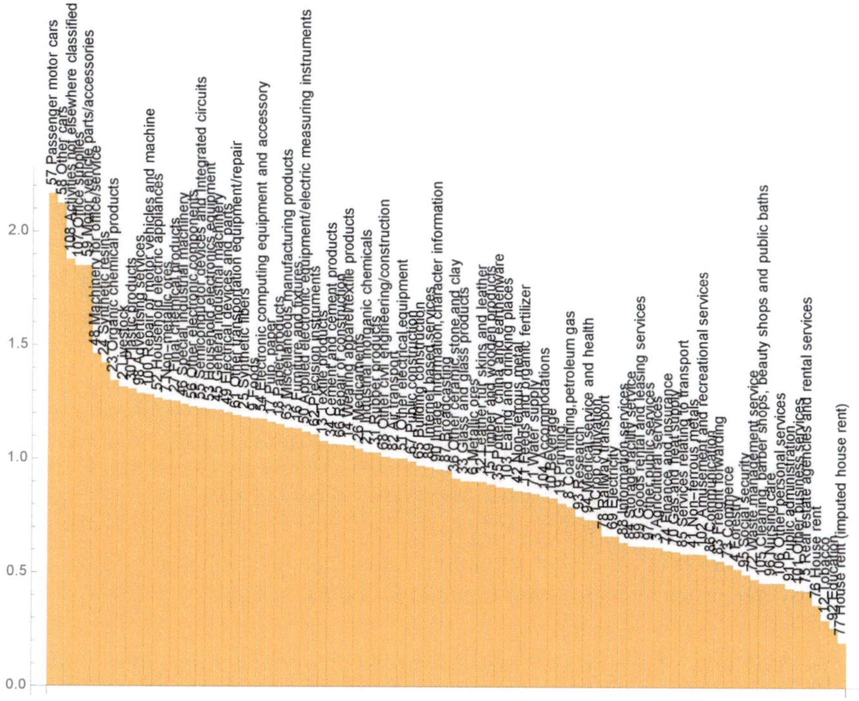

Fig. 6.10 Ranking of AI indices for industries characterized by competitive imports

---

Exercises

6.1 Calculate the eigenvalues and the eigenvectors of the next matrix A, and then confirm the maximal value as well as its associated eigenvalue:

$$A = \begin{pmatrix} 0.1 & 0.3 \\ 0.7 & 0.5 \end{pmatrix} \tag{6.15}$$

6.2 Take an input-output system with no joint product, and assume an input matrix ($a_{ij} \geqq 0$) which fulfills Hawkins-Simon condition $\triangle \geqq 0$ as follows:

$$A = \begin{pmatrix} a_{11} & a_{12} \\ a_{21} & a_{22} \end{pmatrix}; \triangle = (1 - a_{11})(1 - a_{22}) - a_{12}a_{21} \geqq 0 \tag{6.16}$$

Using a price-cost system (6.11) in the text above, prove that

$$(\alpha - a_{11})(\alpha - a_{22}) - a_{12}a_{21} \geqq 0 \tag{6.17}$$

guarantees the nonnegativess of prices.

6.3 Hawkins-Simon condition $\Delta = (1 - a_{11})(1 - a_{22}) - a_{12}a_{21} \geqq 0$ is called "the net-producibility condition." On theother hand, $(\alpha - a_{11})(\alpha - a_{22}) - a_{12}a_{21} \geqq 0$ is called "the non-negative price condition." Prove that if

$$a_{11} + a_{22} + \sqrt{(a_{11} - a_{22})^2 + 4a_{12}a_{22}} < 2,$$

both conditions are fulfilled.

6.4 Using the numerical example A above, calculate $[I - A]^{-1}$ (I is the identiy matrix of 2 by 2). Then verify whether $[I - A^T]^{-1}$ is $([I - A]^{-1})^T$ or not.

6.5 In the text above,

> x_i is the extent of influence that node i carries. A^T is the adjacency matrix, and λ is the principal eigenvalue. The λ outward spreads are balanced by inward spreads. This balance is equivalent in meaning to Sraffa standard commodity (Sraffa, 1960).

How can you describe any other economic role of the balancing proportion chracterized by the principal eigenvector in the input-output system?

6.6 The concepts of graphs and matrices are known to be compatible. Using the numerical example A above, examine that the numerical matrix $[I - A^T]^{-1}$ and $[I - A]^{-1}$ is equivalent in terms of graphical presentation.

6.7 According to the random matrix theory, it holds the relationship between the eigenvalues λ and the variables x[3]:

$$f(x) := \frac{q\sqrt{(\lambda\text{max} - x)(x - \lambda_{\text{min}})}}{(2\pi)x} \tag{6.19}$$

Plot $f(x)$, withing the range $[\lambda_{\text{min}}, \lambda\text{max}]$.

6.8 A is the input-output matrix of the classification of 13 industrial sectors in 1995 in Japanese domestic economy. The eigenvalues of $A^T A$ ("T" means transpose) is then calculated as follows:
$\{6.24801, 2.68701, 1.45099, 1.21919, 0.62855, 0.331741, 0.23072, 0.124978, 0.0396677, 0.0201562, 0.0113797, 0.00761128, -3.75785 * 10^{-16}\}$

[3] The next formula is driven from the next relationships:

$$q = 1; \lambda_{\text{min}} = N\left[-2\sqrt{\frac{1}{q}} + \frac{1}{q} + 1\right]; \lambda\text{max} = N\left[2\sqrt{\frac{1}{q}} + \frac{1}{q} + 1\right] \tag{6.18}$$

Plot the density distribution of these eigenvalues in the form of bar chart by increments of 0.1.

6.9 Integrate both diagrams made out in Exercises 14.7 and 14.8, and then examine the modes outside the random matrix property value distribution.

6.10 The Wolfram Demonstrations project has a useful tool like "Weighted Random Graph" (Tiziano & Garlschelli, 2016). Access to https://demonstrations.wolfram.com/WeightedRandomGraph/ to try some several simulation on which cases you are interested. Examine weight, degree, and strength repectively. Then, investigate what kind of characteristics each distribution represents, and detect any connection among three distributions.

References

Aruka, Y. (1991). Generalized Goodwin theorems on general coordinates. *Structural Change and Economic Dynamics, 2*(1), 66–91.

Brody, A. (1970). *Proportions, prices and planning. A mathematical restatement of the labor theory of value*. Akademiai Kiado North-Holland.

Hawkins, D., & Simon, H. (1949). Some conditions of macroeconomic stability. *Econometrica, 17*(3/4), 245–248.

Hildenbrand, W. (1981). Short-run production functions based on microdata. *Econometrica, 49*(5), 1095–1125.

Iyetomi, H., Nakayama, Y., Aoyama, H., & Fujiwara, Y. (2011). Fluctuation-dissipation theory of input-output interindustrial correlations. *Physical Review E, 83*(12), 016103.

Iyetomi, H., Nakayama, Y., Yoshikawa, H., Aoyama, H., Fujiwara, Y., Ikeda, Y., & Souma, W. (2011). What causes business cycles? Analysis of the Japanese industrial production data. *Journal of Japanese and International Economy, 25*(3), 246–72.

Mariolis, T., & Tsoulfidis, L. (2016). Capital theory 'paradoxes' and paradoxical results: Resolved or continued? *Evolutionary and Institutional Economics Review, 13*(2), 297–322.

Sraffa, P. (1960). *Production of commodities by means of commodities: Prelude to a critique of economic theory*. Cambridge UK: Cambridge UP.

Statistics Bureau. (2016). 2011 input-output tables for Japan.

Tiziano, S., & Garlaschelli, D. (2016). The weighted random graph model.

7 Alternative Developing Tools for Economics

Abstract

An innovative feature of this book is its econocentric structure, focusing on digital designs. From the outset, econocentrism is linked with monetary exchange as the core engine of capitalism. Needless to say, monetary exchange and its ledger system will undergo significant innovations soon, sychronizing with the new stage of communication style backed by pervasiveness of quantum computing. In fact, the new coronavirus pandemic has changed lifestyles worldwide, which are unlikely ever to return to their original form. This great transformation will change the nature of the socio-economic system itself, which will be centered on digital designs. At present, money is stating to undergo a major revolution. Many books dealing with digital designs and innovations have been published, but few if any of them focus on monetary and analytical methods in the way that this present volume does. Dealing with the new attributes brought about by this great change will be beyond the scope of traditional economics. Digital tools such as blockchain, cryptocurrency, and crypt assets as well as distributive ledger systems, require new modes of analysis. First, the evolution of money and complex thinking necessary for understanding that change must be analyzed. Furthermore, the way that goods markets are mutually coordinated and the future of the labor market must be understood, points that are emphasized in the first section of the book. Second, other computational approaches to social dilemmas, crypt graphics, and the supply chain are introduced in the latter part. To facilitate understanding of the core engine of market capitalism, the detailed settlement mechanism in terms of an AI market experiment are also presented.

7.1 A View on the Current Situation Beyond the Older Economics

We are facing to a harsh reality. First, the superstars like Vanguard and BlackRock (extraordinary asset management corporations) has now dominated nearly the world. These corporations directly or indirectly dominated almost 80% of international

Y. Aruka, *Evolutionary Economics*, Springer Texts in Business and Economics,
https://doi.org/10.1007/978-981-97-1382-0_7

capitals worldwide. In this century, we cannot miss corporations that operate above the governments. More interestingly, these financial institutes are not regulated by the banking acts. A traditional macro/financial model, whether orthodox or heretical, no longer holds. Second, the reasoning method is also changing. Previously, we believed the reasoning must be achieved from induction to deduction by way of approximation function. We did not believe in an alternative scientific method. However, it may be the new normal to believe in transduction, which is represented by machine learning. In this context, we will also be forced to change our style of communication, whether money or information.

7.1.1 The Harsh Reality and Its Dominance of the Fast Track Path to the Future

Given such a reality, where the free market mechanism has broken down, evolutionary economics needs some game changing ideas. Even Nobel laureates no longer provide us with future insights. Creative Destruction, which is a very famous term of Schumpeter, the pioneer of evolutionary economics, literally is under way in the world. Sometimes this word is replaced with the Great Reset. However, we still have no idea of what the coming system is after the destruction. We have not established any measure on the coming society.

The new coronavirus pandemic has changed lifestyles worldwide, which are unlikely ever to return to their original form. This great transformation will change the nature of the socio-economic system itself and will be centered on digital designs. This direction may suggest agendas which the United Nations (UN) and the World Economic Forum(WEF) proposed around the Sustainable Development Goals (SDGs).[1] In fact, such a fast track to progress will be a dominant factor to determine the future path. However, the human history is not necessarily uniquely established in advance. We may thus avoid identifying the future track with the established acts in this book.

Econocentrism Containing Monetary Exchange

At present, money is beginning to undergo a major revolution. Many books dealing with digital designs and innovations have been published, but few if any of them focus on monetary and analytical methods in the way that this present volume does. Taking into account the new advancement of the monetary exchange, our book will be called econocentric.[2]

---

[1] In the scheme of WEF, "we are stepping into the era of the Internet of Bodies from Things" by collecting our physical data via a range of devices that can be implanted, swallowed or worn.https://www.weforum.org/agenda/2020/06/internet-of-bodies-covid19-recovery-governance-health-data/.

[2] The definition of econocentrism seems not necessarily uniquely established in *Oxford Dictionary*, for example. Usually, econocentrism simply means the use of the principle of supply and demand at

7.1.2 The Limits of Older Economics

Dealing with the new attributes brought about by this great change will be beyond the scope of traditional economics. Digital tools such as blockchain, cryptocurrency, and crypt assets as well as distributive ledger systems, require new modes of analysis. First, the evolution of money and complex thinking necessary for understanding that change must be analyzed. Furthermore, the way that goods markets are mutually coordinated and the future of the labor market must be understood, points that are emphasized in the first section of the book. Second, in the latter part, other computational approaches to social dilemmas, cryptographics, and the supply chain are introduced in the latter part. To facilitate understanding of the core engine of market capitalism, the detailed settlement mechanism in terms of an AI market experiment are presented.

To data, traditional economics have chosen to argue "market in general", as symbolized by general equilibrium theory, which was originally established in 1870's. In reality, unfortunately, there is no longer a held "generality" by any means, as Leon Walras firstl expected. To depict the modern market, it may be not only inappropriate but also boldly far-reaching for us to discuss the market in general.

It is difficult for the classical coverage of the economic reasoning to analyze the contemporary system, which we imagine. However, we temporarily illustrate how classical economics approaches the modern macroeconomic system, according to Schefold (2021). Schefold assessed the Cambridge/Keynesian economics inheriting from classical economics in the following manner:

> Piketty shows that larger fortunes tend to be associated with higher rates of return on financial investments, and in this modern reality is different (Piketty, 2014), but we cannot analyse here how the rich get richer. ... I only want to stress that the Cambridge economists could not easily leave the narrow framework of steady state analysis, because it was associated with the constant capital-output ratio, but they had no theory for its determination. Schefold (2021, 13)

Here the steady state analysis is connected with the assumption of a constant capital-output ratio. The idea of Joan Robinson, Keynse's best desciple, regarded that there were few reswitchings of the choice of techniques happening excepting around the corner points, in the event that there were held a constant capital-output ratio almost everywhere. So the dynamics of macro economics will be concentrated on the field of investment, in particular, behaviors of investors.[3]

---

least loosely when we formalize "the value of intangible assets like human emotional development or environmental sustainability, and the monolithic implied trustworthiness of market dynamics". The usage does not imply the strict use of the principle of supply and demand. Cited from Urban Dictionary: https://www.urbandictionary.com/define.php?term=econocentrism. In our context, the econocentrism may rather focus on the use of the principle of monetary exchange.

[3] Schefold then assumed that confidence returns, as the pandemic peters out, so that the option to raise interest rates again presents itself (Schefold, 2021, 16).

> [O]nce a production function is given, Keynesian analysis is inherently more flexible, not in the sense of agnosticism, but by emphasizing forces that matter in the real world, principally the behaviour of investors. ... The investment climate can be assessed. Neo-Fisherians believe that moderate rises of interest rates and prices might go together, involving rational expectations. With a constant capital-output ratio, the effect of a small and slow rise of the interest rate similarly seems precarious, but possible for a Keynesian, in what Joan Robinson called a state of tranquillity that is not disturbed by a process of substitution (Schefold, 2021).

Fortunately, we recently acquired two major technological advancements. One is AI in general, the other is Bitcoin or cryptocurrency in particular. The latter is a byproduct in association with blockchain technology. But the impact of either Bitcoin or Ethereum is enormous in theory and in practice. In particular, Ethereum is more interesting in the sense that it also provides with **smart contract**. This has the potential power to innovate the economic system, quite possibly, the social system.

A Note on Quantum Financial System (QFS)

Finally, we need to take note of the new advent of quantum financial system (QFS). As IMF noted in Fall 2021, "Quantum computers could crack the cryptography that underpins financial stability"[4] QFS could be also an alternative to Bitcoin and so on. Quantum bit may be superior to 0, 1 bit. However, the current crypto money will still stay in the power of decentralization and community consensus.

How the Contemporary System Differs Much from the Image of Classical Economics

We are instead interested in how the contemporary system differs substantially from the image of classical economics. Fortunately, we recently acquired two major technological advancements. One is AI in general, the other is Bitcoin or cryptocurrency in particular. The latter is a byproduct in association with blockchain technology. But the impact of either Bitcoin or Ethereum is enormous in theory and in practice. In particular, Ethereum is more interesting in the sense that it also provides with **smart contract**. This has the potential power to innovate the economic system, quite possibly, the social system.[5]

[4] https://www.imf.org/external/pubs/ft/fandd/2021/09/quantum-computings-possibilitiesand-perils-deodoro.htm.

[5] Aruka (2022) focuses on the settlement mechanism of the Bitcoin Exchange, discussing its uniqueness and commonality as compared with the stock exchange. We then introduce our new idea of digit length frequency distribution when we are interested in fully random iterated cellular automata (FRICA). Finally, we apply the length distribution to the price time series generated by the U-Mart acceleration experiment tool and examine the neutralizing effects by the change of the market transaction strategy composition, which may suggest some possible criteria whether the market may be rigged or not.

7.1.3 Some Instances of Using Blockchain

It is noted that blockchain is not simply a technology for crypt-currencies. Blockchain also is used a censor technology, e.g., in order to retrieve a defective lot in a factory system of the manufacturing industry.

Currency Exchange

Among them, we note the IBM blockchain applied to the currency exchange, which provides the financial institutions with a better opportunity by way of a world wire network (API): either are transformed into "a stable coin" as the digital asset, which can achieve a simultaneous exchange between the two. Here messaging, clearing, and settlement for the desired exchange will be integrated by blockchain technology without falsifying bookkeeping. The latter usage may be classified into a hybrid application of blockchain in a sense that blockchain is incorporated as a sub-system of the currency exchange. **IBM Blockchain** is an instance to deliver value around the world. See https://www.ibm.com/blockchain

A Simple Auction Design on the Ethereum Platform

In 1993, Nick Szabo described how users could input data or value/then regain it from the transfer system as if it were a digital vending machine. **Ethereum** shares the same function as Bitcoin in a sense that **the network** can transfer value from one to another. Different from Bitcoin, Ethereum provides each node with additional information account, which could function as the distributive ledger for each, while Bitcoin only transfers the value of currency (Fig. 7.1).

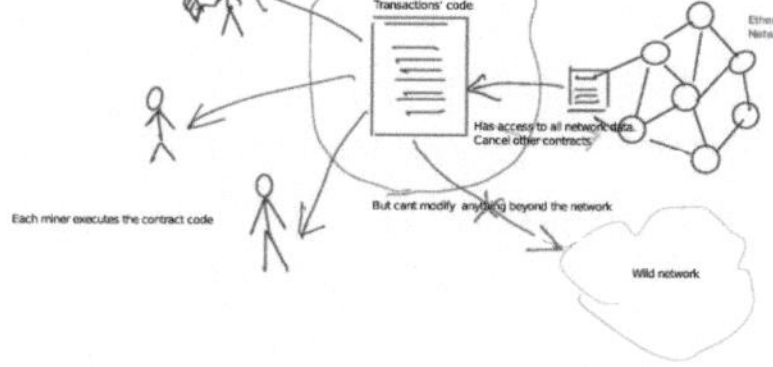

Fig. 7.1 Smart contracts on the Ethereum platform. *Cited from https://vas3k.com/blog/ethereum/ but the chart was originally produced

Turing Completeness and Smart Contract

Ethereum is called a system written in Turing complete language. As a Turing Complete system means a system in which a program can be written that will find an answer, Ethereum, if it is, allows to program **autonomous agents**. The contract will be called **smart contract**.[6]

The features of smart contract is summed up as follows.

- Smart contracts are fulfilled with multisignature accounts, which imply that "funds are spent only when a required percentage of people agree".
- Smart contracts can manage agreements between users, say, if one buys insurance from the other.
- Smart contracts provide utility to other contracts (similar to how a software library works).
- Smart contracts can store information about an application, such as domain registration information or membership records.

7.2 Some Fundamental Changes of the Socio-Economic System

The economics of production of the last century depend on capital and labor. In the 19th Century, the factors of production was land and labor. Land has been replaced with capital as the capitalistic production develops. This suggests that production style is not always fixed. To our understanding, the style is now transitioning, when a universal tool making machine actually appears. Siemens has already provided this kind of entity.[7]

Almost every input will be invisible excepting program codes. In this entity, substitution between factor inputs will not matter in view of cost comparison. In other words, this entity will no longer guarantee the idea of a continuous substitution between physical factor inputs. Thus, this kind of the entity will not only drastically reduce the time of production and the related cost of labor input but will also make invalid the traditional idea of a choice of techniques. Now, the economic distributive principle will not be guaranteed by a so-called production function analysis; thus, we must prepare a new analysis of production, although we are faced with too many corrective tasks to establish it along the traditional grounds. In this chapter, we rather just refer to some fundamental problems of traditional production analysis.

---

[6] The items described below is cited from https://www.coindesk.com/information/ethereum-smart-contracts-work.

[7] See **Siemens' website** page titled: Automation systems for all requirements https://new.siemens.com/global/en/products/automation/systems.html.

7.2.1 The Short-Run Production Function and Its Aggregation Form

Hildenbrand's production function study was published in Econometrica 1981 (Hildenbrand, 1981), but did not see the light of day until (Dosi et al., 2016) drew attention to it. As is well known, the law of returns is assumed a priori in the traditional production function. However, Hildenbrand (1981) drew a short-run production function using the example of the Norwegian tanker industry in 1967 (377 vessels with a load capacity of over 15,000 tons). The tankers were of various types, 57 were turbine-driven and 320 were motor-driven, and their production dates ranged from 1950 to 1966. The output of the tanker industry is tonnes per day times miles transported. Following tradition, only two inputs are considered: fuel and labour. Referring to the work of Johansen and Eide, the production function for the Norwegian tanker industry is shown in the upper panel of Fig. 3 of Hildenbrand (1981, 1100). As shown in his figure, the techniques used in the industry may represent some combinatorial compositions. A simple understanding on firms' technology will contradict reality. In fact, the industrial technology is based on a wide range of *unequal* productivities reflecting a complex technology. Thus the real isoquant of the industry will not compose a typical isoquant on the material(capital)-labor plane.

According to Hildenbrand (1981), this idea differs from the traditional production function. We define the projection of Y on the input space $\Re^l_+$:

$$D = \{V \in \Re^l_+ | (V, X) \in Y \texttt{ for some } X \in \Re_+\}$$

It then hods **the traditional production function**:

$$F(V) = \max\{X \in \Re_+ | (V, X) \in Y\}$$

The operator max in the above has excluded the possibilities of "certain institutional barriers to factor mobility in aggregating the individual production sets" (Hildenbrand 1981, 1097).

In general, the *ex post* technology of a production unit is a vector is a production activity a that produces, during the current period, a_{l+1} units of output by means of (a_1, ..., a_l) units of input. **The size of the firm** is the length of vector a, i.e., a multi-dimensional extension of the usual measure of firm size (Fig. 7.2).

7.2.2 An Alternative Production Set of Zonotope-Basis

Given $Y = (a_1, \ldots, a_l)$, a set of generators for n, the zonotope Y is the convex hull of all vectors of the form a; that is (Y) is the Minkowski sum of all segments $[0, a_i]$, where $a \in Y$, i.e., $\sum_{a_i \in Y} a_i$. Also $Z(Y)$ is the shadow of the r-dimensional cube $[0, 1]^r$ via the projection in $\Re$:

$$Vol(Y) =: \sum_{1 \le i_1 \le i_2 \cdots \le i_l \le N} |\Delta i_1, \ldots, i_l|$$

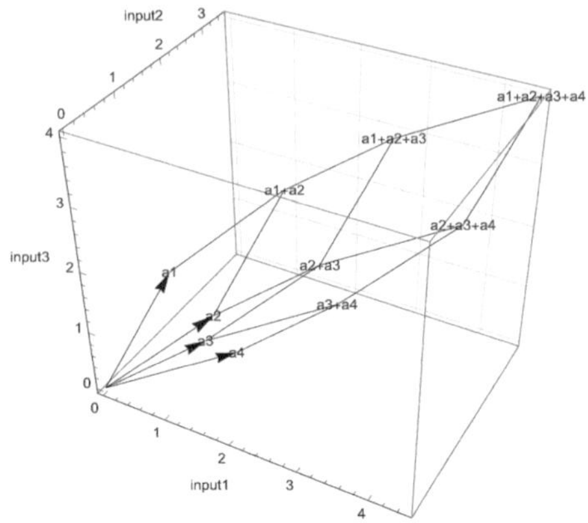

Fig. 7.2 Hildenbrand's short-run production set and its three-dimensional zonotope. *The author depicted this figure by Mathematica

Here $|\Delta i_1, \ldots, i_l|$ is the module of the determinant. This kind of discussion will suggest a new growth/innovation theory of production. It is noted that $Vol(Y)$ measures the volume of a rugby ball. The idea of **Volume** is defined by Dosi et al. (2016). The abosolute measure is the Gini volume of the zonotope, which could be regarded as a generalization of the well known Gini index. Let $Vol(P_Y)$ be the volume of the paralletop P_Y of diagonal $d_Y = \sum_{n=1}^{N} a_n$, that is the maximal volume we can get when the industry production activity $\sum_{n=1}^{N} a_n$ is fixed. It then hold the Gini volume:

$$Vol(Y)_G = \frac{Vol(Y)}{Vol(P_Y)}$$

Thus we can empirically measure the productivity growth by the change of inequality. It also is noted that the idea of smaller firm size does not necessarily generate greater growth of the industry.

7.2.3 The Effect of Financial Industry on the Real Economy

The present economic system seems to be keenly examined in terms of several insights of the new coordinates. The advent of financial big bang was too shocking to lose sight of the effectiveness of production economy. However, it is easy to verify that the effect of financial activities is extremely small in view of value added or income creation if we measure its effect by a macroscopic GDP aggregate. As Table 7.1 shows, the contribution to GDP of the financial industry, even altogether with the insurance industry is merely 3.2%. This ratio is also within 10% even in the United States. Readers will be surprised to know how small the income creation capability the financial industry is, despite the extraordinary financial wealth creation. Therefore, in summary, we are forced to recognize the dichotomy of economy into the real one and the financial economy. Both linkage is really thin.

Table 7.1 The input-output table of 13 sector, 2015, Japan at production prices

Industry	Value added (million yen)
Agriculture, forestry and fishery	11310425
Mining	21116028
Manufacturing	202892254
Construction	3699380
Electricity, gas and heat supply	20506251
Commerce	32587127
Finance and Insurance	17327829
Estate	11884118
Transport and postal services	34909649
Information and communications	28703703
Public administration	1157289
Services	78757323
Activities not elsewhere classified	4728298
Total of inter./mediate sectors	469579674
Total of gross value added sectors	548238714

7.2.4 The Landscape of Exchange Systems

Now we inspect how the market exchange will be constructed. The classical image of market exchange breaks down by reflecting both the rapid change of the market organization and the communication system. For the market organization, as shown by Mirowski (2007), a market is repeatedly either spun off or complemented from the underlying market, forming a highly complicated layered system in the evolution of market. On the other hand, as a rapid change of the communication system locally and globally, a series of new exchange mechanisms has appeared. These may be an essential concept for understanding the modern market system and the contemporary societal system. Incidentally, non-symbolic methods may reflect fast thinking, while symbolic methods may reflect slow thinking, as Kahneman (2011) pointed out.

> Among financial technologies, HFT is a striking factor. The operation speed is on the order of microseconds, preventing much working from being performed by human intelligence. In fact, the average processing speed of Bitcoin is about 10 min, leading us to excessively depend on computing ability such as "proof of work". ..... [On the other hand, the] horizontal axis shows the type of processing, from less symbolic to more symbolic. Symbolic processing implies the so-called programming based one. Through the recent rapid progress of pattern recognitions due to machine and deep learning, nonsymbolic processing will begin a new stage of AI work to replace previous human works (Aruka, 2020, 380).

Through the recent rapid progress of pattern recognitions due to machine and deep learning, nonsymbolic processing will begin a new stage of AI work to replace previous human works.

The Hyper-Speed Domain: Relaxed Static Stability

This observation may call us "the relaxed static stability". Depending on the idea of "fail safe", structural stability has been important in designing planes and ships up to now. On the contrary, a modern stealth fighter like Lockheed F35 is designed by the idea of relaxing "static stability". It is well known that bicycles behave much more quickly than tricycles, and attempt to restore its instability by resort to their countermotion. The countermotion will be controlled by computational powers. Thus, we expect that some nonlinear effect is implemented behind the financial flash crashes, always accompanying a countervailing power.[8]

The Slow-Speed Domain: Distributive System of P2P Exchange Network

In contrast with the hyper speed domain, it matters "the slow speed" to employ blockchain technology. Here the word "slow" may be interpreted as "nonhyper-speed" or "nonmicrosecond". In view of a certain scaling, blockchain may be enough speedy excepting the mining speed of Bitcoin. In this sense, it is easy to identify the crypt-currency using blockchain technology with a slow speed technology. More interestingly, there currently exists a world wide nodes network at the basis of **P2P transaction**. It is interesting to see a global bitcoin node distribution which is alway accessed from the homepage https://bitnodes.earn.com/nodes/live-map/.

The Difference Between the Traditional Transaction and the P2P Transaction

Even HFT transaction requires an "auctioneer". Although the "auctioneer" is a computer server, even HFTs usually assume a centralized system of both double auction and batch auction on the restrictive administration of two rules: time priority and price priority. Thus, no trade holds without matching coordination or the continued announcement of the matching results. However, the size of information generated in the HFT transaction rapidly increases due to the faster speed of settlement.

P2P Transactions also Generate a Rapid Growth of Information

P2P transaction on the basis of blockchain mining. As the number of transaction node increases, a geometrically rapid growth of transaction information is generated due to its network properties. A practical application of P2P transaction may be feasible just when the grand infrastructure for mining is arranged at any rate.

[8] See Arthur (2009, 73).

7.2.5 Transductive/Symbolic Reasoning

It was noted in the earlier section that symbolic/non-symbolic coordinates will be a key coordinate to identify the parts of the socio-economic landscape. We will then examine this reasoning. Brownlee (2017) compactly illustrates transductive learning as follows:

Transduce	To transduce means to convert something into another form, i.e., to convert (something, such as energy or a message) into another form essentially sense organs transduces physical energy into a nervous signal. *Merriam-Webster Dictionary* (online), 2017
Transducer in engineering	It is a popular term from the field of electronics and signal processing, where a transducer is a general name for components or modules converting sounds to energy or vice versa. *Digital Signal Processing Demystified*, Broesch (1997).[9]
Transduction in biology	The action or process of transducing; especially:the transfer of genetic material from one microorganism to another by a viral agent (such as a bacteriophage). *Merriam-Webster Dictionary* (online), 2017 (Fig. 7.3).

Transductive Learning

It is an interesting framing of supervised learning where the classical problem of "approximating a mapping function from data and using it to make a prediction" is seen as more difficult than is required. Instead, specific predictions are made directly from the real samples from the domain. No function approximation is required.

> The model of estimating the value of a function at a given point of interest describes a new concept of inference: moving from the particular to the particular. We call this type of inference **transductive** inference. Note that this concept of inference appears when one would like to obtain the best result from a restricted amount of information (Vapnik, 1998, 169)

Example of k-NN classification
The test sample (green dot) should be classified either to blue squares or to red triangles. If $k = 3$ (solid line circle) it is assigned to the red triangles because there are 2 triangles and only 1 square inside the inner circle. If $k = 5$ (dashed line circle) it

[9] All signal processing begins with an input transducer. The input transducer takes the input signal and converts it to an electrical signal. In signal-processing applications, the transducer can take many forms. A common example of an input transducer is a microphone.

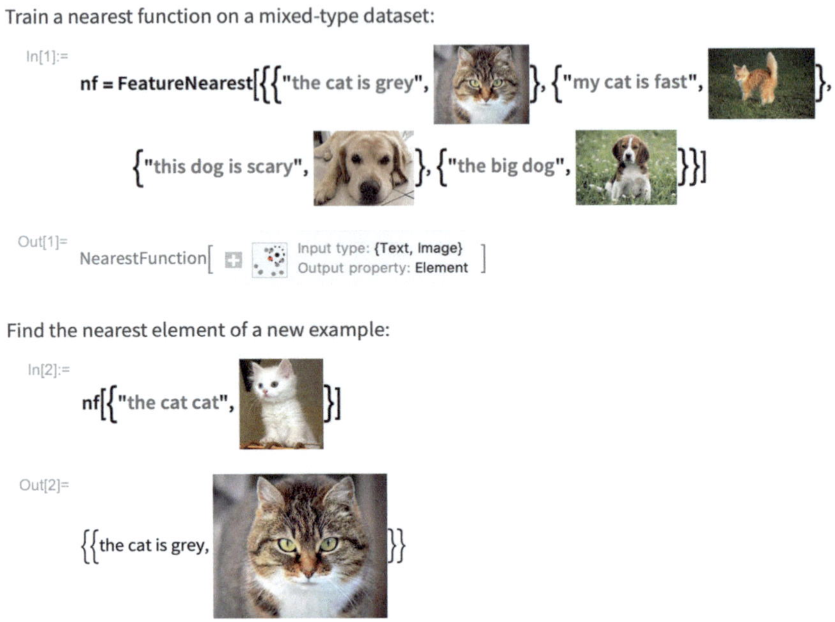

Fig. 7.3 A symbolic processing. **Source* Made from Mathematica

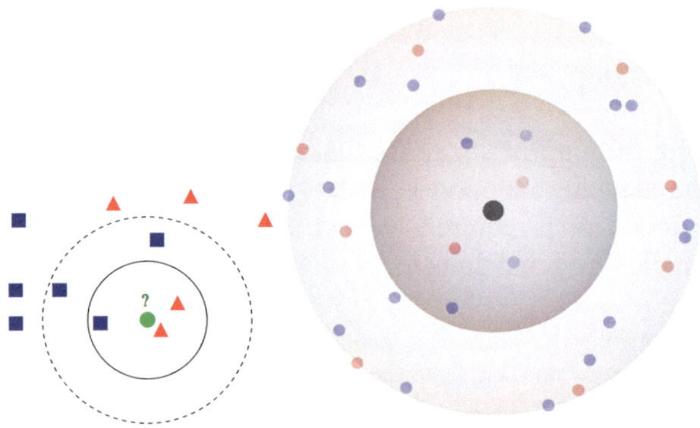

Fig. 7.4 K-nearest neighbors algorithm and its generalization *The right figure is a three dimensional extension of the left figure. The left figure is cited from Wikipedia article's figure https://en.wikipedia.org/wiki/K-nearest_neighbors_algorithm#/./media/step/File: KnnClassification.svg

is assigned to the blue squares (3 squares vs. 2 triangles inside the outer circle). Cited from Wikipedia https://en.wikipedia.org/wiki/K-nearest_neighbors_algorithm. The right figure of Fig. 7.4 is an extended version of the left figure. The center point should be estimated whether blue or red.

7.2.6 Science and Ethics

Until now, prediction has inevitably been associated with the following problems, as Klaus Mainzer, professor emeritus at the Technical University of Munich and philosopher of science, has pointed out. In his book Mainzer (2007), Mainzer discusses the "prediction problem" in terms of the Joseph effect (persistence) and the Noah effect (discontinuity). According to Mainzer (2007), we discussed science and ethics.[10]

> We have a particular type of self-fulfilling prophecy like the Oedipus effect. According to this effect interpreted by Robert K. Merton, a true prophetic statement—a prophecy declared as truth when it is not—may sufficiently influence people, either through fear or logical confusion, so that their reactions ultimately fulfill the false prophecy. This implies that the collective macrostate of social various orders (order parameter) can be averaged over its parts. We apply this self-fulfilling rhetoric to our rational expectation hypothesis. This hypothesis might be self-fulfilling either through fear or logical confusion, of course. But this prophecy must be faced with some logical failure. It could be verified in the framework of complex dynamics that this hypothesis only referred to a unilateral direction of the whole dynamics in which direction a single rational individual had to contribute to the rational macrostate of economy. Moreover, we need the other aspect of the full feedback: "Its order parameters strongly influence the individuals of the society by orientating (enslaving) their activities and by activating or deactivating their attitudes and capabilities" (Mainzer, 2007, p. 395). This is just the slaving principle as a whole elucidated as synergetics by Haken (1977) and Weidlich (2000). These dynamics are thus encompassed by critical values, outside of which the system falls into an unstable situation. So to be fulfilled, the prophecy might be circumvented.

Consideration in this dimension will contain some ethics by judging whether the effect of Joseph(persistence) or Noah(discontinuity) should be placed.

However, what we are now convinced of is that the advent of the quantum computer age will fundamentally change the system of information communication, including monetary exchange. At that time, the traditional analysis of induction-deduction will be replaced by an analysis based on transduction (machine-learning inference), which will make it possible to make predictions that traditional analysis has missed, and this will make traditional predictions themselves obsolete. The idea is MIT is already working intensively on new predictions (time machines?) based on this understanding. However, the basis of the Great Reset will still be a revolution in computing power and the associated revolution in communication.

To be sure, we are faced with this kind of prediction difficulties. In a near future, however, a new science should get over them in the era of galantic space development by humans, if extraterrenial factors were taken into account. Thus we will explore the networks structure of the time series, i.e., something causal.

Although we attempt to grip only a slight indication, in the following, we will cast a new light on the time series prediction in view of visibility graph. This will suggest

---

[10] This part summarizes (Aruka et al., 2009, 311).

a new inferential procedure as a means to obtain something causal to connect the time series with a network structure.[11]

7.3 The Time Series in View of Horizontal Visibility Graph

7.3.1 The Visibility Graph

Firstly we define **the visibility graph**.

> By definition, in **the visibility graph**, each node indicates a sample that is connected to another node if visibility between the two exists.

The operation to connect the segments is then explained in the following manner.

- According to **the rule of visibility graph** in between the highest node and the second highest node, we can connect each other of the values. In other words, two vertices(nodes) are connected by an edge if the corresponding events in the time series are larger than all the events between them.
- Thus a time series will be transformed into a visibility graph as follows. The bars represent the values of the time series. Suppose the initial node is the starting node. Choose the values consecutively until a higher value than the initial value is found. Then, specify the higher value as the end node.
- Otherwise no lower value than the initial value, the next value after the first will be chosen the end node. Replace the end node with the initial one and repeat the same procedure. The batch of the procedure will be regarded as a cycle.
- Due to Kaurov (2013) in Wolfram demonstration project, we focus on the starting node of each batch to connect them to form **a graph-theoretic shortest-path algorithm** (Fig. 7.5).

A *horizontal* time evolution is thus constructed in view of visibility graph as follows[12]:

The Shortest Path

This study develops both of the time evolution of CA and the network formation in view of HVG. According to Kaurov (2013), we call this development **an evolution of a finite elementary cellular automaton (ECA)**. This can be done in a few different ways. We can consider every step of an ECA evolution to be a binary number and calculate its decimal form by counting digits from **left** to right or in reverse.

---

[11] We already learned that something causal will sometimes cause chaotic behaviors if a nonlinear relationship is given. However, something causal must be necessarily condition for an exact prediction.

[12] More details are discussed in Wolfram Community titled Kaurov's "Visibility Graphs: Dualism of Time Series and Networks"https://community.wolfram.com/groups/-/m/t/33771.

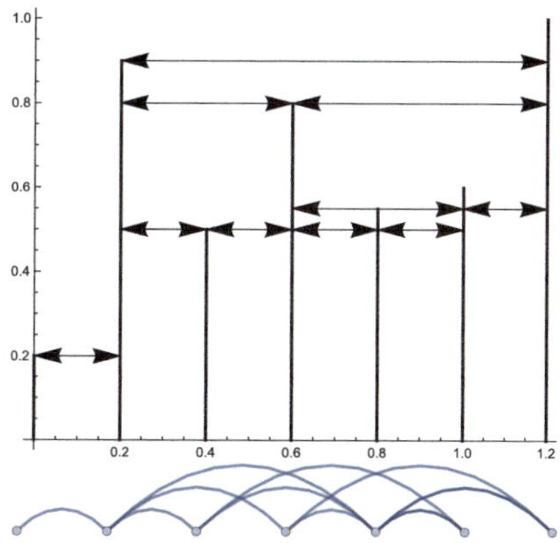

Fig. 7.5 A simple illustration of HVG and its network. **Source* The author depicted these figures by referring to the figures appearing from: Lacasa et al. (2008) (By definition, in **the visibility graph**, each node indicates a sample that is connected to another node if visibility between the two exists)

The shortest path consists of each starting node of each cycle in view of network formation. We may then measure a difference between each event and each node of the shortest path with realized matching. In his smart demonstration, Kaurov has shown **a graph-theoretic shortest-path algorithm** by connecting the starting nodes of each cycle in view the HVG. This path is depicted in *yellow* colors on his HVG network.

Fully Random, Rule-Based Iterated Cellular Automata (FRICA)

In our recent studies like (Aruka et al. 2019, 2020), we focus on the horizontal evolution of our time series generated by the **FRICA**. Rule 110 proves itself to reproduce such structures. Much more interestingly, Wolfram's research group has also discovered these from the behaviors of Fully Random, Rule-based Iterated Cellular Automata (**FRICA**) with multiple rules. FRICA is employed to access *how damaging* the inclusion of a given rule is to the universal behavior of rule 110, for instance. Thus, we can then detect some critical conditions that may make a certain local structure collapse by changing a selection of the rules. This new observation may bring us a new perspective, at least, a useful hint, on how to measure the market performances.

We apply the ideas of shortest path algorithms to the FRICA to get Fig. 7.6.

7.3.2 Exponential Distributions Reflecting Events Recurring at Random in Time

Next, we look on some application of the horizontal visibility graph. Lacasa et al. (2008) has given The exponential distribution derived from the HVG. They then dealt with the cases where "*the algorithm captures the random nature of the series, and the particular shape of the degree distribution of the visibility graph is related to the*

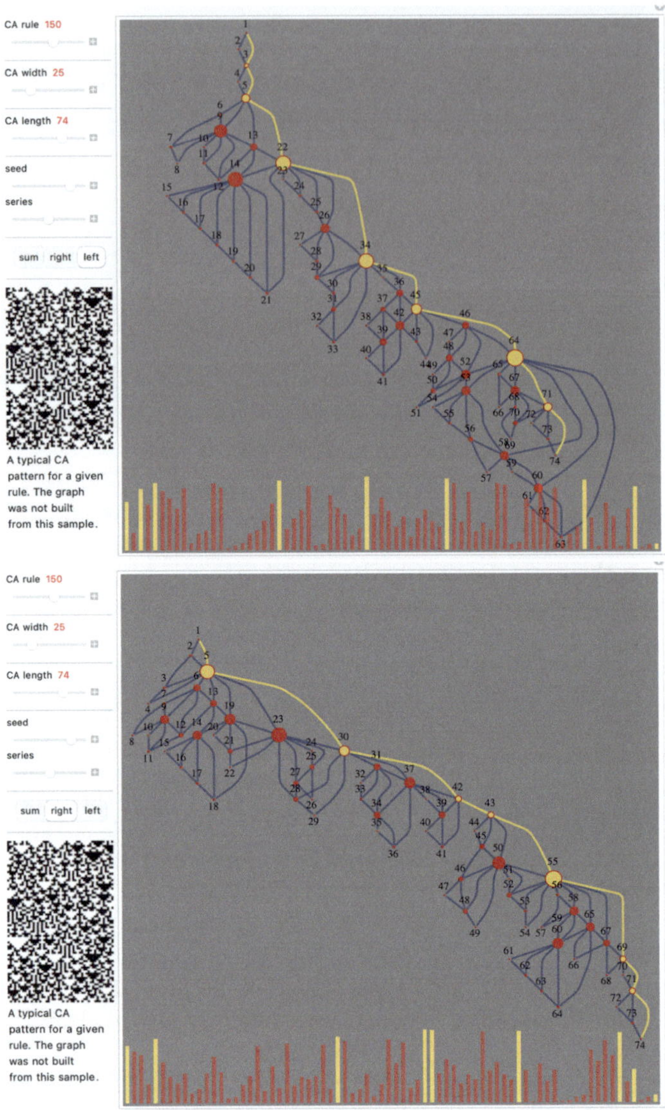

Fig. 7.6 The HVG and its graph-theoretic shortest-path algorithm in the left/right sided case of the FRICA (rules 150, 25 and 74) *These figures are simulated by the use of Kaurov (2013)

particular random process."[13] It is thus seen that exponential distributions have a close link to events recurring "at random in time".

It is then interesting to know the logical links of other distributions. **Mathematica** briefly gives a good illustration of the history of exponential distribution.

> Historically, the exponential distribution has been used most widely to describe events recurring "at random in time", i.e., in circumstances in which the future lifetime of an individual has the same distribution regardless of its present state. The use of the exponential distribution has increased significantly over the last 75 years, due in part to considerable research within the field of order statistics beginning in the early to mid-1950s. Since then, the exponential distribution has been used to model various phenomena over intervals of approximately constant rate, e.g., the number of phone calls placed in a specific time interval each day. In stochastic processes, the exponential distribution describes the lengths of interarrival times in homogeneous Poisson processes. The exponential distribution is also used in credit risk modeling, queueing theory, reliability theory, physics, and hydrology.[14]

Mathematica also gives the logical links between exponential distribution and other distributions. This figure must be helpful to know the internal relationships between them. Usually in econophysics, we like to see a particular link between power law distribution and exponential distribution. But it is also important to observe the other distributions through the exponential distribution.

We refer to the relationships between the exponential distribution and the other well-known distributions in our field.[15]

Power Distribution	Power distribution is a transformation of an exponential distribution; Exponential distribution can be obtained from power distribution,
Pareto Distribution	Pareto distribution is a transformation of exponential distribution; Transformation of a Pareto distribution yields an exponential distribution.
LogisticDistribution	Logistic distribution is a transformation from exponential distribution; Logistic distribution is a transformation from exponential distribution.
Poisson	The parametric mixture of poisson distribution and exponential distribution follows geometric distribution.

[13] In their Fig. 3 of Lacasa et al. (2008), the "first 250 values of $R(t)$, where R is a random series of 106 data values extracted from $U[0, 1]$". On the other hand, the "degree distribution $P(k)$ of the visibility graph associated with $R(t)$ (plotted in semilog). Although the beginning of the curve approaches the result of a Poisson process, and *the tail is clearly exponential.* This behavior is due to data with large values (rare events), which are the hubs".

[14] This part is cited from Mathematica index. https://reference.wolfram.com/language/ref/ExponentialDistribution.html.

[15] The detailed relationships of not only the mentioned distribution but also the other distributions are found in Mathematica's reference https://reference.wolfram.com/language/ref/ExponentialDistribution.html.

Table 7.2 The default composition

Agent strategy	No. agents
TrendStragey	2
AntiTrendStragey	2
Random	3
*S*Random	3
SRsiStrategy	2
RsiStrategy	2
MovingAverageStrategy	2
*S*MovingAverageStrategy	2
SFSpreadStrategy	2
DayTradeStrategy	2
MarketRandomStrategy	2

7.3.3 Contriving a Simple Market to Be Manipulated

Now we narrow down the manipulation in the market exchange. When we employ a virtual market simulator like U-Mart, it will be an easy work whether the market could be manipulated. We commonly implement a so-called technical analytical agent in the U-Mart. In recent years, we have already discovered a special agent set, i.e., **Nakajima-Mori agent configuration**, to always realize any given real price movement.

The Minimal Nakajima-Mori Agent Set in the U-Mart Futures Price Formation

In the U-Mart experiment, the default standard set of strategies is fixed in the way of Table 7.2. As the bodies of each strategy are simultaneously increased, the possibility to match current orders to settle them may be much bigger. It is noted that the representative strategies of traditional technical analytical agents are employed.[16]

On the other hand, the minimal Nakajima-Mori agent set is driven by many simulations of the U-Mart acceleration experiment in the following way.[17]

7.3.4 Characterizing the Even-Matching in the Market Transaction

In the narrative of double auction, as the transaction continues much longer, the market may sometimes fall into a state of steadiness as a result of even matching forces from both directions of rising and declining. This state of the market is called "even matching".

[16] See the details of the strategies employed in the U-Mart system for Chap. 11 written by Professor Nakajima.

[17] See the details for Aruka et al. (2019) and (2020).

Table 7.3 The minimal composition

Agent strategy	Mini bodies
Random	1
AntiTrend	1
DayTrade	1
MovingAverage	3
Rsi	1
Trend	2
SRandom	6
SFSpread	5
SMovingAverage	4
SRsi	3

As the rising rate declines after the consensus breaks down, we will then catch up again with a sell-off opportunity. The figure illustrates this matching process in the case of rising trend. The right edge of the triangle is the point where the market can move either up or down. Thus, a triangle will be formed just before a breaking out of the price series. The red circle of the figure indicates a breakout point to buy when the price will rapidly increase. The breakout point will also break down if the price no longer rises. This, then, means the end of an even matching process (Table 7.3).

Triangle Formation in the Market Transaction

Interestingly, in view of visibility graph, the initial point of the triangle formation may be regarded as the start of a segment to be connected as **the shortest path**. Thus **the breakdown point** also means the end of the same segment of the shortest path. The triangle of the figure just corresponds to a segment of the shortest path of the price time series.[18]

A Breaking Point on the Shortest Path

In other words, the shortest path of our price time series will be interpreted with a whole path connecting each new segment after each, each time the consensus breaks down and the price is wandering about.

At the state where the triangle is kept shaped longer, there may be accumulated orders that were ordered earlier. These previous orders will contribute to the market price either much lower or above a newly assigned order. As a result, the market price will be **pegged** down to a bottom or a ceiling. The event will often occur in **the narrative of double auction** (Fig. 7.7).

The mentioned event will be reproduced as a jumped futures price if we employ the price time series generated by the Nikkei225 spot time prices daily based.[19]

[18] Dr. Yoshihiro Nakajima, my collaborator, contributed to this interpretation. The author is thankful for his wise advice.

[19] The data of Nikkei225 is partly employed a part of the period from 1965 to 2021 fitted to the experimental tool period range.

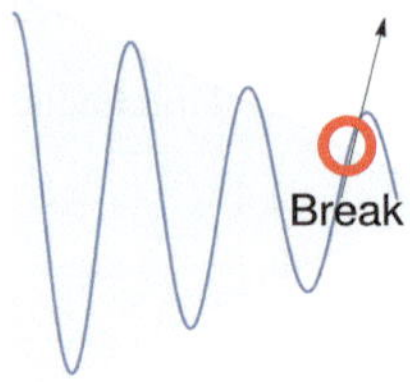

Fig. 7.7 Triangle formation in the case of an ascending price trend

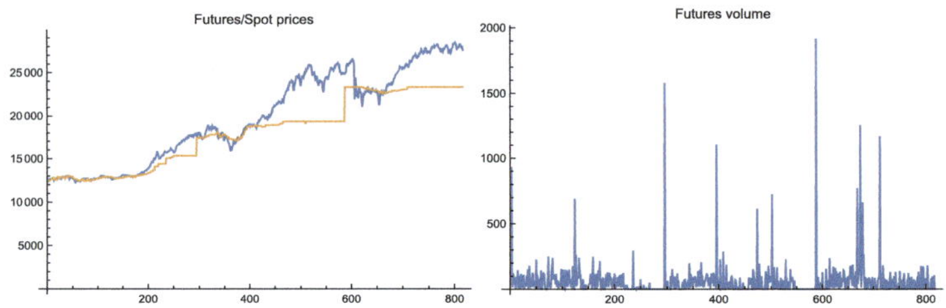

Fig. 7.8 Nikkei225 spot prices case

The Shortest Path of Nikkei225

Finally, we depict the shortest path of this case and its network structure. The latter shows the set of strategies playing the key role in settling down the futures market exchange on the shortest path (Figs. 7.9, 7.10).

Exercises

7.1 Describe the current changes of the style of production, compared to the traditional capitalist economy which was based on machine-made large industry, and mention a set of decisive changes including the change of soical/private life style.

7.2 Try to sort out the attributes brought by the Great Change, connected on the capital-labor system with AI penetrations in your own way. Taking into account transhumanism, discuss this subject.

7.3 Discuss how the stock/currency exchange system were altered by the shift to the HFT (High Frequency Transactions). In particular, discuss if the new change made the original system much more efficient or not.

7.4 List up the usage of blockchain other than financial tools as you currently regard them as promising.

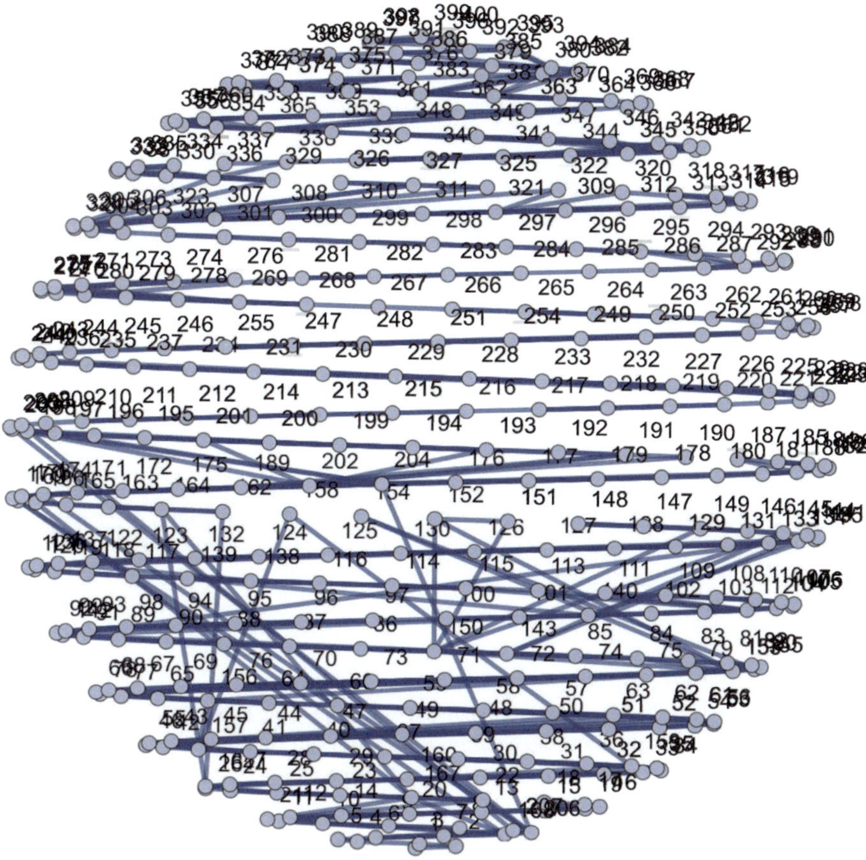

Fig. 7.9 The shortest path derived from the Nikkei225 spot time series

7.5 According to Hildenbrand (1981), the short-run production function was verified to be of zonotope-typed set. Describe in what ways the zonotope-type production function differs from the traditional production function.

7.6 Traditionally, we use some approximation function to infer the values of the function at points of interest. Induction is an operation to draw an approximation function from some examples. On the other hand, deduction is an operation to draw the values of the function at points of interest from an approximation function. In this context, discuss what kind of inference machine learning will achieve (Fig. 7.9).

7.7 The "agglomerate method" is often used, which is a hierarchical clustering method. "Agglomerate" works when clusters have similar densities and are isotropic like "colors." Sometimes symbolic processing is possible. In some case, we need some *training* to tie some pictures with "cat is grey," another picture "cat is fast"

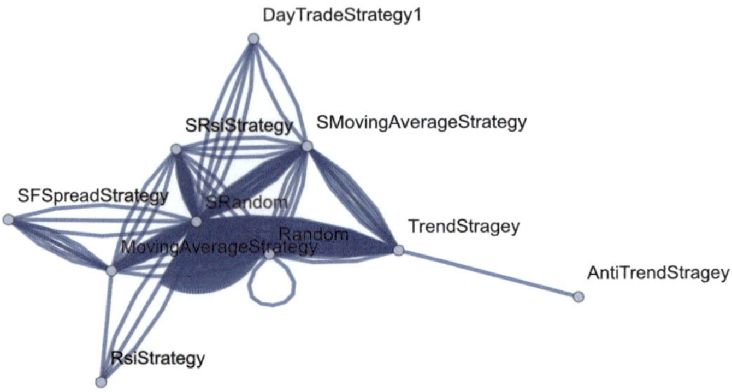

Fig. 7.10 The network structure of the shortest path derived from the Nikkei225 spot time series

and then detect any nearest feature. These detction perform a desired classification/identification between pictures. Learn the "agglomerate method", and then apply it to your target. Hint: Use the operator "Agglomerate" (Machine Learning Method) if you like Wolfram Mathematica.

7.8 In the text above, "[t]he U-Mart system is an artificial intelligent futures transaction system of long-running lifetime initiated by Japanese computer scientists since 1998 (see Aruka (2015, 111–112) and Shiozawa et al. (2008)." In the U-Mart system, the so-called traditional technical agents, either human or algorithmic, can participate in the play. Try to summarize briefly each technical agent of the U-Mart, and discuss the usefulness of the minimal Nakajima-Mori agent set (Fig. 7.10).

7.9 Illustrate the idea of the shortest path of Horizontal Visibility Graph in your own way, and then draw a numerical example of it as you like.

7.10 The Wolfram Demonstrations project has a useful tool like "Horizontal Visibility Graphs for Elementary Cellular Automata" (Kaurov 2013). Access to https://demonstrations.wolfram.com/HorizontalVisibilityGraphsForElementary/CellularAutomata/ to try some several simulation on which cases you are interested. And then discuss some advantage on the visibility graph, i.e., the transformation from the network development to a time series representation in your own way.

References

Arthur, W. B. (2009). *The nature of technology*. Free Press.

Aruka, Y. (Ed.). (2022). *Digital design for money, market, and social dilemmas*. Springer Nature.

Aruka, Y., Nakajima, Y., & Mori, N. (2019). An examination of market mechanism with redundancies motivated by turing's rule selection. *Evolutionary and Institutional Economic Review, 16*(1), 19–42.

Aruka, Y., Nakajima, Y., & Mori, N. (2019). The minimum heterogeneous agent configuration to realize the future price time series similar to any given spot price time series in the AI market experiment. In E. Bucciarelli, S.H. Chen, J. Corchado (Eds.), *Decision economics: Complexity of decisions and decisions for complexity. DECON 2019. Advances in intelligent systems and computing* (Vol. 1009, pp. 85–92). Springer, Cham.

Aruka, Y. (2015). Hodgson's bibliometric report and the reconstruction plan of economics. *Evolutionary and Institutional Economics Review, 15*(1), 189–202.

Aruka, Y. (2020). The evolution of the exchange process: From the decentralized to the distributed digital exchange. *Evolutionary and Institutional Economic Review, 17*(2), 379–398.

Aruka, Y., & Akiyama, E. (2009). Non-self-averaging of a two-person game with only positive spillover: A new formulation of Avatamsaka's dilemma. *Journal of Economic Interaction and Coordination, 4*(2), 135–161.

Broesch, J. D. (1997). *Digital Signal Processing Demystified (Engineering Mentor Series)*. Newnes(Elsevier).

Brownlee, J. (2017) Machine learning mastery: Gentle introduction to transduction in machine learning in deep learning for natural language processing.

Dosi, G., Grazzi, M., Marrengo, L., & Settepanella, S. (2016). Production theory: Accounting for firm heterogeneity and technical change. *The Journal of Industrial Economics,64*(4), 875–907.

Haken, H. (1977). *Synergetics—An introduction: Nonequilibrium phase transitions and mankind*. Springer.

Hildenbrand, W. (1981). Short-run production functions based on microdata. *Econometrica, 49*(5), 1095–1125.

Kahneman, D. (2011). *Thinking, fast and slow*. Farrar, Straus and Giroux.

Kaurov, V. (2013). Horizontal visibility graphs for elementary cellular automata. Available through the Wolfram Demonstrations Project https://demonstrations.wolfram.com/HorizontalVisibilityGraphsForElementaryCellularAutomata/.

Lacasa, L., Luque, B., Ballesteros, F., Luque, J., & Nuño, J. C. (2008). From time series to complex networks: The visibility graph. *PANAS,105*(13), 4972–4975.

Mainzer, K. (2007). Kapitel 7: Zufall in Kultur, Wirtschaft, und Gesselschaft. In *Der kreative Zufall: Wie das Neue in die Welt kommt?* CH Beck.

Mirowski, P. (2007). Markets come to bits: Evolution computation and markomata in economic science. *Journal of Economic Behavior and Organization, 63*(2), 209–242.

Piketty, T. (2014). *Capital in the twenty-first century*. Harvard UP, Cambridge Mass.

Schefold, B. (2021). Transformations of the Cambridge critique contribution to the issue in memory of Krishna Bharadwaj. *Indian Economic Journal, 69*(2), 2411–254.

Shiozawa, Y., Nakajima, Y., Matsui, H., Koyama, Y., Taniguchi, K., & Hashimoto, F. (2008). *Artificial market experiments with the U-mart system*. Springer Series on Agent Based Social Systems (Vol. 4). Springer.

Vapnik, V. N. (1998). *Statistical Learning Theory*. New Jersey: Wiley-Interscience.

Weidlich, W. (2000). *Sociodynamics: A systematic approach to mathematical modeling in the social sciences*. Harwood Academic Publishers; Reprinted by Taylor and Francis 2002, Russian 2004, Paper edition, Dover Publications 2006, Japanese 2007, 2000.

Part III

Evolutionary Reconstruction of Economics

The Reconstruction of the Theory of Production and Preference

8

Abstract

This article was originally designed to comment an unprecedented bibliometric study of evolutionary economics by Hodgson and Lamberg (2016). However, Hodgson only reported the historical trajectory and the current situations of evolutionary economics initiated by since Nelson RR Winter SG Nelson and Winter (1982). He gave an insightful consideration about **the raison d'être** of evolutionary economics. According to his opinion, evolutionary economics is still failing to equip the core theories. We naturally agree with his remarks on the current situations around evolutionary economics. We take this opportunity to *squarely* address the subject about how to insert the core theories into evolutionary economics. We argue that the alternative candidates to be replaced with the main stream core theories are in the following ordering:(1) the theory of production to invalidate myopic optimization, (2) the theory of preference to invalidate myopic optimization, (3) the SMD Theorem to invalidate invisible hand, and (4) the market mechanism to invalidate the efficient market hypothesis. Needless to say, the alternative theories shown in these arguments imply the reconstruction of economics. Finally, we address the current analysis of bibliometrics.

8.1 Toward a Reconstruction Plan of Economics

The work of Hodgson and Lamberg (2016) is an unprecedented work on bibliometric analysis of evolutionary economics in its range and scope. First, this analysis retrieved 8,474 articles. Second, it separated the development of the time profiles in the subsequent five year periods: 1986–1990, 1991–1995, 1996–2000, 2001–2005, and 2006–2010. Thus this study was able to refer to the present trend and the fashions around the different and cross disciplines. In this sense, the observed facts that Hodgson and Lamberg discovered seem to be almost all reasonable from our institutional overview. Furthermore, in connection with the author's great intelligence, this bib-

Y. Aruka, *Evolutionary Economics*, Springer Texts in Business and Economics,
https://doi.org/10.1007/978-981-97-1382-0_8

liometric analysis has finally given an insightfully useful perspective to reconstruct economics for us.

In spite of wider penetrations/success over diverse fields except for economics over years, as Hodgson and Lamberg (2016) stated, it must be true that almost no one was successful in replacing the core engine with the main stream's one. His suggestions fortunately coincide with our original plans appeared in Aruka (2017a) to revive economics **ontologically**. This is the reason why I decided to comment on this article. As Hodgson and Lamberg recommended, **the raison d'être** of evolutionary economics must be the innovation of the core theories of the traditional economics. In other words, the belief of the main stream economics is that *everything is at best*. On the contrary, our belief is that *everything is evolving*. We continue to comprehend that "evolutionary economics" as "economics to be evolved". In this point of view, first of all, the reconstruction of political economy mattered. In this sense, Japan Association for Evolutionary Economics (JAFEE) adopted another purpose against the standard definitions of evolutionary economics at the very outset of the foundation. She was sustaining her effort to construct the core theories, such as the theory of value, as an alternative to the main stream. Based on that, Shiozawa (2007) and (2015) used to sub-tropical algebra to provide a general proof of international trade theory of value in the case of the transaction of three commodities including intermediate goods among three countries. This is the great innovation since Ricardian theory of value. Due to Shiozawa's contributions, the existing theory of comparative cost and its marginal version has lost their justification.

Once upon a time at Cambridge UK, Kaldor (1955) purposed constructing "alternative theories" of distribution in order to replace the neoclassical marginal productivity theory. He and his followers' attempts have never been successful at rejecting the existing core theory of marginal productivity with their doctrine. The Sraffian theory of value survived longer in being an alternative candidate in value and distribution. However, the classical principles of political economy has been throughly replaced with **equilibrium economics**. Equilibrium economics always depends on the belief that **everything is at best**, even in serious depressions. It is interesting to note that the Leibzian idea of **everything is at best** was criticized by *Candide* in [?].

We regard *evolution* as an idea of the antithesis against the everything-at-its-best proposition. The real world of evolution is then irrelevant to the grand design of God. Biological evolution does not contain an original intention to optimize the whole system to coordinate other organs consistently, at least at the outset of mutation. In this context, evolution is rather motivated by **creative coincidence** in Mainzer (2007) as a consecutive source of innovation. The same mechanism that causes the skin's blood to condense causes blood condensation in the brain. In general, evolution does not give any normative optimality at all. Thus the use of the idea of evolution becomes a strong support to the construction of the core theories of production and preference without the idea of optimization and human rationality.[1]

[1] It is noted that there are two kinds of rationality: human rationality and algorithm rationality.

The main stream economics updated herself to survive. Despite of Hirofumi Uzawa's (1928–2014) expectation, the rational expectational hypothesis internationally spread in the economics departments. As demonstrated in Aruka (2015a), it is noted that the idea of bounded rationality is considered the raison d'être of rationality. That is to say, **bounded rationality** is not any modification of rational economics at all but a refined form of it. Reality is always skewed and polluted because the secular world is not the world of God if we are faithful to the tradition of Thomas Aquinas.

8.2 The Preliminaries to Replace the Core Theories of Economics

We first mention the recent prospects to innovate the core theories of economics. Hildenbrand (1981, 1994) has already given us a set of great hints to innovate the theories in both production and consumer preference. Although my exposition is not exhaustive, in the following, we will refer to how several eminent scholars prepared for the alternative theories. In my opinion, the present time is overdue to innovate on the traditional ideas. Now, we mention the main points and illustrate them very shortly.

1. Theory of production to invalidate myopic optimization
    a. Hildenbrand (1981) and the zonotope set of production
    b. A fallacy of the specification on a particular technique and the zonotope set of the international trade
2. Theory of preference to invalidate myopic optimization
    a. A sufficient condition to confirm the positive income effect in Hildenbrand (1994)
    b. The utility theory of imperfect identification in Luce (1959) and Saari (2005)
3. The SMD Theorem to invalidate the invisible hand
    a. A generalization on SMD theorem in Saari (1992)
    b. Aggregation and choice paradoxes
4. The market mechanism to invalidate the efficient market hypothesis
    a. The U-Mart system as an ontological construction of the exchange system by AI
    b. Class 4 of Fully Random Iterated Automata (FRIA)

8.2.1 Theory of Production to Invalidate Myopic Optimization

8.2.1.1 Hildenbrand (1981) and Zonotope Set of Production

There were few to understand the importance (Hidldenbrand, 1981). Dosi (2016b) and Scuola Superiore Sant'Anna noticed its importance. Hildenbrandt proved that the short-run production function was empirically measured did not fulfil the contours of the neoclassical production function but, rather, the form of *zonotopic* set of the discrete basic activities of production in a Minkowski space. This set geometrically forms a shape like a rugby ball. Most importantly, the use of zonotopic production set permits us to analyze the **recursive property** of activities/techniques. Either the neoclassical school or Leontief's input-output analysis were not able to implement a recursive process of production in general.

In short, "[l]eaving the special space restricted by the traditional production function, we can observe various possible combinations to accept institutional effects. Broadening the space, from where technology can be chosen, implies to introduce all possible combinations of activities" (Aruka, 2017a, 410). Dosi (2016a) successfully applied this kind of production set to technical progress by calculating the volume of this set. This must be a great progress in the theory of production to invalidate the myopic optimization in production.

8.2.1.2 A Fallacy of Specialization on a Particular Technique and the Zontopic Set of the International Trade

A good example of the benefit of specialization in a particular techniques is the merger or an integration of two basic activities/plants. However, as Aruka (2017b) demonstrated, this does not depict the effect of specialization in the international trade between two countries. So far, no one was successful to formulate a general model of international trade of intermediate commodities. This was due to the different rates of distribution among both countries are complicatedly intermingled with the **country-wise** profile space and the **commodity-wise** profile space. This interrupted us in confirming equilibrium prices. Fortunately, Shiozawa (2007 and 2015) gave historically great contributions to find equilibrium in this case. By this proof, it was verified that we never required a particular specification of commodity production for the world efficient production.

This theorem permits us to model the international trade between the same industries, even in equilibrium. Thus we have also been released also from the neoclassical bindings in the international trade theory. It is also noted that the world production system of three countries and three commodities are exactly the zonotopic set, as shown in Aruka (2017b).

According to sub-tropical algebra, let denote the max-times semi-ring a set of all positive numbers by $a \oplus_{\max} b = \max\{a, b\}$ and $a \odot b = a \cdot b$

On the other hand, we describe Ricardian economy of M countries and N commodities by

$$\mathcal{E} = \{A = [q_{ij}], q = (q_i) \tag{8.1}$$

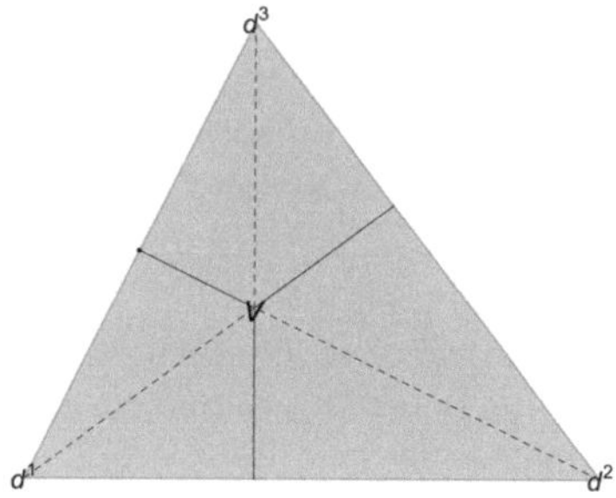

Fig. 8.1 Max-times hyperplane of exotic algebra *The figure was designed by the author by referring to Shiozawa (2015, 188)

Let the wage-price system be

$$(w, p) = (w_1, \ldots, w_M; p_1, \ldots, p_N) \tag{8.2}$$

where w_i is the wage of Country i, p_j is the price of commodity j. It must then holds in economic point of view:

$$w_i a_{ij} \geq p_j, \forall i \in [M] \text{ and} j \in [N]. \tag{8.3}$$

Expressing this in terms of subtropical matrix form, it follows:

$$w \geq p \otimes_{\max} B. \tag{8.4}$$

Here B is a transposed matrix whose (j, i) component is the reciprocal of $1/a_{ij}$.[2] Shiozawa (2015, 188) called the frame simplex such as Fig. 8.1.

Vertices of price simplex represent commodities. The hyperplane for max-times semi-ring separates the simplex into three domains of different types. Correspondingly to this illustration, we define the wage simplex, i.e., subtropical hyperplanes with the min-times semi-ring as detailed later.

8.2.2 Theory of Preference to Invalidate Myopic Optimization

8.2.2.1 A Sufficient Condition to Confirm the Positive Income effect in Hildenbrand (1994)

The great success of Pareto-Slutsky equation (Slutsky, 1915) in analyzing consumer demand was given as one of **the raison d'être** of the main stream economics. But

---

[2] Shiozawa (2015, 187) used the expression $\odot_{\max}$ in order to distinguish the symbol $\otimes$. If these conditions are fulfilled, it then holds:

$$w = w \otimes_{\min} A \oplus_{\max} B, \tag{8.5}$$

$$p = p \otimes_{\max} B \oplus_{\min} A. \tag{8.6}$$

.

this analysis never was completed to derive the law of consumer demand, which says that the demand decreases as the price increases. Despite being able to confirm the direction of income effect, surprisingly, many insisted to call Pareto-Slutsky equation the law of demand with a studied nonchalance. This attitude was considerably frivolous. The usual practice to justify Slutsky equation is to impose the assumption of **gross substitutability** (GS). This assumption is equivalent with respect to the income effect being negligible, despite of the discovery of Giffen effect. It is quite easy to find Giffen effect in the simplest exchange economy of two commodities if the budget is presented in terms of the real endowments of the economy and not using income in terms of monetary units, as shown in Aruka (2015b, 49). That is to say, the Giffen effect is not an exceptional case. The followers of the General Equilibrium Model were too idle to look for a sufficient condition to establish the direction of sings of the income effect.

Hildenbrand (1994) has smartly given several sufficient conditions to establish the positiveness of income effect. One of these conditions is that as income x increases, the spread of demand f, which is the sum of variance and square mean of demand f, increase. In other words, the consumption patterns of the richer class become diverse. Here it is useless to apply a monotheistic idea of myopic optimization. This suggests a great conversion from the neoclassical method of homogeneous agents to the new method of heterogeneous gents. The idea of mathematical closeness both in the commodity space and in terms of personal satisfaction must be a fallacy if we envisage the way in which patterns of consumption will be formed in reality. Outside sophisticated mathematical modeling, we need a different idea of consumption such as shown in Aruka (2015b, 51–62).

8.2.2.2 The Utility Theory of Imperfect Identification in Saari (2005)

The alternative theory of choice must be the probabilistic choice theory of utility given by Luce (1959). However, the generic usage of this theory is almost for a practical one to predict the consumer demand of transportation or sightseeing, including mode choices. This method became well known by McFaden's Nobel Prize in the academic world. When Luce's utility is *algebraically* considered, this is currently dealt with as **the multi-logit model**, which can illustrate either successive choices or mode choices. Alternatively, it may be possible to derive the multi-logit model type utility from the neoclassical assumptions.[3] A restrictive assumption like **independence from irrelevant alternatives** is often imposed. However, almost all of such an attempts depend on the assumption that the set/subset of preference are *universal*.

However, the original version of Luce (1959) does not need to assume universal preference set. In a serial paper of topological geometrical investigation, Saari (2004) showed that **imperfect identification of alternative issues** could generate paradoxes that are sensitive to a small change of circumstances. Given the preference set/subsets, it turns out that there are trivially formed probability profiles and ranking profiles.

[3] See, for instance, Durlauf (1997) and (2000).

Either in voting or commodity exchanges, the ranking result of candidates depends on a *relative position* of the preference subset in relation to the probability profile.

It is noted that the ranking results of candidates may be changed because agent's preferences changes. His/her position never changes but a preference subset to which he/she belongs changes either by forming a coalition of several agents or by the new introduction of an alternative issue, for instance. In short, his/her *relative* distance from the candidates changes. Thus such a change of a *relative* position can be *imperfectly* identified to give rise any counter-intuitive paradox, thus contradicting myopic optimization.

8.3 Durlauf's Random Preferences Influenced by Social Interaction

Luce=Saari's studies will be detailed in the next chapter. In this subsection, we illustrate how the main stream economics deal with a random choice but without leaving methodological individualism.

8.3.1 Individualistic Utility

Durlauf (1997) and (2000) in principle never part with the *methodological individualism* in orthodox economics but depends essentially on the above formulation of interactive network of agents when he seriously is concerned with the effects of *heterogeneous subgroups* on individualistic choice. His case may be regarded as an application of the above minimization problem in view of social costs. In particular, he utilized the *logistic distribution* as a specific form of *random preferences* to derive a probability distribution of choice as resulting some similar idea of Gibbs distribution.

In Durlauf's idea the utility V of agent has been construed as a union of three different types of utility for individual $i \in I$: private utility ω as private and deterministic utility; social interaction S as social and deterministic utility; random shock ϵ as private and stochastic utility.

$$V_i = \omega_i + S + \epsilon_i. \tag{8.7}$$

8.3.2 Private Utility

Binary Choice. We indicate the outcome of binary choice whether an individual $i \in I$ can be a painter or a musician by ω_i, and its support by $\Omega_i = \{-1, 1\}$. $\omega_i = -1$ means painter, $\omega_i = 1$ a musician, for example.

Heterogeneous Agent. Agents playing in the system are heterogeneous, whose property is expressed as X_i.

Random Shocks. We assume independent stochastic disturbances among heterogeneous agents. In the case of $\omega_i = 1$ which suggests to be a musician, if utility of random shock $\epsilon(1)$ is *relevant*, utility of choice for i to be a musician will increase. $\epsilon(1)$ exhibits unobservable musical talent, while $\epsilon(-1)$ unobservable artistic talent.

There may be several possibilities for each individual. A particular one will be realized by a probabilistic distribution of random shocks. We for convenience assume a *logistic distribution* of the probability which the difference of the random shocks on a binary choice $\epsilon_i(-1) - \epsilon_i(1)$ can be within a particular z.[4]

$$\text{Prob}(\epsilon(-1) - \epsilon(1) \leq z) = \frac{1}{1 + e^{-\beta_i z}}. \tag{8.8}$$

The density function of logistic distribution is symmetrically bell-shaped. β_i indexes *unobservable heterogeneity*. The larger β is, the lower a probability which the difference of utility falls within a certain value of z may be.

8.3.3 Social Utility

Agent i has his own belief on choices of the other members of the group I based on a certain information: $\mu_i^e(\omega_{-i}|F_i)$.[5] Individuals are inclined to conform to or deviate from others' choices of the group. When all the members have the same choice, social utility for individual is of zero. When each deviates from each other, social utility for agent i is negative.

$$S(\omega_i, X_i, \mu_i^e) = -E_i\left(\sum_{j \neq i} \frac{J_{i,j}}{2}(\omega_i - \omega_j)^2\right). \tag{8.9}$$

Weight on interaction $J_j(X_i)$ simply is denoted by $J_{i,j}$, as relating the choice for i to one for j. Thus the square $(\omega_i - \omega_j)^2$ will give *conformity effects*. Hence social utility S is just a subjectively expected value as based on agent i's belief of the distribution of social interaction $[J_j(X_i)]$.

8.3.4 Derivation of the Probability on Individual Choice

The decision process of individual i is as follows:

$$\omega_i = \arg \max_{\omega \in \{-1,1\}} V(\omega, X_i, \mu_i^e, \epsilon_i). \tag{8.10}$$

---

[4] Here $\beta(X_i) \geq 0$.

[5] The suffix $-i$ shows the remaining members except for i.

Linearization of Utility Function

A linearized function of utility is given where a slope is h_i, an intercept k_i[6]:

$$u(\omega_i, X_i) = h_i\omega_i + k_i. \tag{8.11}$$

Under a certain set of information, a choice ω_i is generated only if the gain of the choice is greater than the opposite. A conditional choice $\mu(\omega_i)$ is the probability when the gain of ω_i is greater than the gain of $-\omega_i$.

$$\mu(\omega_i|X_i, \mu_i^e) = \mu(V(\omega_i, \epsilon_i(\omega_i)) > V(-\omega_i, \epsilon_i(-\omega_i)). \tag{8.12}$$

Taking account of the above (8.7) and (8.9) into (8.12), it follows:

$$\begin{aligned}
&\mu(h_i\omega_i - E_i\sum_{j\neq i}\frac{J_{i,j}}{2}(\omega_i - \omega_j)^2 + \epsilon_i(\omega_i)\\
&> -h_i\omega_i - E_i\sum_{j\neq i}\frac{J_{i,j}}{2}(-\omega_i - \omega_j)^2 + \epsilon_i(-\omega_i))\\
&= \mu(h_i\omega_i + \sum_{j\neq i} J_{i,j}\omega_i E_i(\omega_i) + \epsilon(\omega_i) > -h_i\omega_i - \sum_{j\neq i} J_{i,j}\omega_i E_i(\omega_j) + \epsilon_i(-\omega_i))\\
&= \mu(\epsilon_i(\omega_i) - \epsilon_i(-\omega_i) > -2h_i\omega_i - \sum_{j\neq i} 2J_{i,j}\omega_i E_i(\omega_j)).
\end{aligned} \tag{8.13}$$

Since the random shocks are assumed to be subject to the *logistic distribution* (8.12), the probability distribution on the choice of individual i, i.e., ω_i can be solved:

$$\mu(\omega_i|X_i, \mu_i^e) \propto e^{\beta_i h_i\omega_i + \sum_{j\neq i}\beta_i J_{i,j}\omega_i E_i(\omega_j)}. \tag{8.14}$$

The joint probability distribution of the whole population on the choice of ω then is:

$$\mu(\omega|X_1, \ldots, X_n, \mu_1^e, \ldots, \mu_n^e) = \Pi_i\mu(\omega_i|X_i, \mu_i^e) \propto \Pi_i e^{\beta_i h_i\omega_i + \sum_{j\neq i}\beta_i J_{i,j}\omega_i E_i(\omega_j)}. \tag{8.15}$$

8.3.5 A Generalization of the SMD Theorem to Invalidate Invisible Hand

8.3.5.1 A Generalization on SMD Theorem in Saari (1992)

A serial theorem argued by Sonnenschein (1972, 1973), Mantel (1974), and Debreu (1974) is called **the SMD Theorem**. SMD states that the aggregate excess demand

[6] Choose such h_i and k_i that $h_i + k_i = u(1, X_i)$ and $-h_i + k_i = u(-1, X_i)$.

function can always be constructed only by the classical assertions about continuity, homogeneity and Walras' Law. There is no need any other general properties. Hence the SMD theorem, at first look, seems the most robust theorem to guarantee an equilibrium in any circumstance to justify the invisible hand. Furthermore, many are convinced that the Walrasian market mechanism are universal almost in any circumstance. Due to this conviction, many are willing to generalize this result in the financial market. This enthusiasm still supports the belief of efficient market hypothesis (**EMH**) in financial markets.

On the other hand, Saari (1992), in the context of the original Luce theory, carefully inspected this theorem to generalize this theorem and provide an alternative proof to show that to prove a general equilibrium of the market is essentially equivalent to prove the winning process of voting.

> [Saari's generalized theorem (Saari, 1992)] asserts that almost anything imaginable can happen! Examples can be created where Smith's invisible hand grasps nothing. Using only diagrams of the form used in a freshman economics course, examples can be created that support Adam Smith's story for all pairs of commodities, but, with the same agents, the price dynamic is chaotic for all triplets, then all sets of four commodities have several equilibria where some are attractors and other are not, and then... (Saari, 2015, 134)

8.3.5.2 Aggregation and Choice Paradoxes

Roughly speaking, any variation of a purchased commodity changes a next optimal position of the individual. The purchase of "IPad, for instance, can radically change customer demand structure (Saari, 2015, 134)". Suppose that a subset where this change occurs is separated from a larger subset of commodities. We do not need to know the aggregated excess demand of any larger subset. In short, **the aggregated demand function** never specifies how a new equilibrium will be generated by what kind of adjustment process. The same reasoning will also be valid to theory of vote, or social choice. The latter theory is often faced with a dead end like voting paradoxes.

Additionally, here, the method of aggregation matters. It is quite interesting to see that an intervention of aggregation rather causes to reflect **the peculiarities of the particular rule** but not the real data (Saari, 2015, 125).

> "Positional elections" (or "positional election rules")[7] is the name attached to election rules where ballots are tallied by assigning points to candidates according to how they are positioned (i.e., ranked) on the ballot. The widely used "plurality vote," where each voter votes for one candidate and the candidate with the largest number of votes wins, assigns one point for a top-ranked candidate and zero for all others. (Saari, 2004, 232)

To be sure, we are used to use an extreme evaluation like plurality vote. Therefore, a small positional change of candidates will give rise chaos.

[7] Sometimes it is called "positional voting".

8.3.6 The Market Mechanism to Invalidate the Efficient Market Hypothesis

8.3.6.1 The U-Mart System as an Ontological Construction of the Exchange System by AI

In the above subsections, we referred to the invalidation of myopic optimization in theoretical point of view. Economics depicted the market as the integration of production and preference. General equilibrium theory is simply one of the pictures to sketch the market economy. Thus, it must be indispensable for us to argue how the market mechanism really is working, without introducing myopic optimizing agents.

The AI market is no longer a virtual market. This is actually a real market. It is not realistic to argue about the stock exchange without referring to the high frequency transaction(HFT). The computerization of the market does not guarantee a purity of competitiveness of the market. In April 2018, **Japan Exchange** decided to adopt the policy of the advanced registration of the HFT agent. This may not be a natural outcome for the general equilibrium and/or the invisible hand's supporters.

The AI market based on **algorithm rationality** is evidence that the market can accept another principle different from **human rationality**. Constructing the AI market system is an attempt to construct the market transaction without resorting to the neoclassical principles. In the real market, dominant agents are the so-called **technical agents** rather than the myopic optimizing and/or rational expectation agent. On the contrary, we can employ the AI market simulator like the U-Mart System[8] to run our experiments without damaging the functional terms structured by existing entities of the real market.

8.3.6.2 The Role of Randomness/No-intelligence in the Market

In an actual market, participating agents are sending orders either randomly or non-intelligently, even though they depend on their own unambiguous strategies. It is also noted that purely random orders often bring the best performance in the market. Thus the market system may be a system with many redundancies.[9]

In this century, it turned out that the automaton of the **Wolfram rule 110** fulfilled the criteria of Turing completeness. This is among major problems that continued to interest Stephen Wolfram.[10] Now, the rule 110 and the similar rules are being explored. The cellular automaton has a simple structure, but it is potent in terms of generating complicated behavior like **Class 4**:

[8] The U-Mart system is an artificial intelligent futures transaction system of long-running lifetime initiated by Japanese computer scientists since 1998(See Aruka (2015b, 111–112) and Shiozawa et al. (2008).

[9] This part depends on Aruka's mimeo paper (Aruka, 2018).

[10] In particular, see *A New Kind of Science* (Wolfram, 2002).

Class 4 Nearly all initial patterns evolve into structures that interact in complex and interesting ways, with the formation of local structures that are able to survive for long periods of time.[12]

Now, we accommodate the idea of **Class 4** to the market system. In the market, at first, the participants of various types are locally formed, and then they mutually interact in complex and interesting ways, with the formation of local structures that are able to survive for long periods of time. The Wolfram ICA simulations examined a kind of attractor formation. Conversely, in the market experiment of the U-Mart system, we often observe a certain correspondence generated in a relationship between an initial strategy configuration and its final performance configuration. A final performance is represented by some special form, like attractor. We can examine whether a final performance configuration is wired to its initial strategy configuration or not. A similar set of strategies, in spite of different environments and experimental modes of the market, may fall into a similar result. Irrespective of the rigid assumption of myopic optimization or rational expectation, we can run the analysis of the market.

8.4 Micro-based Theories for Evolutionary Economics

8.4.1 Methodological Biases

Also In the financial society established since the 1990s, economists has strangely learned to generalize the "efficienct market hypothesis" to financial markets.

Mysterious situations have thus been dominant as follows:

1. First of all, the expected utility theory is often used in financial theory. But the basis of this theory is given by Daniel Bernoulli. Its basis does not have any intersection with the classical utility theory at all. In the first place, the domain for both theories is different. The argument of expected utility is money or income. On the other hand, the argument of the classical utility theory is usually defined as physical quantities or services enjoyed. Moreover, in addition to utility theory and expected utility theory, mode selection based on Luce's discrete selection theory in Luce (1959) provides a sequential utility theory. However, as we will see later, an alternative geometrical analysis such as found in Saari's works proves that traditional utility functions do neither contribute to selection theory, nor can Luce's selection theory contribute to unique decisions. The so-called social choice theory such as Amartya Sen is also under pressure to change significantly (Lin & Saari, 2008; Saari, 2006).
2. In financial markets, especially in the artificial market for securities or stock trading, we know that so-called zero intelligence is the agent that is not defeated.

[12] Cited from Wikipedia article **Cellular automaton** at https://en.wikipedia.org/wiki/Cellular_automaton.

We know a reason why this agent is a winner, but random agents are not intellectually rational in terms of traditional economics. Interestingly, however, it is not defeated by an intellectually complex agent. This is what economics, which insists on intellectual optimization, should explore properly.

3. In addition, Mirowski (2007) has already pointed out that when the market is stacked on top of the market, the original market meaning is lost. Financial markets are typical of hierarchical markets. In such a hierarchical network, the working of the individual market will have to be examined by computer simulation. However, there is little sign that economics will solve the problem of hierarchical interaction. Now financial markets themselves are more essential to technical efficiency calculations than economic efficiency calculations. With the advent of HFT, microsecond payments are now made, which means that physical distance determines the settlement. Originally, the Zaraba rule was a time-first principle, but the Zaraba rule itself was custom to stabilize the transaction. But under HFT, the economic meaning of the rule has changed, and even the traditional stock market rule of membership has virtually changed with the lending of high-performance servers on stock exchanges.

8.4.2 Encounters with New Science and Innovation in Economics

As Arthur (2009) pointed out, the aircraft structure of modern state-of-the-art fighters does not incorporate stability for fail-safe. It increases the room to become uneasy structurally of the aircraft, and enables agile action. This is because ICT technology can restore instability instantaneously.

Relaxed Static Stability

This observation may call us "the relaxed static stability". Depending on the idea of "fail safe", structural stability has been important in designing planes and ships up to now. On the contrary, a modern stealth fighter like Lockheed $F35$ is designed by the idea of relaxing "static stability". It is well known that bicycle behaves much more quickly than tricycle, and tries to restore its instability by resort to its counter motion. The counter motion will be controlled by computational powers. Thus we expect that some nonlinear effect is implemented behind the flash crashes, always accompanying a countervailing power (Fig. 8.2).

As symbolized by Germany's Industrial Policy **Industry 4**, it goes without saying that now that ICT is essential to infrastructure, the scope of economic policy applications needs to be reconsidered. However, there is only a great emotional backlash against Arthur's theory of technology, and few people, like Arthur, seriously consider the true situation of modern society. It was not actually realized from the theory of financial and economics the reason why **the option market** has publicly become opened again at the end of the last century. In order to reopen it, technological advances that can accurately calculate high risk by polynomial calculation, that is, a

Fig. 8.2 Lockheed Martin F-35 Lightning II, Wikipedia

dramatic increase in computer computing power, were indispensable. That's Arthur's point, but in a recent example, the same is true of the emergence of Bitcoin in 2008.

Bitcoin assumes **a Peer-to-Peer payment network** based on **an open source protocol**. The task of booking transaction settlements for this kind of other person is not possible without **the establishment of Git-hub technology**. The Git-hub system has made it possible to create a new system without server management, but bitcoin is only feasible with such a technical foundation. Of course, Bitcoin also has many properties in common with other regional currencies and recently emerged digital coins, but it should not be forgotten that they are inherently different. Bitcoin can be an important entity of the society's economic system, and so it will also carry the risk of system destruction. Bitcoin is a prime example, but for survival, the "computability problem" always comes with it, which essentially leads to the "Turing problem". It should be noted that it is not a problem of economics by any way. Economics often emphasizes economic decisions, but it will be necessary to explore how much economic decisions contribute to "economic problem" decisions.

Wolfram's New Science

Mathematica's Stefan Wolfram's *New Kind of Science* (Wolfram, 2002) is not very famous in the world of economics. John Conway simplified the Turing problem with life games and contributed to the development of cellular automata (see Gardner (1970)). Cellular automata promoted the rise of computer science in the 1990s with the development of John Holland's complex adaptive systems and genetic algorithms. With the spread of agent-based modeling ABM, computational electronics is now one of the standards. The important point here is that these developments follow Turing traditions properly. ABM can be criticized by economics for its lack of a theoretical basis. However, ABM itself has a mathematical basis in the Turing sense if the algorithm can be proposed neatly like the bucket relay algorithm of the gene. It is equally important that interactions containing nonlinear interactions that cannot be solved by mathematical analysis have no choice but to simulate in ABM.

In the 1930s, the theoretical basis of genetic research was almost established. The problem was that it was computationally possible, as was the optional risk calculation, so it would take more than 50 years to demonstrate the theory. It will be condesteming in the reader's understanding of the theory of light of Wright (1932) and Turing (1952) about the morphological model (Aruka, 2017a).

> In the era of classical political economy, the method was ontological centric. But, in the last century, the method was replaced with the belief of so-called hypothesis testing, in particular, efficient-market hypothesis testing. The idea of hypothesis testing generally presumes that an object to be tested is really unknown. This is reminiscent of agnosticism. In statistical test, while there is some unknown process f in itself, there are supposed to be alternative statistical models to represent an imprecise but a supposed nearly true process. A best practical way to detect f may be then a comparison of alternative statistical models $\{g_1, g_2\}$ by the famous Akaike Information Criterion (AIC), for example.
>
> 1. This kind of statistical customs, however, is categorized within null-hypothesis orientation.
> 2. The acceptance or rejection does not mean any visualization of the unknown process under test.
>
> The statistical test of efficiency can simply judge whether there exists market whose attribute is more efficient or not. Even if a model with statistically higher efficiency were chosen, the test would never state how such an efficient-market was constructed. The test only states that *an unknown market might be efficient*. Thus, even if any stochasticity should be incorporated into some general equilibrium model, the stochastic parts would make the system neither realistic nor empirically verified, so that a dynamic stochastic general equilibrium model will not be bestowed reality. An unknown market is not resolved at all. In ontology, on the contrary, **how to exist** matters. An entity specific to a particular domain is constructed by ontological blocks, which are either virtual or physical existing in the domain.

8.5 Ontological Method of Production Theory

Ontology in information science, a fortiori, makes us build some ontological construction, whether virtual or physical, using artificial intelligence. Due to a drastic change of the social system, the efficient-market hypothesis has lost its validity. It seems to us unavoidable to restore **ontology** to economics. However, this does not mean to return to the approach of classical political economy again. We should learn a new ontology defined in information science. It is noted that **entity** is already embodied as operator/function in Wolfram's Mathematica. Entity can be of functional form in information science.

As artificial intelligence is employed to run entities, it is easier to argue their classes, instances, attributes, their relationships, and functional terms among complex interactions which are mathematically not identified in advance. Thus, an ontological reasoning on the market domain easily brought an idea to apply agent-based modelling (ABM) to emulate an actual entity such as actual market, macro economy, and so on. Among them, a market simulator such as U-Mart system can emulate an actual exchange market, potentially in some cases become **a miniature of an actual market** itself. That is to say, the artificial market is an ontological experiment in the market domain to reproduce a market. To employ ABM, without restricting excessively a domain under research and/or damaging functional terms structured by existing entities, we will be able to reproduce some complicated interactions.

To part with the efficiency hypothesis in the domain of production, some ontological consideration may be required. A custom sanctified by long practice in production was to presuppose optimizers and their environments fitted to them. As Hildenbrand (1981) noticed, the traditional production function is described as the projection of Y on the input space for some X of the input space is V:

$$\text{Maximize } X \text{ for } (V, X) \text{ in } Y$$

As an optimizing rule/agent is imposed in advance, the domain of technology set is then limited to a convex set of original single activities.

Hildenbrand (1981, 1097) mentioned:

> [T]he economic relevance of the efficient production function is questionable. Other concepts of production functions for an industry are indeed conceivable; one might take into account certain institutional barriers to factor mobility in aggregating the individual production sets.

Leaving the special space restricted by the traditional production function, we can observe various possible combinations to accept institutional effects. Broadening the space, from where technology can be chosen, implies to introduce all possible combinations of activities. By nature, on the other hand, a zonotope of production permits to represent all possible combinations of activities. It then turns out that traditional economics is entirely irrelevant to an ontological thinking about how the production function exists. Given four basic activities, a zonotope of production is described in Fig. 7.2 of the previous chapter.

The same consideration as a zonotope of production applies to gene analysis, as Wright (1932) described a diversity of huge size, which allelomorphs of genes can generate, as Fig. 8.3. Figures 7.2 and 8.3 are of formally similar forms. Furthermore, we can immediately grasp a common idea between both figures.[13]

Interestingly, Alan Turing exhibited a model of the Chemical Basis of Morphogenesis in Turing (1952). Here, he suggested that concentrations and asymmetries are keys to understanding evolution starting from the embryo. Evolving dynamics is modeled as a single activator a single inhibitor model to generate various singularities. There exists an asymmetry between the inhibitor and the activator. The inhibitor's diffusion from one cell to another is much bigger than the activator's one. More interestingly, Turing in 1952 properly predicted that artificial intelligence would reproduce this theory. In 2006, Stefanie Sick et al. by computer simulation on the growth of hair has shown that two types of molecules that play an important role in the growth of hair have all the characteristics of Turing's morphogens.[14]

[13] We notice that both are based on the same ontological reasoning.

[14] Stephen Wolfram, recently in his blog referred to "The Practical Business of Ontology: A Tale from the Front Lines". Here, he mentioned the Philosophy of Chemicals. To employ artificial

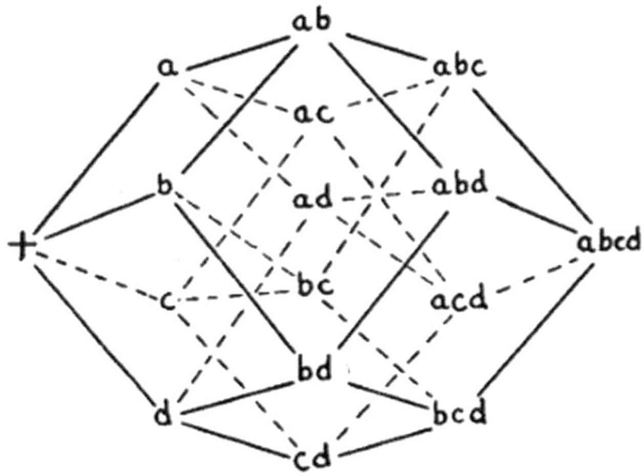

Fig. 8.3 The 16 homozygous combinations: a; b; c; d are allemorphs. *Cited from Wright (1932, 357)

It is noted that the article of Rosser and Rosser (2017) shares with the spirit common to Wright (1932) and Turing (1952). By resorting to Thorstein Veblen, this article examined the basis for increasing returns, multiple equilibria, and bifurcations in the evolution of institutions.

8.6 Production Theory and Zonotope Production Set

8.6.1 Traditional Production Functions

With the birth of economic physics, the problems of so-called "aggregate production functions" have theoretically come to be recognized at a deep level. The theory of production functions starting with Knut Wicksell has completely lost its original meaning in the last century. Originally, the variables of the production function were land and labor, both as the original production element, but in the 20th century, land was replaced with capital artificially produced. Naturally, economists intentionally abandoned this problem. Speaking precisely, capital must be manufactured by the production function as long as it is an artifact.

We discuss the problem of the short-term production function. First, we describe a production function of thee factors of production. It is noted that the third factor of production x_3 is measured by the z on the cube. Namely, the figures here are drawn so that the output level increases in a stepped direction toward the upper right corner

intelligence, in particular, cellular automaton, a practically ontological reasoning will be achieved by resorting to ABM thinking.

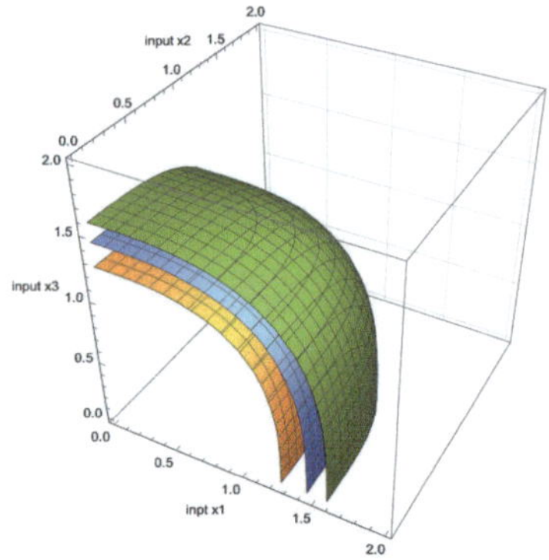

Fig. 8.4 A production function of increasing return

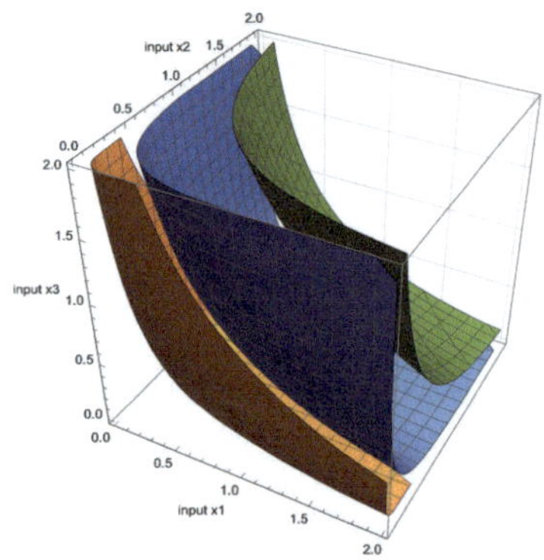

Fig. 8.5 A production function of decreasing return

of the box. In the following diagrams of Figs. 8.4, 8.5, all coordinates of composed by the x_1,x_2, x_3, show the input amounts.

Figure 8.4 shows a production function of increasing return to scale such as the type:

$$y = x_1^3 + x_2^3 + x_3^3. \tag{8.16}$$

On the other hand, Fig. 8.5 shows a production function for diminishing returns to scale such as the type:

$$y = x_1^{0.33} + x_2^{0.33} + x_3^{0.33} \tag{8.17}$$

8.6.2 Recursive Properties of Production Technology

Wassily Leontief is well known for his formulation of input-output table, but it is not well known that he examined the recursive nature of technology in his paper "The Internal Structure of Functional Relationships" (Leontief, 1947). Recursing, i.e., self-reference, is when describing something, a reference to itself appears in the description. x_1 and x_2 need each other for their own production. Hence The function f^1 represents the recursive relationship.

Now we assume that the production function $F(x_1, x_2, x_3)$ is continuous and can be second-order differential. It then hols:

Proposition 8.1

$$\frac{\partial(\frac{\partial F}{\partial x_1}/\frac{\partial F}{\partial x_2})}{\partial x_3} \equiv 0, \tag{8.18}$$

$$i.e., \frac{\partial R_{12}}{\partial x_3} \equiv 0 \tag{8.19}$$

If and only if the condition is fulfilled, it exists the two functions $f^1(x_1, x_2)$ and $f^0(f^2(x_1, x_2), x_3)$ satisfying

$$F(x_1, x_2, x_3) \equiv f^0(f(x_1, x_2), x_3) \tag{8.20}$$

Here, R_{12} is the so-called marginal substitution rate.

It is noted that this proposition can be generalized for over 3 arguments x_i.

Theorem 8.1 *Let S be a partial set of $\overline{X}$. Also be S a complement set of S. S, a partial set of X is then separable if and only if*

$$\frac{\partial R_{s_i s_j}}{\partial \overline{s}} \equiv 0 \, for \, all \, \overline{s} \in \overline{S} \tag{8.21}$$

Primitive Inseparable Relationships

The following function is called a primitive inseparable function:
$f^1(x_1, x_2) = f^1(f^2(x_1, x_2), f^3(x_1, x_2))$

8.6.3 Zonotope Production Set

In this subsection, we would like to consider the recursive relationship between production technologies through the Zonotope production set.

Well, I want to start from the introduction to theory of production function by Hildenbrand who is a giant head of mathematical economics. It was published in the journal Econometrica (Hildenbrand, 1981), but this work was not reconsidered at all until (Dosi et al., 2016b) enlighted on it in his own new reformulation.

Hildenbrand's Short-Run Production Function

> As is well known, the law of profit maximization is assumed in advance to derive traditional production functions. However, Hildenbrand (1981) drew a short-term production function using the Norwegian tanker industry (377 vessels, load capacity of 15,000 tons or more) in 1967 as an numerical example. This figure was produced as Fig. 3 of Hildenbrand (1981). The shape is of zonotope, i.e., a ruggby ball. This remebers Fig. 7.2. In this figure, the types of tankers are 57 turbine-driven, 320 motor-driven, and the date of manufacture is varied from 1950 to 1966. The tanker industry produces tons of transport miles per day. In keeping with economics tradition, the inputs are assumed to be only two elements: fuel and labor. Inputs are valued by the price and wages of a given base year. Hildenbrand then cited the work of Johansen and Eide to reproduce the production function of the Norwegian tanker industry.

After all, traditional production functions are not trying to see the relationship between input and output only in areas limited by operator max. It is different from the actual production functions that Hildenbland tested in the Norwegian tanker industry. On the other hand, the actual production set was a zonotope production set.

Figure 8.6 is a productivity set consisting of a possible combination of basic activities. Combinations are not limited to efficient combinations like traditional production functions. They contain all possible combinations, institutional, practical and policy combinations. Figure 8.7 depicts changes in the input surface when the

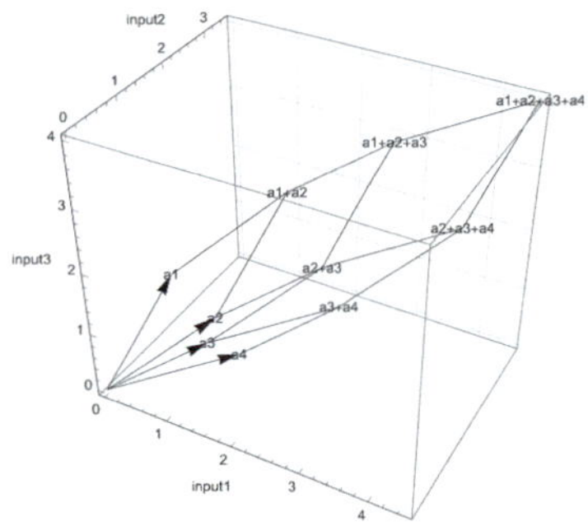

Fig. 8.6 The activity analysis of zonotope-basis

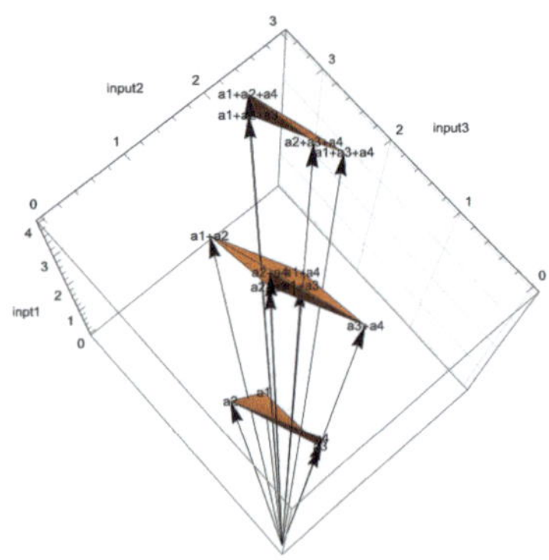

Fig. 8.7 The zonohedron, given the original 4 activities $\{a_1, a_2, a_3, a_4\}$: $\sum_{i=1}^{4}[0, a_i] \subset R^3$

input scale is increased by $1x$, $2x$, and $3x$ at the same time. The scale of the input is increasing toward the upper right side of the box, but the surface of the isoquant of equal input varies according to the input scale. The bottom isoquant faces down toward the bottom, the middle one is relatively closer to the plane, and the upper level is depicted convex toward the top. As seen from Figs. 8.4 and 8.5, the upper isoquants exhibit increasing returns, while the lower isoquants exhibit decreasing returns. Thus, a zonotope production set, in general, will not establish some unique returns to scale.

8.6.4 Production Set in the Minkowski Space

We describe the ex post technology of a production unit as follows:

$$(a_1, ..., a_l, a_{l+1}) \in \Re$$

We then observe the production set Y. Given a family $\{a_n\}_{n \in N}$, the short-run total production set is written in the following manner:

$$Y = \sum_{n \in N} [0, a_n]$$

In economics, there were few to discuss production in context of **zonotope**. **Zonotope** is one of the **Minkowski space** family. A convex polygon is a zonotope if and only if all its 2-dimensional faces have a center of symmetry. By the use of this idea, we can observe all possible combinations for production without resort to any restriction of efficiency.

Hildenbrand in (1981) defines the short-run total production set associated to them as the **zonotope**. The short run production possibilities of an industry with N units at a given time is a finite family of vectors $\{a_i\}_{1 \leq i \leq N}$ of production activities.

$$Y = \{y \in \Re_+^{l+1} | y = \sum_{i=1}^{N} \phi_i a_i, 0 < \phi_i < 1\}$$

According to Hildenbrand, this idea differs from the traditional production function. We define the projection of Y on the input space $\Re_+^l$:

$$D = \{V \in \Re_+^l | (V, X) \in Y \texttt{ for some } X \in \Re_+\}$$

It then hods **the traditional production function**:

$$F(V) = \max\{X \in \Re_+ | (V, X) \in Y\}$$

The operator max in the above has excluded the possibilities of "certain institutional barriers to factor mobility in aggregating the individual production sets" (Hildenbrand, 1981, 1097).

In general, the *ex post* technology of a production unit is a vector is a production activity a that produces, during the current period, a_{l+1} units of output by means of $(a_1, ..., a_l)$ units of input. **The size of the firm** is the length of vector a, i.e., a multi-dimensional extension of the usual measure of firm size.

Given $Y = (a_1, ..., a_l)$, a set of generators for n, the zonotope Y is the convex hull of all vectors of the form a; that is (Y) is the Minkowski sum of all segments $[0, a_i]$, where $a \in Y$, i.e., $\sum_{a_i \in Y} a_i$. Also $Z(Y)$ is the shadow of the r-dimensional cube $[0, 1]^r$ via the projection.[15] It is noted that the application of znotpoe to production set was recently achieved by Dosi et al. in (2016a). They employed **the volume of zonotope** Y in $\Re$:

$$Vol(Y) =: \sum_{1 \leq i_1 \leq i_2 \cdots \leq i_l \leq N} |\Delta i_1, ..., i_l|$$

Here $|\Delta i_1, ..., i_l|$ is the module of the determinant. This kind of discussion will suggest a new growth/innovation theory of production. This approach may be classified into **the complex adaptive system**. This matter may be referred by the author elsewhere.

Exercises

8.1 Discuss the ontological background when it can be concluded that Leibzian idea of **everything is at best** will be justified

8.2 According to the main stream random choice theory, formulate descriptively the private utility, the social utility, and its interaction. Then examine whether this kind of simplification could be joustified in case that the set/subset of preference are not universal.

8.3 Explain the differences between this theory and Ruth's random choice theory. In particular, discuss what difficulties exist with many multi-logit utility models.

8.4 Try to sort out the difference between the mainstream random choice theory and the original Luce-Saari theory of random choice.

8.5 Give a numerical example of discrete basic production activities of 3 sectors in Minkowski space, and make out the diagram. Then calculate the volume of this zonotope set.

---

[15] Under the projection $(t_1, ..., t_r) \mapsto \sum_{i=1}^{r} t_i a_i)$, the shadow of the r-dimensional cube $[0, 1]^r$ is $Z(Y)$.

8.6 In the text above, Class 4 property of cellular automaton was interpreted by exemplifying the AI market transactions. Detect another economic instance of Class 4 property.

8.7 Explain descriptively why the efficient market hypothesis is indispensable for the SMD theorems in the barter transactions but the efficient market hypothesis will be invalidated if it were incorporated into the finanical market.

8.8 Brian Arthur employed the term "the relaxed static stability" to characterize one of new features of the new innovation. Find another instance other than the F-35 to discuss the new direction of the current innovation.

8.9 Create a numerical example of a production function with the primitive inseparable relationships and verify Theorem 8.1.

8.10 We have a traditionally analytical tool such as indifference curve either of the production function or the utility function. Ensure that the idea of Zenohedron is also available for utility functions, and then try to make out such a figure in the 3-dimensional space.

References

Arthur, W. B. (2009). *The nature of technology*. Free Press.

Aruka, Y. (2015a). *Evolutionary foundations of economic science: How can scientists study evolving economic doctrines from the last centuries? (Springer series: Evolutionary economics and social complexity science)* (Vol. 1). Springer.

Aruka, Y. (2015b). The rise of pure economics under a new form of scholasticism in view of the present socio-economic system. *Evolutionary and Institutional Economic Review, 13*(1), 3–29.

Aruka, Y. (2017a). Special feature: Preliminaries towards ontological reconstruction of economics: Theories and simulations. *Evolutionary and Institutional Economic Review, 14*(2), 409–414.

Aruka, Y. (2017b). Some new perspectives on the inter-country analysis of the world production system. *Evolutionary and Institutional Economic Review, 14*(2), 467–498.

Aruka, Y. (2018). Interpreting the iterated dilemma games using the presentation like cellular automatons. *Evolutionary and Institutional Economic Review, 15*(2), 351–365.

Debreu, G. (1974). Excess demand functions. *Journal of Mathematical Economics, 1*(1), 15–21.

Dosi, G., Grazzi, M., Marrengo, L., & Settepanella, S. (2016a). Production theory: Accounting for firm heterogeneity and technical change. *The Journal of Industrial Economics, 64*(4), 875–907.

Dosi, G., Grazzi, M., Marrengo, L., & Settepanella, S. (2016b). Production theory: Accounting for firm heterogeneity and technical change. *The Journal of Industrial Economics, 64*(4), 875–907.

Durlauf, S. N. (1997). Statistical mechanics approaches to socioeconomic behavior. In W. B. Arthur, S. N. Durlauf, & D. A. Lane (Eds.), *The economy as an evolving complex system II* (pp. 81–104). Addison-Wesley.

Duraluf, S. N. (2000). A framework for the study of individual behavior and social interaction.

Gardner, M. (1970). Mathematical games: The fantastic combinations of John Conway's new solitaire game "life". *Scientific American,223*(4), 120–123.

Hildenbrand, W. (1981). Short-run production functions based on microdata. *Econometrica, 49*(5), 1095–1125.

Hildenbrand, W. (1994). *Market demand*. Princeton University Press.

Hodgson, G. M., & Lamberg, J. A. (2016). The past and future of evolutionary economics: Some reflections based on new bibliometric evidence. *Evolutionary and Institutional Economics Review, 15*, 167–187.

Kaldor, N. (1955). Alternative theories of distribution Nicholas. *Review of Economic Studies, 23*(2), 83–100.

Leontief, W. (1947). A note on the intersection of subsets of independent variables of a continuous function with continuous first derivatives. *Bulletin of the American Mathematical Society, 53*, 343–350.

Li, L., & Saari, D. G. (2008). Sen's theorem: Geometric proof, new interpretations. *Social Choice and Welfare, 31*(3), 393–413.

Luce, R. D. (1959). *Individual choice behavior: A theoretical analysis*. Wiley.

Mainzer, K. (2007). (Kapitel 7: Zufall in Kultur, Wirtschaft, und Gesselschaft. In *Der kreative Zufall: Wie das Neue in die Welt kommt?* CH Beck.

Mantel, R. (1974). On the characterization of aggregate excess demand. *Journal of Economic theory, 7*(3), 348–353.

Mirowski, P. (2007). Markets come to bits: Evolution computation and markomata in economic science. *Journal of Economic Behavior and Organization, 63*(2), 209–242.

Nelson, R. R., & Winter, S. G. (1982). *An evolutionary theory of economic change*. Belknap Press of Harvard University Press.

Rosser, B. J., & Rosser, M. V. (2017). The evolution of behavioural institutional complexity. In Y. Aruka & A. Kirman (Eds.), *Economic foundations for social complexity science-theory, sentiments, and empirical laws* (pp. 67–88). Springer.

Saari, D. G. (1992). The aggregate excess demand function and other aggregation procedures. *Economic Theory, 2*, 359–388.

Saari, D. G. (2004). Geometry of chaotic and stable discussions. *American Mathematical Monthly, 111*(5), 222–230.

Saari, D. G. (2005). The profile structure for luce's choice axiom. *Journal of Mathematical Psychology, 49*, 226–253.

Saari, D. G. (2015). Social science puzzles: A systems analysis challenge. *American Mathematical Monthly, 12*(1), 123–139.

Saari, D. G., & Petron, A. (2006). Negative externalities and Sen's liberalism theorem. *Economic Theory, 111*(5), 222–230.

Shiozawa, Y., Nakajima, Y., Matsui, H., Koyama, Y., Taniguchi, K., & Hashimoto, F. (2008). *Artificial market experiments with the U-mart system*. Springer series on agent based social systems (Vol. 4). Springer.

Shiozawa, Y. (2007). A new construction of Ricardian trade theory a many-country, many commodity case with intermediate goods and choice of production techniques. *Evolutionary and Institutional Economics Review, 3*(2), 141–187.

Shiozawa, Y. (2015). International trade theory and exotic algebras. *Evolutionary and Institutional Economics Review, 12*(1), 177–212.

Slutsky, E. (1915). Sulla teoria del bilancio del consumatore. *Giornale Degli Economisti e Rivista Di Statistica, 51*(1), 1–26.

Sonnenschein, H. (1972). Market excess demand functions. *Econometrica, 40*(3), 649–663.

Sonnenschein, H. (1973). Do Walras' identity and continuity characterize the class of community excess-demand functions? *Econometrica, 6*(4), 345–354.

Turing, A. (1952). The chemical basis of morphogenesis. *Philosophical Transactions of the Royal Society of London B, Biological Sciences, 237*, 37–72.

Wolfram, S. (2002). *A new kind of science*. Wolfram Media.

Wright, S. (1932). The roles of mutation, inbreeding, crossbreeding, and selection in evolution. *Proceeding of International Congress of Genetics, Ithaca, USA (VI), 1*, 356–366.

Choice Axioms and a Geometrical Analysis of Rankings

9

Abstract

The discrete utility theory is treated in this chapter. In view of mainstream, the alternative one to the traditional choice theory must be the probabilistic choice theory of utility given by Luce (1959). Later, this method became well known by McFadden's Nobel Prize in 2007 (McFadden, 1974) in the academic world but before the event rather famous in the practical field. Shortly after the release of Luce (1959), unfortunately, Debreu (1960), one of the most respectful general equilibrium theorist, declared that "Luce's choice axiom" is inconsistent. Subsequently, therefore, the theoretical study of Luce's choice axioms had only sporadic development in the academic world, and this type of Luce utility theory was rather limited to practical analysis. When Luce's utility is algebraically considered, this is currently dealt with as the multinomial logit model, which can illustrate either successive choices or mode choices. Alternatively, it may be possible to derive the multinomial logit model type utility from the neoclassical assumptions. A restrictive assumption like Independence from Irrelevant Alternatives (IIA) is often not only required to be imposed but also to depend on the assumption that the set/subset of preference are universal. However, Saari pointed out that Debreu's criticism was off the point, as Saari found (2005), that Debreu's example on Luce's theory was discussing a problem in which the number of constraint expressions was too excessive than the number of unknowns to deal with, and then that nothing could be determined. On the contrary, Saari escaped the narrow deterministic arguments to expand significantly the theoretical coverage of choice theory. In his framework, even Arrow's Possibility Theorem (Namba, 1951) is simply a special case.

Y. Aruka, *Evolutionary Economics*, Springer Texts in Business and Economics,
https://doi.org/10.1007/978-981-97-1382-0_9

9.1 Review of Luce's Choice Axiom and the Ranking Decision Problem

Hildenbrandt has not just opened up the possibility of a new production set definition by introducing zonotope as seen above. Market demand (Hilednbrand, 1994) also defined a new set of consumption consisting of heterogenous interacting agents. Here the condition that the income effect becomes positive was confirmed. Therefore, until the end of the last century, Hildenbrandt showed the possibility of new theories in both production and consumption. It is noted that Aruka (2015, Chap. 2) details the theory of consumption demand in Hildenbrand. In this section, we refer to the essential points of choice theory in the context of Donald G. Saari, at University of California, Irvine, who is a well-known mathematician on multi-body issues, has also opened up the importance of tropical geometry in the field of choice theory.

Saari noted that "Luce's choice axiom" did not mention the determining rules, and analyzed the relationship between choice axioms, voting profiles, and probability profiles in geometric analysis, suggesting the applicability of tropical geometry.

Shortly after the release of Luce (1959), Debreu (1960), general equilibrium theorist, declared that "Luce's choice axiom" is inconsistent. Subsequently, the theoretical study of Luce's choice axioms had only sporadic development, and Luce utility theory was rather limited to practical analysis. However, Saari pointed out that Debreu's criticism was off the point, and that Debreu's example on Luce's theory was discussing a problem in which the number of constraint expressions was too excessive than the number of unknowns to deal with, and then that nothing could be determined.

Luce's utility theory originally faces the underdetermination problem in that the number of constraint is short of the number of unknowns. We have two kinds of problem of voting profiles (Fig. 9.1b) and probability profiles (Fig. 9.1c). By introducing these, Saari has solved the underdetermination problem.

> It is needless to propose a set of universal choice alternatives as the general equilibrium theory suggests in her choice axiom. Originally, Luce's set of choices was not a universal set, but rather a set of choices where their set variates. Interestingly, the choice probability can be defined on this set.

Luce's utility theory defines both probabilities of the case of perfect discrimination, which implies to be fully identified, and the case of imperfect discrimination. An introduction of universal choice set will invalidate a lot of useful information around Luce choice axiom. Thus Saari was successful to develop Luce's choice axiom into a theory of ranking decision. Saari's innovative contribution is to examine the rationality of the choice based on new information that can be analyzed from the composition of the rankings born from the choice axiom. Modern society has become such a society to accepts"ranking of anything" without criticism. It is an essential social task to consider ranking decision-making problems in depth.

9.2 Profiles of Choice Axiom

Discrete choice theory originating from Luce (1959) can deal with sequential choices. For example, when traveling, you can handle **mode choices** such as using an airplane, using a railway, or using a bus. These probabilities can be estimated by the maximum likelihood method from the actual data. Since probability calculation can be easily performed from the polynomial logit model, it was put into practical use early in tourism demand analysis as a kind of applied analysis by probability preference modeling.

Durlauf (1997, 2000) also showed that multinomial logit utility could be derived from the mainstream assumptions without using Luce's choice axiom. Here we assume that a random binary choice. We then consider the gap between the binary choices due to external random shocks as the utility difference of the chosen objects. Suppose that the difference can be fitted within the logistic distribution. The binary logit utility, which Luce obtained, will be then obtained.

Following Luce (1959), we denote "the probability that A is judged to be the superior element in T according to some specified criterion by $P_T(A)$. Luce' choice is called "discrete choice".

> Luce's axiom has the effect of endowing each alternative with an intrinsic level of likelihood that is independent of the particular set. Thus, while P_T denotes a probability defined over set T, this notation does not imply that T is the universal set. Saari (2005, 228)

Axiom Luce's choice axiom

1. The conditional probability P_S is defined on S, if $S \subset T, 0 \leq P_T \leq 1$. It is denoted the probability of the event A by $P(A)$. It is also denoted that

$$P(A, B) = P_{\{A,B\}}(A);\ P(B, A) = P_{\{A,B\}}P(B).$$

2. **The case of imperfect discrimination on alternatives:** This case is represented by

$$P_T(R) = P_S(R)P_T(S) \text{ for all } A_i, A_j \in T \text{ if } P(A_i, A_j) \neq \{0, 1\} \tag{9.1}$$

for $R \subset S \subset T$. Thus the conditional probability is written

$$P_T(R|S) = \frac{P_T(R \cap S)}{P_T(S)} \tag{9.2}$$

It then holds that

$$P_S(R) = P_T(R|S) \text{ for } R \subset S \subset T. \tag{9.3}$$

3. **The case of perfect discrimination on alternatives:** This case is represented by

$$P_T(S) = P_{T-\{A_i\}}(R)P_T(S - \{A_i\}) \text{ for all } A_i, A_j \in T \text{ if } P(A_i, A_j) = 0 \quad (9.4)$$

for every $R \subset S \subset T$. It then holds

$$P_C(s) = \frac{\nu}{\sum_{s \in U} \nu(s)}. \quad (9.5)$$

Hence it exists the function $\nu : C \to R$. This function is called utility function in the discrete choice theory.

Let the alternatives be the two a, b. We substitute $\exp^{\mu V_a}$ into $\nu(a)$, $\exp^{\mu V_b}$ into $\nu(b)$, respectively. It then holds the binary logit probability as follows:

$$P_{\{}a, b\} = \frac{\exp^{\mu V_a}}{\exp^{\mu V_a} + \exp^{\mu V_b}}. \quad (9.6)$$

This probability is called logit probability because it is of logit form $\frac{1}{1+\exp^{-z}}$.

First, we employ 3 alternatives $\{A, B, C\}$ to analyze the probability in the case of imperfect discrimination identification. Suppose X, Y, Z to be surrogate variables of A, B, C. It then holds the following relationships:

$$P(X) = \frac{P(X, Y)P(X, Z)}{P(X, Y) + P(X, Z) - P(X, Y)P(X, Z)} \quad (9.7)$$

$$P(B, C) = \frac{P(A, C)P(B, A)}{P(A, B)P(C, A) + P(B, A)P(A, C)} \quad (9.8)$$

As seen in the above, it is noted that $P(x, y) = P_{\{x,y\}}(x)$ for any x, y.

$$P(A) = \frac{P(A, B)P(A, C)}{P(A, B) + P(A, C) - P(A, B)P(A, C)}; \quad (9.9)$$

$$P(B) = \frac{P(B, A)P(B, C)}{P(B, A) + P(B, C) - P(B, A)P(B, C)}; \quad (9.10)$$

$$P(C) = \frac{P(C, A)P(C, B)}{P(C, A) + P(C, B) - P(C, A)P(C, B)}; \quad (9.11)$$

$$P_T(A) = a, P_T(B) = b, P_T(C) = c, P(A, B) = \frac{a}{a+b}, P(B, A) = \frac{b}{a+b}, P(A, C) = \frac{c}{a+c} \quad (9.12)$$

It then holds:

$$P(A) = \frac{a}{a+b+c}, P(B) = \frac{b}{a+b+c}, P(C) = \frac{c}{a+b+c}$$

It also holds:

$$P(B, C) = \frac{b}{b+c}.$$

In the 3 alternaitve choice, we need the two kinds of approach to determine the choice procedure:

1. **Best-first approach** (or Descending approach)
First, choose the top ranked alternative A with the likelihood $P_T(A)$, and then choose B among the remaining alternatives $\{B, C\}$ with the probabilities $P(B, C)$. It is written the choice procedure in the following manner:
$$R(A \succsim B \succsim C) = P_T(A)(B, C) \tag{9.13}$$

2. **Worst-first approach** (or Ascending approach)
First, choose the bottom ranked alternative C with the likelihood $P_T^*(C)$, and then choose B among the remaining inferior alternatives $\{A, B\}$ with the probabilities $P^*(B, A)$. It is written the choice procedure in the following manner:
$$R^*(A \succsim^* B \succsim^* C) = P_T^*(A)P^*(B, C) \tag{9.14}$$

We need some restrictive condition to make the two approaches coincident in the following manner:

Theorem 9.1 (Luce's theorem (Luce, 1959, 69)) *Suppose the probability space P and P^* to be defined on $T = \{A, B, C\}$. Also suppose that P and P^* satisfy the choice axiom in the case of imperfect discrimination. It then holds that the necessary and sufficient condition to be*

$$R(A \succsim B \succsim C) = R^*(A \succsim^* B \succsim^* C) \tag{9.15}$$

is

$$P(A, B) = P(B, C). \tag{9.16}$$

9.2.1 Counting the Number of Equations and the Unkowns

As stated above, the choice axiom does not refer to anything about the choice procedure. On the other hand, if we try to keep the choice axiom regardless of the choice procedure, we are forced to impose an unrealistic necessary and sufficient condition

$P(A, B) = P(B, C)$. According to Saari's works, however, we would like to examine the above system from the "problem of counting the number of equations and the unknowns".

Let $x = P_T(A)$, $y = P_T(B)$. It then holds

$$1 - x - y = P_T(C).$$

Let $u = P_T^*(A)$, $v = P_T^*(B)$. It also holds

$$1 - u - v = P_T^*(C).$$

The choice axiom demands the next three constraints:

$$P(A, B) = P^*(B, A), \tag{9.17}$$

$$P(A, C) = P^*(C, A), \tag{9.18}$$

$$P(B, C) = P^*(C, B) \tag{9.19}$$

It then holds from these three conditions as for the arguments $\{x, y, u, v\}$:

$$\frac{x}{x + y} = \frac{u}{u + v}, \tag{9.20}$$

$$\frac{x}{x + (1 - x - y)} = \frac{1 - u - v}{u + (1 - u - v)}, \tag{9.21}$$

$$\frac{y}{x + (1 - x - y)} = \frac{1 - u - v}{(1 - u - v) + v} \tag{9.22}$$

By the way, neither the three constraints nor the relationships between the four variables x, y, u, v are independent. Therefore, two constraints correspond to four unknowns, and it can be seen that the system has two degrees of freedom. Hence it has been seen that the unrealistic requirement of the choice theorem is only a way to reduce the excessive degrees of freedom of the system. In order to consider alternatives, in the case of imperfect discrimination, Saari introduced a voting profile and a probability profile to make the relationship between these and the choice axiom been analyzed geometrically.

9.3 A Geometrical Analysis of Ranking

We employ a numerical example shown in Table 9.1, which Saari (2005, 232) used, to show how the ranking will be generated. According to Saari, there is assumed to be 6 different types $\{1, 2, 3, 4, 5, 6\}$ and the alternatives A, B, C embedded in our probability space.

We also employ a unit simplex $\triangle ABC$ as an analytical device to represent ranking situations. Here the vertices of the triangle $\{A, B, C\}$ indicate the ideal points of choice. The triangle $\{A, B, C\}$ is divided into 6 subtriangles $\{1, 2, 3, 4, 5, 6\}$.

Table 9.1 Rankings of the three alternatives

Types	Ranking	No. votes	Probability
1	$A \succsim B \succsim C$	7	0.2
2	$A \succsim C \succsim B$	2	0
3	$C \succsim A \succsim B$	4	0.3
4	$C \succsim B \succsim A$	6	0
5	$B \succsim C \succsim A$	0	0.2
8	$B \succsim A \succsim C$	7	0.3

Vertex A is supported by voters within the domain of the subtriangle $\triangle 1, 2$. Vertex C is supported by voters within the area of the subtriangle $\triangle\{3, 4\}$. Vertex B is supported by voters within the area of the subtriangle $\triangle\{5, 6\}$.

Figure 9.1a, in the initial situation, consists of the subtriangles $\{\triangle 1, \ldots, \triangle 6\}$, each of which is labelled $\{1, \ldots, 6\}$ respectively. The diagram shows the interior points of the subtriangles are all closest to A, then to B. Therefore, $A \succsim B$. In addition, it is farthest from C. Hence the ranking $A \succsim B \succsim C$ holds. The subtriangles $\triangle_1$ and $\triangle_2$ suggest the region where the best ranking holds. This region is dark gray colored. The subtriangles $\triangle_3$ and $\triangle_6$ suggest the region where the second-best ranking holds. This region is lightly gray colored.

The perpendicular from the vertex C to the edge AB shows that A and B are indifferent in the binary choice. Since the center of gravity of the triangle $\triangle ABC$ is the same distance to any of the vertices, it holds that $A \sim B \sim C$.

9.3.1 Voting Profile Space

First, we define the voting profile space in the following manner: j indicates a binary preference and n_j indicates the number of votes for preference j. VP(voting profile) is defined such as

$$\mathcal{VP} = \{n = (n_1, \ldots, n_6) \in R^6 | n_j \text{ is a nonnegative number}\}. \tag{9.23}$$

9.3.1.1 Making a Voting Profile from the Numerical Example

The subtriangles $\triangle_1, \triangle_2, \triangle_3$ on the left edge of the midpoint of the edge AB are binary choices $\{A, B\}$ and support A. Therefore, $7 + 2 + 3 = 13$ votes are confirmed.

In the voting decision rule, the positional election rule that gives a weighted value of the voter's choice is important. First, in extreme cases, the highest ranked option is weighted by 1 and the other alternatives are weighted by 0. This is called the relative majority plurality rule. The exact opposite rule gives 0 for the lowest ranked choice and 1 for all other choices. In the case of $n = 3$, it then holds

$$w^3 = (w_1, w_2, w_3) = (1, s, 0) | w_j \geq w_{j+1} \text{ for} j = 1, 2 \tag{9.24}$$

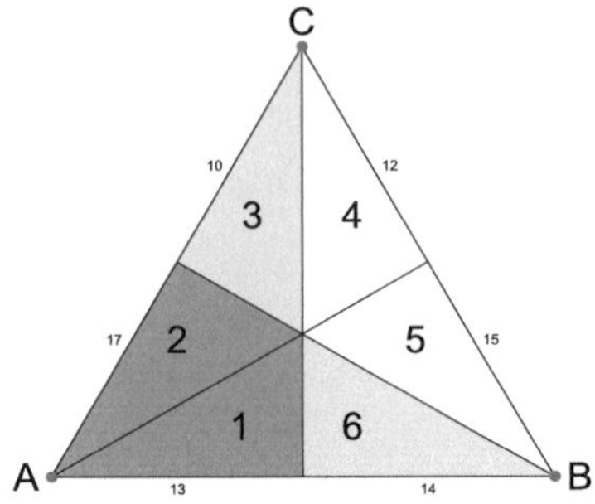

(a) Geometrical presentation: the types of ranking and the initial situation

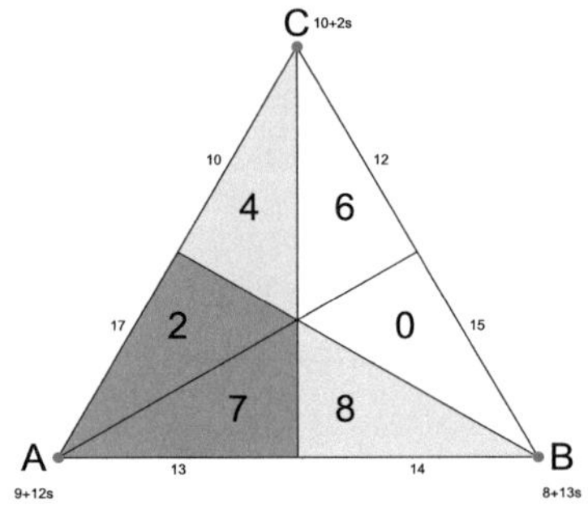

(b) Geometrical presentation: the voting profile

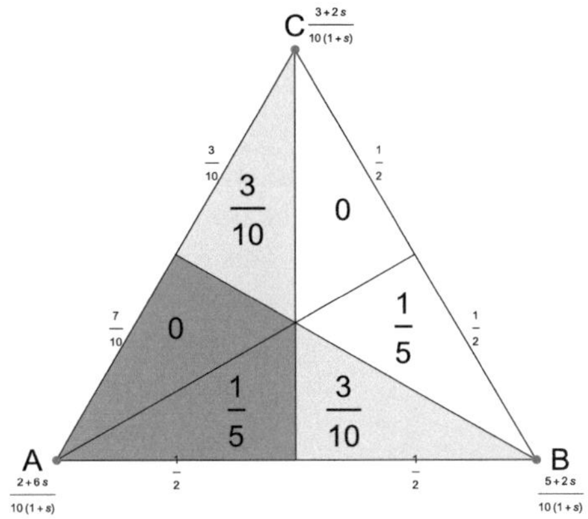

(c) Geometrical presentation: the probability profile

Fig. 9.1 Geometrical presentations

"Positional elections"(or "positional election rules") is the name attached to election rules where ballots are tallied by assigning points to candidates according to how they are positioned (i.e., ranked) on the ballot. The widely used "plurality vote", where each voter votes for one candidate and the candidate with the largest number of votes wins, assigns one point for a top-ranked candidate and zero for all others.

The antiplurality votes where one point is given to all but the last-ranked candidate who is assigned zero points (Saari, 2004, 232).

The total score by weighted w^3 can be expressed by the following formula. Number of voters who evaluate A as the top ranked + $s\times$ number of voters who evaluate A as the second ranked. In other words, this will be displayed as:

> The number of votes for the subtriangles Δ_1 and Δ_2
> $+ s\times$ the number of votes for the small trianglesΔ_3 and Δ_6.

The weight s can be arbitrarily given within the range of the condition $w_j \geq w_{j+1}$ for $j = 1, 2$.

If the weight $s = 0$, the election then follows **the relative majority rule** (plurality rule).

If the weigh $s = 0.5$, the election then follows **the Borda rule**.

Even if there are only three options, the number of method of giving the weights s will be infinite within the range of [0, 1].

Let a condition such as $w_j \geq w_{j+1}$for$j = 1, 2, \ldots, n$ be added. Define to select the value of w_j among

$$w^n = (w_1, \ldots, w_n) = (1, \ldots, 0)|w_j \geq w_{j+1}\text{for}j = 1, 2, \ldots, n.$$

It is easily seen that the ways to assign the weights will be enormous number.

9.3.2 Probability Profile Space

In the same example, "probability profile space" can be formally described as follows. j indicates a binary preference, and p_j indicates the probability that preference j will occur. The probability calculation of the vertices is calculated as follows with reference to the probability profile based on Fig. 9.1c.

Referring to this figure, first of all, calculate the total sum of the weights w_j:

$$\sum_{j=1}^{n} w_j = 1 + s + 0 = 1 + s. \tag{9.25}$$

Then normalizethis sum such as

$$\sum_{j=1}^{n} = \frac{1}{1+s} + \frac{s}{1+s} + 0 = 1. \tag{9.26}$$

Therefore, the vertex A of the probability profile is calculated as follows:

$$\frac{1}{1+s}(7+2) + \frac{s}{1+s}(8+4) = \frac{2+6s}{(1+s)10}. \tag{9.27}$$

Thus the probabilities of the vertices B and C can be achieved similarly as to how we calculated above, if we refer to Fig. 9.1c. Hence the probability profile of this example will be completed.

9.3.3 Majority Rule Decision on Classical Utility Theory

> The most important point is that there is certainly nothing inherent in utility theory which would assure the existence of an equilibrium. (Plott, 1967, 791–792)

Multinomial logit utility is epoch-making in that it enables sequential choice theory from a viewpoint that traditional utility theory did not deal with. Below,we would like to investigate the effect of utility theory on majority voting. First, we discuss the relationship between classical utility theory and "majority rule." Charles Plott, who later became prominent as an experimental economist at CALTECH, showed in American Economic Review in Plott (1967) that "majority rule equilibrium" can only be obtained by chance, and that utility theory contributes nothing to equilibrium. In fact, this problem was formulated by Sonnenschein (1972) as a question to Adam Smith's invisible hand, and was finally solved by Saari (1992, 1995). For the overall outlook, see Saari (2015).

Suppose m individuals prefer each of n variables $(x_1, \ldots, x_n)$ according to m classical utility functions U^i $(i = 1, ..., m)$. We then consider a specific small change in the variables $(dx_1^*, \ldots, dx_n^*)$ from some existing situation. This change is called "motion". Let some existing situation be $\bar{X}$ in Euclidian n-space. Individual i would then vote for the motion over the existing situation $\bar{X}$, if

$$\nabla U^i b_k = \frac{\partial U^i}{\partial x_1} dx_1^* + \cdots + \frac{\partial U^i}{\partial x_n} dx_n^* > 0. \tag{9.28}$$

The individual i then decides his/her preference on this action b_k according to the following inequality sign. Support if

$$\nabla U^i b_k > 0.$$

Be indifferent if

$$\nabla U^i b_k = 0.$$

Be against if

$$\nabla U^i b_k < 0.$$

In other words, if the angle formed by the individual utility gradient ∇U^i with respect to the grandient b_k is acute, the individual i support *for* minute motion; if the angle is perpendicular, he/she is *indifferent* to it; if the angle is obtuse, he she is *against* it. Thus the relationship is geometrically illustrated by using gradients as Fig. 9.4. Here IC is the indifference curve of individual i (Fig. 9.2).

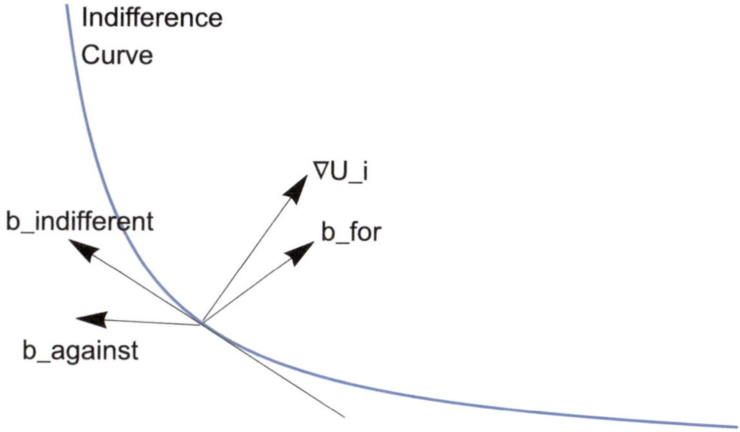

Fig. 9.2 Gradient analysis of binary choices

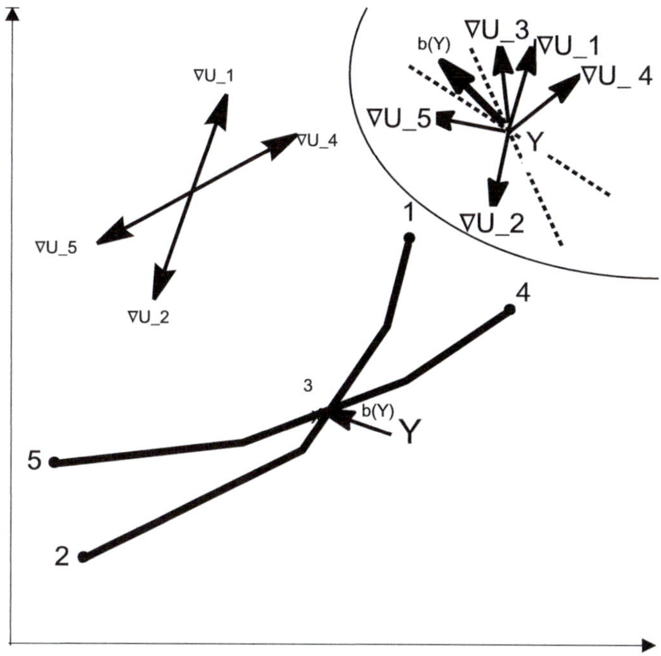

Fig. 9.3 A gradient method by Plott (1967)

Saari (2004, 380, Fig. 2) used Fig. 9.3 to show the coalition formation by voters. The triangle vertices $\{a, b, c\}$ in Fig. 9.3 indicate the ideal point of the voter. The circle is drawn around the ideal point of each voter. Each circle passes through the diamond $\diamond$ centered on the figure. The inner point of each circle is close to the ideal

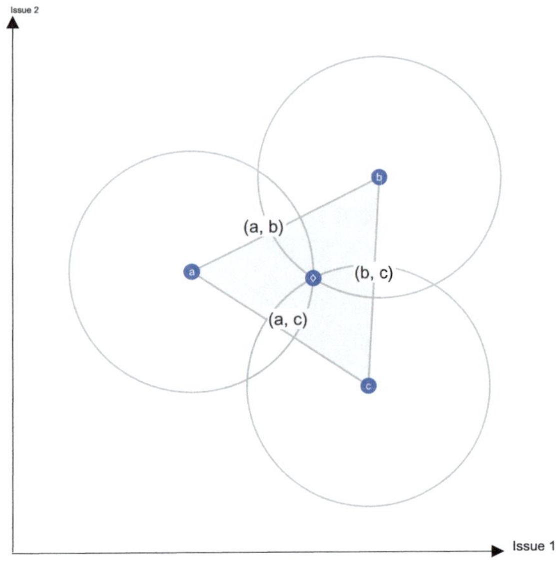

Fig. 9.4 A coalition formation by Saari (2004)

point of each voter. On the contrary, the outside of the circle is not preferred for each voter. Therefore, voters prefer interior point of their own circles to $\diamond$. Now, there are three voters $\{a, b, c\}$. The "majority" or "alliance" is $\{a, b\}$, $\{b, c\}$, $\{a, c\}$. Each of these corresponds to one of the "three leaves." Inside the triplane, majority voters in either case prefer the area inside the leaf to $\diamond$., and can propose a better improvement than the present situation. This means that any majority can always better than $\diamond$ by forming any coalition. To tell the truth, this conclusion is only a rephrasing of the above Pot's conclusion that the majority equilibrium cannot be decided. Plott illustrated the two alternative choice problem. Saari further develops geometry that can handle three choice problems (Fig. 9.4).

9.3.4 A Final Comment on the Rule Based Decisions

In the above discussion, decisions are not only necessarily uniquely established but also the individualistic basis for choices may be locally volatile or floating to promote an evolution of choices. However, there are often observed the rules and aims in the field for discussion to be excessively fixed. Here we briefly look that justification for a selected solution cannot be separated from a preference of the rules/aims specification. In the event, a strict confinement to a particular principle will exclude a possible evolution.

The idea is motivated by Koji Namba. He is pathologist and philosopher whose authored the book: *Death and life studies as preparedness* (Namba, 2004, 97–99). Take, for example, the "horse thief's claim" that actually occurred at the end of the Heian period (794–1192 A.D.) of Japan.

The lord, a samurai, ordered his servant to procure horses. You will be killed if you deceive your main order, but you will not be killed if you steal a horse (the death penalty was abolished in the Heian period). Now we would like to infer that the thief will be blocked if there is a death penalty. However, there may be an alternative enforcement to make the lord and the perpetrator "a joint criminal" to suppress thef.

Taking intou account reconsidering this kind of argument, it is seen that the "field" for argument depends on a particular system. In many cases, if some evolving improvemnt is to be allowed, "special fields" for choices should not be absolute.

For more enlightening, we cite the example as for "How to divide the heritage of 17 horses with 3 children". Now the three children are faced to the heritage of 17 horses after their father died. The testament of this heritage imposes the following two requirements.

1. **Minimum Guarantee Amount**
   1/2 or more for the eldest son, 1/3 or more for the second son, 1/9 or more for the third son
2. **Residual equal distribution**
   Since the remainder of this distribution is $17 - (8 + 5 + 1) = 3$, the remaining 3 horses are redistributed to the eldest son, the second son, and the third son. At this time, the order invariance is still maintained with 9 the eldest son $>$ 6 second sons $>$ 2 third son.

The **minimum guarantee amount** in association with the **residual equal distribution** will bring us the confirmed solution. That is, the inheritance has been achieved by aid of the village elder to establish the following allocation. That is to say, the village elder brought one horse to add to the existing 17 horses, by command, the elder allocated 9 horses to the eldest son, 6 horses to the second son and 2 horses to the third son. Finally, the elder then brought back one extra horse to go home. It is noted that the applied allocation principle will be somewhat restrictive since horse cannot be divisible. So the personal right will be not necessarily perfectly satisfied. Incidentally, it is easy to see that this example is the same problem as the "Talmud's solution" that Aumann and Maschler (1985).

In this context, we examine the reason why we need elders. **The ultimatum game principle** is used in association with **the equal distribution of residuals**. In other words, the principle is that even if the elder offers merely one horse for the third son, it is irrational to refuse it *since one horse increases*. If this principle is followed, the side that does not receive even one will always refuse the offer. However, according to the imposed rule, if it is refused, the distribution of the offerers will also be all confiscated. Therefore, we need someone to confiscate. This must be an elder. If the eldest son demands all three, the elder says that the eldest son's share will be confiscated unless even one is distributed to the second and third sons. As a result, in the case of horses, one cannot be divided, so two of the three must be given to the second and third sons. In short, the above allegations always set up a "special field" with an "elder" as an absolute power.

Exercises

9.1 Triangles are used to illustrate three-dimensional probability spaces, and rectangular triangles can be used to check three-dimensional coordinates in an elementary way. Using a right-angled triangle, try to draw a three-dimensional probability space with each of the three vertices as the origin of an event.

9.2 In Luce's theory of discrete choice, give specific examples for each of the cases of both perfect and imperfect discrimination.

9.3 Give a descriptive account of the differences between the Descending (Best-first approach) and Ascending (Worst-first approach) approaches in the case of incomplete discrimination in Luce discrete choice theory.

9.4 Produce different examples of both approcahes of the best-first and the worst-first.

9.5 In Luce's utility theory, there are two kinds of problem of voting profiles and probability profiles. Discuss how the probability profile is affected by the voting profile. Furthermore, study the background behind the scene where "Arrow's Possibility Theorem" holds.

9.6 As an elementary usage, multinomial logit utility theory and Arrow's possibility theorem often assume 'independence from alternatives' (IIA). How is IIA treated if the preference set is not universal?

9.7 In the probability profile depicted by Fig. 9.1c, calculate the vertices B, and C.

9.8 As Plot (1967) pointed out, "there is certainly nothing inherent in utility theory which would assure the existence of an equilibrium." Explain descriptively this phrase in your own way.

9.9 State the shortcomings of the rule-based decision-making.

9.10 The ultimatum game principle is used in association with the equal distribution of residuals. Discuss if this principle could be achieved without the elder.

References

Aruka, Y. (2015). Hodgson's bibliometric report and the reconstruction plan of economics. *Evolutionary and Institutional Economics Review, 15*(1), 189–202.

Aumann, R. J., & Maschler, M. (1985). Game theoretic analysis of a bankruptcy problem from the Talmud. *Journal of Economic Theory, 36*(2), 195–213.

Debreu, G. (1960). Review of 'individual choice behavior: A theoretical analysis'. *American Economic Review, 50*, 186–188.
Durlauf, S. N. (1997). Statistical mechanics approaches to socioeconomic behavior. In W. B. Arthur, S. N. Durlauf, & D. A. Lane (Eds.), *The economy as an evolving complex system II* (pp. 81–104). Addison-Wesley.
Duraluf, S. N. (2000). A framework for the study of individual behavior and social interaction.
Hildenbrand, W. (1994). *Market demand.* Princeton University Press.
Luce, R. D. (1959). *Individual choice behavior: A theoretical analysis*. Wiley.
McFadden, D. (1974). Conditional logit analysis of qualitative choice behavior. In P. Zarembka (Ed.), *Frontiers in econometrics* (pp. 105–142). Academic Press.
Namba, K. (1951). *Social choice and individual values*. Yale UP.
Namba, K. (2004). *Death and life studies as preparedness (in Japanese).* Bunshun Shinsho.
Plott, C. (1967). A notion of equilibrium and its possibility under majority rule. *American Economic Review, 57*(4), 787–806.
Saari, D. G. (1992). The aggregate excess demand function and other aggregation procedures. *Economic Theory, 2*, 359–388.
Saari, DG. (1995). Mathematical complexity of simple economics. *Notices of American Mathematical Society, 42*(2), 222–230.
Saari, D. G. (2004). Geometry of chaotic and stable discussions. *American Mathematical Monthly, 111*(5), 222–230.
Saari, D. G. (2005). The profile structure for luce's choice axiom. *Journal of Mathematical Psychology, 49*, 226–253.
Saari, D. G. (2015). Social science puzzles: A systems analysis challenge. *American Mathematical Monthly, 12*(1), 123–139
Sonnenschein, H. (1972). Market excess demand functions. *Econometrica, 40*(3), 649–663.

The Evolution of Exchange Process 10

Abstract

There exists an ambiguous attitude in economic theory toward referring to the details of exchange mechanisms as a social system. To date, in classical theories, the main research target has been the exchange mechanism for commodities in general. Instead of studying the exchange of the broader social or community system, recently, much work has focused on auction mechanisms for particular goods in the context of experimental design. However, the advent of the community currency and crypto-currency suggests that we should study the feasibility and sustainability of the broader system. In this article we will focus on systems of exchange with auctioneers and without auctioneers. We then examine the properties of bilateral exchange between randomly selected traders without auctioneers and explore the resulting properties of iterations of such transactions. Finally, we mention special issues of cryptocurrency in the face of the Byzantine General Problem and discuss a well-coordinated distributed system involving digital tools such as blockchain.

10.1 The Landscape of the Exchange System

The classical image of market exchange has been drastically changed recently. Mirowski (2007) described that a market is repeatedly either spun off or complemented from the underlying market forming a highly complicated layered system in the evolution of market. This may be an essential concept for understanding the modern market system. On the other hand, a series of new exchange mechanisms has appeared. In this article, we focus on these new events to depict the modern market reconstruction. Thus we firstly follow the traditional subject of classical exchange with an auctioneer.

Before going further into the details, we roughly describe the landscape of exchange systems. Here we utilize some auxiliary ideas to classify systems dealing with of market exchanges. These system are constructed and construed by Artificial

Y. Aruka, *Evolutionary Economics*, Springer Texts in Business and Economics,
https://doi.org/10.1007/978-981-97-1382-0_10

Intelligence (AI). The remarkable operation of AI will be revealed by the speed of coordinations and transactions: fast vs slow. Its other characteristics will be divided by the ways of processing: non-symbolic vs symbolic. Non-symbolic way may reflect the way of fast thinking, while symbolic way may reflect slow thinking, as Kahneman (2011) pointed out. From both of these standpoints, thus, there are several footholds to support the structure of the exchange systems. Among financial technologies, HFT is a striking factor. The operation speed is on the order of microseconds, preventing much working from being performed by human intelligence. In fact, the average processing speed of Bitcoin is about 10 minutes, leading us to excessively depend on computing ability such as "proof of work". This characteristics is depicted on the vertical axis, from fast processing to slow. The horizontal axis shows the type of processing, from less symbolic to more symbolic. Symbolic processing implies the so-called programming based one. Through the recent rapid progress of pattern recognitions due to machine and deep learning, nonsymbolic processing will begin a new stage of AI work to replace previous human works. Thus, we summarize the rough profile of AI usage of the modern society as Fig. 10.1. It should be noted that our society currently relies on AI in the above multilayered ways. We will return to Fig. 10.1 again at the end of **Concluding remarks**.

10.1.1 Exchange with Auctioneers

We first take the case of auctions with auctioneers to observe how to exchange either a unit commodity or certain units. Here, we leave aside the realistic *broader* exchange systems to consider a particular smaller exchange such as "auction". It should be

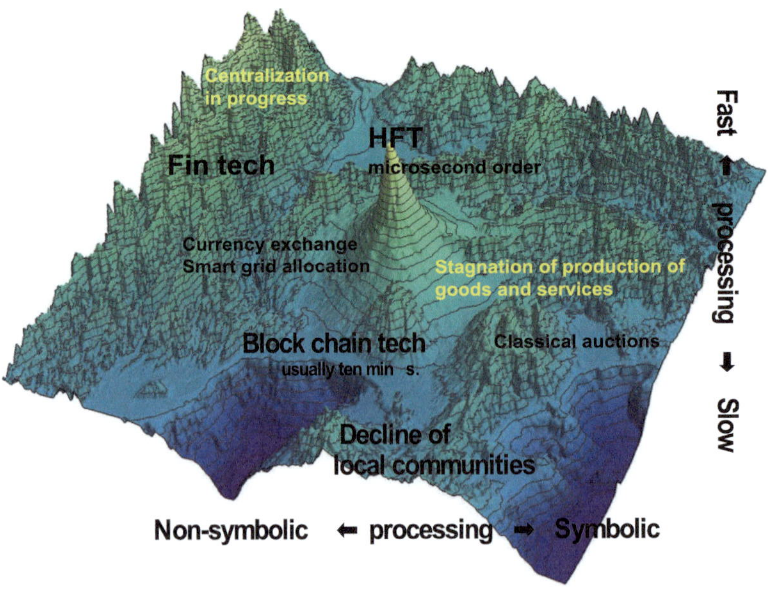

Fig. 10.1 The landscape of exchange systems

noted that the theories of auction merely refer to a limited domain of specialities on goods, estates, and fine arts. The results, as it is, will never provide a general understanding of the market which can contribute to the capitalistic production.

The reader may be reminded of "internet auction" and so on. In this type of setting, the auctioneer or the organizer is assumed in advance. In general, there are two types of auctions: sellers' and buyers' auctions. We then call the exchange system a financial market when any agent either sells or buys. Typically, when we use the term auction, it indicates a complete separation between seller and buyer: the seller only asks and the buyer only bids.[1] In this sense, the exchange environment of auction is a special case for a market exchange in general. Among classical auctions, it is most common to see whose organizer is the seller. Usually, the object will be of a unit or a few units of a good. The latter type is called a multi-unit auction. Usually, the true value of the good is not objectively established, that is, no one knows the true value of it. Otherwise, we do not need to hold auction to collect information.

10.1.2 Auction Where the Sellers Select the Buyers

In fact, auction discussions have been popular in game theory and experimental economics. In many cases of auctions, the sellers selects the buyers. Conversely, there are also auctions such as **reverse auctions** in which the buyer selects the sellers. Let us first take up the discussion of auctions where sellers choose buyers. Currently, mainstream school are also conscious of big data. Bood-Creed et al. (2021) is a paper by the authors at UC Berkeley, University of Chicago, and Harvard University, which was recently accepted in *The Review of Economic Studies*. Here, an **eBay** auction is chosen and, in detail, the efficiency of Kindle sales on eBay is simulated. eBay obtains a uniform price equilibrium with a multi-unit auction, but specifically, the framework itself is specially limited, with 2 unit auctions. Their analysis results show that this auction does not always achieve efficiency.

10.1.2.1 Generalized Second-Price Auction

Generalized second-price auctions are used by Google and Yahoo advertising programs. Clickthrough rates are important in web advertising. The click rate of an advertisement is the number of clicks divided by the number of views. There are n bidders and they choose k $(n > k)$ different slots. According to the "slot allocation rule, slots with higher click probabilities are allocated in descending order of bid prices. The bidder with the highest bid is assigned the slot with the highest click rate, and the next bidder is assigned the slot with the next click rate. However, the highest bidder gets the slot at the price of the runner-up bidder, and the runner-up bidder gets the slot at the price of the third highest bidder. The probability that each slot is clicked is $\alpha_i > 0$. $n - k$ slots are dummies $\alpha_m = 0$ $(k + 1 < m \leq n)$. The bidder's

[1] Aruka (2015) noted that it may be required for the buyer to temporarily be a seller, and vice versa, when the batch auction is applied in a commodity exchange market.

utility is $u_i = \alpha_i(v_i - p_i)$ when assigned slot i. However, it is easy to see that this rule does not guarantee a **Nash equilibrium**. Now, it is assumed that there are two slots $\alpha_1 = 1, \alpha_2 = 0.4$; three bidders with valuations $v_1 = 6, v_2 = 5, v_3 = 1$; bids $b_1 = 6, b_2 = 5, b_3 = 1$. From the settings, $p_1 = b_2 = 5$ and $p_2 = b_3 = 1$. At this time,

$$u_1 = \alpha_1(v_1 - p_1) = 1(6 - 5) = 1 \tag{10.1}$$

$$u'_1 = \alpha_2(v_2 - p_2) = 0.4(4 - 1) = 1.2 \tag{10.2}$$

That is, Bidder 1 can change the bid price from 5 to 4 to increase utility. Therefore, the bid price of this auction is not a Nash equilibrium. Such auctions are held on the Web. Auctions handled by auction theory are "technically artificial designed" even if they are actually human-operated. These kinds of design create the gap between theory and reality. We will not go into details because this article is not a place to study auction theory, but we present some profiles of the basic auction frameworks.

10.1.2.2 Japanese Auction

We call the auction fulfilling following conditions Japanese auction:

a. The initial price is set 0 or the seller's lowest price.
b. Buyers entering the auction house indicate their willingness to buy at the price offered.
c. Buyers can leave at any time but are not allowed to re-enter.
d. The offered price is continuously raised, for example, for 1 yen each time.
e. When there is only one buyer left, the auction stops and the buyer buys at the offer price.

Japanese auction has some advantages over **Vickrey auction**. As the clock progresses, the mechanism is that the buyer indicates at each point whether he or she wishes to remain or leave. Therefore, privacy is preserved because there is no need to express anything other than the second highest price. Further, even if there is a person who follows the behavior of the buyer, the behaviour of the buyer is not ultimately restricted. On the other hand, since Vickrey auction is a sealed bid, the bid price of the other party cannot be confirmed, so a bidder must choose the highest price to win. Therefore, a bidder has to make a successful bid for more than the true value of the item. However, with a Japanese auction, the true value of the other party can be confirmed as time passes, so a bidder can decide whether to stay or leave according to the bidder's true value. In comparison with English auctions, this system has the following advantages: In Japanese auction, prices are continuously bid up like the Walrasian adjustment process in stability discussion, so there is no sudden jump in auction prices as in English auction.

10.1.2.3 Evaluation of Traditional Auctions

Many auctions can be designed in addition to the above in auction theory. The idea of **correlation equilibrium** may also suggest some sophisticated associations with auction games for further generalizations. However, as shown by the mathematician Kono (2008a, 2008b), the assumption of first-order independence of strategy sets among agents is indispensable in proving the existence of a correlation equilibrium.

In most discussions, we introduce a variable s to represent a signal in addition to the true value v and the bid price b, but it is difficult to judge whether a signal is an accident, noise, or an artifact. Inducible signals cannot rule out the possibility of independence assumptions.

We also have some problems with the true value. When the seller discusses it, it may be considered to be **the reservation price**. When the buyer discusses it, it may be a private, true value by connecting it with the utility function. However, it may be difficult to determine the uniqueness of the decision in the probability space in view of discrete utility function of Luce (1959). These considerations must be taken into account when the term *truthfully revealed* is employed.

10.1.3 Auctions Where the Buyer Selects the Sellers

Next, we will discuss auctions in which the buyer selects the sellers. This is used in *tenders* held for government procurement. One of the auction mechanisms adopted by tenders is **the reverse auction** proposed by Glen Meakem in 1995. However, in Japan, this has since been applied to the procurement process between businesses, including cost negotiations between private companies, and has developed as a large-scale mechanism, replacing the aspect from traditional theory with an engineering aspect.

10.1.3.1 Japanese Reverse Auctions

First, consider Japanese reverse auction. In this type of auction, the organizer starts by calling the opening price. Here the participants are the sellers, who decide whether to accept or withdraw the price. When all the participants' responses to this price are determined, the software that implements the scoring function determines a price level lower than the opening price and announces it to the sellers, and the remaining sellers then decides whether to accept at the new price. This is continued until the sellers no longer bids. Unlike traditional auctions based on buyer selection, the procurement business targets so-called platform goods. In that sense, it is already in a different aspect from the previous auctions. Techniques such as **VA** (value analysis) and **VE** (value engineering) are used for scoring. Therefore, the simple classical "discovery principle" as explained in Kreps (1990, 680–703) and Aruka (1996, Chap. 1, Exercise 2) is not valid. The latter work discussed the mechanism by which sellers reveal **the true cost**.

10.1.3.2 Magic Number Scams

In fact, it is not easy for a seller to confess the truth. According to Ayres (2007), bribery cases often occur in public works bidding, and auction organizers and bid companies then collude. In 1992, there was a famous scandal called *Magic Number Bidding* in the school construction business in New York City is famous. Seven companies have obtained the total winning bids of 23 million due to fraud (Ayres, 2007, 44). The details of this bribery were clarified in a judicial transaction, after which a study was conducted to explore the bid price of bribery companies (scammers) by quantitative analysis of these auctions.

First, we explain the specifications of the fraud called *Magic Number Bidding*. The auctioneer organizes a collusion with certain operators, and bribing companies inform the organizer of their reservation price in advance. Since it is a reverse auction, the seller who offers the lowest bid price wins. Since the bid price will be presented by the sellers within a predetermined time, the conspirators will bid the bribing company near the end time if the bribing company's reserve price is lower than any of the other bids. The organizer should say the bid price of the bribing company is slightly lower than the lowest bid price (true bid price). The false bid price should be higher than the reservation price. Therefore, a study after the elucidation of the case, Ingraham (2005) found that the difference between the true bid price and the false bid price was extremely small in the bribery auction. It should be noted that if the bribing company's reserve price was higher than the bid prices of other bidders, the conspirators would not offer a false bid price.

In the 1992 scandal, it was important for the conspirators to spoof a fake bid price near the end of the auction. However, Chandler (2011) proposed a new version of the Magic Number Bidding simulator at the Wolfram Demonstration Project. Magic Number Bidding, of course, is a crime, but the following variations are given. In the classic Magic Number bid, the timing of the false bid was near the end time, but the timing can be chosen to be early. This has the effect of hindering surveillance the timing. Therefore, Chandler (2011) designed the game in which the conspirator is free to choose the timing of the false bid price presentation. On the other hand, there are two ways to determine the false bid price: choosing it to be either near the true minimum price or near the reservation price. The latter option is not risk prone, but rather is risk-averse attitude, and in that case, the method will produce little profit even if a successful bid is made.

10.1.3.3 Auction Theory and Practice

Theoretically, "Benford's Law"(Benford, 1938) can be used to probe fraud in measuring **e-voting**, but this does not necessarily eliminate voting fraud. The skills of fraud may be improved. We recall that in 2011, the Democratic Government of Japan at the time adopted the "reverse auction" and was told that only good things would happen with the introduction of this auction. According to Krishna (2002, 1), the historical origin of auction is stated as follows:

> In 193 A.D., having killed the Emperor Pertinax, in a bold move the Prætorian Guard proceeded to sell off the entire Roman Empire by means of an auction. ...Auctions have

> been used since antiquity for the sale of a variety of obejects. Herodotus reports that auctions were used in Babylon as early as 500 B. C.

To be sure, there are many objects of the auctions, ranging from land to the crude oil reserves. But the value should not be known in advance. No one knew the value of the emperor status. In short, auctions are originally "mechanisms" that economically process things of which the "true value" is not known, so we should not target things whose production costs can be objectively expressed. According to **eBay** founder Pierre Omidia, the first successful bid was a "broken laser pointer".[2] It is difficult for both the exhibitor and the successful bidder to determine the "true value". If anything, the reservation price is the bid price b. For example, in the reverse auction example, it is possible to classify around the reservation price as indicating risk avoidance and that near the bid price as indicating risk preference. However, the reservation price may be given on the basis of the objective cost. Therefore, the true value is not necessarily connected with the reservation price.

Economics tends to believe that even if an economic person is bounded rational and the auction mechanism is pertinently designed, the best choice will be naturally revealed through signals. It has already been mentioned that such beliefs do not always hold. In the reverse auction described in the previous subsection, the situation is completely different in a procurement auction conducted between private companies. Secondary costs are incurred in procurement auctions due to engineering cost estimates such as VA and VE. Revealing or detecting true value is no longer complete by relying on subjective rationality and cost efficiency.

10.2 Alternative Market Mechanism Without Auctioneer

We believe that there is an alternative approach to this discussion in market mechanism research. The stance of revealing "true value" from the rationality of microeconomic economic agents is idealistic. It is necessary to consider the cranial nerve reaction in order to clarify the micro motive of economics. It is difficult for motives and decisions to lead to independence. In fact, the process of decision making based on motivation is also an intrinsic thinking process. To date, no history of metastasis or change in this intrinsic process has been presented in objective terms such gene sequences.

Mainzer (2007, 186;228) cited **Libet's experiment** (Libet, 2002) to call the attention on the decision idealism.

> Just as the brain can be subject to illusions about apparent connections to the outside world, so it can also create an illusion of itself. In any case, it is subject to its own time quotations, which are more or less random due to metabolic reactions and signal processing in different parts in the course of evolution. This includes the discovery, in Benjamin Libet and others,

[2] See the article of eBay in Wikipedia:https://en.wikipedia.org/wiki/EBay.

> that actions are inadvertently initiated more quickly before they are deliberately perceived as acts. Mainzer (2007, 186);
>
> But what about the freedom of us humans to decide? Here …the non-linear dynamics of human brains should be taken into account as an example of complex systems. After the Libet experiments, intentions and intents are unwittingly defined earlier than they are recognized in consciousness. But that does not mean that our behavior is determined by them. Rather, the neocortex can take corrective action. Mainzer (2007, 228)

In contrast to the Libet experiment, this kind of argument in economics is currently subject to experimental economics verification. Thus the test of the null hypothesis cannot be avoided in economics. "Ideal propositions" such as rational postulates can be judged only by the null hypothesis. According to "Bayes' theorem", the possibility of false positive is included in the positive judgment, and false negatives are included in a negative judgment. Only the possibility of behavioural success is discussed, and the proposition cannot be completely affirmed or denied.

10.2.1 The Exchange Economy Without Auctioneers

It is strange that motivation analysis becomes the most important issue in the analysis of economic problems. The motive of a crime will affect the criminal's sentence, but the consequences of a crime have social influences. In examples such as currency exchange, it is the outcome of the exchange that is of social importance. Whether it is used for pleasure or for welfare is at the discretion of the individual, and whether the individual is "optimally" consuming is not directly reflected in the optimality of society. Therefore, in the following, we focus on an approach that does not involve microscopic motivation analysis.

In the following, we treat the subject of the exchange that does not assume an "auctioneer". Such exchanges can be classified as k-lateral exchanges that do not go through an organized exchange. Historically, bilateral exchange has been discussed in the framework of "negotiation theory" using duopoly theory between companies, typically by the use of Edgeworth's box diagram. However, bilateral can be generalized to multilateral or k-lateral. Axtell (2005) calls such an entire exchange without auctioneer *a decentralized exchange*. However, in the following, the random expansion of a relative or bilateral exchange may be called a *distributed exchange*. **P2P** (Peer to Peer) exchange is adopted for cryptocurrencies using blockchain, which is bilateral exchange. Such an exchange is usually called a distributed exchange because a distributed ledger is implemented.

10.2.1.1 Money Holdings Generated from Random Money Transfers

Aruka (2015a) in his first chapter discussed the mechanism for the "rich-get-richer" phenomenon. Here, he gave a simulation of the monetary economy and distribution law based on Wright (2005). First, we explain the core part of the model of Dragulescu and Yakovenko (2000) that motivated the work of Wright (2005, 2011) in Wolfram Demonstration Project.

First, the exchange is an interaction between agents i and j, and in this case, the interaction is to change the possession of a certain amount of money Δm. This result is

$$[m_i, m_j] \rightarrow [m_i', m_j'] = [m_i - \Delta m, m_j + \Delta m] \tag{10.3}$$

The amount of money does not change, so the conservation law holds.

$$m_i + m_j = m_i' + m_j' \tag{10.4}$$

On the other hand, if the system is divided into two small systems 1 and 2, the exchange rule (addition) is added in terms of the amount of money. It then holds:

$$m = m_1 + m_2 \tag{10.5}$$

Since the multiplication $P = P_1 \times P_2$ holds for probability,

$$P(m_1 + m_2) = P_1(m_1)P_2(m_2) \tag{10.6}$$

This equation gives the solution

$$P(m) = Ce^{(m/T)} \tag{10.7}$$

Therefore, the probability distribution of currency exchange follows **the Boltzmann-Gibbs distribution**. If the normalization conditions

$$\int_0^\infty P(m)dm = 1, \quad \int_0^\infty mP(m)dm = \frac{M}{N}$$

are imposed, the constant becomes

$$C = \frac{1}{T}, \quad T = \frac{M}{N}$$

Then, the average amount of money per agent is T (effective temperature). The monetary axis is divided into bins b of size dm continuously in the range $0 \le m \le \infty$; let b's index be $b = 1, 2, \ldots$. If the number of agents per bin b is N_b, the total number of agents is

$$N = \sum_{b=1}^{\infty} N_b$$

An agent in bin b has the currency m_b. The total amount of money is

$$M = \sum_{b=1}^{\infty} m_b N_b$$

The probability that a particular set of occupancy N_b will be the actual set is proportional to the number of ways that a bin holding N agents can be distributed:

$$\frac{N!}{N_1!N_2!\cdots}$$

Taking the logarithm of this probability gives the entropy.

$$\ln N! - \sum_{b=1}^{\infty} \ln N_b!$$

Since N_b is a large number, applying **the Stirling formula**,[3] the entropy per agent is

$$\frac{N \ln N! - \sum_{b=1}^{\infty} N_b \ln N_b!}{N} = -\sum_{b=1}^{\infty} \frac{N_b}{N} \ln \frac{N_b}{N} = -\sum_{b=1}^{\infty} P_b \ln P_b \tag{10.8}$$

Here, P_b is the probability that the agent owns money m_b.[4]

In Dragulescu and Yakovenko (2000), the Boltzmann-Gibbs distribution formation is examined by simulation under the assumption that the initial distribution of money holding is even and random exchange is performed. They also consider the role of debt and note that the formation of Boltzmann-Gibbs distribution then collapses from random exchange.

According to Wright (2005), the simulation is performed as follows:

Step 0 In the initial state, the money holdings of the agents are evenly distributed.
Step 1 Randomly select two arbitrary agents and transfer a fixed amount of money from one agent to the other.
Step 2 Reset the previous round and repeat Step 1 until the given round is reached.

Figure 10.2 shows the results when the above steps were repeated 50 times, assuming that the number of agents is 500 and the initial initial holding money amount is 100. When the entropy is calculated here, it gradually approaches the maximum value. In addition, as the number of steps is increased, the so-called 20 : 80 law is observed. In other words, the bottom 80% can be observed to be an exponential distribution and the top 20% to be a Pareto distribution.

[3] Stirling formula is stated as:

$$\ln N! \approx N \ln N$$

.

[4] The Boltzmann-Gibbs distribution is derived by maximizing the entropy S and the occupancy N_b using the Lagrange multiplier method with a total monetary amount M and a total number N of agents as constraints.

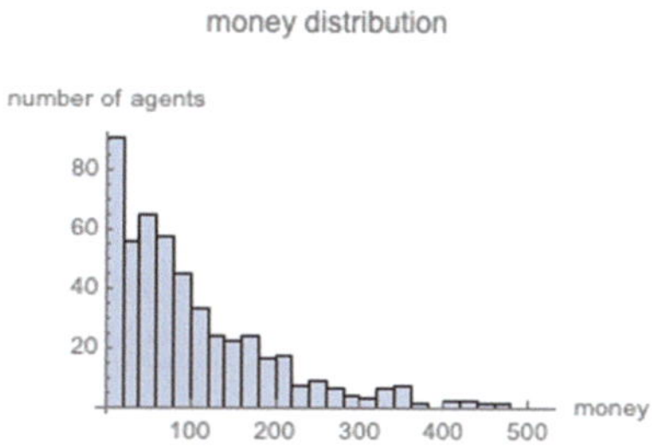

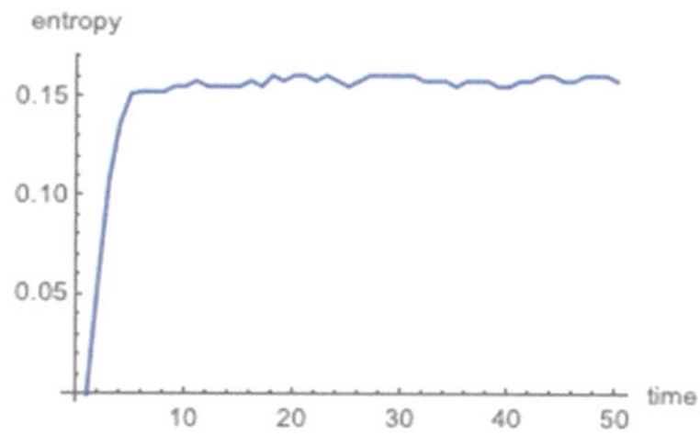

Fig. 10.2 Random monetary exchange and the system entropy

10.2.1.2 Computational Complexity of an Auctioneer-Free Exchange Economy

Axtell (2005) studied "k-lateral exchange without auctioneers" in a paper called "Complexity of Exchange".

If there is no auctioneer coordinator, the equilibrium is a function of the number of agents and the number of products. The set of agents is $A = 1, .., A$, and the set of products is $N = 1, ..., N$. Let $T = 1, 2, ..., \tau$ be a set of times, and let its elements be the physical time series in which a transaction occurs. The exchange happens at T, and agent i owns the distribution $x^i(t) \in R_+^N$ at each time t. Therefore, $x^i(0)$ is the initial endowment. Axtell (2005) further assumes that, according to tradition, the agent's preference set is continuous and strongly convex. Here, the utility function of agent i is a non-decreasing function of $U_i : R_+^N \to R$. Under the above assumptions, a certain number of groups of agents k trade a certain number of goods at each period $t \in T$. Axtell (2005) calls this k-lateral exchange. However, in general, multiple groups of agents can trade multiple products at specific times, but agents cannot be members of multiple trading groups at specific times.Let π^t be the total set of agent groups that make a transaction contract, where $t \in T$. The transaction history $\Pi = \{\pi^1, \ldots, \pi^T\}$ records the agent group that trades a specific good at each time point. Overall, the exchange process can be represented by the mapping:

$$\mathcal{T}_\Pi : R_+^{AN} \to R_+^{AN}$$

In other words, the exchange process may be represented as

$$x(t+1) = \mathcal{T}_\Pi[x(t)]$$

In the exchange process, the equilibrium will be fixed if the operator $\mathcal{T}_\Pi$ is in the order of $AN \times AN$, that is, $O[(AN)^2]$ is bounded above.

Here, the exchange process is defined on the dimension of the product AN (allocation space) of the agent set A and the product set N, while the utility of the agent i is a mapping from the product dimension N to the one-dimensional range. With reference to Uzawa (1962), Axtell (2005) evaluates the exchange process $x(t+1) = \mathcal{T}_\Pi[x(t)]$

with the following **Lyapunov function** V for the equilibrium of k-lateral exchange.

$$V[x(t)] \equiv \sum_{i \in x} U^i[x^i(t)]$$

This Lyapunov function converges geometrically with $\beta < 1$ (Axtell, 2005, Propositions 2 and 3). After all, Axtell (2005) thought that to see the convergence of the exchange process, it would be best to see how β depends on the agent set A and the product set N, that is, on the allocation space. In order to fit the equilibrium in ϵ approximation in τ steps, τ is obtained in the range of the following equation is obtained.

$$\epsilon \equiv \frac{V* - V[x(t)]}{V* - V[x(0)]} \leq \beta^{\tau} \tag{10.9}$$

$$\tau \leq \frac{\ln(1/\epsilon)}{\ln(1/\beta)} \tag{10.10}$$

Then, the following proposition holds:

Proposition 10.1 (Axtell, 2005, Proposition 10) *The number of interactions is bounded above with* $A^2N^2\tau(\epsilon, \beta)$ *as the upper bound, which leads to the k-lateral exchange. Therefore, computational complexity P is defined.*

If the k-side exchange is limited to bilateral exchange for each pair of people, the following proposition holds.

Proposition 10.2 (Axtell, 2005, Proposition 11) *The computational complexity of bilateral exchange is bounded above by* $AN^2\tau(\epsilon, \beta)$.

In the previous subsection, we discussed an exchange process in which the exchange of money between any two persons is repeated and deployed throughout the system. It can be seen that the previous discussion on a two-sided exchange may somewhat suggest moderately a deduction of computational complexity.

10.3 Blockchain Technology and the Digital Exchange Economy

In the previous section, we have seen that Axtell (2005) took into account the complexity of finding an exchange equilibrium solution and derived a condition for solving a complicated exchange on a large allocation space where the exchange is performed, and performed a simple simulation. In the following, the **P2P** network obstacle problem is discussed.

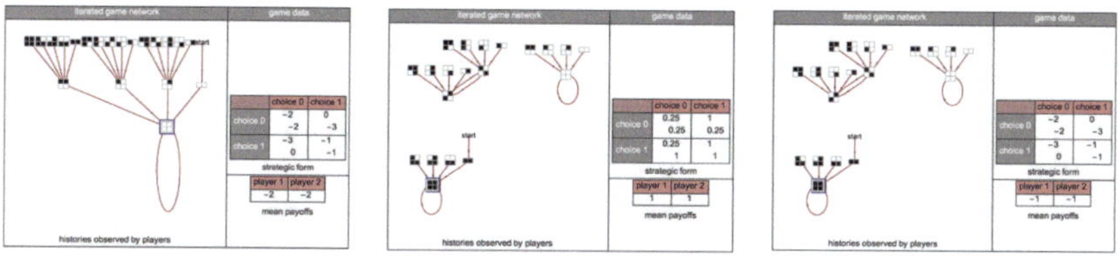

(a) PD (b) Avatamsaka (c) PD with TFT

Fig. 10.3 Mean payoffs in the 2 by 2 games with memory

10.3.1 Rationality and the Consensus-Building Under Huge Amount of Information

In Aruka (2018) and Aruka and Kirman (2017), **algorithm rationality** is important in an ICT society where computer science is important, while it is usually overlooked in the definition of economic rationality in dealing a great deal of information in a complicated network. Aruka (2018) gives a calculation about the amount of information in a two-player game that retains two periods ago in a simple two-player two-strategy game. This is a kind of **P2P** network problem. The player plays the game by referring to the game history every two periods. Certainly, the information content of the game is astronomical numbers.

1. The game tree has a total of $1 + 4 + 16 = 21$ states.
2. With 2 strategies and 2 players, the number of possible actions in the game is $2^{21} \times 2^{21} = 2^{42}$ [4.4 trillion].

We calculated the mean payoffs in three different settings in Fig. 10.3. The first diagram shows the Prisoners' Dillemma game, the second the Avatamsaka Game, the third the TFT case in Avatamsaka Game[5]:

Stephen Wolfram, Mathematica founder, successfully committed to developing his own new kind of science Wolfram (2002), in computability and proposed an ontological approach. A world consisting of a set of types, properties, and types of relationships that can be described on a computer describes modes of existence. In particular, it becomes important to identify the relationship between entities. Schelling (1960) pointed out the importance of "common knowledge" in consensus building, and clarified that an agreement is reached only when there is a unique signal that is mutually recognized.[6] However, common knowledge rationality does not presuppose the malicious intent of the parties to the agreement. In other words, "common knowledge" rationality envisions an environment in which all agents are rational. However, in network problems, defense from malicious intent is of utmost

[5] See the details in Aruka (2018).

[6] See "Common Knowledge", Stanford Encyclopedia of Philosophy, https://plato.stanford.edu/entries/common-knowledge/.

concern. In the following, we consider the consensus building problem in the case of maliciousness.

10.3.2 Blockchain Technology and Malicious Traders

Blockchain technology makes a distributed consensus algorithm. In a blockchain that uses **Proof of Work** (PoW), miners mine a certain block through a series of trial calculations by using a hash function until it is located. This system exclusively depends on the uniqueness of **the hash function**, although it sometimes does not hold true. If uniqueness is shown, the block is approved as correct, and the reward is paid to miners. Whether the mining result is correct can be immediately confirmed in other blocks. In this remittance network, tampering will not be worth the time cost, because it takes much time by checking all the block calculations from the tampering point but also to catch up with the ongoing blockchain.

In addition to Bitcoin, there is a cryptocurrency system that implements the idea of **a smart contract**. Since each node can have accounting information, smart contracts provide computer protocols intended for smooth verification, enforcement, execution and negotiation of contracts. A feature of smart contracts is that they can process a transaction with a secured credit, without going through a third party. This idea was proposed by Nick Szabo in 1994. The smart contract has the following features:

Non-Turing complete type: There are smart contracts (such as Bitcoin Script) that have non-Turing-complete characteristics such as loop processing not being possible.

Turing complete type: This type cannot execute a contract whereby some complications for the iterated process are implemented but the resource necessary for operation can be expected before the operation is terminated. Here the virtual machine working on the cryptocurrency like **Ethereum** is called EVM (Earned Value Management).

However, even in systems such as smart contracts, **malicious traders** will occur as shown in Fig. 10.4.[7] One of the essences of the digital society is that duplication cannot be distinguished when a token is issued. In this sense, fraud is likely to occur at any time; in digital society, copying can be done at almost no cost, and the recipients of transmitted and received currency cannot identify fraud. Therefore, new technologies such as mining and proof of work have come into use. In fact, consensus building on the network is accompanied by another problem of obstacles to consensus formation in contracts. Consensus building fails when there is malicious intent or system failure. This problem has been formulated as the "**Byzantine General Problem**"(BGP) and was already discussed in 1980 as **the Network System Failure Problem** by Pease,

[7] See Aruka (2019) for the details of making a vicious circle.

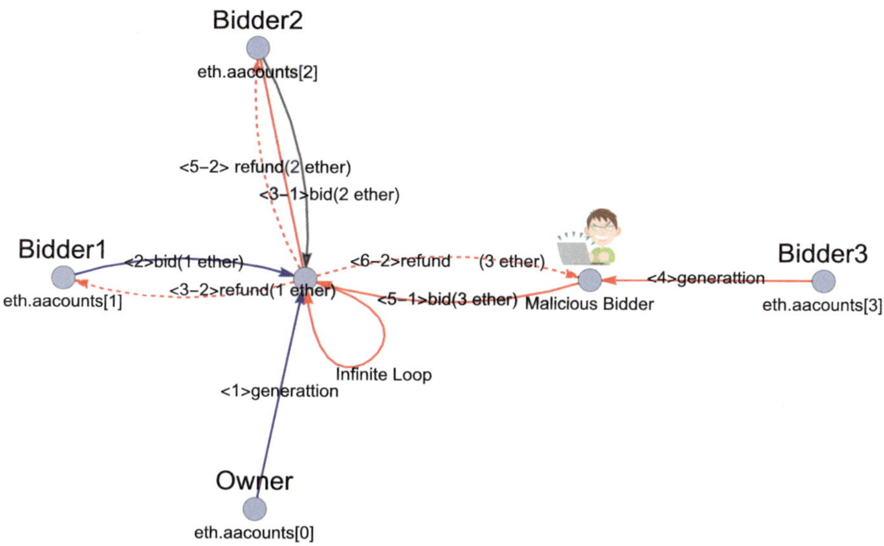

Fig. 10.4 Malicious trader and his effects

Shostak, Lamport (1980). Here, we show the diagram of how a malicious trader makes an infinite loop in a currency transmission/reception system.[8]

10.3.3 Byzantine Generals Problem

The Byzantine Generals' issue implies that when consensus is formed on a decentralized network, it is not possible to form a consensus with credibility if there is a malicious person. This suggests that the malicious existence mentioned in the previous subsection must be resolved on the **P2P** system of cryptocurrencies such as Bitcoin. In the following the Byzantine Generals Problem is abbreviated as **BGP**.

BGP and its consensus formation Suppose that Generals of the Ottoman Empire who attack Constantinople, the capital of the Eastern Roman Empire (Byzantine Empire), lead their corps and surround the city. The generals want to agree on an urban attack plan. In the simplest form of the problem, the generals only decide whether to "attack or withdraw." Some generals must agree on the conclusion of the offensive. In other words, it is clear that the attack will be defeated by only some generals. This is a metaphor that has nothing to do with historical facts, of course.

[8] The previous version of Fig. 10.4 was produced by the reference of Takago (2017). See Fig. 5 in Aruka (2019, 11).

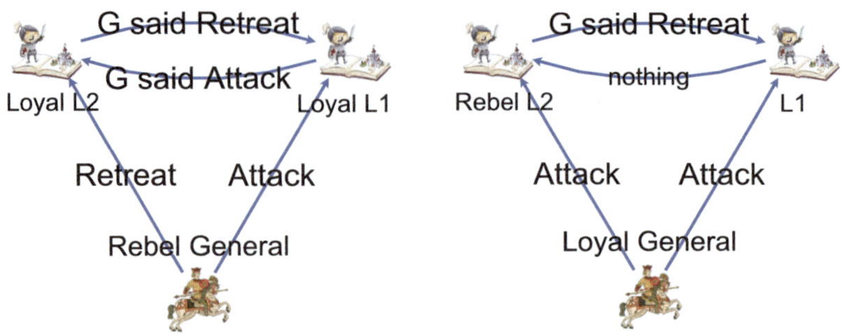

(a) Loyal general case (b) Rebel general case

Fig. 10.5 Impossibility of consensus formation **G**: General; **Li**: Lieutenant *i*

10.3.3.1 BGP and Its Impossibility Proposition

There are fortifications that cannot be dropped by a single attack, and the attack must be carried out by two generals. In this terrain, two generals can communicate with each other only by sending a messenger. Whether to attack at the scheduled attack time depends on the content of the agreement by communication between the generals.

According to Siddharth (2011), we assume at least the supreme commander and two lieutenant generals.[9] First, the two generals need to communicate with each other, agree on an attack time, and each confirms that the other party knows the agreement. Consensus building can result in an infinite loop, so we give the two generals a rank of general commander and deputy commander. However, we imagine the next situations, as shown in Fig. 10.5. Here, we assume that every lieutenant are loyal.

The general commander decides the attack time, and transmits the attack order to the lieutenant's army through a messenger, and waits for the lieutenant's consent to be transmitted. If a reply is not received, it is either a messenger (sending) accident or a betrayal by the aide. However, it is generally impossible to design algorithms that can be safely agreed upon.[10]

[9] See Siddharth (2011) and Aruka (2019) for the details of the proof.

[10] We need the next additional conditions if we employ oral messages due to easy sending. See Aruka (2019,14).

1. The messages to be sent are assumed to be transmitted properly. In other words, rebels cannot interfere with communications between two generals.
2. The recipient has knowledge of the sender of the message. In other words, rebels can't obscure messages by sending additional messages.
3. It can be confirmed whether oral messages can be sent or not. We may promise the default message as "Retreat", for example. Otherwise,"Attack" will be confirmed.

Thus it then follows:

Proposition 10.3 *If no more than 2/3 of the generals are loyal, no solution can be found. Even with 3 generals, the protocol will not work if there is one rebel.*

10.3.3.2 Generalization of the Two-Generals Problem

The points of interest for solving the BGP are as follows:

1. If all the lieutenant generals were loyal, they would move on the same action plan.
2. If the number of rebels is small, they will not be moved to the opposite plan.

The verbal message recursion algorithm then follows:

Verbal message recursion algorithm: All lieutenant generals forward received values to lieutenants other than themselves. The commander sends his value to all aides. Each deputy communicates the order of the commander to everyone, including deputies who have different values than the commander. The final value of i is the majority among the values received by the aide i. To distinguish the messages that change in different rounds, we classify them by the name of the aide.

This recursive algorithm thus shares the implications of majority voting, delivery of outgoing messages, and verification of outgoing transmissions.

1. Majority voting is an input synchronization scheme where every input process has the same decision value. If the input is not false, the non-false incoming stream uses the above values.
2. All messages sent will be delivered correctly. Communication media failure can be viewed as another form of rebellion.
3. The recipient of a message knows who sent it. A fully connected network is then formed. If signed messages are used, the recipient does not need to know who sent them.
4. To detect the absence of message transmission, a timeout mechanism must be used for message transmission. Communication synchronization is then required.
5. The signature S must not be forged or altered. Additionally, anyone can judge the truth.
6. Message M is signed in the form of node $i = (M, S(M))$. Cryptographic operations and modular arithmetic are used.

Hence, the block chain mechanism fulfills these conditions. We can then understand the basis of how cryptocurrencies such as Bitcoin were algorithmically designed.

In the above environment, define *p-regular* to solve the BGP.

p-regular The set of adjacent nodes of node i (deputy officer) is *regular* when the following conditions are fulfilled: All nodes are neighbors of node i. A node that does not belong to the rule set has a route that originates from the node of the set and does not pass through node i. A graph is said to be p-regular if every node has p-regular neighbours, i.e., they are adjacent nodes. Therefore, a $3m$-regular graph is defined by a minimum of $3m + 1$ nodes.

We can then prove the following proposition using the idea of p-regular:

Theorem 10.1 *If there are m rebels, no solution can be found unless there are* $3 \times m + 1$ *generals. This is regardless of whether the agreement is strict.*

In short, the Byzantine General Problem implies that "when a consensus is formed on **a decentralized network**, if there is a malicious person, it is impossible to form an agreement that can guarantee reliability". This is a problem that must be solved on a **P2P** system such as a virtual currency.[11] Thus we newly require amending system faults in a decentralized network. An answer to this problem has been confirmed by **blockchain technology**, which is connected with **the distributed ledger system**.

10.4 Concluding Remarks

A blockchain is a system that uses probability theory to test the hash value of a data block in each iteration with a combination of a hash function and a nonce. Therefore, since the **PoW** is used, the settlement speed of Bitcoin is about 10 minutes on average. This is a *slow* transaction compared to microsecond settlement of **HFT** (High Frequency Transaction) in securities transactions. Figure 10.1 in the above shows the "two digital economies" of the economy with "the high-speed securities trading" and "the low-speed blockchain trading" in mind. In general, the economy is divided into processes that are very fast and those that are time consuming for processing.[12] The difference of processing speed is a key to understand the whole digital economy. Thus we have adopted two pivotal coordinates to describe the contemporary landscape of exchange systems in Fig. 10.1: (a) Fast/Slow processing and (b) Symbolic/Non-symbolic processing.

According to Kahneman (2011), Izumi (2020), the digital economy may be classified into the fast thinking and the slow thinking from the viewpoint of **symbol processing**.

[11] Obtained from https://note.mu/rottenmarron/n/ne98508d1b958.

[12] It is noted that the financial investments is not limited to HFTs. Non-life insurance and pension investment funds may often move only approximately once a year.

> In the current artificial intelligence technology, non-symbol processing artificial intelligence including deep learning is centered on supporting **System 1**(fast thinking) in the field of economic finance, and symbol-processing artificial intelligence mediated by humans is **System 2** (The main focus is to support slow thinking.) (Izumi, 2020, 34–35)

Machine learning has been especially popular. The modern economic system has produced **digital coins**, **cryptocurrencies** and **new smart contracts** by digitization; digitization is now spreading in local currencies, and technological innovation is progressing in this direction. In particular, "Symbol processing artificial intelligence mediated by humans is innovating in **System 2**(slow thinking)".

Currently, Mr. Yoshikazu Takasaki, President of **Doreming**, who has currently attracted the world's attention, has undertaken an innovation in the digital deposit system design and development.[13] This system is the world's first integrated platform *ubiquitous* for human resources, payroll & financial services all over the world. The latter is the human-mediated symbolic artificial intelligence system 2(slow thinking).

Since the 1980s, economics has lost interest in the theory of distribution. The classical theory of marginal productivity of distribution became rapidly powerless in an economy in which the joint-production was predominant, and the financial big bang was powerful enough to deplete interest in fair distribution. In contrast, Doreming's "Digital Deposit System Design" is a system that allows real-time management by linking attendance management, payroll calculation, and payment in real time, and the use of this system itself may then give a design specification for **sharing economy**. When IT became popular at the end of the last century, LINUX OS realized the sharing communities of IT world, and GIT HUB realized micro-level IT asset sharing and decentralized management. Without taking into consideration the sharing economy of the IT society, the distribution theory of the "digital economy" of this century will never be determined. This should be a popular issue in economics.

Exercises

10.1 The general consensus is that auctions produce efficient results. Moreover, auctions have a long history, having been identified in the Babylonian period of 500 B. C. State how you would rate the entire Roman Empire by means of an auction. Use the term "true value."

10.2 The convergence property of Lyapunov functions was often used in equilibrium economics. Apart from the above cases, state any other economic problems where Lyapunov functions are applied.

10.3 Summarize briefly the batch auctions and the continuous double auctions in a single market. Compare them with Bickrey-style auctions.

[13] As for the details, see the company's homepage:https://www.doreming.com.

10.4 The above text describes the advantages of Japanese-style auctions over Bickrey-style auctions in a single market. Consider why a Walrasian adjustment process can produce a more stable process than an English auction in a single market.

10.5 It is interesting to note that there are two types of fermentation in beer brewing: continuous and batch fermentation. The results are naturally different. Let us compare a batch auction with a continuous double auction in one stock market. Furthermore, study how the results differ from each other given the same initial configuration of the market.

10.6 According to Axtell (2005), we have learnt the computational complexity of an auctioneer-free exchange economy. With reference to Cryptocurrency transactions, discuss how the complexity of P2P exchange could be reduced.

10.7 Devise specific examples of BGPs and specify the problems they cause in order to keep from happening rebels.

10.8 The Byzantine General Problem (BGP) was raised by the Network System Failure Problem. As stated above, the BGP implies that "when a consensus is formed on a decentralized network, if there is a malicious person, it is impossible to form an agreement that can guarantee reliability." Discuss if a majority rule in BGP can remove this problem, by taking into account Sect. 10.3.3.2 above, compare the cryptocurrency mining process and the BGP.

10.9 Taking into account Sect. 10.3.3.2 above, compare the cryptocurrency mining process and the BGP.

10.10 The main stream economics never left her target/focus from homo economicus. In the result, malicious agents were not considered. Try to design economics with malicious agent midst homoeconomicus.

References

Aruka, Y. (1996). *Introduction to microeconomics (in Japanese)*. Shinsei-sha.

Aruka, Y. (2015). Hodgson's bibliometric report and the reconstruction plan of economics. *Evolutionary and Institutional Economics Review, 15*(1), 189–202.

Aruka, Y. (2017). *Systemic risks in the evolution of complex social systems*. In Economic foundations for social complexity science: Theory, sentiments, and empirical laws. Springer.

Aruka, Y. (2018). Interpreting the iterated dilemma games using the presentation like cellular automatons. *Evolutionary and Institutional Economic Review, 15*(2), 351–365.

Aruka, Y. (2019). The rise of smart contract and its complex impacts on the digital ecosystem. In S. Sato , S. Iwanaga, & A. Ishii (Eds.), *Proceedings of the 23rd Asia Pacific Symposium on Intelligent and Evolutionary Systems* (pp. 4–16). Springer Nature.

Axtell, R. (2005). The complexity of exchange. *Economic Journal, 115*(504), 193–210.
Ayres, I. (2007). *Super crunchers: Why thinking-by-numbers is the new way to be smart*. Bantam Books.
Benford, F. (1938). Noncooperative game in cooperation: Reformulation of correlated equilibria. *Proceedings of the American Philosophical Society, 78*(4), 551–572.
Bodoh-Creed, A. L., Boehnke, J., & Hickman, B. (2021). How efficient are decentralized auction platforms? *Review of Economic Studies, forthcoming, 88*(1), 91–125.
Chandler, S. (2011). Iterated games. Retrieved from http://demonstrations.wolfram.com/IteratedGames/.
Dragulescu, A., & Yakovenko, V. M. (2000). Statistical mechanics of money. *The European Physical Journal B, 17*(4), 723–729.
Ingraham, A. (2005). A test for collusion between a bidder and an auctioneer in sealed-bid auctions). *Contributions to Economic Analysis and Policy, 4*(1), 1–32.
Izumi, K. (2020). Current status and challenges of artificial intelligence technology in financial markets(Kinyushijo niokeru jinkochino no genjyo to kadai). In Y. Aruka (Ed.), *Value creation and the distributive market design (Kachi-sozo to bunsangata-shijosekkei) in Japanese* (pp. 85–92). Chuo UP.
Kahneman, D. (2011). *Thinking, fast and slow*. Farrar, Straus and Giroux.
Kono, N. (2008a). Noncooperative game in cooperation: Reformulation of correlated equilibria. *The Kyoto Economic Review, 77*(2), 107–125.
Kono, N. (2008b). Noncooperative game in cooperation: Reformulation of correlated equilibria (II). *The Kyoto Economic Review, 78*(1), 1–18.
Kreps, D. M. (1990). *A course in microeconomic theory*. Princeton UP.
Krishna, V. (2002). *Auction theory*. Academic Press.
Libet, B. (2002). *Mind time: The temporal factor in consciousness*. Harvard UP: In Perspectives in cognitive neuroscience.
Luce, R. D. (1959). *Individual choice behavior: A theoretical analysis*. Wiley.
Mainzer, K. (2007). Kapitel 7: Zufall in Kultur, Wirtschaft, und Gesselschaft. In *Der kreative Zufall: Wie das Neue in die Welt kommt?* CH Beck.
Mirowski, P. (2007). Markets come to bits: evolution computation and markomata in economic science. *Journal of Economic Behavior and Organization, 63*(2), 209–242.
Pease, M., Shostak, R., & Lamport, L. (1980). Reaching agreement in the presence of faults. *Journal of the ACM, 27*(2), 228–234.
Schelling, T. (1960). *The strategy of conflict*. Harvard UP.
Siddharth, C. (2011). Regarding the Byzantine general problem. Retrieved from https://www.slideshare.net/siddharthchaudhry/byzantine-general-problem-siddharth-chaudhry?from_action=save
Takago, T. (2017). *Kenro-na smart contract kaihatsu-no-tameno blockchain nyumon (Introduction of blockchain to develop a robust smart contract), in Japanese*. Gijutsu-Hyoron-sha.
Uzawa, H. (1962). On the stability of Edgeworth's barter process. *International Economic Review, 3*(2), 218–232.
Wolfram, S. (2002). *A new kind of science*. Wolfram Media.
Wright, I. (2005). The social architecture of capitalism. *Physica A: Statistical Mechanics and its Applications, 346*(3/4), 589–620.
Wright, I. (2011). Statistical mechanics of money. Wolfram Demonstration Project http://demonstrations.wolfram.com/StatisticalMechanicsOfMoney/

A Theory of International Trade

11

Abstract

When production theory is discussed in traditional economic custom, somehow, either intermediate goods or price determination are often not examined precisely. The prices are usually fixed, while scarcity of resources is exceptionally attached importance. The efficiency of production is consequently forced to be adapted to a given price system of goods. However, this kind of restrictive treatments of production came up against several difficulties when the theory of international trade is argued in terms of Ricardo and Heckscher-Ohlin, i.e., **comparative cost theory**. The object of international transactions may not be limited to such resources as regulations are often imposed. It is rather important to trade not only among the different intermediate goods but also even among the same kinds of intermediate goods empirically shown in Ikeda (2016). Thus the introduction of intermediate goods for production is indispensable to develop the theory of international trade. Even in the 21st century, however, economists were still frustrated to escape from a special two country-two commodity case. Fortunately, by remarking geometry, Shiozawa (2007, 2016), Shiozawa et al. (2017), has been successful to establish **a price determination** in a more general case of three country-three commodity. In Shiozawa (2016), he smartly employed a sub-tropical geometry to examine a general case of international trade, i.e., three country-three commodity case. Behind his idea, there is the idea of Minkowski space of production, in particular, zonotope. This approach will give a different view of production set, and possibly suggest a further generalization more than three of the number of country and commodity. First of all, this article gives a brief look of the new essence of Shiozawa's theory, and then gives by some numerical simulation a new characterization of international trade in line with Shiozawa's theory. Furthermore, this article examines the effect of the introduction of free international trade. The introduction of the optimization rule to international trade results in drastic changes in network structures. Finally, the link with the network analysis and econophysics will be argued.

Y. Aruka, *Evolutionary Economics*, Springer Texts in Business and Economics,
https://doi.org/10.1007/978-981-97-1382-0_11

11.1 An Introductory Review on the International Trade

11.1.1 An Integration of Two Production Systems Through Specialization

It is well known that an integration of any two production systems $\{A, B\}$ will bring some more efficient production as a whole than a simple sum of the production amounts over the two independent systems. For simplicity, we suppose that each system can produce two goods $\{x, y\}$ common to the two systems. We then give a simple example. We have two states of each production system where any system can specialize her production to some particular good of any two goods. Thus we may have a state with specialization and a state without specialization to some particular good.

It is shown that can increase the total production of A and B for both goods x and y. An efficient total production can only be achieved if either A or B specializes in producing the good in which they have **a comparative advantage**. We assume that a production possibility frontier is linear. In comparison between given two systems, a comparative advantage of any system will be then revealed as for the production of one of two goods. For instance, the system A has a comparative advantage in the production of y. The system B has a comparative advantage in the production of y. If it is the case, the production possibilities frontier of the systems A and B will be then depicted in Fig. 11.1. Thus the frontiers of both countries have their maximum production on each good respectively. We denote the system A's maximum capacity on good x by X_{maxA}, on good y by y_{maxA}, for instance. The same notations are applied to X_{maxB}, on good y by y_{maxB} for the system B.

Now we employ a numerical example as shown in Table 11.1.

In our instance shown by Table 11.1, there are two modes of production: independent mode and integrative mode, i.e., the mode "without specialization" and the mode "with specialization."

In an integrative mode, A can produce 50 units of X, while B can produce 100 units of Y. Here $x \in X$ and $y \in Y$. On the other hand, either A or B can only produce less than her maximum amount which they can specialize their production. We set $\alpha = \frac{Y_{\max B}}{X_{\max A}}$. Hence it depends on the ratio α whether A or B should specialize. In our example, if $\frac{Y}{X} \geq \alpha$, A must specialize in the production of X, and *vice versa*. We may then allow an intermediate case that A can produce both goods but B can specialize to produce Y. This illustrates how a comparative advantage in integration for specialization can occur given some independent systems. The result is represented by the activity analysis of Fig. 11.1. In Fig. 11.1, the specialization to a particular commodity due to its comparative advantage in the system A is demonstrated. But this kind of specialization does not refer to and/or specify at all how the outputs will be exchanged among the systems. The transactions among the systems should be complex if the outputs were also used as the intermediate goods for production. This is the reason why the classical international trade theory was not updated until Shiozawa (2007, 2016) has mathematically innovated by the use of subtropical geometry.

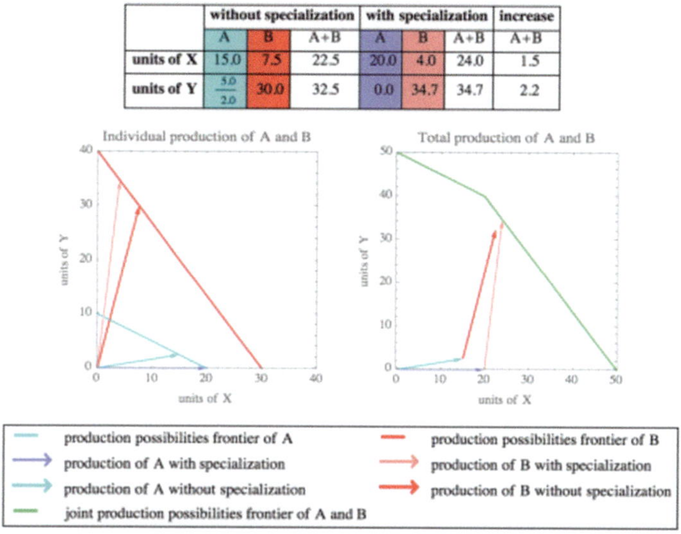

Fig. 11.1 The activity analysis of integration of two independent production system through specialization. Drawn by Brechtefeld (2012)

Table 11.1 A numerical instance

System	Independent		Integration	
Commodity	*A*	*B*	*A*	*B*
x	15	7.5	20	4
y	2.5	30	0	34.7

In the following, we will argue **an integration through international trades.** Taking into account international trades, however, the effect of integration of independent systems must be more complex. The effect could not be confirmed by a simple comparison of comparative advantage in terms of real productivity among the independent systems. We will require a more roundabout reasoning on the idea of comparative advantage.

11.1.2 Shiozawa's Innovative use of Zonohedron

Another more sophisticated/innovative instance is recently has been shown by Shiozawa (2016) when he argued the international production system of 2 country—3 goods case (Shiozawa, 2016, 13): Some New Topics in International Trade Theory). Here he dealt with intermediate goods in the international trade. See Fig. 11.2. **Shiozawa's diagram** (Shiozawa's polygon) is interpreted as Minkowski sum of any two triangles (any two countries A and B). Firstly each triangle is composed by the

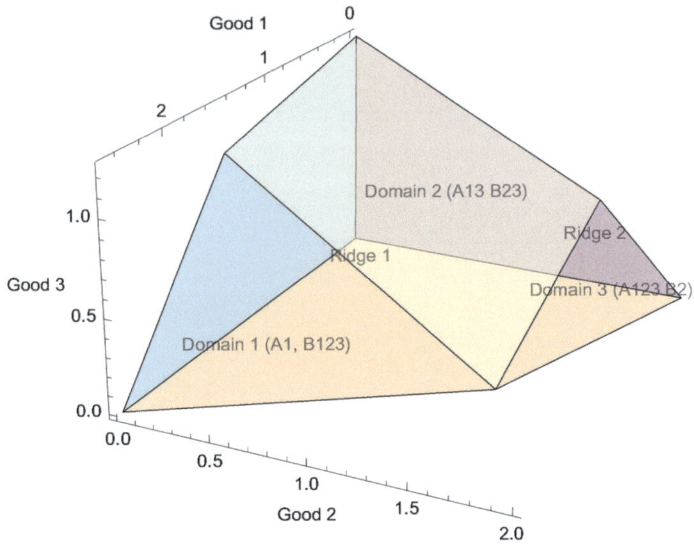

Fig. 11.2 Shiozawa's diagram

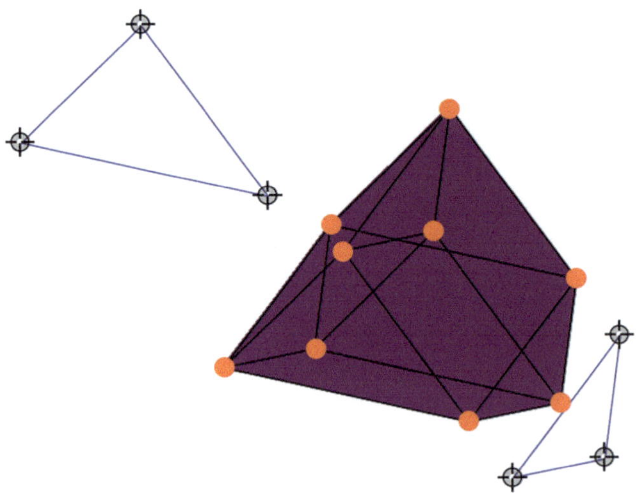

Fig. 11.3 Minkowski sum of any two triangles

commodities space each country separately. But the composition of two triangles will generate a **zonohedron** of many facets.

In the following, we will see the double observations how the countries and the commodities are mutually interacted. In other words, a Minkowski sum of any 2 systems will reveal some complex relationships newly generated by the international trade between two countries. This formation is easily shown graphically in Fig. 11.3.

11.2 Ricardian Economy with International Trade

A Ricardian trade economy, or Ricardian economy, is an economy with M countries and N kinds of commodities, where M and N are positive integers. The usual convention $[M] = 1, \ldots, M$ and $[N] = 1, \ldots, N$ is used. The economy is given a set of production processes or production techniques, expressed by a rectangular matrix A with M rows and N columns. An entry a_{ij} of A denotes the labor input coefficient for the production technique in country i producing commodity j. Thus, a_{ij}'s of labor is required to produce s units of commodity j in country i. Each country has a fixed labor force q_i. This is the maximum quantity of labor available for production in a country. E comprises the set $\{A, q\}$, where A is a set of $M \times N$ positive numbers a_{ij} (i.e., $A = [a_{ij}]$ and the vector q is a set of M positive numbers q_i. Thus, a Ricardian economy is simply the couple $\{A, q\}$.

No body has successfully proved the existence proof in its general case of M countries and N kinds of commodities with intermediate inputs. Jones (1961) only gave a sufficiency proof in the special case of $M = N$. But the number of commodities is actually far bigger than the number of countries. We were keen to generalize Ricardian trade theory. A general case must contain a production of commodities by means of commodities. In this point of view, **Yoshinori Shiozawa** was the first scholar who successfully proved a general case of Ricardian trade theory in Shiozawa (2007). Here he employed **barycentric coordinates** for his proof.

11.2.1 Shiozawa's Ricardian International Trade Theory of Subtropical Form

$$w = p \otimes \max B$$

First of all, Shiozawa's new proof Shiozawa (2016) employs **the max-times semiring**. Every country has an industry in which employers can pay maximal wage rate. Let B to be a matrix in which the (j, i) element is $1/a_{ij}$. If the equation holds, every country i has a commodity $j = j(i)$, such that

$$w_i = p_j/a_{ij} \text{ and } p_j/a_{ij} \geq p_i/a_{ik} \text{ for } \forall k \in [N].$$

This means that every country has an industry in which employers can pay the maximal wage rate. This has been equivalent to the same effects as cost minimization according to Fujimoto's empirical observations of innovation processes of the manufacturing industries Fujimoto (2007), Fujimoto and Shiozawa (2012). Hence he confirmed **the conjugacy between wage rates and prices**. In the event, a list of **major conjugate relations** in Ricardian economy has been established.

Shiozawa (2016), secondly, confirmed in the Ricardian economy that the subtropical hyperplane arrangement with full commodity apexes (in case of min-times semi-ring) and with full country apexes (in case of max-times semi-ring) could determine the range of wage rate vectors and price vectors in a self-replacing steady state.

Table 11.2 Commodity-wise view

Comodity 1	Commodity 2	Commodity 3
↓	↓	↓
Country 2,3	Country 2	Country 2

Table 11.3 Country-wise view

Country 1	Country 2	Country 3
↓	↓	↓
ψ	Commodity 1,2,3	Commodity 2

Here Shiozawa regarded the competitive type at a point as *spanning*, namely, sharing and covering. Therefore, we get the diagrams of spanning core in commodity simplex and spanning core of **country simplex**. In this elegant arrangement, Shiozawa formulated the world production set in terms of **Minkowski sum**. This formulation is also innovative for mathematical economies. It is noted that Fig. 11.2 is driven by Fig. 11.3 by incorporating the above **major conjugate relations**.

11.2.2 The Application of Hyperplanes of Tropical Geometry to the International Trade

Leaving a rigorous proof given by Shiozawa et al. (2017), we can easily summarize how the goods and countries generate a complex network structure. In the following, by the use of simplex geometry, we firstly depict that domains in which each country has **cost advantage**. We employ this to embed relative prices into this simplex to establish **the price simplex** of the world production system diagrammatically. We then incorporate **the wage simplex** into **the price simplex** to prove "commodity's cost advantage" in countries. In this procedure, we finally find **competitive types** of country domains in a superposition of the price simplex and the wage simplex.

In order to develop our idea, we have two ways to express the state of transactions between commodities and countries: commodity-wise notation and country-wise notation. In this illustration, we will employ the latter (Tables 11.2, 11.3 and 11.4).

We then allocate the cost-advantage of any commodity to any country. We give the next selection of cost-advantage for our argument shown in Fig. 11.4.

The apex of a tetrahedron is degenerated/flattened on a plane. Thus V is called the apex of commodity space represented by a two-dimensional triangle. We argue

Table 11.4 A selection of cost advantage allocation

Country 1	Country 2	Country 3
↓	↓	↓
Commodity 2	Commodity 3	Commodity 1

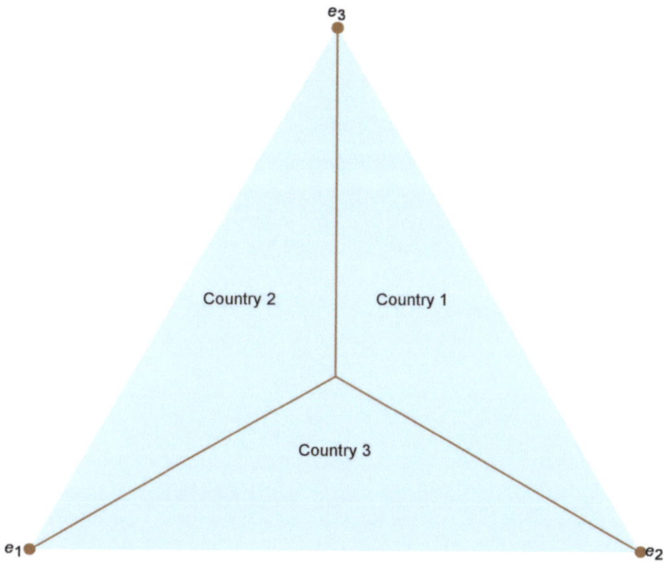

Fig. 11.4 Cost advantages in the country-wise notation

the cost advantage when the wage vector $w = (w_1, w_2, w_3)$ is given in the triangle $V^1e_1e_2$. The cost of production for commodity 1 is then the lowest in country 3. As the wage vector changes to move to $V^1e_2e_3$, country 1 has the lowest cost of commodity 1. If the wage vector is found in $V^1e_3e_1$, country 2 has the lowest cost of commodity 1. Similarly as in commodity 1, we can also argue the cost advantages for commodity 2 as well as commodity 3. So, as Fig. 11.5 shows, we have three apexes such as v^1, v^2, v^3, and **10 domains** in the triangle, which correspond to the different types of cost advantages, i.e., the different competitive types.

It is noted that $(1, 2, 1)$ means commodity 1 has the lowest cost in country 1, commodity 2 has the lowest cost in country 2, and so on.

We take the set of production coefficients of commodity 1 among 3 countries as a_{11}, a_{21}, a_{31}. By using a scalar c, we normalize v_i by letting

$$v_1 = \frac{c}{a_{11}},\ v_2 = \frac{c}{a_{21}},\ v_3 = \frac{c}{a_{31}}.$$

It then holds

$$v_1 + v_2 + v_3 = 1 \tag{11.1}$$

$$c = \frac{1}{a_{11}} + \frac{1}{a_{21}} + \frac{1}{a_{31}} \tag{11.2}$$

Figure 11.6 can establish the comparative costs, by focusing on $w1$ and $v3$ on the line e^2e^3. It then follows the next relationships:

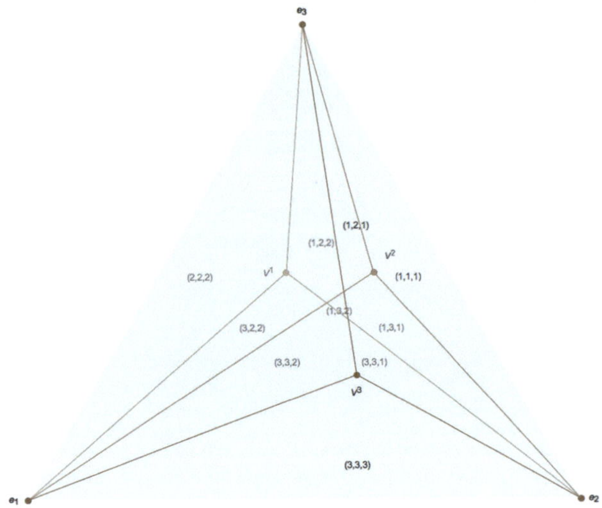

Fig. 11.5 This is 10 domains in the triangle corresponding to the different types of cost advantages

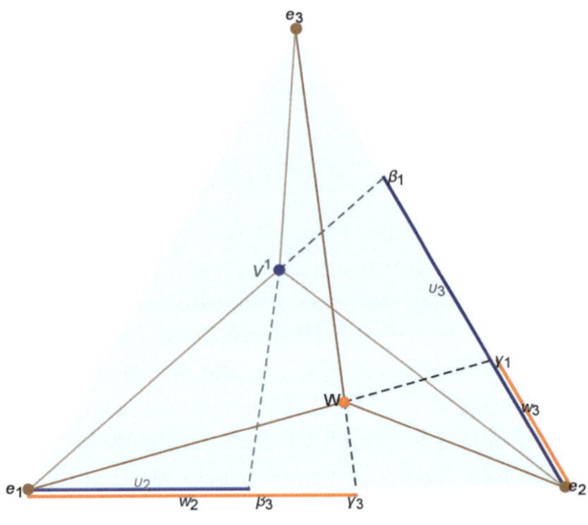

Fig. 11.6 The comparison of cost advantages between country 2 and country 3 given V^1 or given that the lowest cost is the commodity 1

$$\left.\begin{array}{l} w_2 : w_3 > \ v_2 : v_3 \\ v_2 : v_3 \ = \dfrac{1}{a_{21}} : \dfrac{1}{a_{31}} \\ w_2 : w_3 > a_{31} : a_{21} \end{array}\right\} \Longrightarrow w_2 a_{21} > w_3 a_{31} \tag{11.3}$$

If we focus on the line $e^3 e^1$, Fig. 11.7 can confirm the next:

$$w_1 a_{11} > w_3 a_{31}. \tag{11.4}$$

Hence it is verified that the cost of production for commodity 1 is the lowest in country 3. As stated in the above, the cost advantages for other commodities than

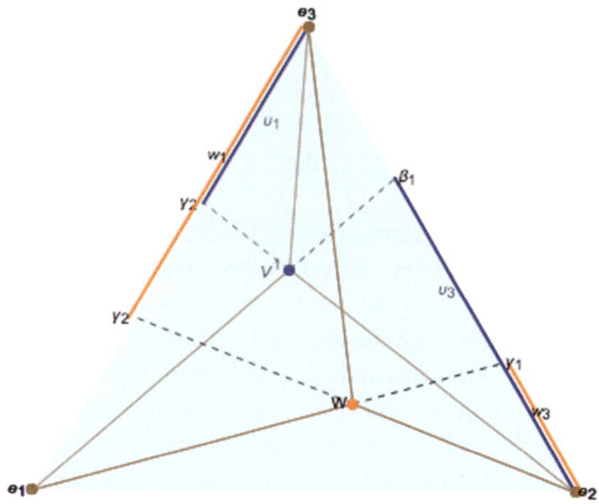

Fig. 11.7 The comparison of cost advantages between country 1 and country 3, given V^1 or given that the lowest cost is the commodity 1

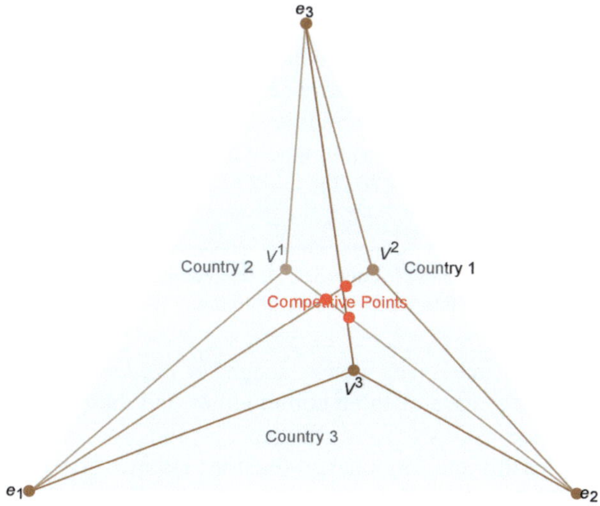

Fig. 11.8 Existence of the competitive points

commodity 1 will be confirmed. So, as Fig. 11.8 shows, that **the competitive points** will be established at the intersections of e_1v_2 and e_2v_1 and e_3v_3.

11.3 A Verification of Shiozawa's International Trade Theory

In the first section when we argued a comparative advantage of an integration of any two independent systems, we noticed that the effects of international trade would give rise to much more complex interactions. Shiozawa (2016) successfully found that this kind of interactions were revealed by some new mathematical transformation like sub-tropical geometry. In short, the essence is no other than wage-price variations among countries through international trades. Needless to say, there is a big difference between a simple comparative advantage of productivity of commodities and the cost advantages between the relationship of commodities and countries. Moreover, we also observed that an idea of comparative advantage would no longer bring any pure specialization of production each country. As an empirical test showed, there may occur an internationally bilateral transaction on the same commodities between any two countries. This must invalidate the old justification of international trade by specialization of production each country, as Shiozawa (2007, 2016) mathematically showed. Thus we finally verify an occurrence of transaction of the same commodity between countries and some associated meanings of the network order of production. We will achieve this verification by the **country-based simulation**.

In the following, we employ the idea of **multiregional input-output model** mainly given by Raa (2006). Raa applied **the make minus use tables** to formulate a new type of input-output model. Needless to say, **the net make less use tables** based on the input-output table inherit some restrictions the I/O table by itself retains. The variables appearing in this table are limited to flow variables for a year basis. In our case, there is the sole factor of production, i.e., labor. This assumption rather reveals the main point on which Shiozawa (2007, 2016) focused. We also note that the I/O table always deals with commodities as intermediate goods. Thus we can verify the international trade equilibrium where intermediate goods are imported /or exported. According to Nettleton (2011),

> the model is quite sophisticated in implementing tableau networked production functions across multiple industries in multiple countries, all interconnected by trade, settled simultaneously in volume and price through linear programming.

Nettleton, moreover, has given a new insight to *randomize* the net make less use tables. We show the case of three commodities and three countries randomly generated, for instance.

Nettleton regarded this inter-regional production system as one of *before* deregulation. "Deregulation" means the free international trade. Thus "*before* deregulation" will suggest a state which cannot move entirely to the free trade for some reason (Table 11.5).

As for the remaining countries in this inter-regional system **Country 2 and 3**, it then follows the result of the *before* deregulation. We firstly show the state transition of **Country 2** (Table 11.6).

We finally show the state transition of **Country 3** (Table 11.7).

11.3.1 The Make Minus use Table and the Network Diagram

In order to argue the input-output system, we need to notice the several versions of the input-output system so far discussed previously. The statistical bureau often announces the input output tables where the input coefficient is defined as an input amount required to produce a unit of the commodity. On the contrary, **the make minus use tables** focuses on the net output structure of the production system as

Table 11.5 The state of *before* deregulation of country 1

Country 1	Country 1 infrastructure			Net export from country 1 to 2			Net export from country 1 to 3			Country 1
Limited trade	Indst.1	Indst.2	Indst.3	Indst.1	Indst.2	Indst.3	Indst.1	Indst.2	Indst.3	Consumption
Industry 1	51	−12	−15	−10	0	0	−4	0	0	−10
Industry 2	−18	33	−10	0	2	0	0	3	0	−10
Industry 3	−16	−13	31	0	0	10	0	0	−2	−10
Labour	−59	−30	−62	0	0	0	0	0	0	0

Table 11.6 The state of *before* deregulation of country 2

Country 2	Net export from country 2 to 1			Country 2 infrastructure			Net export from country 2 to 3			Country 2
Limited trade	Indst.1	Indst.2	Indst.3	Indst.1	Indst.2	Indst.3	Indst.1	Indst.2	Indst.3	Consumption
Industry 1	10	0	0	25	−15	−12	2	0	0	−10
Industry 2	0	−2	0	−16	34	−15	0	9	0	−10
Industry 3	0	0	−10	−15	−12	49	0	0	−2	−10
Labour	0	0	0	−17	−100	−27	0	0	0	0

Table 11.7 The state of *before* deregulation of country 3

Country 3	Net export from country 3 to 1			Net export from country 3 to 2			Country 3 infrastructure			Country 3
Limited trade	Indst.1	Indst.2	Indst.3	Indst.1	Indst.2	Indst.3	Indst.1	Indst.2	Indst.3	Consumption
Industry 1	4	0	0	−2	0	0	42	−14	−20	−10
Industry 2	0	−3	0	0	−9	0	−17	51	−12	−10
Industry 3	0	0	2	0	0	2	−17	−16	39	−10
Labour	0	0	0	0	0	0	−12	−43	−89	0

well as the inter-regional system. The entry in the table indicates a net output if it is positive, otherwise a net input. As shown in the tables, the matrix of net output and input will not be an adjacency matrix. It will be rather a *weighted* adjacency matrix. We then examine the next theorem.

Kirchhoff's theorem for directed multigraphs
Kirchhoff's theorem can be modified to count the number of oriented spanning trees in *directed* multigraphs. The matrix Q is constructed as follows:

1. The entry q_{ij} for distinct i and j equals $-m$, where m is the number of edges from i to j;
2. The entry q_{ii} equals the in-degree of i minus the number of loops at i. **The number of oriented spanning trees** rooted at a vertex i is the determinant of the matrix gotten by removing the i_{th} row and column of Q.

We focus on **the number of oriented spanning trees rooted at a vertex** i in our tables. According to Kirchhoff theorem on the adjacency matrix, usually, the off-diagonals of the matrix are -1. But we note that our table are not an adjacency matrix but rather a *weighted* adjacency matrix. The make minus use table is fitted to the definition of **weighted Kirchhoff matrix**. Thus we apply the weighted Kirchhoff matrix to our table.[1] Incidentally, it may be useful to depict a *directed* network structure of the make minus use tables by the *directed* graph if the table is *asymmetrical*.[2]

In our modeling, the produced goods are all allowed to be utilized as the intermediate goods for the self and the production of others.Thus it follows to apply the definition of Kirchhoff entries to the net input/output. Let the entry of *net* input or *net* output of good j in the productive sector (process) i be a_{ij}, and the exogenous final consumption in the sector j be c_j.

Hence we show the *directed* network structure of the make minus use Table 11.5 by the use of **Kirchhoff diagram**. Here the number of directed arrows indicates the size of net variables (Fig. 11.9).

$$\begin{aligned} \textbf{objective } c &= (0,0,0,0,-1,0,0,0,0,0,-1,0) \\ \textbf{objective function} &= \sum_{i}^{12} c_j y_{ij} \end{aligned} \tag{11.5}$$

[1] The function titled "KirchhoffGraph" of **Mathematica** is quite helpful to depict the strength of the oriented spanning trees. See, for example, "Weighted Kirchhoff Matrix?" (https://mathematica.stackexchange.com/questions/23122/weighted-kirchhoff-matrix).
[2] See KirchhoffWiki (2017), Kirchhoff (2015), and Maurer (1976).

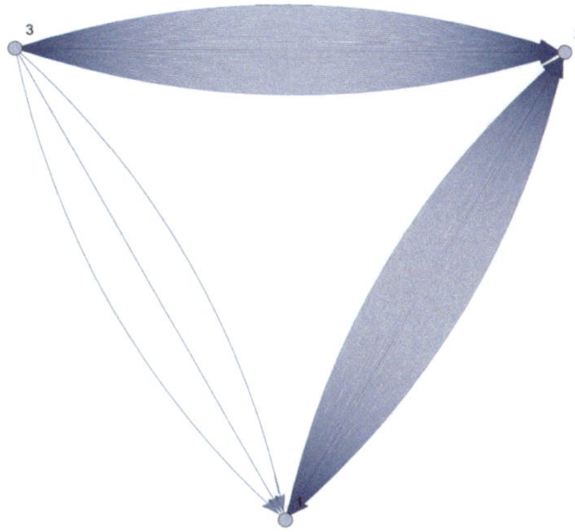

Fig. 11.9 Table 11.5 shows that industry 3 provides industry 1 with net input of 3 in country 1. The directed arrow from industry 3 to industry 1 consists of **3 lines** in Kirchhoff diagram

11.3.2 The Traditional View of the Landscape of the Production System

Now, first of all, we deal with the quantity system of supply and demand. The production system of country k is then represented each country as follows:

Here m_{ij} is the import coefficient of good j in the productive process i. z_{ij} is the export coefficient of good j. $m_{ij} - z_{ij}$ will be the net export coefficient.[3]

$$w^{[k]}l_i^{[k]} \geqq \sum_{j=1}^{n} \{a_{ij}^{[k]} p_i + (m_{ij}^{[k]} - z_{ij}^{[k]}) p_i^{[k]}\} \tag{11.6}$$

$$\text{cost} \geq \text{price}$$

Here the wage rate of country k is denoted by $w^{[k]}$. On the other side, it follows the price system subject to the nonzero excess profit condition:[4]

$$c_j^{[k]} \leqq \sum_{i=1}^{n} \{a_{ij}^{[k]} x_j + (m_{ij}^{[k]} - z_{ij}^{[k]}) x_j^{[k]}\} \tag{11.7}$$

$$\text{demand} \leq \text{supply}$$

As we have learned in the above, it is important to know that we cannot actually regard the domestic production system as the so-called independent system without taking into account any inter-country transactions, i.e., imports and exports. So the statistical bureau practically is providing us with the next three types of input-output tables MIACJapan (2016):

[3] The objective function will be given by the form: min $\sum_{j=1}^{n} x_j l_j$

[4] The objective function will be given by the form: max $\sum_{i=1}^{n} p_i c_i$.

- Type $[I - A]^{-1}$
  The construction of input-output table A is based on the assumption of competitive imports. In this table, domestic and imported products are viewed neutrally and no distinction is drawn between them.
- Type $[I - [I - M]A]^{-1}$
  Construction of the import coefficient matrix M entails the removal of imported products from the above described competitive table A. This is based on the common ratio of the imported product to the total input among all of the products. All of the export outputs are assumed to be domestic products.
- Type $[I - A_D]^{-1}$
  Based on the assumption of non-competitive imports, the actually detected ratio of the imported products to the total input of each industry can be calculated. Subsequently, a non-competitive table A_D was constructed according to the extent of our knowledge.

In the following, we give a sight of the landscape of the actual traditional input-output table of 37 sectors classification in Japan in 2011. In Fig. 11.10, the axes perpendicular to the traditional input plane is limited to the non-negative numbers.This is one of the differences from the make minus use table. On the other hand, Fig. 11.11 shows **the density distribution** of the input coefficients of the same table. The scale of the vertical axis is measured in logarithm.The actual distribution of inputs of the sectors, at first glance, seems randomly distributed. But the author examined this distribution did not necessarily become a random distribution. According to the ran-

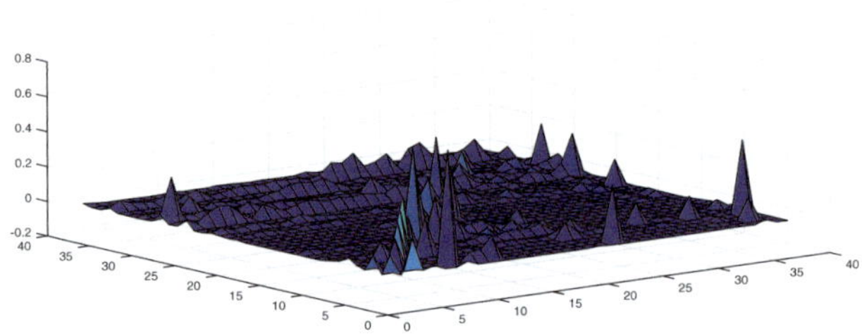

Fig. 11.10 The input output table of 37 sectors in 2011, Japan

Fig. 11.11 The density distribution of the input coefficients of the same table in 2011

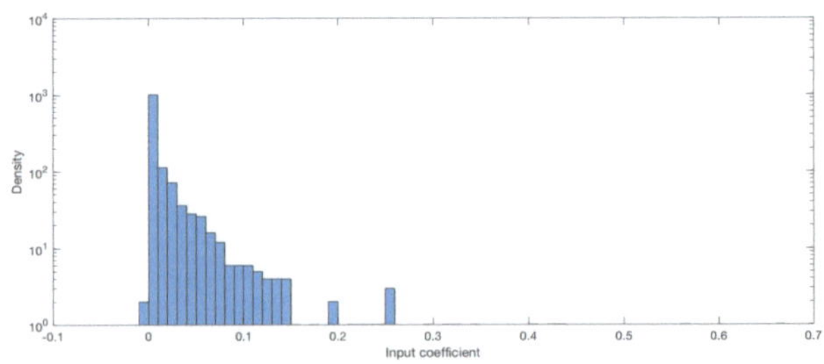

dom matrix theory, we will find some principal modes outside the estimated random distribution of eigen modes of the production system. This analysis was achieved in Chap. 6 of this book, and Aruka and Kirman (2017) and elsewhere. In this chapter, we focus on another property of a network structure of the inter-country production system.

11.3.3 The Case of the International Trade of the Intermediate Goods

The above formulation never contains any selection process of international transaction of intermediate goods (industries) between countries. It could no longer stand the world system of international trade. We must move to a new augmented profile to embrace all the interaction of import and export between countries. We then construct a new array, i.e., **commodities matrix** B. The matrix is "arrayed" by a *specific* rule taking into account the mutual interaction of productive relationship between countries by the international trade.

The mutual interaction of multiple countries and many industries will generate a more complicated network difficult to grasp a whole relation. In order to avoid difficulties of new notations, it seems easily understandable to employ a numerical example to present how to construct the competitive process of international transaction of intermediate goods between countries. This operation will suggest the introduction of the free trade system to all the inter-regional system. We, only for convenience of illustration, take the smallest case of 3 industries and the 2 countries, although our simulation refers to a more general case of the 3 countries- 3 industries case later.

11.3.3.1 The Commodity Matrix of 2 Countries by 2 Industries Case

We assume **the make minus use table** of 2 countries and 2 intermediate goods as follows (Tables 11.8 and 11.9).

Given the above tables, we incorporate some *slack variable* to join two countries production systems and then construct the commodities space by the commodities matrix B as well as the activity variables y in the following manner (Table 11.10)

We thus specified the labels of the activities by the next rules to Country 1 in the smallest economy of the world production system containing the international trade. It then follows our optimization problem of the world production system.

Table 11.8 The table of country 1

Country 1	Country 1 infrastructure		Net export from country 1 to 2		Country 1
Limited trade	Industry 1	Industry 2	Industry 1	Industry 2	Consumption
Industry 1	25	−12	−3	0	−10
Industry 2	−10	25	0	−5	−10
Labour	−30	−18	0	0	0

Table 11.9 The table of country 2

Country 2	Net export from country 2 to 1		Country 2 infrastructure		Country 2
Limited trade	Industry 1	Industry 2	Industry 1	Industry 2	Consumption
Industry 1	3	0	17	–10	–10
Industry 2	0	5	–15	20	–10
Labour	0	0	0	–12	–1

Table 11.10 The corresponding activity levels of Country 1 in the smallest international economy

Country 1	Country 1 infrastructure		Net export from country 1 to 2		Consumption	Slack variable
	Industry 1	Industry 2	Industry 1	Industry 2	Consumption	S
Industry 1	b_{11}	b_{12}	b_{13}	b_{14}	b_{15}	b_{16}
Industry 1	y_{11}	y_{12}	y_{13}	y_{14}	y_{15}	y_{16}

On the other hand, the present example gives the commodities matrix B being generated by taking into account *slack variables*. The next B will be of the sparse form:

$$B = \begin{pmatrix} 25 & -12 & -3 & 0 & -10 & 0 & 0 & 0 & 0 & 0 & 0 & 0 \\ -10 & 25 & 0 & -5 & -10 & 0 & 0 & 0 & 0 & 0 & 0 & 0 \\ -30 & -18 & 0 & 0 & 0 & 0 & 0 & 0 & 0 & 0 & 0 & 0 \\ 0 & 0 & 0 & 0 & 0 & 0 & 3 & 0 & 17 & -10 & -10 & 0 \\ 0 & 0 & 0 & 0 & 0 & 0 & 0 & 5 & -15 & 20 & -10 & 0 \\ 0 & 0 & 0 & 0 & 0 & 0 & 0 & 0 & -2 & -71 & 0 & 0 \\ 0 & 0 & -3 & 0 & 0 & 0 & 3 & 0 & 0 & 0 & 0 & 0 \\ 0 & 0 & 0 & -5 & 0 & 0 & 0 & 5 & 0 & 0 & 0 & 0 \\ 0 & 0 & 0 & 0 & 0 & 1 & 0 & 0 & 0 & 0 & 0 & 0 \\ 0 & 0 & 0 & 0 & 0 & 0 & 0 & 0 & 0 & 0 & 0 & 1 \end{pmatrix} \tag{11.8}$$

The activities y corresponding to the B as well as the boundary condition on y will be given as follows:

$$\textbf{actitvities } y = \begin{pmatrix} y_{11} \\ y_{12} \\ y_{13} \\ y_{14} \\ y_{15} \\ y_{16} \\ y_{21} \\ y_{22} \\ y_{23} \\ y_{24} \\ y_{25} \\ y_{26} \end{pmatrix} \quad \begin{matrix} y_{11} = 0 \\ y_{12} = 0 \\ y_{13} = -\infty \\ y_{14} = -\infty \\ y_{15} = 1 \\ y_{16} \geq 0 \\ y_{21} = -\infty \\ y_{22} = -\infty \\ y_{23} = 1 \\ y_{24} = 0 \\ y_{25} = -\infty \\ y_{26} = -\infty \end{matrix} \quad \textbf{limits} = \begin{pmatrix} 0 \\ 0 \\ -\infty \\ -\infty \\ 1 \\ 0 \\ -\infty \\ -\infty \\ 1 \\ 0 \\ -\infty \\ -\infty \end{pmatrix} \tag{11.9}$$

In addition, we note the boundary conditions on the activities y by **limits** in the above relations.

Finally, we specify the resources. The production system requires the primary resources. In our example, just the labour is used differently from country to country.

$$\textbf{resources } l = \begin{pmatrix} 0 \\ 0 \\ -48 \\ 0 \\ 0 \\ -82 \\ 0 \\ 0 \\ 0 \\ 0 \end{pmatrix} \tag{11.10}$$

$$\textbf{objective function} = \sum_{i}^{12} c_j y_{ij} \text{subject to } \mathbf{B}y \ngeq l \tag{11.11}$$

Hence we can formulate the linear programming of the world production system internally incorporated by the international trade. The prime problem is arranged *Minimizing Problem* in *Mathemetica* formula.

It is noted that $\ngeq$ implies the relations y imposed on the above. In **Mathemetica** formula, we summarize our optimization problem in the following manner:

$$\textbf{LinearProgramming [objective, commodities, resources, limits,} \\ \text{Method} \rightarrow \text{InteriorPoint]} \tag{11.12}$$

11.3.3.2 The Establishment of Shadow Prices Including the Wage Rate

It must be helpful to formulate the dual linear programming problem of the above prime problem:

$$\textbf{objective function} = \sum_{i} p_i l_i \text{ subject to } p\mathbf{B} \nleq y$$

$$\textbf{DualLinearProgramming [objective, commodities, resources, limits,} \\ \text{Method} \rightarrow \text{InteriorPoint]} \tag{11.13}$$

In usual forms, it follows that

$$\begin{aligned} p &= (p_{11}, p_{12}, p_{13}, p_{14}, p_{15}, p_{21}, p_{22}, p_{23}, p_{24}, p_{25}) \\ p &= (p_{11}, p_{12}, p_{11}, p_{12}, w_1, p_{21}, p_{22}, p_{22}, p_{23}, w_2) \end{aligned} \tag{11.14}$$

Here p is set as follows:

$$\textbf{Domestic} \quad \begin{matrix} p_{11} = p_{13} & p_{21} = p_{23} \\ p_{12} = p_{14} & p_{22} = p_{24} \end{matrix} \quad \textbf{International}$$

Here it is also noted that the commodity price must be uniform both for the domestic price and the price for international transaction, i.e.,

The shadow price to support the optimization of the world production system is then established. It is important to know the shadow price of labour in the context of Shiozawa's international trade theory. Needless to say, **the wage rate** is just the shadow price of labour. In our dual programming, the wage rate must be different from country to country, on one hand. On the other hand, the prices of the commodities must be uniform in equilibrium each commodity all over the countries. As **Shiozawa's theory** confirmed, the driving force of the international trade is just **the cost advantage due to the wage rate**. Our dual programming has verified this fact by employing the idea of Nettleton (2011). The simulation has been achieved by re-arranging the program of Nettleton (2011) on the Wolfram Demonstrations Project.

Finally, we mention the shadow prices of our numerical example of two countries by two industries case as a result of running the dual linear programming on the Table 11.11.

It is apparent that **the wage cost advantage** is better in Country 2 than in Coutry 1, i.e., the wage rate of Country 2 is lower than it of Country 1. Thus Country 1 was forced to give up the full operation of both industries. The table after deregulation of this case will be of the next form (Tables 11.12 and 11.13).

Even in the case of the smallest world production system of the 2 countries by 2 industries, the simple idea of mutual specialization of industry composition between

Table 11.11 The shadow prices of the 2 countries by 2 industries case

Countries	Commodities	Shadow prices
Country 1	Commodity 1	0.047
Country 1	Commodity 2	0.053
Country 1	Labour	0.041
Country 2	Commodity 1	0.047
Country 2	Commodity 2	0.053
Country 2	Labour	0.008

Table 11.12 The *after deregulation* table of country 1

Country 1	Net export from country 1 to 2		Country 1 infrastructure		Country 1
Limited trade	Industry 1	Industry 2	Industry 1	Industry 2	Consumption
Industry 1	0	–32	43	0	–11
Industry 2	0	67	0	–56	–11
Labour	0	–48	0	0	0

Table 11.13 The *after deregulation* table of country 2

Country 2	Country 2 infrastructure		Net export from country 2 to 1		Country 2
Limited trade	Industry 1	Industry 2	Industry 1	Industry 2	Consumption
Industry 1	–43	0	67	–9	–15
Industry 2	0	56	–59	18	–15
Labour	0	0	–8	–65	0

two countries does not hold. Thus we will focus on a network analysis on the structural change after deregulation int the final subsection.

11.3.3.3 The 3 Countries by 3 Industries Case

Finally, we focus on the change of the network structure of the inter-country systems before and after deregulation by means of **Kirchihoff matrix** as we already introduced. For a later reference, we show a numerical example randomly generated of the 3 countries by 3 industries case. We firstly specify the labels of the activities by the next rules to Country 1 (Tables 11.14 and 11.15).

As for the remaining countries in this inter-regional system **Country 2 and 3**, it then follows the result of the *after* deregulation. We firstly show the state transition of **Country 2** (Table 11.16).

We finally show the state transition of **Country 3** (Table 11.17).

11.3.4 Validity of the Comparative Advantage Among Countries Mutually Transacting

Inspecting the items of net export among countires, the same industry of Country A gives the net export to Coutry B, vice versa. As shown in Tables 11.6 and 11.10, Industry 1 either in Country 1 or Country 3 can give the net export mutually, for instance. The international trade rather demonstrates the international transaction around the same intermediate good. The simulation result coincides with the empirical analysis.[5]

- The deregulation may generally expand the net outputs of the world.[6]
- But the expansion of the international trades will not necessarily generate either the specialization of a particular industry or the balanced growth of inter-industries.
- It may be rather observed that the productive network in some country is entirely destroyed to prevent from self-reproducing ever before.

[5] As for the empirical econophyics verification, see Ikeda (2016).

[6] It is apparent because deregulation implies maximizing the total net output common to all the participating inter-country systems. Also see an example of the simulation by Nettleton (2011).

Table 11.14 The corresponding activity levels of country 1

Country 1	Country 1 infrastructure			Net export from country 1 to 2			Net export from country 1 to 3			Comsumption	Slack variables	
	Indst.1	Indst.2	Indst.3	Indst.1	Indst.2	Indst.3	Indst.1	Indst.2	Indst.3	Consumption	S_2	S_1
Industry 1	b_{11}	b_{12}	b_{13}	b_{14}	b_{15}	b_{16}	b_{17}	b_{18}	b_{19}	b_{10}	b_{11}	b_{12}
Industry 1	y_{11}	y_{12}	y_{13}	y_{14}	y_{15}	y_{16}	y_{17}	y_{18}	y_{19}	y_{10}	y_{11}	y_{12}

Table 11.15 The state of *after* deregulation of country 1

Country 1	Country 1 infrastructure			Net export from country 1 to 2			Net export from country 1 to 3			Country 1
Limited trade	Indst.1	Indst.2	Indst.3	Indst.1	Indst.2	Indst.3	Indst.1	Indst.2	Indst.3	Consumption
Industry 1	10	–56	0	36	0	0	36	0	0	–26
Industry 2	–4	153	0	0	–62	0	0	–62	0	–26
Industry 3	–3	–60	0	0	0	45	0	0	45	–26
Labour	–12	–139	0	0	0	0	0	0	0	0

Table 11.16 The state of *after* deregulation of country 2

Country 2	Net export from country 2 to 1			Country 2 infrastructure			Net export from country 2 to 3			Country 2
Limited trade	Indst.1	Indst.2	Indst.3	Indst.1	Indst.2	Indst.3	Indst.1	Indst.2	Indst.3	Consumption
Industry 1	50	0	0	0	0	–64	50	0	0	36
Industry 2	0	58	0	0	0	–80	0	58	0	–36
Industry 3	0	0	–112	0	0	261	0	0	–112	–36
Labour	0	0	0	–144	0	0	0	0	0	0

Table 11.17 The state of *after* deregulation of country 3

Country 3	Net export from country 3 to 1			Net export from country 3 to 2			Country 3 infrastructure			Country 3
Limited trade	Indst.1	Indst.2	Indst.3	Indst.1	Indst.2	Indst.3	Indst.1	Indst.2	Indst.3	Consumption
Industry 1	−86	0	0	−86	0	0	216	−27	0	−17
Industry 2	0	4	0	0	4	0	−87	98	0	−17
Industry 3	0	0	68	0	0	68	−87	−31	0	−17
Labour	0	0	0	0	0	0	−62	−82	0	0

Now we characterize our simulation result on **the network properties** of before and after deregulation of the inter-country production and transaction system. In simulation, the numerical values are generated randomly. It then seems natural that the network structures from country to country are uniformly random. In this sense, each network structure seems similar among countries before deregulation. As the world production system moves to deregulation, however, we will see a drastic breakdown of egalitarian network structures among countries. We give a simulation result in the case of 5 countries.

11.3.4.1 The Transition of the Landscape Before and After Deregulation

Firstly, we see the transition of the landscape of the use minus make table. Then we see the drastic change of the network structure among countries (Figs. 11.12, 11.13, 11.14 and 11.15).

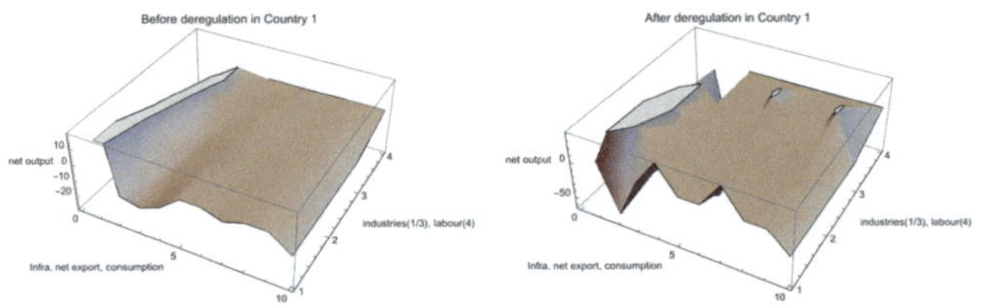

Fig. 11.12 All in one of the landscape of the smallest international economy

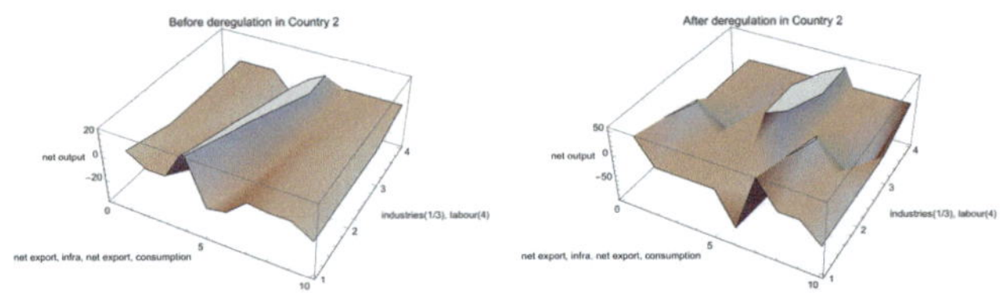

Fig. 11.13 The transition of the landscape of the smallest international economy before and after deregulation in country 2

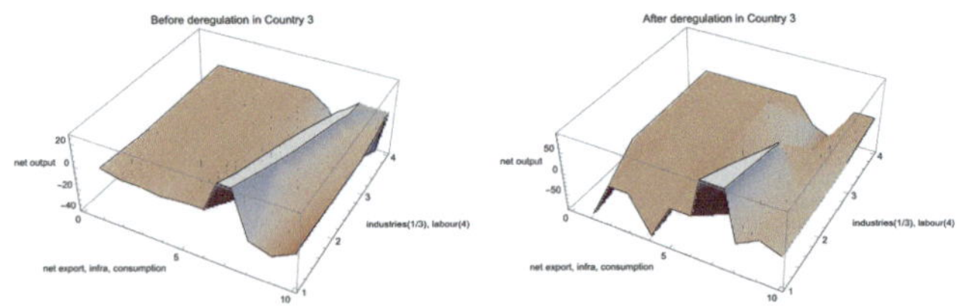

Fig. 11.14 The transition of the landscape of the smallest international economy before and after deregulation in country 3

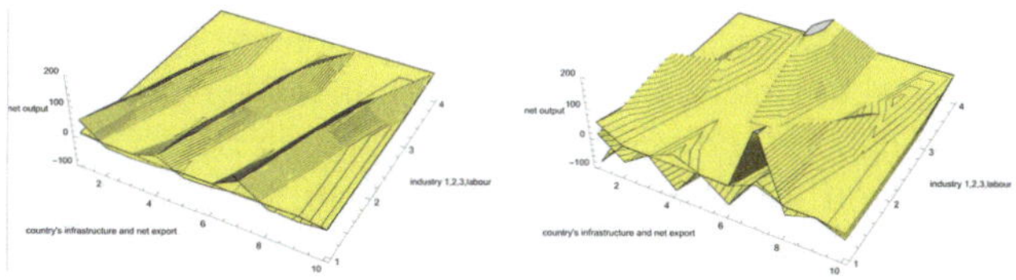

Fig. 11.15 All in one of the landscape of the smallest international economy

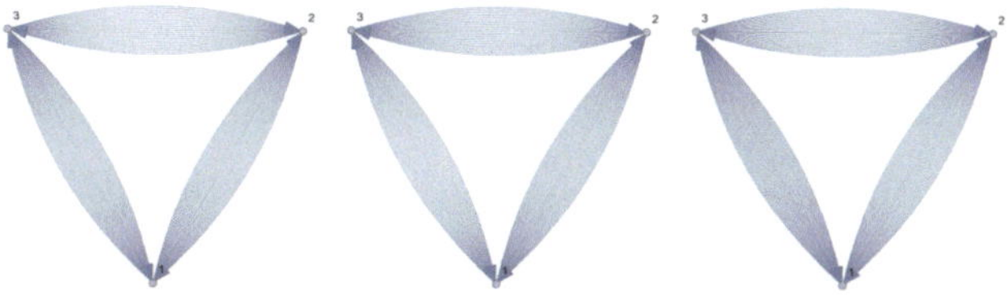

Fig. 11.16 Kirchhoff diagrams of the smallest international economy before deregulation

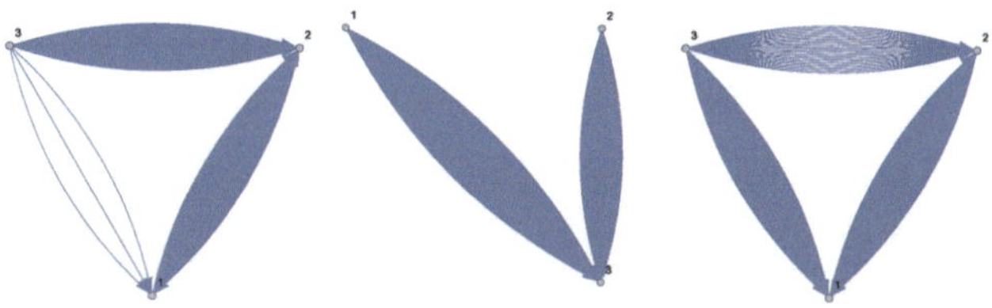

Fig. 11.17 Kirchhoff diagrams of the smallest international economy after deregulation

11.3.4.2 The Transition of the Kirchhoff Diagram Before and After Deregulation

In turn, we depict the change of the network structure by Kirchhoff diagram, as we already illustrated. This directed diagram can demonstrate the importance of the inter-industrial relationship explicitly. The thickness of the directed arrow represents the weight of input inwards the targeted nodes (industries). In our numerical example of 3 countries case, it follows the next transition of network structure (Figs. 11.16 and 11.17).

11.4 Concluding Remarks

The economy essentially is sustained periodically through mediating industries (intermediate commodities), which is preparing for the next year's growth. In this process, on the other hand, the international trade must play a decisive role to *re-connect* the inter-industrial activities. The networked production and the international trade are then the cooperative factors for the growing/decaying process of the national/regional economy. In this point of view, Ikeda (2016) seems smartly navigating an empirically based analysis of the worldwide economy by employing the world input-output data and the international trade data. In Ikeda (2016), the fundamental set of the analysis for this purpose is neatly well defined in view of econophysics. The community structure of the system is interestingly driven according to the idea of the modularity benefit function, for instance. An undirected multiplex network may then be employed in order to detect the community structure in a time-dependent network.

In order to deal with the dynamics of the world economy and to explore the structural controllability of the world system, it is also pointed out by Ikeda (2016) that the idea of "driver nodes" (partially and globally) is "identified by the maximum matching in the bipartite representation of the network" due to Newman (2006). Here an integer linear programming is applied.

It is quite interesting to learn the driven propositions in this paper. Although there are many interesting findings, among them, the next two findings of Ikeda (2016) are very interesting:

1. "[T]he increase of the number of driver nodes during economic crisis is explained qualitatively by the heterogeneity in terms of degree distribution."
2. These community structure means that international trade is actively transacted among same or similar industry sectors.

In view of the proposition (2), the traditional international trade doctrine should be reconsidered. In fact, the free trade will not give rise some industrial specialization between countries. A new approach seems much more excellent in examining the effects of the international trade. But Ikeda (2016) does not necessarily fetch the true interaction of inter-country interaction through the import and export. Because the idea of relative prices and distributive factors like wage rate are not explicitly argued similarly as in econophysics analysis. In particular, the wage rate must play a decisive role for the international trade. If the wage rate comparison should be explicitly taken into account, the perspective of their paper could be much improved.We wished to show their point of view here.

The effect of the international trade is decisively different from a merger of any independent units. But an analysis of the world production system requires a more complicated idea of production system. A possibility set of production composed of two countries may be generated as a *zonotope* of two facet of country's production. The sphere the activity analysis targets is merely a part of the zonotope set. Thus, according to Shiozawa (2016), we employ a new *tropical* geometry and were successful to introduce a hyperplane of wage-price coordinates, and argued a price competition in a general case of the international trade of multiple intermediate commodities between multiple countries. Hence Shiozawa was successful to demonstrate properly that any idea of industry specialization in country is irrelevant to confirm any cost advantage of the international trade. The cost advantage holds without any idea of optimization. We however examined the effects to introduce the framework of free trade, i.e., *deregulation* each country. According to a network analysis, the introduction of free trade suggests a drastic change of *industrial networks* each country. The result may be disastrous for employment of some country.

Exercises

11.1 In the numerical examples of Sect. 11.1.1, there are no primary factor of production like labor or land. Add the labour input to each country to create the so-called Ricardian comparative cost of production model.

11.2 In a two-commodity, two-country trade proposition in which commodity production is fully specialised within each country to only those commodities whose production is relatively superior, investigate whether different conclusions are reached when relative advantage is measured in terms of linear production technology or in terms of marginal productive forces.

11.3 Create an instance that integrates the views by commodity-wise and the view by country-wise, referring to Table 11.4.

11.4 As stated above, the wage rate must play a decisive role for the international trade. However, cite any historical examples of production of the same good where, if wages are relatively low, you cannot gain an advantage over your competitors. If not, cite a case where a relative advantage was lost due to wage increases.

11.5 As noted in the text above, (1, 2, 1) means commodity 1 has the lowest cost in country 1, commodity 2 has the lowest cost in country 2, and so on. Change the selection of cost advantage allocation represented in Table 11.4 to any other allocation between countries and commodities. Then make out the figure of Cost advantages in the country-wise notation by referring to Fig. 11.4.

11.6 Using the same case as you adopted in the previous exercise, make out the triangle corresponding to the different types of cost advantages by referring to Fig. 11.5.

11.7 Give any relationship on the comparative cost advantage based on the wage difference among three countries, and then try to create the figure by referring to Fig. 11.6.

11.8 We already learnt the random matrix theory and its application in Chapter 6. Look at Fig. 11.11, and then review how the industrial configuration given by this figure has been constructed in view of the random matrix theory.

11.9 Make another commodity matrix of 2 countries by 2 industries case other than the matrices represented by Tables 11.9 and 11.10, and then calculate the shadow prices including the wage rate of their productionsystems.

11.10 In this chapter, "before deregulation" is defined a state which cannot move entirely to the free trade for some reason. Thus the world production system "after deregulation" is calculated by applying the dual linear programming to the original system. In the result, we then learnt that, starting with the national economies of the three countries importing and exporting, each national economy that its total production cost is minimizedin terms of world production have to be transformed significantly, compared with the original economies. Examine the implications of the consequences of the free trades in the case of international trade policy.

References

Aruka, Y., & Kirman, A. (Eds.). (2017). *Economic foundations for social complexity science: Theory, sentiments, and empirical laws*. Springer.

Brechtefeld, F. (2012). Efficient total production through specialization. wolfram demonstrations project.

Director-General for Policy Planning (Statistical Standards). (2011). *Input-output tables for Japan* (p. 2016). Ministry of Internal Affairs and Communications Japan: In Input-Output Tables for Japan.

Fujimoto, T. (2007). Architecture-based comparative advantage—A design information view of manufacturing. *Evolutionary and Institutional Economics Review, 4*(1), 55–112.

Fujimoto, T., & Shiozawa, Y. (2012). Inter and intra company competition in the age of global competition: A micro and macro interpretation of Ricardian trade theory. *Evolutionary and Institutional Economics Review, 8*(2), 193–231.

Ikeda, Y., et al. (2016). Econophysics point of view of trade liberalization: Community dynamics, synchronization, and controllability as example of collective motions. *RIETI Discussion Paper Series, 16*(E26), 1–35.

Jones, R. W. (1961). Comparative advantage and the theory of tariffs: A multi-country. *Multi-commodity Model. Review of Economic Studies, 28*, 161–175.

Maurer, S. B. (1976). Matrix generalizations of some theorems on trees, cycles and cocycles in graphs. *SIAM Journal on Applied Mathematics, 30*(1), 143–148.

Nettleton, S. J. (2011). Computable general equilibrium (CGE) of multiregion input-output model. Wolfram Demonstrations Project.

Newman, M. E. J. (2006). Finding community structure in networks using the eigenvectors of matrices. *Physical Review E, 74*(036104).

Raa, T. (2006). *The economics of input-output analysis*. UK: Cambridge UP.

Shiozawa Y. (2016). Some new topics in international trade theory. *mimeo: Hausdorff School of Economics and Tropical Geometry*.

Shiozawa, Y., Oka, T., Tabuchi, T. (Eds.). (2017). *A new construction of Ricardian theory of international values: Analytical and historical approach*. Springer Nature.

Shiozawa, Y. (2007). A new construction of Ricardian trade theory a many-country, many commodity case with intermediate goods and choice of production techniques. *Evolutionary and Institutional Economics Review, 3*(2), 141–187.

Wikipedia. Kirchhoff's theorems. https://en.wikipedia.org/wiki/Kirchhoff%27s_theorem

Wolfram Language and System Documentation Center. (2015). Kirchhoff Matrix. Wolfram Language and System Documentation Center.

Part IV

Elementary Stochastic Methods for Economics

Elementary Tools for Stochasitc Analysis

12

Abstract

Lambert Adolf Jacob Quételet (1796–1874), the astronomer, first attempted to ground statistical sociology with the 'average man' (l' homme moyen). He then exhibits an interesting question about the difference between criminals and ordinary people. Even if the probability distribution of crime occurrence is Gaussian, different theoretical backgrounds arise depending on whether crime is regarded as acquired or innate. If it is considered acquired, there will be a uniform population with a certain probability of becoming a criminal, whereas if all criminals are congenital, there is a probability of being born a criminal. Quételet is also currently well known by the body mass index (BMI) scale, originally called the Quetelet Index. The obesity index is also attributed to him. He proposed that society be modeled using mathematical probability and social statistics, which brought the 'enthusiasm for normal distributions' of natural and social scientists in the 19th century. Indeed, from the discoveries of Bernoulli and de Moivre, it came to be thought that large amounts of data on completely chance events could be used to argue for nonchance regularities. Moreover, the large amounts of data that came to be accumulated with the industrial revolution were also thought to apply to population, industry and society. This was the birth moment of social statistics. It came to be thought that distribution laws such as the Gaussian normal curve could be recognised everywhere. In other words, if we can consider 'normal size', we can also talk about 'normal distribution'. Clearly, everyone has the freedom to be or not to be a criminal. However, the probability may be already determined at birth. In this circumstance, unlimited freedom and responsibility could not be guranteed. From the dawn of the Enlightenment, the ideals of freedom and probabilistic design have not always been compatible. The enthusiasm of probability distribution, on the contrary, was rather irrelevant to ethics. As time evolved since the enthusiasim due to Quételet, various problems were addressed, such as 'the existence of dependence or interaction between individual data, or the occurrence of unusually large scatter and fluctuations', and the assumption of normality in asset price fluctuations, for example in economic examples, was dismissed. This

Y. Aruka, *Evolutionary Economics*, Springer Texts in Business and Economics,
https://doi.org/10.1007/978-981-97-1382-0_12

is nothing but an achievement of econophysics, but this is a very recent one. Finally, we learn the Polya urn process as a good reference mechanism to grasp the evolution of the system.

12.1 A Brief Summary of the Efficient Market Hypothesis

12.1.1 Disengagements from the Efficient Market Hypothesis

We note that the efficient market hypothesis cannot really explain the current state of financial markets, nor the global financial crisis, because it relies on the idea of the market operating by a series of random walks.

A stock price time series under the **random walk hypothesis** may be represented as:

$$P_t = P_{t-1} + \epsilon_t = P_0 + \epsilon_0 + \epsilon_1 + \cdots + \epsilon_t \tag{12.1}$$

P_t will follow a Gaussian distribution. Here ϵ is regarded as white noise. The expected price is calculated around P_0, so the expected distance from P_0 has a finite value. Each price change will be estimated from the next $\epsilon_0 + \epsilon_1 + \cdots + \epsilon_t$. Each price change will therefore be the stochastic variant of a normal distribution. This is the simplest illustration of the efficient market hypothesis.

There are several variants of this:
Auto-regressive model **AR(p)**: $y_t = a_1 y_{t-1} + \cdots + a_p y_{t-p} + \xi_t$
Moving average model **MA(p)**: $y_t = \xi_t - b_1 \xi_{t-1} - \cdots - b_p \xi_{t-p}$
Auto-regressive moving average model **ARMA(p, q)**: $y_t = a_1 y_{t-1} + \cdots + a_p y_{t-p} + \xi_t - b_1 \xi_{t-1} - \cdots - b_p \xi_{t-p}$[1]

These auto-regressive models are *linear*, and are therefore described as *linear auto-regressive models*. There are several differences between **AR** and **MR**. **The auto-correlation function** will decrease and approach zero in AR, but in MR, it will instantly be zero whenever the parameters exceed a critical point. **The partial auto-correlation function** in AR will instantly be zero whenever the parameters exceed a critical point, but will decrease and approach zero in MR. **The power spectrum** has a peak in AR, which will emerge around zero if the fluctuations are small. In MR, a valley emerges around zero if the fluctuations are larger.

We now show a simulation of $AR(2)$, i.e., a second-order auto-regressive simulation. This Wolfram Demonstration uses a random variable drawn from a normal density with mean zero and variance unity. It is governed by the equation:

$$AR(2) : y_t = a_1 y_{t-1} + a_2 y_{t-2} + \xi_t \ (i = 3, \ldots, N) \tag{12.2}$$

Here ξ_t is a random variable, N is the length of the series and the constants a are auto-regressive. If $a_1 + a_2 < 1$, $a_2 - a_1 < 1$, and $-1 < a_2 < 1$, then the series is

[1] A more sophisticated version of this is the auto-regressive integral moving average model, $ARIMA(p, q, r)$. $MA(1)$ is an approximate function of $AR(\infty)$.

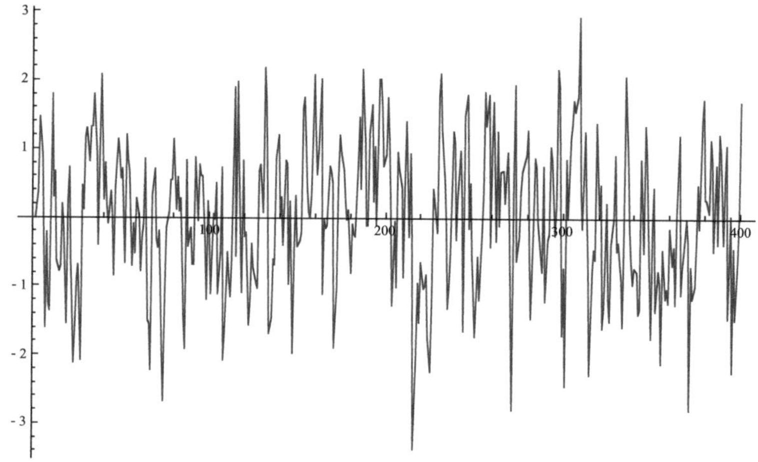

Fig. 12.1 A second-order auto-regressive model. [a]http://demonstrations.wolfram.com/AutoRegressiveSimulationSecondOrder/

stationary. A series of length 400 is created in every case in this Wolfram Demonstration (Fig. 12.1).

We then move to a more sophisticated regression, with two different regimes into and out of which the variable can move. Each regime follows a similar Gaussian/random process. We remove the trend item from the model, and make the process stationary and geometrically ergodic. In this case, however, the expected value $E(x)$ generated by the two-regime model is not necessarily zero. The regimes may then be described by the condition:

$$x_{t-1} < k \tag{12.3}$$

$$x_{t-1} \geq k \tag{12.4}$$

We therefore obtain a two-regime threshold auto-regressive (TAR) first-order process:

$$x_t = \begin{cases} \alpha_1 + \beta_1 x_{t-1} + \epsilon_t < k \\ \alpha_2 + \beta_2 x_{t-1} + \epsilon_t \geq k \end{cases} \tag{12.5}$$

We set the constants α_i as 0, and $\beta_1 = -1.5$ in the first regime, $\beta_2 = -0.5$ in the second regime. The series contains large upward jumps when it becomes negative, and there are more positive than negative jumps (Fig. 12.2).

We then denote the actual profit of security i at term t by r_{it}. It is then *assumed* that:

$$r_{it} = E(r_{it} \mid I_{t-1}) + \epsilon_{it} \tag{12.6}$$

Here I_t is the information set available everywhere at term t. r_{it} is a random error at t. It then holds that:

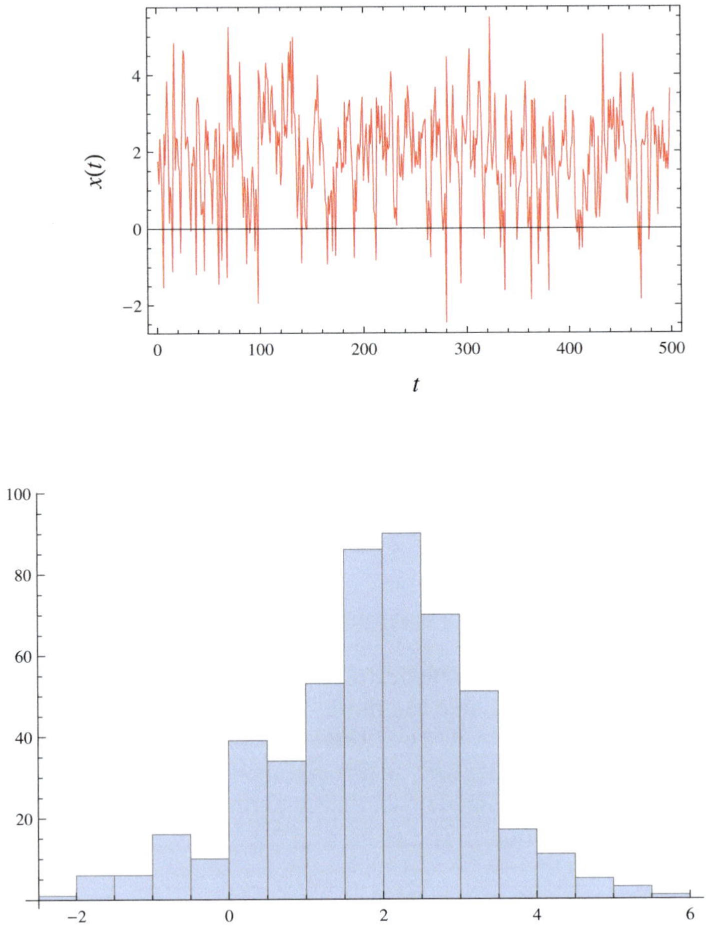

Fig. 12.2 Two-regime threshold auto-regressive model simulation: $\alpha_1 = 1, \alpha_2 = 1, k = 1$. [a] Two-regime threshold auto-regressive model simulation. http://demonstrations.wolfram.com/TwoRegimeThresholdAutoregressiveModelSimulation/

Efficient Market Hypothesis (Fama 1970).[2]

1. If the market were *efficient*, all usable information could affect market prices.

$$E\ (\epsilon_{it+s}\epsilon_{it} \mid I_{t-1}) = 0 \quad s = 1, 2, \ldots \tag{12.7}$$

$$E\ (\epsilon_{jt+k}\epsilon_{it} \mid I_{t-1}) = 0 \quad k = 0, 1, 2, \ldots \tag{12.8}$$

$$E\ (\epsilon_{jt+k}\epsilon_{jt} \mid I_{t-1}) = 0 \quad k = 0, 1, 2, \ldots \tag{12.9}$$

[2] Also see Fama (1965).

2. The efficiency of the market can measure all the responses of prices, given all the information I_t.
3. If anyone can obtain excess profit from some particular information, this market is not efficient in relation to this kind of information.

$$E(\epsilon_{it} E(r_{it} \mid I_{t-1}) = E(\epsilon_{it}) E(r_{it} \mid I_{t-1}) = 0 \tag{12.10}$$

A weak form. Using price information, technical analytical traders can earn excess profit.

A semi-strong form. Basic information gives any trader a chance to earn excess profit.

A strong form. Insider information gives any trader a chance to earn excess profit.

In summary, in the world where the hypothesis holds, errors should *not be systematically* generated. This implies that:

$$E(\epsilon_{it} \mid I_{t-1}) = 0 \tag{12.11}$$

12.1.2 Self-similarity in the Random Walk

A random walk process never excludes the emergence of self-similarity. We may therefore find a strange attraction in the efficient market hypothesis. It is clear that:

Random walk $\Rightarrow$ Fractal motion
Fractal motion $\neq$ Random walk

We now show a simulation of a random walk to generate self-similarity. This is unchanged for any scaling as well as period length (Fig. 12.3).

In the next section we verify the historical implications of the Gaussian distribution and the central limit theorem (CLT), and will then argue a generalization of the CLT. We will see that any distribution other than the Gaussian may benefit from a generalized CLT. It is also clear that the CLT would be valid even if there was no variance.

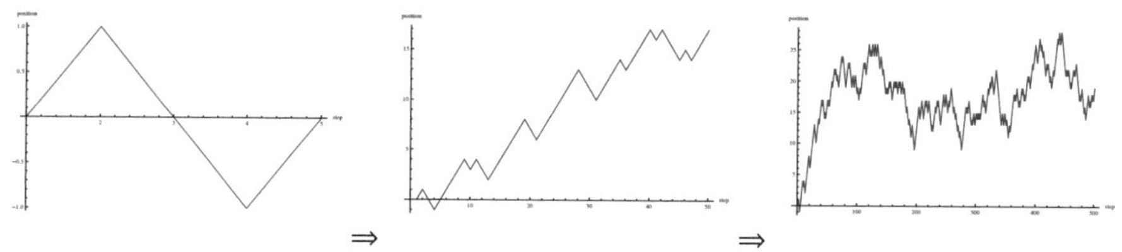

Fig. 12.3 Self-similarity in the random walk: scale = 5, 50, 500. http://demonstrations.wolfram.com/SelfSimilarityInRandomWalk/

12.2 Moving Away from the Social Philosophy Around the Gaussian Distribution

12.2.1 The Historical Penetration of the Gaussian Distribution and Galton's Ideas

Lambert Adolphe Jacques Quételet(1796–1874) is still well known as the proposer of the Quételet index or Body Mass Index. His enthusiasm penetrates various social ideas even to this day. However, advances in science are uncovering the fictitious background to Quételet's ideas.

> A key role is played by the astronomer and sociologist Lambert Adolf Jacob Quételet, who, in 1835, for the first time, challenged others to think of the 'average person' as well as statistics. Does it matter that there are large error calculations in the natural sciences or in investigations of 'normal distributions' in society? It is today hardly comprehensible that natural and social scientists of the 19th century took large numbers and normal distributions as a universal rule in nature and society (Mainzer, 2007, 48; trans. by the author).

Modern probability theory suggests that the Gaussian or normal distribution is not universal, instead taking the normal distribution as a special case **stable distribution**. This also changed the implications of the CLT. Unfortunately, many economists still hold to Galton's conviction of the dominance of the normal distribution by means of the CLT.[3]

Galton demonstrated an approximation of a binomial distribution using a nail board (see Fig. 12.4). Each time a ball hits a nail, it has a probability of bouncing either left or right. The balls accumulate in the bins at the bottom.

> A visualization of the Bernoulli distribution can be traced back to Galton. On a perpendicularly standing board, nails are set at a constant distance in n parallel rows (see Fig. 12.4). Each nail is exactly in the gap between two nails in the row above. If balls of the diameter of the distance between nails are dropped from a funnel above the board, they may fall through without being affected by friction from the nails. If a ball hits a nail, it can fall either to the right or to the left. This procedure repeats itself in each row. The ball therefore falls in a random way on the nail board, being diverted to the right or left with equal probability. After going through the n rows, the balls land in the $n+1$-th box. A ball would fall into box i if it were diverted i times to the right and $(n-i)$ times to the left. This process leads to a Bernoulli distribution of the balls. (Mainzer, 2007, 49; trans. by the author)

It is interesting to use simulation to verify and compare the frictionless and frictional cases. Even in the physical world, using an experimental method, we cannot

[3] The British physician and natural scientist Francis Galton (1822–1911), who first tried to measure intelligence, stressed the law of the large number: "I hardly know anything other than this whose imagination is influenced in such a way like the marvelous form of cosmic order, which is expressed by the law of the error frequency. It prevails with bright serenity, and complete self-denial in the middle of the wildest confusion. The greater the rabble, the greater the obvious anarchy. Its influence is surely the highest law of senselessness".

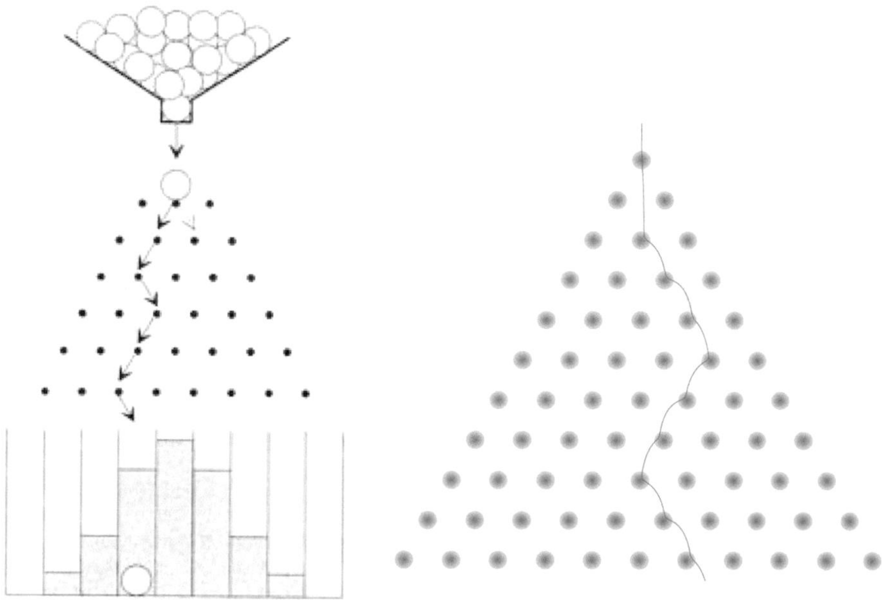

Fig. 12.4 Flexible Galton Board to generate a binomial distribution: $p = 0.5$, bin number= 10. [b] In this figure in Mainzer (2007, 50). [a] http://demonstrations.wolfram.com/FlexibleGaltonBoard/

Fig. 12.5 A Galton board with frictionless and frictional cases. The details of parameters in this simulation are: [a] Earth acceleration 2; friction coefficient 0; initial position 0; initial velocity 0; initial angle $\pi/2$; [b] Earth acceleration 2; friction coefficient 2;initial position 0; initial velocity 0.5; initial angle $\pi/2$; *c* Nail parameters for both figures: thickness 0.2; strength 0.1; surface softness 2 http://demonstrations.wolfram.com/GaltonBoard/

reproduce an ideal state, and so it is hard to justify a world of normal distributions (Fig. 12.5).

Galton's belief therefore does not hold, as the CLT states. The CLT can be generalized to random variables without second (and possibly first) order moments and the accompanying self-similarity of the stable family. Even if the first moment is infinite, we can find an existing stable distribution, such as the power law distribution. A new definition of stable distributions thus contains the normal distribution as a special case. These findings were largely responsible for the focus on Gaussian distributions. The role of non-Gaussian distributions was first noted by Benoît Mandelbrot, who proposed that cotton prices followed **an alpha-stable distribution** with α equal to 1.7, a Lévy distribution.[4]

12.2.1.1 Generalized Central Limit Theorem (GCLT)

It has often been argued recently that the "tail" behavior of sums of random variables determine the domain of attraction for a distribution. The classical CLT is merely the case of finite variance, where the tails lie in the domain of attraction of a normal distribution. Now, however, interest has moved to infinite variance models, bringing a new generalized CLT. This describes distributions lying in the domain of attraction of a stable distribution, or:

> A sum of independent random variables from the same distribution, when properly centered and scaled, belongs to the domain of attraction of a stable distribution. Further, the only distributions that arise as limits from suitably scaled and centered sums of random variables are stable distributions.[5]

We now consider the generalization of the CLT. This explanation draws heavily on John D. Cook's note "Central Limit Theorems".[6]

The propagation of the idea of a Gaussian distribution was inseparable from the powerful role of the CLT. More interestingly, however, it has recently transpired that the theorem was applicable to non-identically distributed random variables, meaning that distributions other than Gaussian are possible in the context of the CLT. Under the , distributions other than Gaussian will be guaranteed a similar powerful role.

The classical CLT requires variables with three conditions: independence, identical distribution and finite variance. Let X_n be a sequence of independent, identically distributed (IID) random variables. It is assumed that X has finite mean $\mu = E(x)$ and finite variance $var(X) = \sigma^2$. We then observe its normalized average as:

$$Z_n = \frac{X_1 + X_2 + \cdots + X_n - n\mu}{\sigma\sqrt{n}} \tag{12.12}$$

The CLT then states that Z_n converges point-wise to the cumulative distribution function (CDF) of a standard normal (Gaussian) random variable.[7]

---

[4] See Mandelbrot (1963). Lévy distributions are also found in nature, e.g., in spectroscopy, with many cases seen in solar flare data. See Lévy (1925).
[5] http://demonstrations.wolfram.com/GeneralizedCentralLimitTheorem/.
[6] See Cook (2010).
[7] See Appendix in Aruka (2015): "An elementary derivation of the one-dimensional central limit theorem from the random walk".

The CLT is not necessarily limited to identically distributed random variables with finite variance. There are, therefore, two different types of generalized CLT, for non-identically distributed random variables and for random variables with infinite variance.

We now discuss a generalized theorem for non-identically distributed random variables. We assume that X_n is a sequence of independent random variables, at least one of which has a non-degenerate distribution. We then define the partial sum and its variance:

$$\text{the partial sum } S_n = X_1 + X_2 + \cdots + X_n \tag{12.13}$$

$$\text{finite variance } s_n^2 = \sigma_1^2 + \sigma_2^2 + \cdots + \sigma_n^2 \tag{12.14}$$

We use the **Lindeberg-Feller theorem** to check the convergence of $\frac{S_n}{s_n}$ using the Lindeberg condition for the CLT for non-identically distributed random variables. The Lindeberg condition is both necessary and sufficient for convergence. Let F_N be the CDF of X_n, i.e., $F_n(x) = P(X_n < x)$. The Lindeberg condition is:

$$\lim_{n\to\infty} \sigma_n^2 \int_{x>\epsilon s_j} x^2 dF_j(x) = 0 \text{ for all} \epsilon > 0. \tag{12.15}$$

The Lindeberg-Feller theorem therefore holds and:

Sufficiency İf the Lindeberg condition holds, $\frac{S_n}{s_n}$ converges to the distribution of a standard normal random variable.

Necessity İf $\frac{S_n}{s_n}$ converges to the distribution of a standard normal random variable, then the Lindeberg condition holds.

We now remove the assumption of finite variance while keeping that of independence, i.e., X_0, X_1, X_2 following IID:

Definition 12.1 The distribution of random variables is called **stable** if there is a positive c and a real d such that $cX_0 + d$ has the same distribution as $aX_1 + bX_2$.

In stable distributions, the shape is characterized by four parameters. The exponent parameter α is probably best known. The parameter will work in the range of $0 \le \alpha \le 2$. If $\alpha = 2$, it follows a Gaussian distribution. For $\alpha < 2$, then:

The Probability Density Function (PDF) for $\alpha < 2$	is asymptotically proportional to $\|x\|^{-\alpha-1}$.
The CDF for $\alpha < 2$	is asymptotically proportional to $\|x\|^{-\alpha}$ as $x \to \pm\infty$.

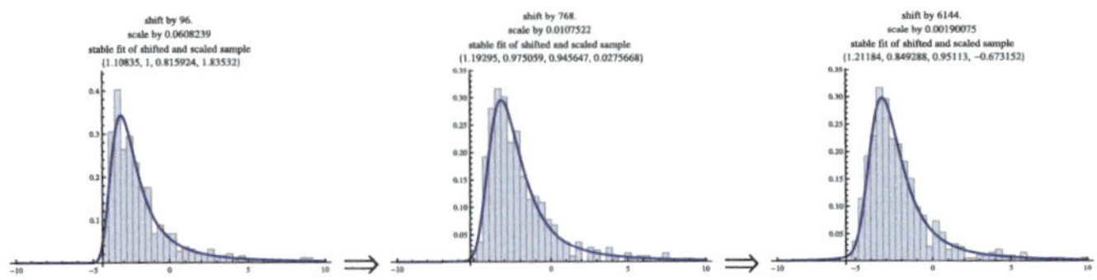

Fig. 12.6 A generalized CLT of the Pareto distribution: $\alpha = 1.2$, number of sums = 16, 128, 1024. http://demonstrations.wolfram.com/GeneralizedCentralLimitTheorem/

All stable distributions other than the normal will therefore have thick tails and non-finite variance. In general, density functions for stable distributions are not possible in closed form, although there are three exceptions: normal, Cauchy, and Lévy distributions.

We can check the convergence of the *aggregation* of random variables X_i for $\alpha < 2$. Let $F(x)$ be the CDF for X, and the slowly varying function $h(x)$ so that:

$$\frac{h(cx)}{h(x)} \to 1, \text{as}\, x \to \infty \text{ for all}\, c. \tag{12.16}$$

The necessary and sufficient conditions on $F(x)$ may therefore be:

$$F(x) = (c_1 + o(1))|x|^{-\alpha} h(x) \text{as}\, x \to -\infty^8 \tag{12.17}$$

$$1 - F(x) = (c_2 + o(1))x^{-\alpha} h(x) \text{as}\, x \to \infty \tag{12.18}$$

$F(x)$ will therefore look something like $|x|^{\alpha}$ in both the left and right tails.[8] The aggregate random variables will be similar to the limiting distribution, giving a generalized CLT for infinite variance.

Figure 12.6 shows a simulation of the generalized CLT on the Pareto distribution[9]:

$$\text{Pareto distribution}[k, \alpha] = \left(\frac{x}{k}\right)^{-\alpha}, x \geq k \tag{12.19}$$

12.3 Heavy Tail Distributions with Heavier Randomness

We have already seen a self-similarity emerging in the random walk. We now turn to heavy tail distributions.[10] The term **heavy tail** means that there is a higher probability of getting very large values. This contradicts the popular image of the normal distribution with a slender tail, reflecting the considerably wider range of possible fluctuations seen in price volatility and financial returns.

[8] $o(1)$ represents a function tending to 0.

[9] http://mathworld.wolfram.com/ParetoDistribution.html.

[10] See Nolan (2005, 2020).

Fig. 12.7 Lévy distribution: $\sigma = 0.5, 1, 2$

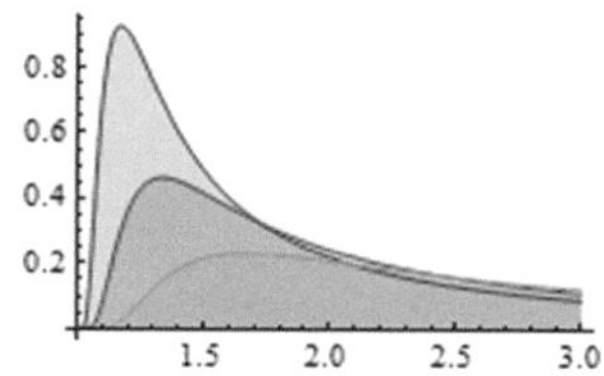

Many econophysicists investigated a particular subclass of heavy tail distributions as **power-laws**, where the PDF is a power.[11] Such a distribution does not usually have finite variance, i.e., not all moments exist for these distributions. This will give rise to some technical difficulties, because of the characteristic functions for stable distributions.[12] A stable distribution is defined in terms of its characteristic function $\phi(t)$, which satisfies a functional equation where for any a and b there are c and h such that $\phi(at)\phi(bt) = \phi(ct)\exp(\mathrm{i}ht)$. The general solution to the functional equation has four parameters. Stable distributions allow $0 < \alpha \le 2, -1 \le \beta \le 1, where \mu$ is any real number, and σ any positive real number. A characteristic function of stable distributions is a continuous α:

$$\exp\left(\mathrm{i}\mu t - \sigma \mid t \mid \left(1 + 2\mathrm{i}\frac{\beta}{\pi}\operatorname{sgn}(t)\log(\mid t\sigma \mid)\right)\right) \quad \text{for } \alpha = 1$$

$$\exp\left(\mathrm{i}\mu t - \mid t\sigma \mid^{\alpha}\left(1 + \mathrm{i}\beta\tan\left(\frac{\pi\alpha}{2}\right)\operatorname{sgn}(t)(\mid t\sigma \mid^{1-\alpha} - 1)\right)\right) \quad \text{for } \alpha \ne 1$$

This can be written in closed form in terms of the four parameters mentioned above.[13] In general, however, the density functions for stable distributions cannot be written in closed form. There are three exceptions: normal, Cauchy, and Lévy distributions (Fig. 12.7).

The probability density for value x in a **Lévy distribution** is proportional to:

$$\frac{e^{-\sigma/(2(x-\mu))}}{(x-\mu)^{3/2}} \tag{12.20}$$

Here the Lévy distribution allows μ to be any real number and σ to be any positive real number. A Lévy distribution with $\mu = 0, \sigma = 0.5$ is a special case of **the inverse gamma distribution** with $\alpha = 0.5, \beta = 0.5\sigma$.

---

[11] The power law differs from the power distribution The probability density for values in a power distribution is proportional to x^{a-1} for $0 < x \le 1/k$ and zero otherwise.

[12] A linear combination of independent identically distributed stable random variables is also stable.

[13] As already noted, the generalized CLT still holds.

12.3.1 Hazard Rates

We focus on the lifetime of a person over the random variable x with probability density function $f(x)$. The probability of surviving at least up to time x is:

$$R(x) = \int_{x}^{\infty} f(x)dx = 1 - F(x) \tag{12.21}$$

dx is a small interval of time, so the probability of death in time interval dx is $f(x)$, the probability density function. Thus the instantaneous death rate at age x, i.e., **the force of mortality**, is defined as:

$$r(x) = \frac{f(x)}{1 - F(x)}. \tag{12.22}$$

If this ratio $r(x)$ is applied to the failure rate in manufacturing processes, it is called **the hazard rate**. It is clear that the distribution is possible whether the ratio rises or decreases with x; that is, whether it has increasing failure rate (IFR) or decreasing failure rate (DFR).[14] The lognormal distribution becomes a DFR only beyond a point, while the Pareto distribution is a DFR throughout its range.

The probability density for value x in a Pareto distribution is proportional to $x^{-\alpha-1}$ for $x > k$, and zero for $x < k$. **The survival function** for value x in a Pareto distribution corresponds to:

$$\begin{aligned}
\text{Pareto distribution} &= \left(\frac{x}{k}\right)^{-\alpha} \quad \text{for } x \geq k \\
\text{Pareto distribution} &= \left(1 + \frac{x-\mu}{k}\right)^{-\alpha} \quad \text{for } x \geq \mu \\
\text{Pareto Distribution} &= \left(1 + \left(\frac{x-\mu}{k}\right)^{1/\gamma}\right)^{-\alpha} \quad \text{for } x \geq k
\end{aligned} \tag{12.23}$$

In the first form of the Pareto distribution $[k, \alpha]$, the mean is (Fig. 12.8):

$$\frac{k\alpha}{-1+\alpha} \text{ for } \alpha \geq 1 \tag{12.24}$$

and the variance is:

$$\frac{k^2\alpha}{(-2+\alpha)(-1+\alpha)^2} \text{ for } \alpha \geq 2 \tag{12.25}$$

[14] DFR indicates that the ability to make more money might increase with one's income (Singh & Maddala, 2008, 28).

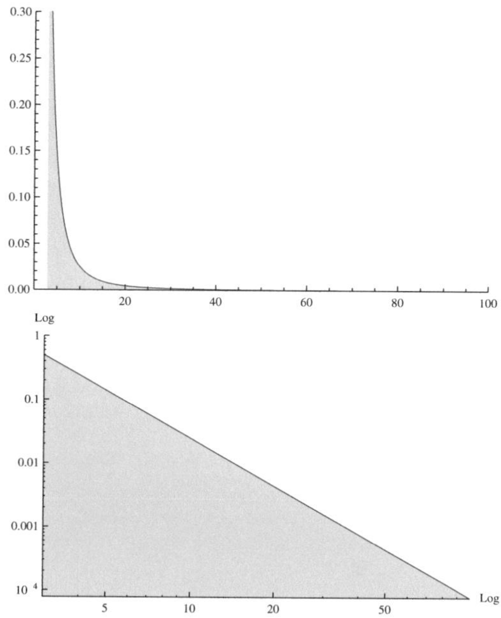

Fig. 12.8 Pareto distribution: $\alpha = 3, k = 1.5$

We now derive the Pareto distribution following Singh and Maddala (2008). It is convenient to transform x into $z = \log x$. We then find the hazard rate with respect to $\log x$:

$$r^*(z) = \frac{\frac{dF}{dz}}{1 - F} \tag{12.26}$$

Taking the negative form of the Pareto transformation, let y, z be:

$$y = -\log(1 - F)$$
$$z = \log x$$
$$y = f(z);\ y' > 0,\ y'' > 0$$

By the log transformation of x, y' is interpreted as **the proportional failure** (Fig. 12.9).

If we then suppose:

$$y'' = ay'(\alpha - y')\ i.e., \tag{12.27}$$

$$\frac{y''}{y'} = a\alpha - ay' \tag{12.28}$$

a is constant. The formula then implies that the rate of change of y' (the acceleration rate) depends on itself, and acceleration should move in a negative direction.

To solve this differential equation, we make three assumptions about $r^*(z)$:

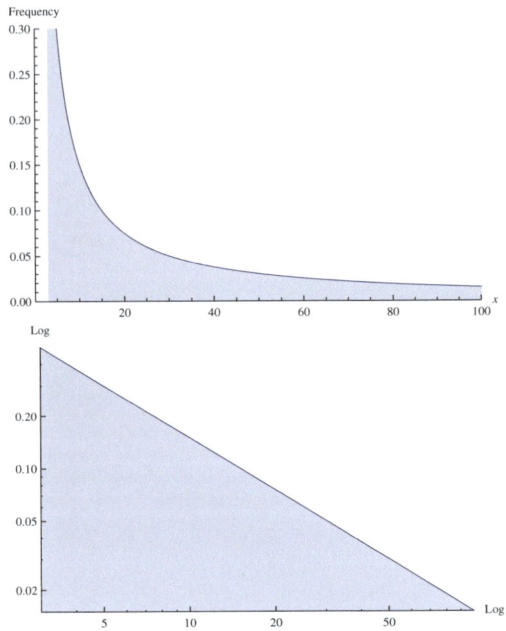

Fig. 12.9 Hazard distribution of a Pareto distribution: $\alpha = 3, k = 1.5$

Assumption 1 : $r^*(z)$ approaches a constant value asymptotically.
Assumption 2 : $r^*(z)$ increases with accelerating rate, then with decreasing rate.
Assumption 3 : $\frac{r^*(z)}{dz}$ tends to zero as $r^*(z) \to 0$.

Taking account of $ay' = y''/(\alpha - y')$, Eq. (12.27) may be rearranged into:

$$\frac{y''}{y'} + \frac{y''}{\alpha - y'} = a\alpha \tag{12.29}$$

The integration of both sides will give:

$$\log y' - \log(\alpha - y') = a\alpha z + c_1 \tag{12.30}$$

c_1 is an integral constant. The solution y' or **the proportional failure** is:

$$Y' = \frac{\alpha e^{a\alpha z + c_1}}{1 + e^{a\alpha z + c_1}} \tag{12.31}$$

We can then easily derive:

$$\log y = \frac{1}{a} \log(1 + e^{a\alpha z + c_1}) + c_2 \tag{12.32}$$

c_2 is another integral constant.

We have then arranged to derive the distribution function. We note that:

$$y = -\log(1 - F)$$
$$z = \log x$$

We also note that:

$$c = \frac{c_2 - c_1}{\alpha}$$
$$b = \frac{1}{e^{c_1}}$$

The distribution function F is therefore described[15]:

$$F = 1 - \frac{b^{1/a}}{(b + x^{a\alpha})^{1/a}} \tag{12.33}$$

12.3.2 An Alternative Derivation in View of Memoryless Processes

The Pareto process depends only on remaining one-sided, so $\frac{dF}{dx}$ depends on $1 - F$ only. Singh and Maddala (2008, 31) called such a process *memoryless*:

$$\frac{dF}{dx} = a(1 - F)^{1+1/a}. \tag{12.34}$$

The most typical memoryless process may be **the Poisson process**:

$$\frac{dF}{dx} = a(1 - F). \tag{12.35}$$

The Weibull process is one into which *memory* is introduced:

$$\frac{dF}{dx} = ax^b(1 - F). \tag{12.36}$$

The motion of x affects its behavior. In general, in an integrated view of memoryless and memory processes, a more general formulation expression is:

$$\frac{dF}{dx} = ax^b(1 - F)^c. \tag{12.37}$$

Specifically, the values of a, b, c will be verified by a concrete form of the process generating a distribution.

[15] c is eliminated. If $x = 0$, $F(0) = 0$. It follows that $c = b^{1/a}$.

Now we allocate further:

$$a_1 = \frac{1}{b}, a_2 = a\alpha, a_3 = \frac{1}{a}$$

It then follows that:

$$\frac{dF}{dx} = \frac{a_1 a_2 x^{a_2 - 1}}{(1 + a_1 x^{a_2})^2} \tag{12.38}$$

Here $a_1 = \left(\frac{1}{x_0}\right)^{\alpha}$ and $a_2 = \alpha$.

The distribution Eq. (12.38) is then rewritten into[16,17]:

$$F = 1 - \frac{1}{(1 + a_1 x^{a_2})^{a_3}} \tag{12.39}$$

12.3.3 Some Empirical Findings in the Market

Empirical findings on the Pareto-Lévy distribution were first confirmed by Manderbrot (1963), who examined (*a*) the New York Cotton Exchange, 1900–1905, (*b*) an index of daily closing prices of cotton on various exchanges in the US, 1944–1958 (published by Hendrik S. Houthakker), and (*c*) the closing price on the 15th of each month at the New York Cotton Exchange, 1880–1940 (published by the US Department of Agriculture). The unit of time t in the time series is different for each. Mandelbrot (2001, Fig. 12.4) shows all three cases (*a*)–(*c*) with positive and negative axes, where all cases are strictly downward sloping. Notice that the variables representing the change rates in terms of logarithm are taken as differently as follows:

$$\begin{aligned} &(a)\ X = \log Z(t+1) - \log Z(t) \text{ is } \textit{daily} \text{ unit based.} \\ &(b)\ X = \log Z(t+1) - \log Z(t) \text{ is } \textit{daily} \text{ unit based.} \\ &(c)\ X = \log Z(t+1) - \log Z(t) \text{ is } \textit{monthly} \text{ unit based.} \end{aligned} \tag{12.40}$$

It may also be helpful to reproduce the scheme of random process classes given by Mantegna and Stanley (2001), Swell (2011) (Fig. 12.10).

Swell (2011, 4) said: "Price-influencing events may be normally distributed, but the likelihood of said events being reported in the news increases with the magnitude of the impact of the event. For the latter distribution, one can factor in the tendency for the media to simplify and exaggerate. Multiply the normal distribution by the distribution according to the likelihood/duration/impact of news reports and one has a much fatter-tailed distribution than a Gaussian."

---

[16] It is clear that $F \to 1$ as $x \to \infty$.

[17] See Champernowne (1953) and Fisk (1961).

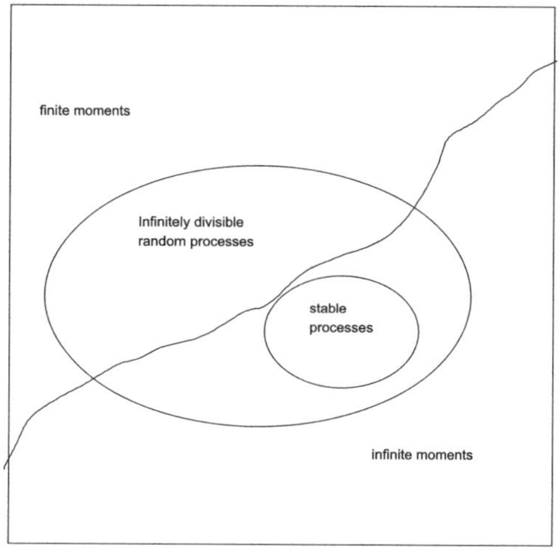

Fig. 12.10 Illustration scheme of classes of random processes. [a] The solid circle denotes the stable Gaussian process. This figure was cited from Swell (2011, Fig. 12.3), though the original figure was replaced with a new one fabricated by the author

The PDF of returns for the Shanghai market data with $\Delta t = 1$ is compared with a stable symmetric Lévy distribution using the value $\alpha = 1.44$ determined from the slope in a log-log plot of the central peak of the PDF as a function of the time increment. The agreement is very good over the main central portion, with deviations for large z. Two attempts to fit a Gaussian are also shown. The wider Gaussian is chosen to have the same standard deviation as the empirical data. However, the peak in the data is much narrower and higher than this Gaussian, and the tails are fatter. The narrower Gaussian is chosen to fit the central portion, but the standard deviation is now too small. It can be seen that the data have tails that are much fatter and have a non-Gaussian functional dependence (Johnson et al., 2003; Swell, 2011) (Figs. 12.11, 12.12 and 12.13).

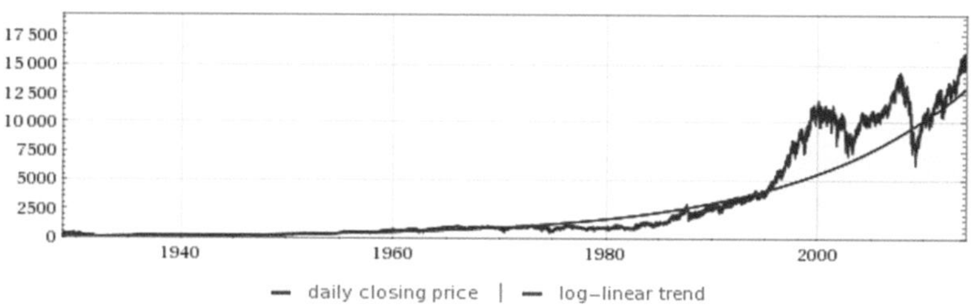

minimum	average	maximum
41.22	2898.8	16 097
(Friday, Jul 8, 1932)		(Wednesday, Nov 27, 2013)

Fig. 12.11 All data from the Dow Jones Index. *Source* Wolfram Alpha. http://www.wolframalpha.com/input/?i=dow+jones

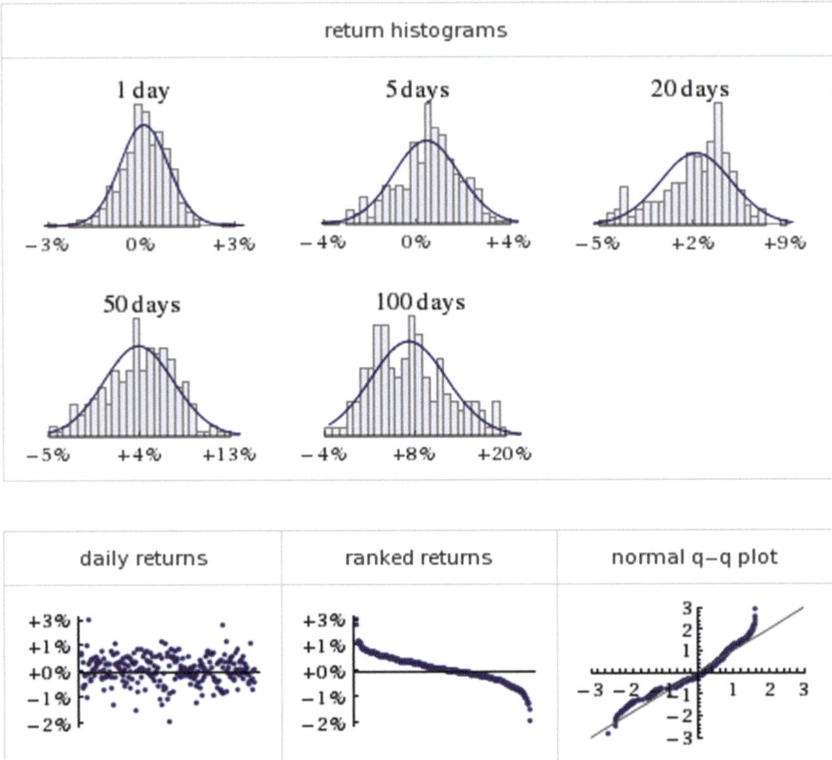

Fig. 12.12 Last year's distributions of the Dow Jones Index on Dec 14, 2013. *Source* Wolfram Alpha. http://www.wolframalpha.com/input/?i=dow+jones

12.4 A Complex Network in Terms of a Polya Urn Process and a Non-growing Network

Complex network analysis cannot explain circumstances with deep logic and information. However, it can be used to show that a monetary exchange system can generate a feedback system.

Recent developments of network analysis since Barabási and Albert (1999) have tended to focus on how a network could generate a scale-free property. As complex network analysis showed, a huge network system is vulnerable to collapse following strategic aggression. This kind of vulnerability is closely connected to the scale-free property. We therefore examine a preferential attachment to a random network to see whether the network evolves as a scale-free system. Reciprocity is one of the important features of networking, and may be dominated by a type choice of preferential attachment. This analysis suggests management of complex networks is possible. More importantly, it is essentially equivalent to a Polya urn process, which may also generate the increasing returns or winner-takes-almost-all process of a modern production system (Table 12.1).

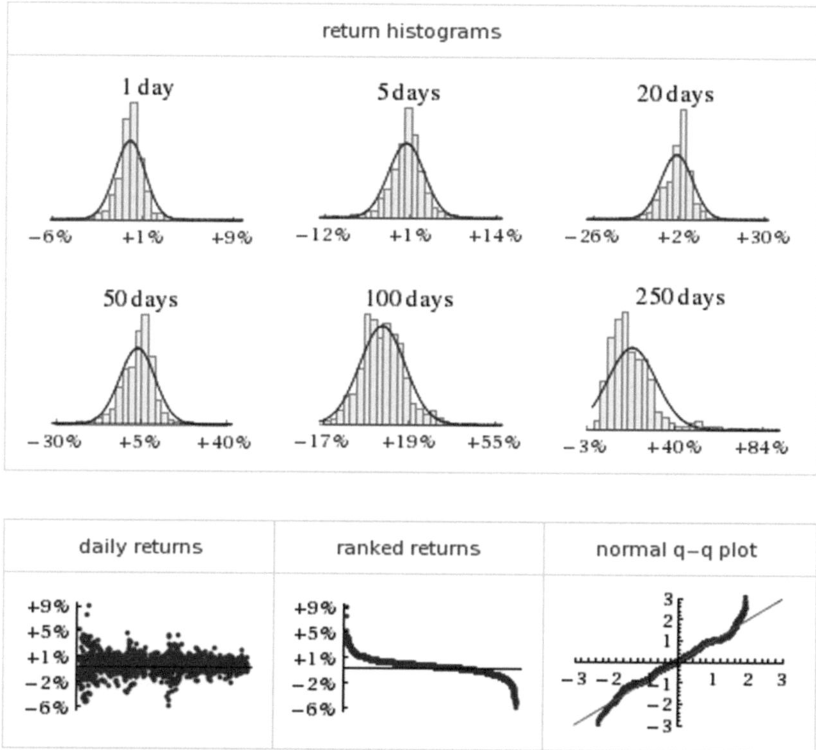

Fig. 12.13 The last 5 years' distributions of the Dow Jones Index on Dec 14, 2013. *Source* Wolfram Alpha. http://www.wolframalpha.com/input/?i=dow+jones

Table 12.1 Barabási rule

Step 0	There is a perfect graph with m nodes Km in an initially random network
Step 1	Add a new node to span a new link to one of the existing nodes with a probability $\pi(k_i) = \frac{k_i}{\sum_i ik_i}$
Step 2.	Iterate Step 1 until a specified number is reached

[a] Barabási and Albert (1999)

A monetary network may be regarded as a random exchange system. Customers, however, often like a preferential attachment. Suppose that a network never grows but reconnects mutually. Ohkubo et al. (2005, 2006) proposed a new rule for this *non-growing*network and also proved that the rule was equivalent to a Polya urn process. We presume a fitness parameter distribution $\phi(\beta) = \{\beta_i\}$ as time independent that is capable of creating a different possibility for network formation. The rule will be (Tables 12.2 and 12.3).

Table 12.2 Ohkubo rule

Step 0	A random network of N nodes and M edges is initially given
Step 1	An edge l_{ij} is randomly specified
Step 2	Replace the edge l_{ij} with an edge l_{im} whose node m is chosen randomly with a probability

[a] Ohkubo et al. (2005, 2006)
[b] Here k_m is the degree of node m, and β_m a fitness parameter of node m

Table 12.3 A polya urn rule

Step 0	Initially, there is a partition of N urns (boxes) and M balls
Step 1	Randomly draw ball n_{ij} from any box i
Step 2	Replace it in a selected urn with a transition rate $W_{n_i} \to W_{n_{i+1}} = (n_{n_i} + 1)_i^{\beta}$

[a] Ohkubo et al. (2005, 2006)

12.4.1 The 'Rich-Get-Richer' Process

Now we can show *the rich-get-richer* phenomenon on k under **the Barabási rule**. The average (mean) is written as:

$$< k >= 2mt. \tag{12.41}$$

The probability that the node added at the $s-$th step becomes degree k is $p(k, s, t)$ and the probability that the node of degree k increases its own degree is $\frac{k}{2t}$. We then have the equation:

$$p(k, s+1) = \frac{k-1}{2t} p(k-1, s, t) + \left(1 - \frac{k}{2t}\right) p(k, s, t), \tag{12.42}$$

which gives the solution:

$$P(k) = \frac{2m(m+1)}{k(k+1)(k+2)}. \tag{12.43}$$

If k is a large number, it leads to **the power law**:

$$P(k) \propto k^{-3}. \tag{12.44}$$

Table 12.4 shows the ways in which the preferential random network and Polya urn process are directly comparable or equivalent.

Table 12.4 Equivalence of the preferential random network and the Polya urn process

	Network reconnection	Polya urn process
Step 0	N nodes and M edges	N urns and M balls
Step 1	Randomly choose an edge l_{ij}.	Randomly draw a ball n_{ij} in any box i
Step 2	$\Pi_m \propto (k_{m+1})^{\beta_m}$	$W_{n_i} \rightarrow W_{n_{i+1}} = \left(n_{n_i} + 1\right)_i^{\beta}$

12.4.2 Interpretation by a Polya Urn Process

Suppose we have a system where there are N urns and M balls. We denote the number of balls in the urn i by n_i. The total number of balls is:

$$M = \sum_{i=1}^{N} n_i. \tag{12.45}$$

We then define the energy of each urn as:

$$E(n_i) = -\ln(n!). \tag{12.46}$$

The Hamiltonian of the whole system is then:

$$H = \sum_{i=1}^{N} E(n_i). \tag{12.47}$$

The definition of energy may lead to attaching the un-normalized Boltzman weight to urn i:

$$p_{n_i} = \exp[-\beta_i E(n_i)] = (n_i!)^{\beta_i}. \tag{12.48}$$

The use of the heat-bath rule gives the transition rate $W_{n_i \rightarrow n_{i+1}}$ from the state n_i to n_{i+1} (Fig. 12.14).

12.5 Key Ideas for the New Economics

The Polya urn process provides us with potentially rich applications to analyze many important problems. In the above, we have examined some particular variations of the Polya urn process. However, one of major challenges to generalize our stochastic arguments depends on how to deal with **the unknown agents**. Without improving such an analytical modeling, we could not deal with how mutants will emerge. So our new economics need to learn how to formulate **the unknown agents** in the Polya urn process. This idea will generalize the framework of economic science.

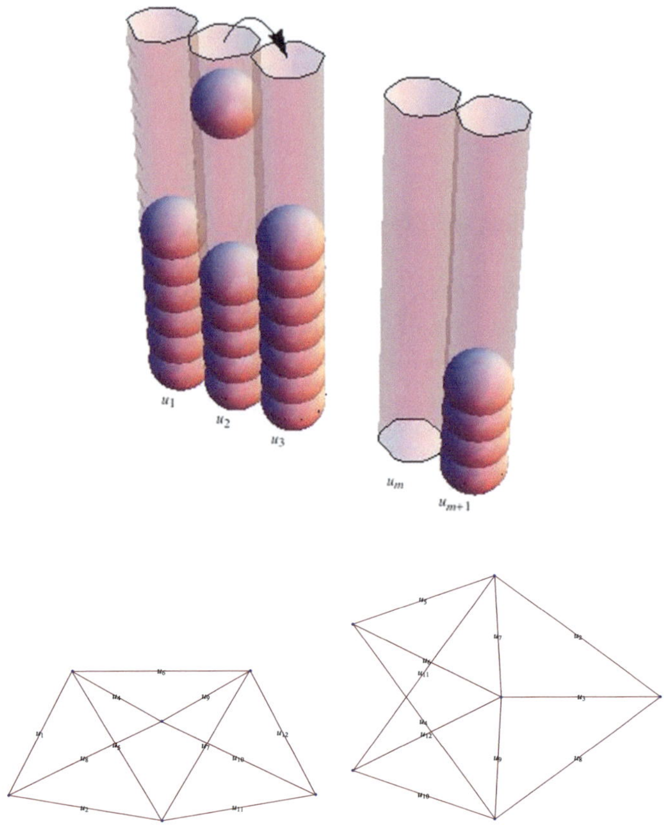

Fig. 12.14 The equivalence between a network connection and a Polya urn process

12.5.1 The Economics of the Master Equation and Fluctuations

The stochastic evolution of the state vector can be described in terms of a master equation, such as the Chapman-Kolmogorov differential equation system. The master equation leads to aggregate dynamics, from which the Fokker-Planck equation can be derived. We can therefore explicitly argue that there are fluctuations in a dynamic system. These settings can be connected with some key ideas, making it possible to classify agents by type in the system, and to track the variations in cluster size (Aoki, 2006).

In Aoki's new economics, there are exchangeable agents in a combinatorial stochastic process, like the urn process. The exchangeable agents emerge by the use of random partition vectors, as in statistical physics or population genetics. **The partition vector** provides us with information about the state. We can then argue the size-distribution of the components and their cluster dynamics with the exchangeable agents.

Suppose a maximum countable set in which the probability density of transition from state i to state j is given. In this setting, the dynamics of the heterogeneous interacting agents gives the field where one agent can become another. Unknown agents can also be incorporated.

A K-dimensional Polya distribution

We make a K-dimensional Polya distribution using parameter θ. We then have **a transition rate**:

$$w(\mathbf{n}, \mathbf{n} - \mathbf{e}_i + \mathbf{e}_j) = \frac{n_i}{n} \frac{n_j + \theta_j}{n - 1 + \theta}$$

where:

$$n = n_1 + \cdots + n_K; \theta_j > 0$$

And:

$$\theta = \sum_j^K \theta_j$$

The next step is a jump Markov process in a stationary state:

$$\pi(\mathbf{n}) w(\mathbf{n}, \mathbf{n} - \mathbf{e}_i + \mathbf{e}_j) = \pi(\mathbf{n} - \mathbf{e}_i + \mathbf{e}_j) w(\mathbf{n} - \mathbf{e}_i + \mathbf{e}_j, \mathbf{n}) \tag{12.49}$$

$$\pi(\mathbf{n}) = \frac{w(\mathbf{n} - \mathbf{e}_i + \mathbf{e}_j, \mathbf{n})}{w(\mathbf{n}, \mathbf{n} - \mathbf{e}_i + \mathbf{e}_j)} \pi(\mathbf{n} - \mathbf{e}_i + \mathbf{e}_j) \tag{12.50}$$

We therefore have **the stationary distribution**:

$$\pi(\mathbf{n}) = \frac{n!}{\theta^{[n]}} \prod_{i=1}^K \frac{\theta_i^{[n_i]}}{n_i!} \tag{12.51}$$

where:

$$\theta^{[n]} = \theta(\theta + 1) \cdots (\theta + n - 1) \tag{12.52}$$

12.5.2 A General Urn Process

Suppose that **balls** (or agents) and **boxes** (or urns) are *both indistinguishable*. We then have a **partition vector**:

$$\mathbf{a} = (a_1, a_2, ..., a_n)$$

a_i is the number of boxes containing i balls. The number of balls is:

$$\sum_{i=1}^{n} i a_i = n$$

The number of categories is:

$$\sum_{i=1}^{n} a_i = K_n.$$

K_n is the number of occupied boxes.

The number of configurations is then:

$$N(\mathbf{a}) = \frac{n!}{\prod_{j=1}^{n} (j!)^{a_j} a_j!} = \frac{n!}{(1!)^{a_1}(2!)^{a_2}\cdots(n!)^{a_n} a_1! a_2! \cdots a_n!}$$

A new type entry in an urn process

Let $\mathbf{a}$ be a state vector. Suppose that one new type agent enters an empty box. We then have the equation:

$$w(\mathbf{a}, \mathbf{a} + \mathbf{e}_1) = \frac{\theta}{n + \theta} \tag{12.53}$$

Suppose too that an agent enters a cluster of size j. We add one to size $j + 1$ while reducing one from size j. We then have:

$$w(\mathbf{a}, \mathbf{a} + \mathbf{e}_{j+1} - \mathbf{e}_j) = \frac{j a_j}{n + \theta} \tag{12.54}$$

Suppose that an agent leaves a cluster of size j. We add one to size $j - 1$ while reducing one from size j. We then have:

$$w(\mathbf{a}, \mathbf{a} - \mathbf{e}_j + \mathbf{e}_{j-1}) = \frac{j a_j}{n} \tag{12.55}$$

We then use **Ewens' sampling formula**:

$$\pi(\mathbf{a}) = \frac{n!}{\theta^{[n]}} \prod_{j=1}^{n} \left(\frac{\theta}{j}\right)^{a_j} \frac{1}{a_j!} \tag{12.56}$$

where:

$$\sum_{j=1}^{n} j a_j = n; \ \sum_{j=1}^{n} a_j = K_n$$

The probability that the number of clusters is k

The probability that the number of clusters is k will be the sum of **a newcomer** who comes in a new cluster with probability $\frac{n}{n+\theta}$ and one who comes in an existing cluster with probability $1 - \frac{n}{n+\theta}$:

$$q_{n,k} := \Pr(K_n = k|n) \tag{12.57}$$

$$q_{n+1,k} = \frac{n}{n+\theta} q_{n,k} + \frac{\theta}{n+\theta} q_{n,k-1} \tag{12.58}$$

In this case, **the boundary conditions** will be:

$$q_{n,1} = \frac{(n-1)!}{\theta^{[n]}} \tag{12.59}$$

$$q_{n,n} = \frac{\theta^n}{\theta^{[n]}} \tag{12.60}$$

The solution is then:

$$q_{n,k} = \frac{\theta^k}{\theta^{[n]}} c(n,k) \tag{12.61}$$

where

$$\begin{aligned}
c(n+1,k) &= nc(n,k) + c(n,k-1) \\
\theta^{[n+1]} &= \sum_{m=0}^{n} s(n,m)\theta^m = \theta(\theta+1)(\theta+2)\cdots(\theta+n-1)(\theta+n) \\
&= \theta^{[n]}(\theta+n) = \theta \cdot \theta^{[n]} + n \cdot \theta^{[n]} \\
\theta \cdot \theta^{[n]} &= \sum_{m=0}^{n} s(n,m)\theta \cdot \theta^m = \sum_{m=0}^{n} s(n,m)\theta^{m+1} \\
&= \sum_{m-1=0}^{n} s(n,m-1)\theta^m = c(n,k-1) \\
n\theta^{[n]} &= n\sum_{m=0}^{n} s(n,m)\theta^m = n\sum_{m=0}^{n} s(n,m)\theta^m
\end{aligned}$$

The final equation is called the signless **Stirling Number of the first kind**.

12.5.3 Pitman's Chinese Restaurant Process

We suppose that there are an infinite number of round tables in the Chinese restaurant that are labeled by an integer from 1 to n. The first customer, numbered 1, takes a seat at table number 1. Customers No. 1 to No. k in turn take their seats at their tables from No. 1 to No. k. The c_j customers take their seats at the j-th table.[18]

The next arriving customer has two options: either a seat at the k-th table, with the probability:

$$\frac{\theta + k\alpha}{\theta + n}$$

or at table j, one of the remaining tables $j = 1, \ldots, k$, with the probability:

$$\frac{c_j - \alpha}{\theta + n}$$

Two parameters, θ and α, are used, so we obtain the solution:

$$\frac{n!\theta^{[k:\alpha]}}{\theta[n]} \prod_{j=1}^{n} \left(\frac{(1-\alpha)^{[j-1]}}{j!} \right)^{c_j} \frac{1}{c_j!} \tag{12.62}$$

where:

$$\theta^{[j]} = \theta(\theta + 1) \cdots (\theta + j - 1)$$
$$\theta^{[j:\alpha]} = \theta(\theta + \alpha) \cdots (\theta + (j-1)\alpha)$$

Ewens' sampling formula Ewens (1972) gives the invariance of the random partition vectors under the properties of exchangeability and size-biased permutation. The Ewens sampling formula is the case with one parameter, a special case of two-parameter Poisson-Dirichlet distributions:

$$\frac{n!}{\theta^{[n]}} \prod_{j=1}^{n} \left(\frac{\theta}{j} \right)^{a_j} \frac{1}{a_j!}$$

In the case of the two-parameter Poisson-Dirichlet model, we will be faced with a *non-averaging* system as the limit.

Exercises

12.1 Whether it is either batch auction or continuous double auction, orders are settled board by board, but there are residual orders carried over from the previous period's board, and settlement is made by adding up the orders placed on the current session's board and the surviving orders from the previous board, with the remaining portion being finally carried over to the next day's session. Now we model the trading process by using the hazard function, i.e., a hazard modelling of order generation.

[18] See Pitman (1995), Yamato and Sibuya (2000), and Yamato and Sibuya (2003).

The agent decides at which clause the order order is placed. The probability of an agent submitting an order at a clause t or less is denoted by the next expression:

$$F(t) = \Pr(\text{board intervals} \leqq t) = \int_0^S f(s)ds \tag{12.63}$$

The probability of the remaining agents with more than t clauses to place an order is

$$S = 1 - F(S).$$

It then holds the hazard rate $h(t)$

$$h(t) = -\frac{d\ln(1 - F(t))}{dt}.$$

Prove that

$$F(t) = 1 - \exp^{-\int_0^t h(s)ds} \tag{12.64}$$

12.2 The hazard rate is not a probability and need not be summed to 1. On the other hand, the order density function at t is a probability density function. Prove the following.

$$f(t) = h(t)S(t). \tag{12.65}$$

12.3 x_i is denoted the spot price at t_i which is given by the observed data. Hazard rates are assumed to be determined by time-dependent base rates $\lambda(t)$ and dynamic explanatory variables x_i. It then holds

$$h(t, x(t)) = \lambda(t)\exp^{\beta x(t)} \tag{12.66}$$

Find the cumulative hazard function.

12.4 The probability of agent i actually placing an order at t_i from among the subgroups $J(t_i)$ that have not yet done so would be the ratio of the hazard rate of $J(t_i)$ at t_i to the hazard rate at i expressed by

$$\Pr(i|t_i) = \frac{h(t_i, x_i)}{\sum_{j\in J(t_i)} h(t_i, x_i)} \tag{12.67}$$

Find this expresssion to be equivlaent to the multinomial logit probability.

Table 12.5 Choice costs

Session	Mode 1	Mode 2	Chosen mode
1	30	50	Mode 1
2	20	10	Mode 1
3	40	30	Mode 2

12.5 In this case, the mode choices are the next two binary modes of "Submit Order" and "Do not place an order." x is regarded as the difference between the moving averages $\bar{x}$ up to before t_i for the difference between the spot price $\bar{x}^s$ and the futures price $\bar{x}^f$. In this case, the cost of choosing mode j is as follows:

$$x = f(\bar{x}^s - \bar{x}^f),\ f' > 0. \tag{12.68}$$

The agent is considered to be calculating costs in proportion to this difference. In the case that agents employ a 'trend following' strategy, examine if you may buy, or sell. Also in the case that agents employ a 'trend following' strategy, examine them.

12.6 Observations show that mode 1 is chosen at $t = 1$, mode 1 is chosen at $t = 2$, and mode 2 is chosen at $t = 3$. Calculate each probability chousen at $t = i$ according to the multinomial logit Formula (12.67) by reffering to Table 12.5.

12.7 The probability at $t = i$ if mode j is denoted P_{ij}. Using the table given in the last exercise, its log-likelihoods P_{11} is calculated as follows:

$$P_{11} = \frac{1}{1 + \exp(20\beta)} \tag{12.69}$$

Use the other two probabilities P_{12}, P_{23} in the same table.

12.8 Using the answers of the last exercise, it then holds the log-likelihood LL as follows:

$$LL = \sum_{j=1,2} \sum_{t=1,2,3} \delta_{jt} \ln(P_j t) \tag{12.70}$$

Here δ_{jt} is Kronecker's delta. Find the optimal β by putting $LL = 0$.

12.9 In the line of Arhtur et al. (1994), we describe a generalization of path dependent process in terms of our repeated game. X_i is denoted a proportion in the total possible points which Player i gains. The initial total *potential* of gains for each player is defined $2N - 1$, if players all mutually cooperate. In the next period 2, the total maximal gains will grow by the number of players $2N$. In the period n, therefore, the proportion for Player i at time n will be $X_i^n = \frac{b_i^n}{(2N-1)n}$. Let $q_i^n(x)$ define

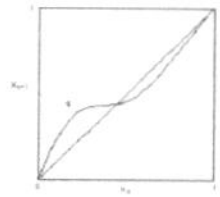

Fig. 12.15 A nonlinear function form of q

a probability of player i to *earn* a point by means of Strategy C in period n. We assume the ratio of cooperation, or C-ratio for each player with the proportion of the total possible gains for each player. If X^n, as a random variable giving a proportion x, appeared at a low level, a value of X^{n+1} might be greater than the previous value of X^n. By our assumption, a low level of proportion in gain can induce an increase of the ratio of cooperation in an individual strategy. If q is nonlinear, a nonlinear dynamics may be generated. Using the pahse diagram represented by Fig. 12.15, explain the path dependency process in our iterated game.

12.10 Try to select an economic process like a technical process which may be fitted to the Pitman's Chinese restaurant process, and sketch its model.

References

Aoki, M., & Yoshikawa, H. (2006). *Reconstructing macroeconomics: A perspective from statistical physics and combinatorial stochastic processes* (p. 333). Cambridge University Press.

Arthur, W. B. (1994). *Increasing returns and path dependence in the economy*, Japanese ed. University of Michigan Press.

Aruka, Y. (2015). Hodgson's bibliometric report and the reconstruction plan of economics. *Evolutionary and Institutional Economics Review, 15*(1), 189–202.

Barabási, A. L., & Albert, A. L. (1999). Emergence of scaling in random networks. *Science, 286*(5439), 509–512. October.

Champernowne, D. G. (1953). A model of income distribution. *Economic Journal, 63*(2), 318–351.

Cook, J. D. (2010). Central limit theorems. Wolfram Demonstrations. http://www.johndcook.com/central_limit_theorems.html linked from Cook (2010): How the central limit theorem began? http://www.johndcook.com/blog/2010/01/05/how-the-central-limit-theorem-began/

Ewens, W. J. (1972). The sampling theory of selectivity neutral Allels. *Theoretical Population Biology, 3*, 87–112.

Fama, E. (1965). The behavior of stock market prices. *Journal of Business, 38*, 34–105. https://doi.org/10.1086/294743.

Fama, E. (1970). Efficient capital markets: A review of theory and empirical work. *Journal of Finance, 25(2)*, 383–417. https://doi.org/10.2307/2325486.JSTOR2325486.

Fisk, P. R. (1961). The graduation of income distributions. *Econometrica, 20*(4), 171–185.

Johnson, N. F., Jefferies, P., & Hui, P. M. (2003). *Financial market complexity: What physics can tell us about market behaviour*. Oxford University Press.

Lévy, P. (1925/2016). *Calcul des probabilités*. Gauthier-Villars, Cambridge.

Mainzer, K. (2007). Kapitel 7: Zufall in Kultur, Wirtschaft, und Gesselschaft. In *Der kreative Zufall: Wie das Neue in die Welt kommt?* CH Beck.

Manderbrot, B. (1963). The variation of certain speculative prices. *Journal of Business, 36*(4), 394–419.

Manderbrot, B. (2001). Scaling in financial prices. *Quantitative Finance, 1*(6), 641–649.

Mantegna, R. H., & Stanley, H. E. (2001). *An introduction to econophysics: Correlations and complexity in finance*.

Nolan, J. P. (2020). *Univariate stable distributions: Models for heavy tailed data*.
Nolan, J. P. (2005). *Stable distributions: Models for heavy tailed data*. Birkhäuser.
Ohkubo, J., Yasuda, M., & Tanaka, K. (2005). Preferential urn model and nongrowing complex networks. *Physical Review E, 72*(065104), 1–4. December.
Ohkubo, J., Yasuda, M., & Tanaka, K. (2006). Replica analysis of preferential urn mode; erratum, *76*(4), 1, article no. 048001; (2007, April). *Journal of the Physical Society of Japan, 75*(074802), 1–6.
Pitman, J. (1995). Exchangeable and partially exchangeable random partitions. *Probability Theory and Related Fields, 102*, 145–158. November.
Singh, S. K., & Maddala, G. S. (2008). A function for size distribution of income. In D. Chotikapanich (Ed.), *Modeling income distributions and Lorenz curves (Chapter 2:24–32)*. Springer.
Swell, M. (2011). *Characterization of financial time series*.
Yamato, H., & Sibuya, M. (2000). Moments of some statistics of pitman sampling formula. *Bulletin of Informatics and Cybernetics, 32*(1), 1–10.
Yamato, H., & Sibuya, M. (2003). Pitman sampling formula and related topics (in Japanese). *Proceedings of the Institute of Statistical Mathematics, 51*(2), 351–372.

Stochastic Methods from the Simplest Transaction Dynamics to the Complex Networks

13

Abstract

In previous chapters we have seen the advent of a new society, with the growing complexity of the market and technological innovations. We demonstrated the move away from the Gaussian world towards that of heavy tail distribution. To fully understand the latter distribution, we need to recognize a generalized central limit theorem, where the Gaussian distribution is simply a special case. We are therefore able to investigate several stable distributions and expand our idea of price equilibrium as a stable distribution. We will also discuss the central issue of how the market economy can generate complex dynamics. First, we use the simplest trader dynamics system designed by Philip Maymin, and recreate his simulation dynamics for an automaton. This explicitly takes into account traders' decisions in combined multiple layers: actions, mind states, memories of the trader and the market. These factors are normally regarded as influential components that govern price movements. In financial transactions, we dispense with psychological effects at individual and aggregate levels. These may no longer be secondary effects. We then observe the stochastic process how a complex network will be generated. Second, we then learn the multiagent trader's dynamics, where the complexity of interactions between heterogeneous traders dominates the market.

13.1 The Simplest Trader Dynamics to Generate Financial Complexity

This section is inspired by Philip Maymin's ingenious demonstrations in the Wolfram Demonstration Project. He attempted to formulate **a single autonomous engine**, based on the application of automata, to recreate *complex* stock price fluctuations. This helps us to understand the essence of the financial market mechanism by taking account of volatile shifts in traders? minds, together with memory effects. The mind state may often accompany the practical employment of a typical technical analytical agent technical analytical agent.

Y. Aruka, *Evolutionary Economics*, Springer Texts in Business and Economics,
https://doi.org/10.1007/978-981-97-1382-0_13

Philip Maymin has focused on the actual aspect of traders' decisions in terms of the combining of multiple layers: actions, mind states, and memories of traders and the market. The environment, here the market, is generated by a rule, but not by factors such as drift and other random factors that often appear in statistical time series analysis. If the market is rising, there are two possible kinds of action. One is **a trend-follower** action: to buy rising stocks. This may reflect a *bearish* or *pessimistic* mind. The other is the **contrarian** action to sell on the way up, or to buy on the way down. This may reflect a *bullish* or *optimistic* mind.

The resulting behavior of the trader depends on the mind state, whether bearish or bullish. Whatever the mind state, behavior may also be influenced by the past (memories) and the market hysteresis. We call this **the internal rule**. Maymin then gives a rule of shift of mind between several states, which plays a role as a **transducer** in the automaton. On the first shift downwards following an upward movement, for instance, the mind may move from optimistic to pessimistic. The trader will be induced to change his attitude from contrarian to trend-follower. Similarly, the same player, faced with an upward movement after a series of downward movements, will be induced to move from trend-follower to contrarian. This flow could cause the market to shift back to the original state. This suggests the shift rule will decide whether the market changes direction. In the model, such a floating rule is *sensitive* to the market change. It is evident that the emerging or floating shift rules will arrange the market in a *periodic* way. More importantly, the model incorporates these induced behaviors. The interactions between mind state, market situation, the trader's memory and the market history can therefore be included.[1] The trader will follow an individual pattern linked to past history.

Figure 13.1 shows this idea in more detail.

13.1.1 Rules to Be Specified

Even if we assume the simplest dealing, we would require several *behavioral* rules to achieve buy, sell and hold, taking into account the market state as well as a trader's memory. The trader's current thinking could be modified during dealing. We usually set several specifications for the trader's dealing rules (Table 13.1).

In the case of two actions {buy, sell}, two states {bearish, bullish}, and {three-period memory}, there are 256 possible rules, including overlapping ones. Some rules may be more important than others. We usually have two rules for state of mind: one that gives **the internal rule**, and one **the shift rule** between the different states of mind. In reality, however, there are many combinations of mind state and market state, as well as actions of buy and sell.

The investor is modeled using an iterated finite automaton iterated finite automaton with only two states: an optimistic contrarian state and a pessimistic trend-following state. The trader starts each day in the optimistic contrarian state,

[1] The number of states may be more than two.

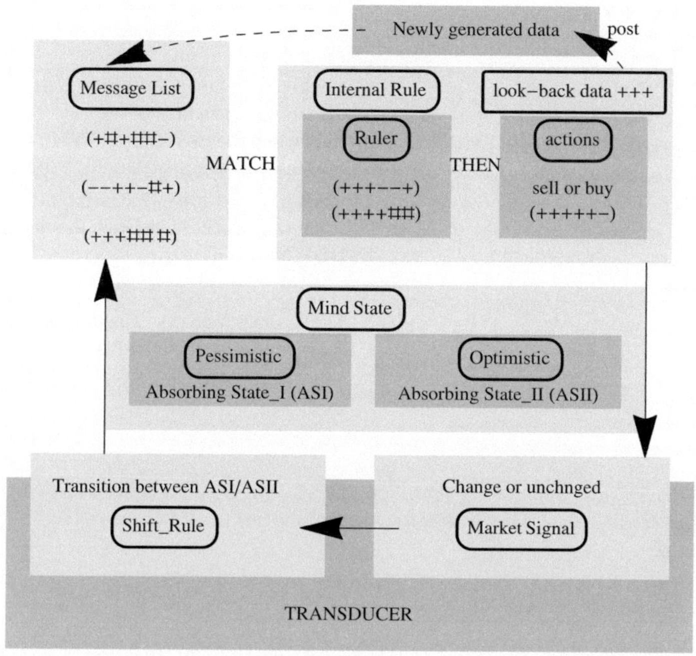

Fig. 13.1 Internal rules in different initial conditions

Table 13.1 Rules

Action rules depending on the mind state
Internal rule
Shift rule (**transducer**)
Look-back rule:
The trader's memory of action associated with the hysteresis of the market

which sells on upturns and buys on downturns, and remains in this state as long as the market keeps going up (Table 13.2).

We take first a simple example. Maymin (2007d: Caption comment) described this model as:

> Pick the rule he follows and the initial conditions for the first three days of the week. The trader looks back over the past three days in considering what to do. The big circles are states, like the emotions of the trader. He always starts in state 1 and then follows the arrows that correspond to the market movement (UP or DOWN) of the day under consideration. The yellow state is the one he was in when he started thinking about the day in question, and the one with the square in it is the one he will move to, based on the yellow arrow that he

Table 13.2 Rules for prices

Action rule	
Internal rule of the trader mind	In the bearish state, the trader sells when the market is UP. In the bullish state, the trader sells when the market is DOWN
Shift rule of the trader mind	Shift to the bearish state so that the trader buys when the market is UP. Shift to the bullish state so that the trader buys when the market is DOWN
Look-back rule	
Memory	The trader's memory of action associated with the hysteresis of the market
Units of time	The last three units of time are used for the look-back

> follows. His "current thinking" is shown on the yellow arrow, too (BUY or SELL), but he only makes his final decision when he has reached the last day that he considers.

According to Maymin, we can imagine the initial conditions shown in Fig. 13.2 .

> The investor follows these transitions by looking at the past few days of price changes, starting with the most recent day. The decision to buy or sell is modeled as his current thinking as he goes through the past few days, and once he reaches the last day of his look-back window, he makes his final decision to buy or sell. The next day, he starts all over.[2] (Maymin, 2007a: Details)

In this instance of "A shift rule sensitive to the market change", the transition of the market will be shown in terms of the **transducer** finite automata:

$$\{\text{state1, input}\} \rightarrow \{\text{state2, output}\} \tag{13.1}$$

Here, the trader is pessimistic and remains in this state as long as the market keeps going down.

In the left-hand side of Fig. 13.3, "[o]n the first downtick, it transitions to the other state, the pessimistic trend-following state. This state is trend-following because it buys on upticks and sells on downticks". In the right-hand side, "[o]n the first uptick, it transitions back to the original state" (Maymin, 2007a: Details). The model can therefore generate periodic motions.

In this rule:

2 Note in the Snapshots how sometimes volatility starts small and then increases, and sometimes it starts large and decreases. A price series that appears stable can suddenly collapse, and after a collapse can remain low, or can come back up. Because the investor looks back a fixed number of days, the price series is guaranteed to eventually cycle. However, this cycle length can be quite long. For example, a 15-business-day look-back, absent any external changes, will cycle in about 130 years.

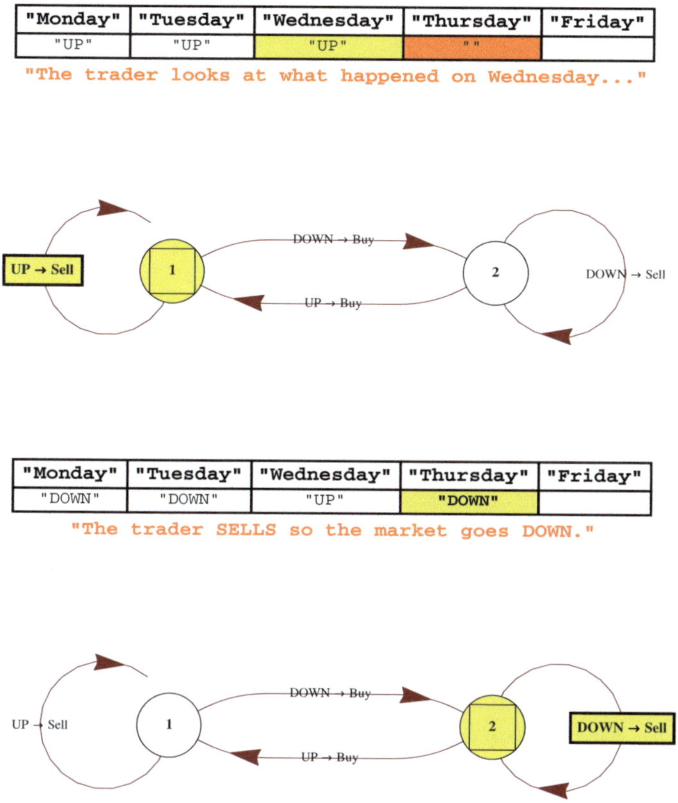

Fig. 13.2 Internal rules in different initial conditions

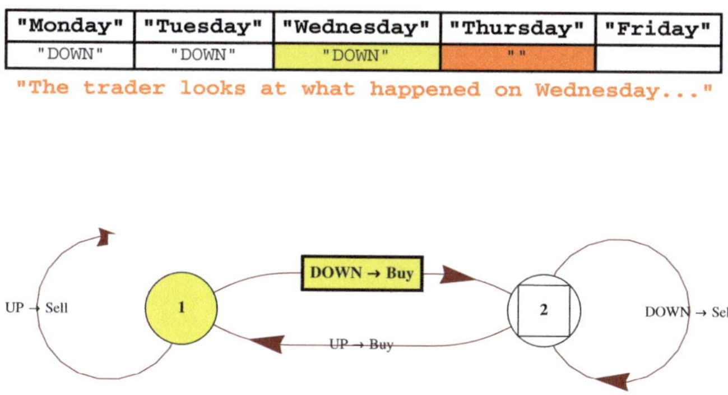

Fig. 13.3 A shift rule sensitive to the market change

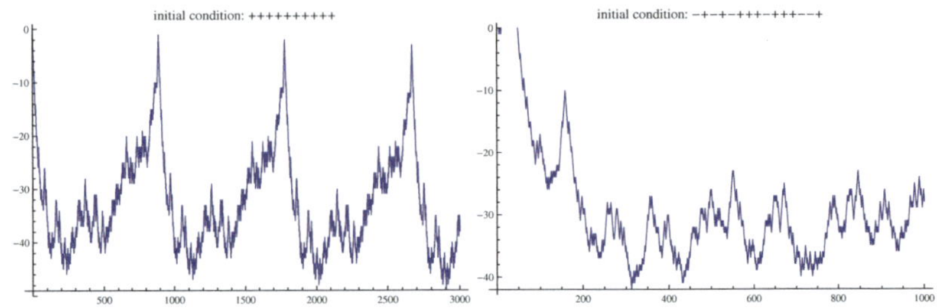

Fig. 13.4 The same trader with 10 look-back windows and price motions under different initial conditions

state 1 is characterized as an **up-absorbing** state.
state 2 is characterized as a **down-absorbing** state.

Consequently, the rule could give the following reduced rule:

1. If the preceding two events are the same, i.e., both up or both down, the trader will sell.
2. If the preceding two events are different, i.e., one up and one down, the trader will buy.

13.1.1.1 An Alternative Interpretation Based on Tick Data

If each event is replaced by a tick,[3] Maymin suggests:

> An investor observes two consecutive ticks. If they are the same sign, i.e., either both up or both down, then he sells. Otherwise he buys. However, his order does not take effect for $w - 1$ ticks. Put another way, his orders face a delay of $w - 1$ ticks, so the minimal model formalizes an investor who looks at consecutive ticks to decide his position and faces a short delay either in mental processing or order execution (Maymin, 2011a).

$$\{\{1, 1\} \to \{1, 0\}, \{1, 0\} \Rightarrow \{2, 1\}, \{2, 1\} \Rightarrow \{1, 1\}, \{2, 0\} \to \{2, 0\}\}. \tag{13.2}$$

Here the first component is the state, 1 (bearish) or 2 (bullish). The second is the trader's action keeping up with the market state:

1: buy at up
0: sell at down.

The trader will follow the **shift rule** as shown by $\Rightarrow$.

We now extend the look-back windows to 10 days or ticks, obtaining a new time series (see Fig. 13.4).

[3] Tick stands for transaction between buyer and seller at the quoted price.

13.1.1.2 A Generalization of the Simplest Trader Dynamics

Maymin proposed to define the domain of his speculative financial market as:

> An investor with s internal states and k possible "actions" with base b and having a look-back window of w days is modeled as an **iterated finite automaton (IFA)**.

Employing the Wolfram IFA numbering scheme, the IFA is run as:

```
ToFARule[m_Integer, {s_Integer, k_Integer}] :=
Flatten[MapIndexed[{1, -1}#2 + {0, k} ->
Mod[Quotient[#1, {k, 1}], {s, k}] + {1, 0} &,
Partition[IntegerDigits[m, s k, s k], k], {2}]]
```

s represents the state of mind of the trader, which is sometimes bearish, sometimes bullish. k represents the action of dealing, usually "buy", "sell", or "hold", although it may be accompanied by the "limit order" or the "market order". For simplicity, we assume dealing is to the market order only, because this is often genuinely possible. When $k = 2$ (Maymin, 2011b), the possible actions are buy and sell. Maymin also proved that the possible actions are buy, sell, and hold if $k = 3$. He introduced a scale of strength of buy or sell, where the possible actions are buy, buy more, sell, and sell more, if $k = 4$[4]

> In general, if k is even, the possible actions are $k/2$ types of buys and $k/2$ types of sells, with differing strengths. If k is odd, the possible actions are the same as for $k - 1$ with the additional possibility of doing nothing, i.e., hold.

There is a basic property of these new trader dynamics, that "[the trader] never learns his own rule. In this modeling, however, the trader is based on "technical analysis", and will trade in reference to a self-chosen technical indicator (Maymin, 2011b, 4). In Maymin's simple model, the trader will not change rule until there is a big loss. It follows that:

> From his point of view, he put in an order to buy and was simply unlucky enough not to have been filled before the market moved away. This happens to him every day, whether he wants to buy or sell. (Maymin, 2011b, 4)

[4] The strength of a buy or sell is an exponent of the base b. For example, when $b = 3$ and $k = 4$, the four possible actions are -3, -1, 1, and 3, meaning sell three times more than normal, sell normally, buy normally, or buy three times more than normal. If $k = 6$, then two additional actions are –9 and 9. According to Maymin, "[i]f a normal buy would increase the market price by one percent, a nine times more fervent order would increase the market price by nine percent" (Maymin, 2011b, 4).

13.1.1.3 How Do the New Traders' Dynamics Differ from Previous Models?

The new dynamics proposed by Maymin decisively differ from previous ideas as they contain rules. In many game theoretic formulations, the players are allowed to change moves by checking the ongoing development of the price. In this case, we specify that the trader can decide his market order, i.e., whether he can buy or sell, by looking back at the preceding price series. In other words, his decision depends on his previous memory. Given the preceding time series DOWN, UP, UP, the trader will buy because of an expectation that the price will go up further. However, his memory is limited to three elements of the last price movement (Table 13.3 and Fig. 13.5).

The consequence may not differ from the new results, but the choice of the shift rules for mind transition could give rise to a big change in the price series.

Table 13.3 Transitory evolution of memory in traditional trader dynamics

Rounds	BUY	BUY	SELL	BUY	BUY	SELL	BUY	
1	{D D U}							
2		{D U U}						
3			{U U U}					
4				{U U D}				
5					{U D U}			
6						{D U U}		
7							{U U U}	
8								{U U D}
⋮			...					

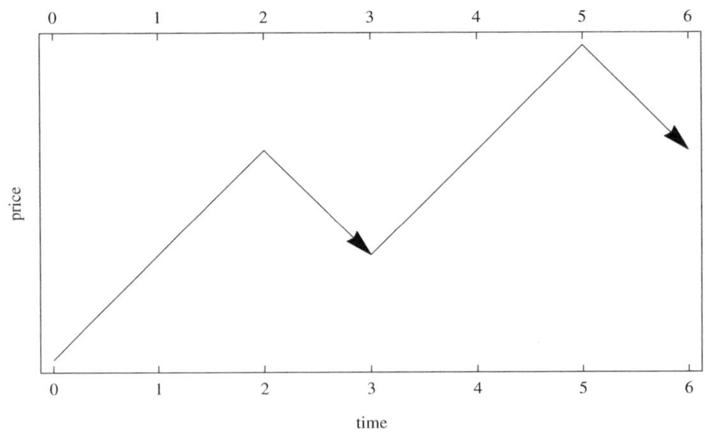

Fig. 13.5 A time series generated

13.1.1.4 Maymin's Justification for the Simplest Trader Dynamics

In the financial market, as described by Maymin, there is no need for multiple traders to create complex price fluctuations. We assume only the initial price ahead of the opening price quotation, on which the trader can act. The preceding price series motivates the trader to make further orders. Maymin (2007a, 2007b, 2007c, 2007d, 2011a, 2011b) gave this price information in the up and down form: $\{up, down\}$. Even this price series is created by the trader himself. The simplest model uses only a single trader, but this may be replaced with the point that in the preceding session, some trades were made, whether our particular trader was involved or not. After moving to the opening price,[5] only one trader will continue to give further orders. In the futures market, self-dealing is acceptable, and in a double auction, it is possible to have simultaneous moves of buy and sell, usually called the day trader method. It is therefore possible to assume a sole agent in the market. Here the interactive effects caused by different agents may not be explicit but the interaction between buy and sell definitely emerges. We can therefore employ the single market simulation to investigate how and why a complex price fluctuation can be created. The market dealings allow moves of only sell, buy or hold, although there are also two kinds of limit order and the market order. A trader may sometimes secure his profit by executing market orders. We therefore take an example of a single trader with market orders. This setting may be reasonable if we comply faithfully with the basic properties of the financial market.

This market will be reflected by the emotions of the trader, which essentially coincides with Thomas Lux (2009) and Raymond Hawkins (2011), where the market could be characterized by the simulation method of emotional interaction irrelevant to the real economy. This is an essential property of the financial market. In the event, through this kind of experiment, we can recognize the new proposition:

Proposition 13.1 *The market is not capable of creating price fluctuations. Instead, the situation is the other way round. A trader, even if there is only one, can create the market, which is simply an institutional arrangement.*

It is important to understand that the market in itself is not capable of creating anything. The agent does not have to be human. In the high-frequency trading (HFT), the main agents are algorithmic ones. This proposition does not imply that human behavior can create a market fluctuation.

Another important feature of the financial market could be compatible with the *sock puppet* sock puppet idea.

Proposition 13.2 *A monologue, i.e., a single trader dynamics, can move the market, whether the action is judged illegal or not.*[6]

[5] In the Tokyo Stock Exchange, the morning or afternoon session under the double auction rule will start after a batch auction on the preceding 30 min of orders.

[6] In the HFT, a cross-transaction is feasible if it can happen more quickly than a trading time unit.

A sock puppet means "an online identity used for purposes of deception".[7] We assume that a sock puppet is the single trader in our market, and call the single trade dynamics required to generate a complex stock price fluctuation "sock puppet dynamics".

In dealings, the trader must have a strategy. The standard classical strategies are still applied in the market, although they date back to the era of the classical stock exchange. They may be used not only by human agents but also by machine or algorithm agents, and the random strategy or zero-intelligent strategy can work well.[8]

The trader can be given alternative options from the same past history, includingt*owards* the trend or *against* it, either the trend strategy or the anti-trend strategy. Either way, the decision could be canceled out before the simulation in either the classical auction or HFT. Throughout, the trader is never required to hold to the first choice of strategy, but can switch strategy either emotionally or intelligently. Needless to say, in the market, an intelligent strategy will never guarantee profits, even if the strategy is very sophisticated. Random strategies, on average, minimize the total loss because of naive risk management.

13.1.2 Complexities in a Dealing Model of an Iterated Finite Automaton

First we need to define complexity. With a look-back window of w with k possible market movements each day, there are only k^w distinct possible price histories on which the trader bases a decision. After k^w days of history, the time series of price changes must have cycled. A complex series is one that takes a long time to cycle, and a simple series cycles quickly.

For example, a rule that always buys will cycle in a single day. Even though the price continues to rise to a unique level each day, the changes are constant. Here, using Maymin's simulator,[9] we can verify some findings of *complex* price motions, a *periodic* motion (see Fig. 13.6).

13.1.2.1 Redundancies and the Depth of Logic Contained in a Complex System

This modeling has definitely generated complex price fluctuations. In general, however, it may be that there are actually not so many *long* complex price motions.

---

[7] According to Wikipedia, "The term—a reference to the manipulation of a simple hand puppet made from a sock—originally referred to a false identity assumed by a member of an internet community who spoke to, or about, himself while pretending to be another person".

[8] **The U-Mart experiment** is helpful in understanding how various random behaviors could intermediate a coordination of contracts in dealings. See Chaps. 7 and 8 of this book.

[9] The minimal model of simulating prices of financial securities using an iterated finite automaton, where length of generated series = initial condition.

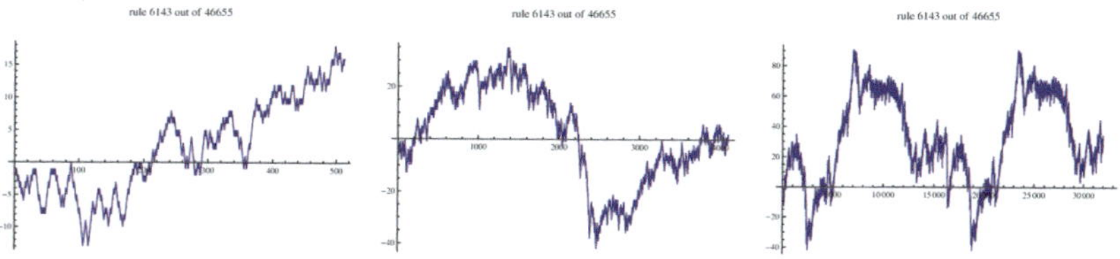

Fig. 13.6 Using 15 look-back windows

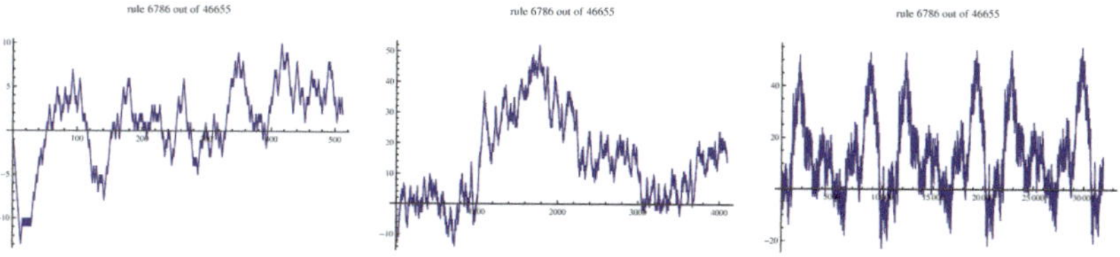

Fig. 13.7 An alternative rule with 15 look-back windows

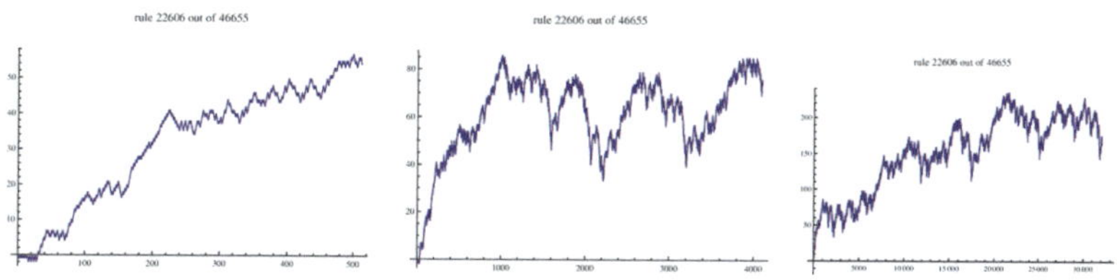

Fig. 13.8 Another alternative rule with 15 look-back windows

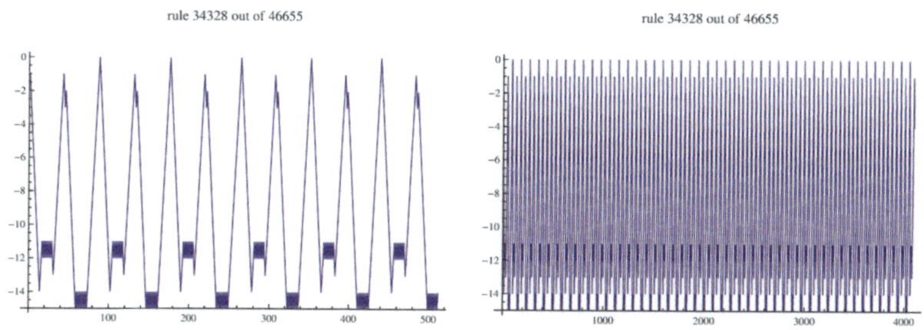

Fig. 13.9 A further rule with 15 look-back windows and periodic motion

Such an observation is usually true of other chaotic movements. Sequences with low complexity are more likely than those with high complexity, as we saw with DNA (Mainzer, 2007, 156) in Chap. 6 (Figs. 13.7, 13.8 and 13.9).

Redundancies and the depth of logic contained in a complex system Redundancy mediated by a coincidence may bring something new. A combinatorial rearrangement found among redundancies suggests the potential for a new idea. If each program to generate a given consequence is smaller, the number of steps calculated by these programs will be increased. As a generated system becomes more complicated, the procedure to reveal the desired system will have a deeper logic, so a simpler program can create a complex system. This is why an organism or a gene can construct a huge complex constitution with a considerably deeper logic in spite of its simple procedure.

Recently, complex systems have often been analyzed as **complex networks**, but the present form of network analysis is insufficient because of the depth of logic and information. Network analysis gives useful findings, but does not yet have a tool to represent the depth of logic and information.

13.1.2.2 Definition of Complexity in Simple Trader Dynamics

Definition: Maymin's complexity

Complexity in a k-action generated price series for a look-back window w means that the periodicity of the rule is greater than $kw/2$. A rule with the maximal complexity would have a periodicity equal to the maximal periodicity (cycle length) of kw, i.e., $2w$. Usually, cycle length $\leq$ the maximum $2w$. Generation of periodicity depends on the initial condition.

A relaxed definition

The minimal complex model must have at least two states and two actions.

Complexity in the price series

Complexity in the price series requires $s \geq 2$ and $k \geq 2$. Cycling does not mean that the market is modeled as repeating, only that this is a characteristic of the model. We can always choose sufficiently large k and w such that the cycle length is longer than the history of the market under consideration.[10]

A rapid growth of complexity due to the HFT in terms of periodicity

We found a two-fold period system in the HFT. Inner look-back windows accompany each time unit, with a new window denoted by w. We estimate the complexity by: $kw\omega/2 > kw/2$. In our simple trader dynamics with HFT, the complexity will therefore rapidly increase.

[10] $k = 15$ and $w = 15$ mean the maximal cycle length is longer than the age of the universe in seconds.

Table 13.4 Set of rules of the rule 110 automaton

Current pattern	111	110	101	100	011	010	001	000
New state for center cell	0	1	1	0	1	1	1	0

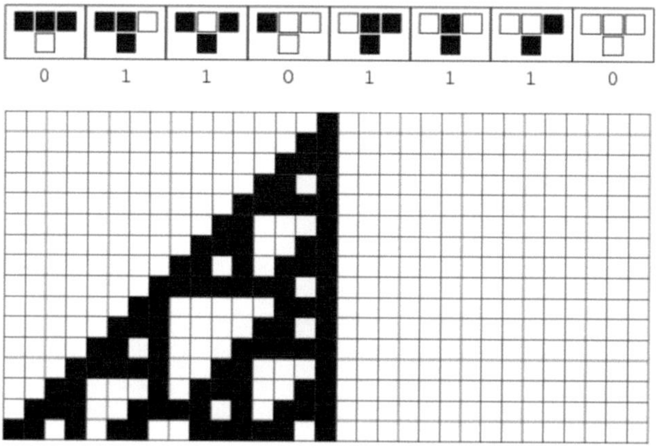

Fig. 13.10 Binary-colored presentation of rule 110. * Black squares: 1; white squares: 0

13.2 A Multiagent Trader's Dynamics Toward Rule Selection

When the number of states is large, it may be challenging for us to formulate an appropriate rule. It then seems difficult to attain the desired purpose and the evolution of the system without finding any *computable* rule. Therefore, in this paper, we research the application of simulations, but in a smarter manner what currently exists (Fig. 13.10).

13.2.1 Wolfram Interactive Cellular Automaton

To examine the rule selection, we cite the experiments on elementary cellular automata. In particular, by the publication, *A New Kind of Science*" (Wolfram, 2002), it turned out that the automaton of **Wolfram rule 110** fulfills the criteria of Turing completeness. This is among major problems that interested Wolfram. Now, the rule 110 and the similar rules are being explored (Table 13.4).[11]

The cellular automaton has a simple structure, but it is potent in terms of generating complicated behavior similar to those in Class 4. The figures of Class 1–4 are reproduced in Fig. 13.11.

[11] "There are 256 such automata, each of which can be indexed by a unique binary number whose decimal representation is known as the "rule" for the particular automaton." See http://mathworld.wolfram.com/CellularAutomaton.html.

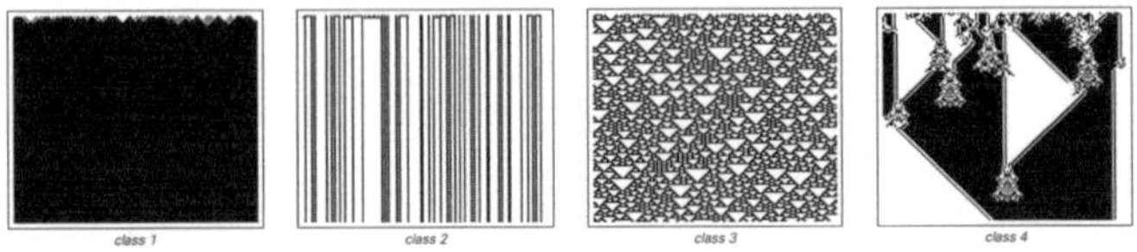

Fig. 13.11 Class 1–4. * Cited from Wolfram (2002): http://www.wolframscience.com/nks/p231--four-classes-of-behavior/

(a) Three ICA: Rules 190, 120, 70 (b) Three ICA: Rules 23, 183, 238 (c) Three ICA: Rules 23, 183, 110 (d) Three ICA: Rules 23, 110, 110 (e) Three ICA: All Rules 110

Fig. 13.12 Three ICA. * These figures are produced by Mitchell and Beyon (2011)'s simulator

> Cellular automata (CA) can be classified according to the complexity and information produced by the behavior of the CA pattern:
>
> Class 1: Fixed; all cells converge to a constant black or white set Class 2: Periodic; repeats the same pattern, like a loop Class 3: Chaotic; pseudo-random Class 4: Complex local structures; exhibits behaviors of both class 2 and class 3; likely to support universal computation (Carvalho, 2011).

By resorting to the **Fully Random, Five-Rule Interactive Cellular Automata (ICA)** Mitchell and Beyon (2011), we can easily examine the effects of the heterogenous interactions of rules. We employ a reduced version of the Five-Rule ICA, i.e., **the Three-Rule** ICA, to examine the effects of the heterogenous interactions of three different rules to easily compare the effects due to heterogeneous interactions of different rules around the rule 110. When only the rule dynamics are considered, we can analyze the effects of rules on the overall dynamics (Fig. 13.12).

> One possible application of FRICAs is a more refined classification system based on, for instance, *how damaging* the inclusion of a given rule is to the universal behavior of rule 110. It is also possible that systems in nature mimic the process of choosing *randomly* for each operation from a limited set of functional rules.

By using the Five ICA, we can determine the effects when rule 110 is increased gradually to five. The initial distribution of the 5 rules is set as {Rule 23, Rule 183, Rule 18, Rule 238, Rule 12}. The first component of the initial distribution is replaced with Rule 110 to be {Rule 110, Rule 183, Rule 18, Rule 238, Rule 12}. By applying the same procedure to the last result, the second component is also replaced with rule 110 to yield {Rule 110, Rule 110, Rule 18, Rule 238, Rule 12}. By repeating a similar procedure, we finally obtain a set in which all components are rule 110. We

(a) Five ICA: Rules 23, 183, 18, 238, 12

(b) Five ICA: Rules 110, 183, 18, 238, 12

(c) Five ICA: Rules 110, 110, 18, 238, 12

(d) ICA Rules 110, 110, 110, 238, 12

(e) Five ICA: Rules 110, 110, 110, 110, 12

(f) Five ICA: All Rules 110

Fig. 13.13 Five ICA. * These figures are produced by Mitchell and Beyon (2011)'s simulator

can observe the different interactive heterogenous rules as the number of rule 110 varies (Fig. 13.13).

13.3 Market Mechanism with Redundancies and a Deeper Logic of Complexity

As Mainzer (2007), a philosopher of science, recommended, the idea of creative coincidence in the human history can be applied to technological innovation. Then, the application of creative coincidence to innovation suggests a new idea that is replaced with J. Schumpeter's creative destruction. See Aruka (2009) for more details.

A momentum of creative coincidence will be revealed by examining the logical depth. Mainzer originally studied the **Turing machine**. The logical depth may be defined in the following manner. With the algorithmic probability P_s for a randomly generated program's output, we now have a measure of the logical depth of s at our disposal. A sequence s has logical depth when the largest proportion of P_s is contributed by short programs that require a large number of computational steps for the production of P_s. The DNA sequences that have evolved over millions of years with many redundancies and contingencies can survive by generating compact programs that require an enormous amount of computational steps for the development of the entire description of a complex organism. In this sense, they have great logical depth, the depth of information generated by a long and complex evolution.

In view of **engineering**, a complex system with a deeper logic may be interpreted with such a program that has various elaboration at each implemented stage. A proper degree of redundancies[12] is rather indispensable for generating innovation. In this sense, a series of small, new inventions will assure a great innovation. In other words, a deeper logic in engineering may imply plentiful, higher precisions, and high-accuracy elaborations. These elaborations in essence are irrelevant to either a pecuniary motive or a market mechanism. It is trivial that such an idea connected with a new invention that is often rooted in our traditional techno-culture. This point

[12] The redundancy of a mathematical system means an excessive degree of freedom. Redundancies in this context mean uncertainties, especially in their availability and usefulness.

of view may be much encouraged by **Brian Arthur** as we describe in the next subsection.

13.3.1 Market Mechanism in Evolution

We follow the essential idea of **Brian Arthur** (2009) who believes that technology is a superclass of economy.[13] In this context, we can say that technology creates itself out of itself.[14] His idea also applies to the market mechanism.

As Arthur (2009) also illustrated, the financial market did not prepare a new system for the safe option market. In contrast, the so-called renovation of financial business was then feasible because computers evolved to solve the complicated risk calculations that were needed for options transactions (Arthur, 2009, 154). The financial market is now exposed to HFT(High Frequency Trading/Transaction). But the HFT is also a product of the evolution of computability. Market theory is utterly irrelevant to the evolution of computer. The evolution of computer has realized HFT. Computers evolved to solve the complicated transactions that were needed for the HFT transactions either in stock exchanges or in currency exchanges. It must be noted that HFT will be changing the institutional setting of the transaction. The prestige of a seat at the Exchange is diminishing because high spec servers are endowed virtually the same membership as that at the stock exchange. More generally, technological innovations can change the qualities of transaction. It has been remarked that market theory does not specify how the actual market system is constructed. In this sense, the existing market theory never been proven to exist.

In examining the example of *Sake Brewing*, there are two ways of brewing: batch and continuous polymerization. The quality and taste of Sake become different when a different brewing process is used. It has been known in the market auction that there are two ways of matching: batch and continuous double auction. The different auction methods apparently bring different results. In the reality of the exchange, even a market equilibrium does not necessarily hold. In the older stock exchanges prior to computer processing, the closing time was often extended to allow them markets to settle down. Actually, it takes much time to arrive at a settlement price. The continuous double auction is generally regarded as an on-the-spot decision to find a matching as soon as possible. The stock exchange is alway monitoring the time series of on-going transactions and seeks to find matches by suggesting a current price band within which current orders could be successfully settled. This is a kind of market engineering.

[13] It arose from the productive methods and legal and organizational arrangements that we use to satisfy our needs. Therefore, it is issued from all these captures of phenomena and subsequent combinations (Arthur, 2009, 3).

[14] Early technologies formed using existing primitive technologies as components. These new technologies in time become possible component "building blocks" for the construction of further new technologies. Some of these in turn go on to become possible building blocks for the creation of yet newer technologies (Arthur, 2009, 21).

The mathematical reasoning of the market process skips through the engineering part of the process. Even if given a particular bundle of binding devices, which the stock exchange cultivated for many years, the dealers cannot always arrive at an equilibrium state by themselves. Any guarantee will not be secured simply by assuming a black box for the market. The architecture of a market must be described each time when a particular market is discussed (see Aruka, 2017). The market architecture is indispensable to establish equilibrium. A mathematical statement of the existence of an equilibrium tells us nothing about the reality of the market mechanism. Mizuno et al. (2010) and Mizuno and Watanabe (2010), who are Japanese econophysicists, have already verified that the results generated by the online market system called "KAKAKU dot Com" (http://kakaku.com) do often not satisfy the conditions of perfect competition as the market theory recommends. It has been noted that the the on-line market is always designed to fulfil the conditions of perfect competition. Contrary to traditional markets, in the on-line market, some firms that adopt a price greater than the lowest price will never be driven away from the market over the course of a year.

13.3.2 A Short History of Japanese Commercial Engineering

In Japan, the shift to the capitalistic mode of production has been certainly prepared by a series of matured circumstances of various spheres until at least 17th Century when the international financial institutions and networks were formed. The underlying industrial capacities, financial capacities, and commercial networks were all sufficient in developing a full-fledged launching point for capitalism. The most typical motivation of the economic and commercial organization in Japan was the Ozaka-dojima Rice-Stamp Exchange. These factors cannot be self-organized by the market forces.[15] Often, these were outcomes of creative coincidences connected with historically ingenious persons. In the case of Ozaka-dojima system, the figure was YODOYA.[16]

The brilliant entrepreneurial the developed both the direct transaction of rice and the indirect transaction by way of the bill exchange of rice stamps during 17th century in Japan. This devise was fully implemented in the institutions that supported modern financial speculation. In particular, the **bill exchange** system brought YODOYA great wealth. In 1730 the indirect exchange was officially taken for granted by Shogun Government of Japan.[17]

This year marked the world- first establishment of a modern **futures market** system. The architecture of the futures market was in fact prepared by the Japanese. This may be regarded as a technological innovation.

---

[15] Of course, the market force could serve as a complementary assistance.

[16] See "Yodoya-Komeichi," the first securities exchange in the nation in Wikipedia article http://marketswiki.com/wiki/Osaka_Exchange.

[17] See Wikipedia articles on "Dojima RiceExchange" and "Osaka Securities Exchange": https://en.wikipedia.org/wiki/Osaka_Securities_Exchange.

The U-Mart system is an artificial intelligent futures transaction system with a long-run lifetime that was initiated by Japanese computer scientists in 1998 (see Aruka, 2015, 111–112; Shiozawa et al., 2008). This system is compatible with both types of batches and continuous double auctions. Moreover, either human agent or algorithm agent can join in the system. The two eminent properties were equipped with the U-Mart system at the beginning. One is the participation system of hybrid agents. After the U-Mart system was released, the reality was closer to the U-Mart. The other is the implementation of the acceleration experiment tool.[18] The latter was indicative of the dominance of the HFT. In this section, we use the acceleration experiment tool. In our context, in an event, it is specially noted that our system originally designed as a virtual system that has turned into an actual realized system. This is called "Equity Index Futures" at the Osaka Exchange, which is a branch of JPX.[19]

The development of the U-Mart system was mainly engineer-driven,[20] and is now internationally recognized as a good platform for AI markets. The source code of the project is open for the public.[21]

13.4 Examining the Futures Market by the U-Mart Simulation in the Default Agent Configurations

One of the most interesting features of the market transaction is that **zero intelligent agent** is a dominant frequent winner of the market game. It has also been easily verified in the U-Mart system that the random agent[22] is often the winner. This is a reason why we should doubt the traditional idea that any rational/intelligent behaviour can optimize the performance of the market. It is also interesting for us to notice that equilibrium cannot not be established without dropping the assumption of homogeneous agents. If all agents select the same behavior of sell, or buy, there may not be any settlement. Therefore, it matters to us what types of agents are implemented. These considerations will motivate us to conduct a realistic simulation using the U-Mart system.

[18] This kit was publicized when U-Mart System ver.2 was released. However, the newest version of the U-Mart System is ver.4. The new experimental tool kit will be released soon when latest version is finally confirmed.

[19] JPX article (Sept 19, 2017): 10th Anniversary of Equity Index Futures and Options Nighttime Trading http://www.jpx.co.jp/english/corporate/news-releases/0060/20170919-01.html.

[20] See the web site of **the U-Mart Organization** http://www.u-mart.org/html/index.html.

[21] **U-Mart** started in 1998 as V-Mart (Virtual Mart) but is now called U-Mart, which is the abbreviation of Unreal Market as an Artificial research Test bed. The U-Mart Project has already many publications either in Japanese or in English. We note two English books on U-Mart. Shiozawa et al. (2008) published a volume of the Springer Series on Agent-Based Social Systems. The last book is Kita et al. (2016) as a volume of Evolutionary Economics and Social Complexity Science. See http://www.springer.com/series/11930.

[22] Speaking precisely, an SRandom agent is one who sends random order around the spot price fluctuation.

As argued in the last section, an evolving system in which the participating agents are *heterogenous* and mutually interact may be a system with many redundancies. In our realistic simulation, the market is an evolving system in which the initial conditions will bring similar results, even though the various heterogenous agents are either intelligently or randomly interacting. In such a complex system, as already discussed, the ICA will deal with the problem on "how damaging the inclusion of a given rule is to the universal behavior". Thus the ICA tries to repeat a similar procedure in order to obtain a certain effect based on the universal rule by referring to the different interactive rules.

Now we incorporate Class 4 as defined in the first section into the market system. In the market, at first, various types of participants are locally formed and then mutually interact in complex and interesting ways. They form local structures that are able to survive for long periods of time. In the first section, the Wolfram ICA simulations examined the attractor formation. Conversely, in the market experiment, we will detect any sensibility that is generated in a relationship between an initial strategy configuration (ISA) and its final performance configuration (FPA). A final performance is represented by some special form. We will examine whether a final performance configuration is sensitive to its initial strategy configuration or not. Then, the shape retention of the performance configuration among the initial strategy configurations and among the experimental modes is addressed.

Here, we rearrange the previous terms that we used in this context. A rule corresponds to a strategy(or agent). The initial distribution is strategy composition. A different interactive rule may find a new mode in our market experiment. By mimicking the Rule-based ICA, we thus prepare for several agents to be tested among the traditional technical agents in the following experimental design.

13.4.1 Experimental Design

Our experiment will be conducted in three different modes from Experiment 1–3. We also examine the effects in several different initial configurations.

13.4.1.1 Different Experimental Modes

- Experimental mode 1: individual match, i.e., each new agent will enter in a round robin tournament against the given technical agent configuration.
- Experimental mode 2: participation by all the members, i.e., all agents including a set of new agents will enter into a round robin tournament against the given technical agent configuration.
- Experimental mode 3: Half of a given set of agents (including all the new agents) are randomly chosen and matched.

In all the experiments, we apply different spot price series by extrapolating data outside the simulation system. In this experiment kit, the contract date of the futures transaction is set 2 months each round. Then, each trading period is then 60

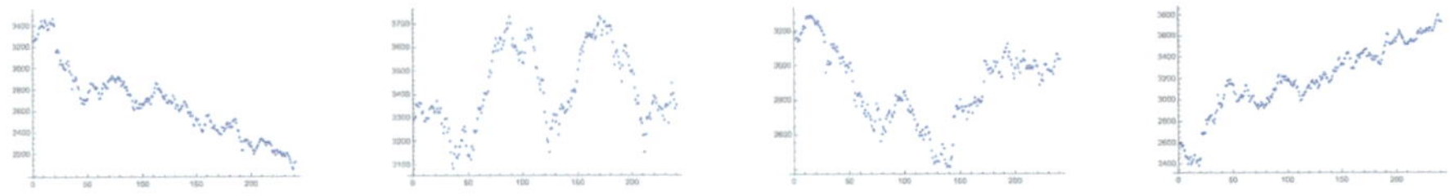

(a) Descending (b) Oscillating (c) Reversal (d) Ascending

Fig. 13.14 Spot price time series to be implemented

days. Thus, the kit will conduct **10** rounds for each type of *spot* price time series (Fig. 13.14):

- descending series: The spot price time series with a large *downward* trend in the long run
- oscillating series: The spot price time series with a large *oscillating* in the long run
- reversal series: The spot price time series that *descends* and then *ascends* in the long run
- ascending series: The spot price time series with a large *upward* trend in the long run.

13.4.1.2 Different Initial Configuration

The default strategies of the U-Mart system is given in Table 13.5 later. We also examine the effects due to three different initial strategy configurations.

- Initial Strategy Configuration 1 (ISC1): the default strategy configuration in the U-Mart system.
- Initial Strategy Configuration 2 (ISC2): the configuration that removes all random strategies, i.e., Random and SRandom.
- Initial Strategy Configuration 3 (ISC3): the configuration that removes all the agents other than random agents, i.e., the configuration composing of random agents except for MyAgents.

It can be seen that ISC3 contain a more randomness because there are only Random and SRandom agents except for MyAgents.

Under the above prescriptions, we adopt the default agents to run the U-Mart system. First, we show their profiles in Table 13.5.

We also give the distribution list of traditional technical agents below in Table 13.6.

We also give the distribution list of traditional technical agents as follows Table 13.6.

In our experiments, we have chosen **SFSpreadStrategy** as opponents to the given list of strategies. In the experimental tool kit, as usual, an agent newly designed is added. But in this article, we focus on SFspreadStrategy as a newly added agent.

Table 13.5 The strategy profiles employed as the default strategies in the U-Mart system

TrendStrategy If the latest spot price is higher than the previous spot price, he/she sends a buy order, and vice versa. The order price is the mean value of a Gaussian distribution, which is estimated by the standard deviation calculated from the latest spot prices; The order volume is offered as a uniform random number within some prescribed breadth, i.e., between the lowest and the highest volume pertinently prescribed
AntiTrendStrategy If the latest price is lower than the previous price, he/she sends a buy order, and vice versa. The prices and volumes of the limit orders are using the same rules as the rules as the Trend Strategy
RandomStrategy The order price is the mean value of a Gaussian distribution, which is estimated using the standard deviation calculated from the latest *future* prices. The order volume is a uniform random number within some prescribed breadth, i.e., between the lowest and the highest prescribed volumes
SRandomStrategy In the RandomStrategy, only the latest *futures* prices are replaced with the latest *spot* prices
RsiStrategy The time series of price is decomposed into upward parts and downward parts. The Relative Strength Intensity (Rsi) is then defined as the ratio of the sum of the price increases and the sum of the price increases and decreases. In the above, the futures price series is employed. If the Rsi calculated using the *futures* price series is greater than the threshold called the "edge band value", the agent sends a sell order, and vice versa. The prices and volumes of limit orders are set using the same rules as the rules of the Trend Strategy
SRsiStrategy In the above, *futures* is replaced with *spot*
MovingAverageStrategy If the moving average of the short term futures price variations is inclined to increase higher than the moving average of the long-term variations, the agent sends a buy order, and vice versa. δP is taken the price difference between the last session and the previous session. Here, the order price is set as follows: the last future price $+ \delta P + (\delta P/4) \times$ the Gaussian mean. Here, the Gaussian mean is the mean of a Gaussian distribution estimated by the calculated standard deviation of the last *futures* prices. The order volume is set using uniform random numbers between the lowest and the highest prescribed volumes
SMovingAverageStrategy In the MovingAverageStrategy, only the latest *futures* prices are replaced with the latest *spot* prices
SFSpreadStrategy If futures price is higher (lower) than spot price, it is bought (sold). The FS spread is defined as the difference between the last futures price and the last spot price. We call the spread ratio the last spot price to the futures price. We also call the threshold value that is chosen empirically (0.01) the—spread ratio threshold. If the FS is broader than the Spread Ratio Threshold, the agent sends a buy order. The order price is the Gaussian mean value of the spot price series whose standard deviation is calculated from the latest prices.The order volume is offered as a uniform random number within some prescribed breadth, i.e., between the lowest and the highest prescribed volumes
DayTradeStrategy Professional traders sometimes send sell and buy orders simultaneously. In terms of sell and buy volumes, this operation guarantees their zero position, i.e., neither the short nor long position.The sell price is set as a price greater than the last futures price. The buy price is set as a price lower than the last futures price. In the U-Mart system, the prices are set by employing the spread ratio R of the spot price P^S to the futures price P^f. The sell price is given by $(1 - R)$ times P^f. The buy price by $(1 + R) \times P^f$. The order volume is a uniform random number within some prescribed breadth, i.e., between the lowest and the highest prescribed volumes

*S indicates *spot* price

Table 13.6 The Pareto rankings and other measures in our experimental mode 1 under the default strategy agent set

Pareto ranking	Agent name	Maximum profit	Mean profit	Winning average	Bankruptcy rate
13	MyStrategy1	10	15	19	1
6	Std01_TrendStrategy	6	10	11	1
21	Std02_AntiTrendStrategy1	21	21	21	1
20	Std03_AntiTrendStrategy2	20	20	20	1
15	Std04_RandomStrategy	12	16	16	1
4	Std05_SRandomStrategy0000	4	4	8	1
3	Std06_SRandomStrategy0001	3	3	3	1
4	Std07_SRandomStrategy0002	5	5	4	1
15	Std08_RsiStrategy	13	17	15	1
10	Std09_SRsiStrategy1	8	13	14	1
13	Std10_SRsiStrategy2	11	8	12	1
10	Std11_SRsiStrategy3	9	7	10	1
15	Std12_MovingAverageStrategy	14	12	13	1
6	Std13_SMovingAverageStrategy1	12	10	6	1
10	Std14_SMovingAverageStrategy2	11	8	6	1
6	Std15_SMovingAverageStrategy3	9	9	4	1
1	Std16_SFSpreadStrategy1	2	1	1	1
1	Std17_SFSpreadStrategy2	1	2	2	1
19	Std18_DayTradeStrategy1	18	19	18	1
18	Std19_DayTradeStrategy2	16	18	16	1
6	MyStrategy2	7	6	9	1

Two agents of SFspreadStrategey are implemented as MyAgent. The behaviors of this agent are akin to human agents who prefer risk averting. In the event, the number of SFspreadStrategy is 4 in total. But interestingly we will see that a newly added agent of SFspreadStrategy is not guaranteed to win although the other added agent of the same type is ranked as top in Pareto ranking (Tables 13.7 and 13.8).

13.4.1.3 Pareto Ranking

We then evaluate the market performance each experiment by employing 4 different measures: maximum profit, mean profit, winning times, and bankruptcy rate.[23] In the U-Mart assessment, we usually evaluate the performance of each of the 4 measures by ranking them over all strategies. It is noted that we need the multi-objective method to conduct the *Pareto ordering* of the agent strategies for the 4 dimensional objectives. Fortunately, our experimental kit provides us with an automatic generation of the Pareto rankings of the 4 objectives.

[23] The bankruptcy does not often occur. In our experiments, any bankruptcy will not be observed. Thus, this measure may be removed in our figures.

Table 13.7 The density distribution of different strategies

Agent strategy	Number of agents
TrendStrategy	1
AntiTrendStrategy	2
RandomStrategy	1
*S*RandomStrategy	3
RsiStrategy	1
*S*RsiStrategy	3
MovingAverageStrategy	1
*S*MovingAverageStrategy	3
SFSpreadStrategy	2
DayTradeStrategy	2

* *S* indicates "spot price"

Table 13.8 MyStrategies adopted in our experiments

MyStrategy1	SFSpreadStrategy
MyStrategy2	SFSpreadStrategy

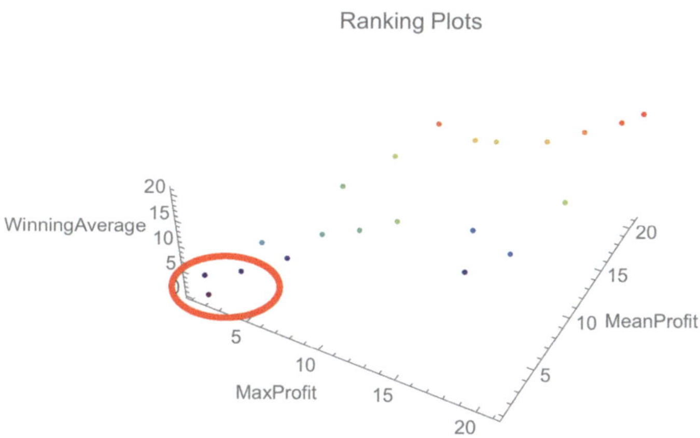

Fig. 13.15 Ranking on the 3-dimensional objectives

In Fig. 13.15, the circled points indicate the top 3 strategies in the *Pareto* ranking: SFSpreadStrategy1, SFSpreadStrategy2 and SRandomStrategy0001. Figure 13.15 shows that the two SFSpread strategies are *Pareto-dominant* in the 3 multi-objective space in the experimental mode 1, as shown in Table 13.7.[24] The second most dominant strategy with respect to Pareto dominance is SRandomStrategy0002.

[24] We removed the bankruptcy from the measures.

13.4.2 The Acceleration Experiments

In the U-Mart system, matching orders in the market are of the hybrid type. That is, the traditional agent that are usually called **technical analytical agents** will match human agents. One of our purposes is to examine the characteristics of agent strategies using experiments. However, the games with human agents are not suitable for long-term experiments. Thus, we adopt the acceleration experiments without human agents. The measures of the simulation results are ordered according to the ranking of their performance from top to bottom in ascending order. Since we employ 4 measures, the evaluation is achieved using the multi-object method that was already mentioned. Now we shall list the simulation results of each mode of the experiments by using radar charts, as shown in Figs. 13.16, 13.17 and 13.18.

The simulation results are summarized in Table 13.9. We focus on any shape retention of performance configuration, i.e., among the initial strategy configurations and among any experimental modes in the radar charts. Table 13.9 indicates that there may be shape retention between ISC1 and ISC2, between Mode 1 and Mode 2, and between Mode 1 and Mode 2 under ISC3, and between ISC2 and ISC3 under Mode 3. By using the acceleration experiments of the U-Mart system, we detected **a block matrix** [ISC$_i$, Mode$_i$] $i = 1, 2$. This matrix block represents the next 4 radar charts: Figs. 13.16a, b and 13.17a, b.

(a) Experimental Mode 1 under ISC1

(b) Experimental Mode 2 under ISC1

(c) Experimental Mode 3 under ISC1

Fig. 13.16 ISA1: Pareto rankings

(a) Experimental Mode 1 under ISC2

(b) Experimental Mode 2 under ISC2

(c) Experimental Mode 3 under ISC2

Fig. 13.17 ISA2: Pareto rankings

(a) Experimental Mode 1 under ISC3

(b) Experimental Mode 2 under ISC3

(c) Experimental Mode 3 under ISC3

Fig. 13.18 ISC33: Pareto rankings

Table 13.9 The effects of the shape retentions of the radar charts

	Mode 1	Mode 2	Mode 3
ISC1	Shape	Retained	No similarity
ISC2			Shape retained
ISC3	Shape	Retained	

1. Here, we found a relatively similar configuration of strategies that is insensitive to neither the experimental modes nor the initial strategy configurations.
2. It is also shown that the SFspread strategy could not absolutely dominate the SRandom strategy, as shown in Figs. 13.16a, b and 13.17a, b. An SFspread can dominate an SRandom, but every SFspread cannot dominate any SRandom. The corollary also holds true.

13.5 Identifying the Fundamental Agent Configuration to Realize any Spot Price Series

The agent configurations examined in the above discussion cannot guarantee an attractive price series like the fundamentals. However, we are now ready to establish a special reference to realize any futures price series similar to a given spot price series. This special agent configuration was already investigated in an insightful simulation by Nakajima and Mori (2005) that resorted to powerful simulations in the U-Mart system.

13.5.1 StdAC: The Standard Agent Configuration

First, we show the agent configuration of Nakajima and Mori (2005) has given in the following manner:

We call this agent the standard agent configuration (StdAC). The traditional "fundamentals" are not internally decided in the market. The market fundamentals must work as a centre of gravitation of the market. This idea must then be *internally* defined inside the agent set to work in the concerned market system. Thus, the composite set of agent strategies should be used as the fundamentals of the market, in the sense that this set can always realize the price series similar to a given spot price series.

We finally employ this set to detect a critical configuration from where the futures price series diverges. Thus, we confirm a new approach to study the market mechanism in this context.

13.5.2 The Simulation Results of Convergence and Divergence Around the Std AC of Technical Strategies

We employ the **Std AC** by using the half scale of **the original Nakajima-Mori figures** mentioned in Table 13.10 to apply the Experimental mode 2 that was defined in the Sect. 13.1.1. We show the simulation results of this environment. Changing the experimental mode will not cause any large variations in the results. Here, we examine the StdAc by means of the spot price series used in Fig. 13.14.

Next, we add 23 bodies of SRandomStrategy agents to the StdAC that is currently adopted. There is not a discernible divergence from a given spot series. However, it is trivial for P-values that the proximity between spot and futures are worse for each given spot price series (Figs. 13.19, 13.20 and 13.21).

Table 13.10 The special agent set is used to realize a futures prices similar to a given spot prices

Agent strategy	Original number†	Adopted number‡
RandomStrategy	8.1	4
AntiTrendStrategy	7.2	3
DayTradeStrategy	8.2	4
Moving AverageStrategy	26.4	12
RsiStrategy	9.3	4
TrendStrategy	13.2	6
*S*RandomStrategy	50.8	23
SFSpreadStrategy	45	20
*S*MovingAverageStrategy	32.8	15
*S*RsiStrategy	22.6	10

* *S* indicates "spot price" English words
† Figures are cited from Nakajima and Mori (2005)
‡ Figures adopted in this article

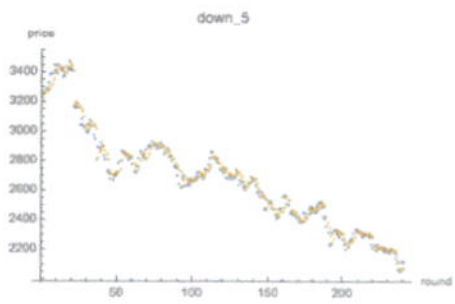

(a) Descending
† Spearman rank's P-value: $1.13122 * 10^{-304}$

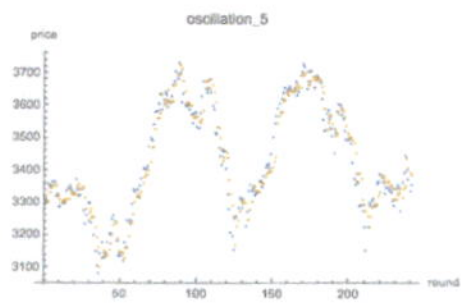

(b) Oscillating
† Spearman rank's P-value: $3.10047 * 10^{-172}$

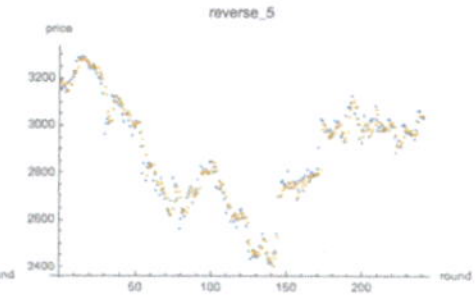

(c) Reversal
† Spearman rank's P-value: $8.49172 * 10^{-192}$

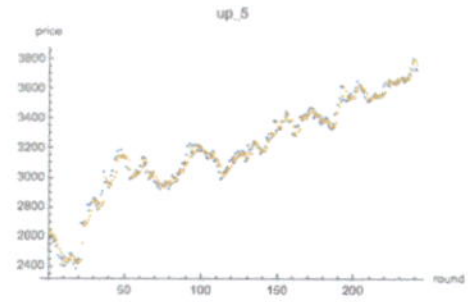

(d) Ascending
† Spearman rank's P-value: $1.340271819962810 * 10^{-308}$

Fig. 13.19 Convergences of Std AC towards each spot price series

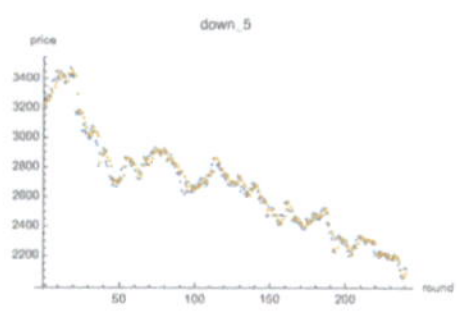

(a) Descending
† Spearman rank's P-value: $2.3555 * 10^{-307}$

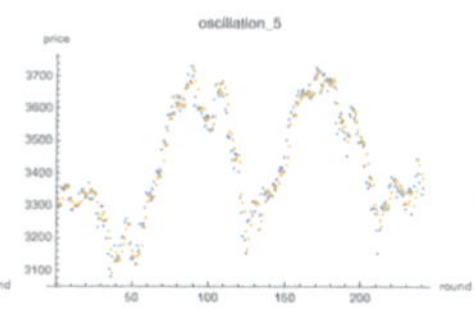

(b) Oscillating
† Spearman rank's P-value: $4.7051 * 10^{-174}$

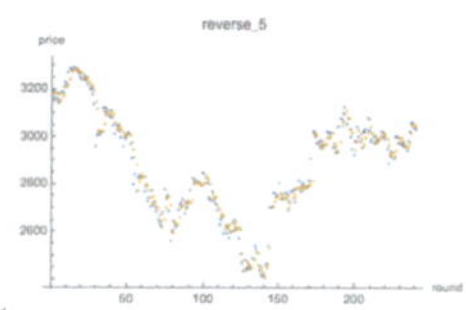

(c) Reversal
† Spearman rank's P-value: $1.21164 * 10^{-197}$

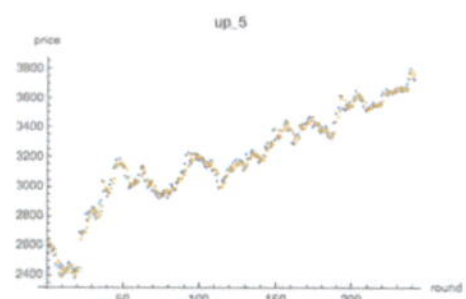

(d) Ascending
† Spearman rank's P-value: $1.297324912844414 * 10^{-314}$

Fig. 13.20 Convergences of the Std AC towards each spot series after 23 SRandom agents are added

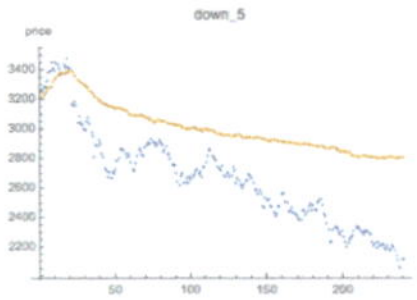

(a) Descending
† Spearman rank's P-value: $6.53379 * 10^{-181}$

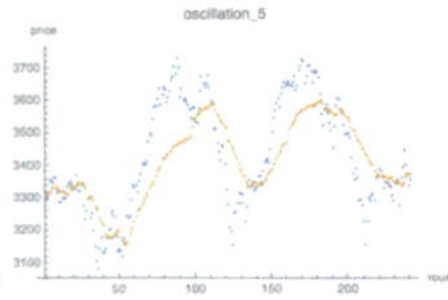

(b) Oscillating
† Spearman rank's P-value: $1.12545 * 10^{-137}$

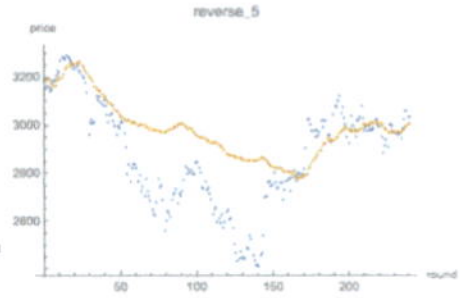

(c) Reversal
† Spearman rank's P-value: $1.02882 * 10^{-31}$

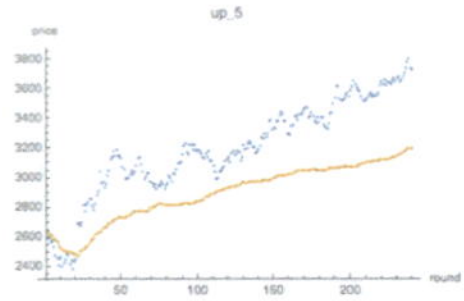

(d) Ascending
† Spearman rank's P-value: $2.31763 * 10^{-182}$

Fig. 13.21 Convergences of Std AC added 46 bodies of Random toward each spot price series

Finally, after removing the SRandom agents from the StdAC, we add 46 Random-Strategy to the StdAC that is currently adopted. The SRandom strategy is defined to randomly place orders around a given spot price, while the Random strategy is the strategy that places orders (sell and buy) without any reference to a given spot price. In this case, the divergence between the spot and futures prices becomes obvious.

13.5.3 A Brief Report of Pareto Rankings in the Average Given the New Fundamental Agent Configuration

Using a similar approach as that above for the Pareto rankings among agents of Std AC, we roughly examine their earning capabilities. For simplicity, we compare the average ranking each strategy.

As long as we employ **Std AC**, the SF spread is always suppressed smaller values. This is the reason why **SFSpread** strategies can earn most effectively. Due to a similar property, **SRandom strategy** may also earn almost equally.Given a big divergence between spot and futures, these advantage will break down as shown in Fig. 13.22c.

13.6 Concluding Remarks

As we sated at the beginning of this article, we examined any sensitivity of performance configurations among the initial strategy configurations and among the experimental modes. Furthermore, by resorting to an intelligent idea of **the standard agent configuration (StdAC)**, we virtually confirmed convergent/divergent behaviours between the spot and futures price series. Thus, we suggest a new approach in agent-based market simulations.

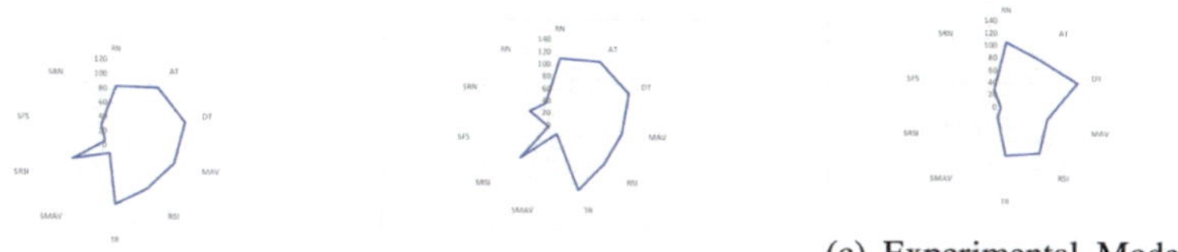

(a) Experimental Mode 2 under StdAC

(b) Experimental Mode 2 under StdAC +23 SRandom agents

(c) Experimental Mode 2 under StdAC -23 SRandom agents + 46 Random agents

Fig. 13.22 Std AC: Pareto rankings

Exercises

13.1 As detailed above, Maymin has given a rule of shift of mind between several states, which plays a role as a transducer in the automaton. It is evident that the emerging or floating shift rules will arrange the market in a periodic way. More importantly, the model incorporates these induced behaviors. The interactions between mind state, market situation, the trader's memory and the market history can therefore be included. The trader will follow an individual pattern linked to past history, which is not generated randomly but by strain tranduced by the system. Figure 13.1 is described by a classifier system. Examine the rules and the conditions in view of the classifier system.

13.2 In the previous chapter, we lerant the time series analysis to remove the effects from randomness. On the other hand, tt is difficult to determine whether the same response occurred randomly or whether a feature of the system produces such an outcome. Even the definition of elasticity on a material, is considered "strain" in systems that can be formulated in Voigt form. Discuss specific examples of "anelastic strain," if any, in financial market price fluctuations.

13.3 There are trendfollowers as well as contralians in the market. In some cases, trendofollower may be contrarian. Such a rule of shift of mind between several states is called a "transducer" in the automaton in this chapter. In this book, "transductive/symbolic reasoning" was discussed in Sect. 7.2.5. Compare the difference of the term of transduction between both. Hint: Transduction sometimes is interpreted with abduction, which can work as amchine learning.

13.4 Even an exchange of goods without production involves a change in the exchanger's holdings, the ratio of the two exchangers' interests changes. In this exchange equilibrium, equilibrium is then said to have been reached when none of the exchangers can any longer increase up their respective utilities. According to a single trader dynamics discuseed above, in the market, however, not only can a trader be a seller or a buyer, but he is also allowed to sell and buy at the same time.

The price fluctuations never change the existing real assets due to the single trader. Describe the differences on the both types of transaction, and explain the differences of the real market and the financial market.

13.5 Redundancies and the depth of logic contained in a complex system was argued in Sect. 13.1.2. Describe the application of "complexities" to the market dynamics in your own way, and then the essential difference between the single trader dynamics and and the multitrader dynamics.

13.6 "Market mechanism in evolution" was argued in Sect. 13.3.1. HFT is a recent example of an evolving market. Mention another instance of the evolving market if any.

13.7 Cellular automata (CA) can be classified according to the complexity and information produced by the behavior of the CA pattern in Fig. 13.11. Examine the properties of class 4 and give examples of events that satisfy class 4.

13.8 The random agents described above are called zero-intelligent agents. This type of agent will not be loser on average and sometimes comes out on top in terms of earned value. First analyse why this is the case, and further examine whether the presence of random agents has a role to play in the price fluctuations of the market.

13.9 The Dojima Rice Exchange, established in Yodoyabashi, Osaka, was the world's first futures exchange. See the historical details for the Japan Exchange's web page https://www.jpx.co.jp/dojima/en/index.html. Investigate briefly the history of exchange system in your country. Hint: Note the difference between the commodity market and the stock market. The Dojima Rice Exchange was not just a commodity exchange. The Dojima was a small area and it was not possible to provide all commodities for settlement. At the Dojima Rice Exchange, rice stamps were used instead of actual commodities.

13.10 From its inception of Rice Exchange in Osaka, "mark to the market" was executed daily before settlement in the futures contract month. Discuss the significance of mark to the market in the exchange system.

References

Arthur, W. B. (2009). *The nature of technology*. Free Press.

Aruka, Y. (2009). The book review: Klaus Mainzer, Der kreative Zufall: Wie das Neue in die Welt kommt (The Creative Chance. How Novelty Comes into the World, C. H. Beck, Müenchen. (2007). 283pp. *Evolutionary and Institutional Economic Review, 5*(2), 307–316.

Aruka, Y. (2015). Hodgson's bibliometric report and the reconstruction plan of economics. *Evolutionary and Institutional Economics Review, 15*(1), 189–202.

Aruka, Y. (2017). Special feature: preliminaries towards ontological reconstruction of economics: Theories and simulations. *Evolutionary and Institutional Economic Review, 14*(2), 409–414.

Carvalho, D. S. (2011). Classifying the complexity and information of cellular automata. Retrieved from http://demonstrations.wolfram.com/ClassifyingTheComplexityAndInformationOfCellularAutomata/.

Hawkins, R. (2011). Lending sociodynamics and economic instability. *Physica A, 390*(7), 4355–4369.

Kita, H., Taniguchi, T., & Nakajima, Y. (Eds.). (2016). *Realistic simulation of financial markets analyzing market behaviors by the third mode of science (Springer series: Evolutionary economics and social complexity science)*, (Vol. 4). Springer.

Lux, T. (2009). Rational forecast or social opinion dynamics? Identification of interaction effects in a business climate survey. *Journal of Economic Behavior Organization, 72*, 638–655.

Mainzer, K. (2007). Kapitel 7: Zufall in Kultur, Wirtschaft, und Gesselschaft. In *Der kreative Zufall: Wie das Neue in die Welt kommt?* CH Beck.

Maymin, P. Z. (2007a). Trader dynamics in minimal models of financial complexity. Available through the Wolfram Demonstrations Project. Retrieved from http://demonstrations.wolfram.com/TraderDynamicsInMinimalModelsOfFinancialComplexity/

Maymin, P. Z. (2007b). Horizontal visibility graphs for elementary cellular automata. Available through the Wolfram Demonstrations Project. Retrieved from http://demonstrations.wolfram.com/TheMinimalModelOfTheComplexityOfFinancialSecurityPrices/

Maymin, P. Z. (2007c). Minimal model of simulating prices of financial securities using an iterated finite automaton. Available through the Wolfram Demonstrations Project. Retrived from http://demonstrations.wolfram.com/TheMinimalModelOfTheComplexityOfFinancialSecurityPrices/

Maymin, P. Z (2007d). Exploring minimal models of the complexity of security prices. Available through the Wolfram Demonstrations Project. Retrieved from http://demonstrations.wolfram.com/ExploringMinimalModelsOfTheComplexityOfSecurityPrices/

Maymin, P. Z. (2011). The minimal model of financial complexity. *Quantitative Finance, 11*(9), 1371–1378.

Maymin, P. Z. (2011). Markets are efficient if and only if p = np. *Algorithmic Finance, 1*(1), 1–11.

Mitchell, E., & Beyon, T. (2011). Fully random, five-rule interactive cellular automata (ICA). Retrieved from http://demonstrations.wolfram.com/FullyRandomFiveRuleInteractiveCellularAutomataICA/

Mizuno, T., & Watanabe, T. (2010). A statistical analysis of product prices in online market. *European Physical Journal, 3B*(76), 501–505.

Mizuno, T., Nirei, M., & Watanabe, T. (2010). Closely competing firms and price adjustment: Some findings from an online marketplace? *Scandinavian Journal of Economics, 112*(4), 673–696.

Nakajima, Y., & Mori, N. (2005). Design of experimental environment for artificial financial market. mimeo.

Shiozawa, Y., Nakajima, Y., Matsui, H., Koyama, Y., Taniguchi, K., Hashimoto, F. (2008). *Artificial market experiments with the U-mart system (Springer series on agent based social systems)*, (Vol. 4). Springer.

Wolfram, S. (2002). *A new kind of science*. Wolfram Media.

Statistical Approach on the Economic System

14

Abstract

Masanao Aoki was a great scholar who sincerely challenged to exit from the secular world fettered by the representative method of economic modeling. He resolutely focused on a stochastic dynamic system, i.e., cluster dynamics with a *finite* number of heterogenous agents of different types, which could change the methodological regime from the pure homogeneous agents to the actual world. The desired model may be described by partition vectors with multiple state. Aoki's model has renovated the traditional restrictive views. In this chapter, by referring to the sole textbook of Masanao Aoki written in Japanese, we will introduce his insightful analytical methods.

This chapter refers to the first and the last textbook single-authored by Professor Masanao Aoki in 2003 titled: *Introduction to Stochastic Dynamic Approach of Heterogeneous Agents* in Japanese (Aoki, 2003). Textbook in general usually surpasses monographs in view of transmission of the author's general mind of way of thinking. We briefly/partially introduce the content of his textbook, and reveal his essential messages of the new approach for the reconstruction of macroeconomics. You will learn the elementary ideas of different type agents, multiple states, partition vectors, stochastic/cluster dynamics, and heterogeneous interaction.

14.1 Ontological Background

14.1.1 Events with Multiplicity

There are over-flooded out many news of macroeconomic problems in the mass media, which are connected with some pushy abduction based on the stereotyped knowledge of the standard economics: Interest cut brings either a rise of investment or decreasing unemployment. Can we believe such a news? We have the simple

Y. Aruka, *Evolutionary Economics*, Springer Texts in Business and Economics,
https://doi.org/10.1007/978-981-97-1382-0_14

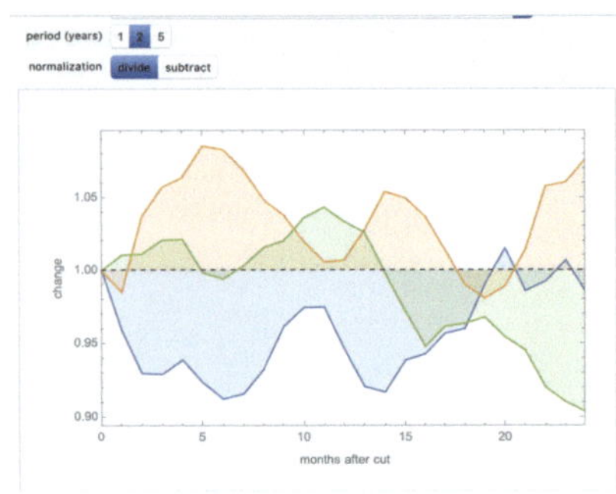

Fig. 14.1 The effects on exchange rate

answer "No". Because we have a very smart historical database given by a piece of the Wolfram Demonstration Project titled: "Macroeconomic Effects of Interest Rate Cuts". Cawley and Meinberg (2011).[1] This simulator gives us a remarkable insight on a macroscopic phenomenon which may coexist with some multiple states. For example, the interest rate cut may make either upward or downward the currency exchange rate or decrease from history to history, and fluctuating from elapsed time to time due to some autocorrelation. We should know that here cannot be escaped such emergence of multiplicity around a certain action like the interest rate cut.

It may be a best way to use the simulator of Cawley and Meinberg (2011) to understand the multiplicity of the subsequential states due to a policy change. It is very interesting to know the profile of this demonstration. The data base categorized three distinguished periods as follows:

Period I — The period before 1979 when interest rates were rising and inflation gradually became a major problem

Period II — The Volcker period in the 1980s, in which interest rates reversed their long-term trend

Period III — The Greenspan-Bernanke period from 1987 to the present (2011).

If we take an example of Period I in this demonstration, we will reproduce the next figures of the historical charts like Figs. 14.1 and 14.2. By inspection from the data base, we will discover many similar events. The idea of ABM (Agent Based Modeling) will also suffice us to methodologically renovate our traditional idealistic modeling structures to permit such a multiplicity emerging in the model.

[1] "Major Fed rate cuts can have wide and varying effects on major macroeconomic variables. This Demonstration shows the change in selected time series following reductions in the Fed Funds rate of 0.5 or more, after a period of rising or level interest rates."

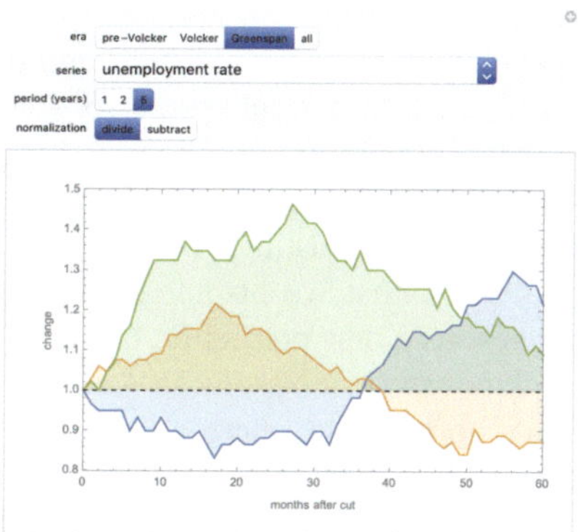

Fig. 14.2 The effects on unemployment

14.1.2 The Fifth Stage of Aoki's Life Work

Professor Aoki has worked with a wide coverage of topics from the 1st to the fifth stage summarized in Aruka-Gallegati-Yoshikawa (2015). His textbook dealt with here belongs to the fifth stage, where "[t]he new method is featured by Statistical Physics and Combinatorial Stochastic Processes. Equilibria is not treated as a fixed points. The system may be subject to non-self averaging and mutant could emerge internally. These studies can rightly establish a set of theoretical foundations to socio-econophysics." The books at this stage include:

Aoki 1996	*New approaches to macroeconomic modeling: evolutionary stochastic dynamics, multiple equilibria, and externalities as field effects*
Aoki 2002	*Modeling aggregate behavior and fluctuations in economics: stochastic views of interacting agents*
Aoki 2003	*Introduction to Stochastic Dynamic Approach of Heterogeneous Agents*
Aoki and Yoshikawa 2006	*Reconstructing macroeconomics: a perspective from statistical physics and combinatorial stochastic processes.*

That is to say, Aoki (1996; 2002; 2003), Aoki and Yoshikawa (2006) had a keen awareness of this multiplicity problem.

Agents involved in the economic system are divided into several subsets (clusters), and the size of the agents changes over time with the probability of entry, exit, and change in agent type. And new subsets emerge as new types of agents enter. Here all sizes and numbers are defined finitely in the discrete system.

In fact, there are as usual various heterogeneous types of people and companies, that is, agents (subjects) interact in society. In other words, agents can be allowed to immigrate in and/or emigrate to other clusters. The type is not necessarily fixed. A new type of agent, who is currently *unknown*, will emerge in the future. Even a given fixed group can also be, to same extent, transformed by the replacement of agents through entry or exit differently according to purpose. Such a group/crowd is forming a common subset/cluster where any component of the group is characterized by exchangeability, or the same kinds. The association of clusters will generate **a cluster dynamics** consisting of several heterogeneous interacting groups. This idea is traditionally inheriting from **the master equation**, or synergetics.[2] In the following, it is noted that we do not know all the types any time. This point of view will suggest us a new prediction based on empirical stochastic distributions. This is just the innovative standpoint in Aoki's textbook.

At some point, there are n agents in the system. Now, in the case that n are classified into K_n types, it needs us to know what type of agent can arrive in the next short span δ by a conditional probability rate. Thus the textbook of Aoki (2003) has consistently demonstrated how to deal with a model to allow **unknown types** selection in stochastic cluster dynamics around the environment of **exchangeability**. Thus, in the finite discrete domain, we can arrange two stochastic analytical frames, i.e., the analytical frame based on the circumstance of exchangeable agents, firstly for the known type, and secondly for the unknown types. In physics, so far, these kinds of formulation have been regarded as **the classic occupancy problem**. According to Aoki, we regard the first frame as the Maxwell-Boltzmann form, and the second as the Bose-Einstein form.[3] In the context of this text book, in the following, we mainly focus on the above two streams chronically. First of all, we start to overview how Aoki argue **the standard master equation** to derive **multiple equilibria**.

The Japanese textbook Aoki (2003) is a relatively small concise book of 187 total pages, which has been published just after the books of Aoki (2002) came out. The contents of both books naturally are overlapping. It isnoted that "non-self-averaging" has been newly focused in Aoki and Yoshikawa (2006) written after his textbook. This is also one of the most important key ideas at the fifth stage. See Aruka and Akiyama (2009) as an application of this idea.

For the sake of the readers' convenience, we introduce the contents of the book:

Chapter 1	Introduction
Chapter 2	Master equations
Chapter 3	Transition rates and the stationary distribution
Chapter 4	Partition vectors
Chapter 5	Generating functions
Chapter 6	Solution method of master equations
Chapter 7	Trees and their dynamics
Chapter 8	A model for the alternatives
Chapter 9	A growth process model for the two industrial sectors
Chapter 10	Distributions of crowds

[2] See Weidlich (2000) for the details of synegetics.

[3] See Aoki (1996, 13) as for the relationship of both distributions. This relationship will be discussed late in Sect. 14.3.2.

Chapter 11 The power law distributions and a stochastic dynamical system with random coefficients quontifications . Criticism against Blanchard-Watson model.

Concluding remarks

Appendices A1. Identical equations of matrices and determinants, A2. Stochastic generating functions, A3. Characteristic curves and auxiliary equations, A4. Differential equations to be fulfilled by generating functions, A5. Examples on the difference between the deterministic system and the stochastic system, A6. The calculation method of Viarengo's order statistics, A7. The Laplace transform, A8. Cauchy's formula, A9. Error functions, A10. The Dirichlet distribution and gamma function, A11. The density function of Z_K, A12. The partition of $[n]$, A13. The two-parametric model, A14. The entry rate with two parameters, A15. The partition vector and the expectation calculation on $E(a_j)$, A16. The growth process of Poisson groups, A17. The growth process for a model of two-typed agents, A18. Distribution functions: Bernoulli, Binomial, Multi-nomial, Lognormal, Beta, random alms (Residual allocation model), GEM, Size-biased replacement, A19. Boltzmann-Gibbs distribution, A20. The minimum sojourn time

14.2 The Standard Master Equation in the Case that Types are Known

We define a Markov chain X_t on the state space S which dynamically describes a flux of probabilities. In a state j at time t, we can imagine a probability $P_j(t) = \Pr(X_t = j)$. We suppose that there are a number of independent agents, each of whom is in one of finite microeconomic states, and its each state evolves according to the master equation

$$\frac{dP_j(t)}{dt} = \sum_{k \neq j}[P_k(t)w_{kj} - w_{jk}P_j(t)]\ j \in S. \tag{14.1}$$

where w_{kj} denotes the transition rates from state j to state k, or the in-flow rates, and w_{jk} the rates from k to j, the out-flow rates.

In the textbook, the fundamental formulas of the master equation are provided in Chap. 2. Here we argue some examples in the alternatives model provided in Chap. 8.

14.2.1 A Gibbs Distribution in Terms of the Master Equation

The system of two states: Then the economy is composed by

$$S = \{a, b\}.$$

Given the nonnegative transition rates $w_{ab}, w_{ba} \geq 0$, the master equation system is constituted by the next two ordinary differential equations:

$$\frac{dP_a(t)}{dt} = P_b(t)w_{ba} - P_a w_{ab}, \tag{14.2}$$

$$\frac{dP_b(t)}{dt} = P_a(t)w_{ab} - P_b w_{ba}. \tag{14.3}$$

Here

$$P_a(t) + P_b(t) = 1.$$

In this case, given an initial condition $P_a(0)$, and $w_{ab} + w_{ba} > 0$, it follows:

$$\pi_a = \lim_{t\to\infty} P_a(t) = \frac{w_{ba}}{w_{ba} + w_{ab}}. \tag{14.4}$$

In general, the master equation may be

$$\frac{\partial P(s,t)}{\partial t} = \sum_{s\neq s'} P(s,t)w(s' \mid s,t) - \sum_{s\neq s'} P(s',t)w(s \mid s',t).$$

In the stationary state or in equilibrium, the probability in-flows and out-flows balance at every state:

$$\pi_j \sum_{k\in S} w_{jk} = \sum_{k\in S} \pi_k w_{kj} \; \forall j \in S, \tag{14.5}$$

$$\pi_j \geq 0, \sum_{j\in S} \pi_j = 1. \tag{14.6}$$

If there exist a j, and a π_j, we call the distribution

$$\{\pi_j, j \in S\}$$

"**an equilibrium distribution**."

If the probability flows balance for every pair of states, it then holds **the detailed balance condition**:

$$\pi_j w_{jk} = \pi_k w_{kj}.$$

Given an **irreducible** Markov chain, for any state s_j, we can find a finite sequence

$$\{s_1, s_2, \cdots, s_j\}$$

starting from some initial state s_0. If the detailed balance condition holds, it follows *a Boltzmann-Gibbs distribution*

$$\pi_j = \pi(s_0) \prod_{i=0}^{j-1} \frac{w_{i+1,i}}{w_{i,i+1}}.$$

Here

$$\pi(s) = K \exp[-U(s)]$$

with

$$U(s_j) - U(s_0) = \sum \ln \frac{w_{i+1,i}}{w_{i,i+1}}$$

implies $U(s)$ to be *a potential.*

The probability distribution is *independent of paths* from s_0 to s_j due to the property of Markov chain process. See Aoki (1996, 118).

14.2.2 Multiplicity of the Microeconomic Configurations

For clarity, now we adopt a more elegant formulation cited from These descriptions are cited from Aoki (1996, 139–141), instead of employing a direct expression in Chap. 8 of the textbook Aoki (2003, 98–101). The total number of states is set N. The $n(t)$ indicates the state variable. We have ${}_N C_n$ ways to realize **the same** $\frac{n}{N}$. In other words, the equilibrium distribution gives the idea of multiplicity of the micro-configuration that produces the same macro value. By use of $\frac{n}{N}$, we employ a variable x such that

$$\frac{x+1}{2} = \frac{n}{N}. \tag{14.7}$$

x measures the fraction from the median. It follows

$$\mathrm{d}x = \frac{2}{N}. \tag{14.8}$$

The base e Shannon entropy, by use of the above variable x, is given by

$$H(x) = -\frac{1+x}{2} \ln \frac{1+x}{2} - \frac{1-x}{2} \ln \frac{1-x}{2}. \tag{14.9}$$

It also is verified

$$\frac{\mathrm{d}H}{\mathrm{d}x} = \frac{1}{2} \ln \frac{1-x}{1+x}. \tag{14.10}$$

The approximation formula thus gives

$${}_N C_n = \exp\left[NH\left(\frac{x+1}{2}\right)\right] + o\left(\frac{1}{N}\right). \tag{14.11}$$

14.2.3 The Microeconomic Birth-and-Death Process in a Discrete Form

Now suppose that the number of microeconomic agents in this subclass is reduced by one(a death), and the number of agents increases by one (a birth). It then follows the master equation in the discrete case:

$$P_{t+1}(n) = W_{n-1,n}P_t(n-1) + W_{n+1,n}P_t(n+1) + W_{n,n}P_t(n), \tag{14.12}$$

where $W_{n,n-1}$ is the probability of transition rate from state n to $n-1$, and where $W_{n,n+1}$ denotes the probability of transition from n to $n-1$.

Let the time step to be small enough.

$$W_{n,n} = 1 - W_{n,n+1} + W_{n,n-1}. \tag{14.13}$$

expresses the probability that the number of agents may remain the same, normally as assumed to be positive.

The detailed balance condition

$$\Pi(n)W_{n,n+1} = \Pi(n+1)W_{n+1,n} \tag{14.14}$$

gives the equilibrium probability Π's. The equilibrium probability distribution will form a *Boltzmann-Gibbs distribution*.

The solution of the above difference equation gives

$$\Pi(n) = \Pi(0)\prod_{k=1}^{n}\frac{W_{k-1,k}}{W_{k,k-1}}. \tag{14.15}$$

In the simplest case, a death shows $W_{n-1,n}$, while a birth $W_{n,n+1}$. Thus, for some constants μ, λ, it holds

$$W_{n,n-1} = \mu n$$
$$W_{n,n+1} = \lambda(N-n).$$

In the following, we set for convenience

$$\mu = \lambda.$$

Let $u_i(x)$ to be a *perceived random benefit* over some unspecified planning horizon of adopting alternative i when fraction x of agents are using it (Aoki, 1996, 138).

Given the two choices 1 and 2, we define the **benefit difference** between two states[4]:

$$\triangle G = \pi_1(x) - \pi_2(x). \tag{14.16}$$

$$\eta_1(x) = \Pr(\pi_1(x) \geq \pi_2(x)). \tag{14.17}$$

Taking some **nonlinear effects** into account, we assume

$$W_{n,n-1} = N\left(1 - \frac{n}{N}\right)\eta_1 \frac{n}{N}, \tag{14.18}$$

$$W_{n,n+1} = N\left(\frac{n}{N}\right)\eta_2 \frac{n}{N}. \tag{14.19}$$

The **potential** is given

$$-\beta N U\left(\frac{n}{N}\right) - \ln Z = \ln \Pi(0) + \ln_N C_n + \sum^{n} \ln \frac{\eta_1(k/N)}{\eta_2(k/N)}.$$

Here

$$Z = \sum_n \exp[-\beta N U\left(\frac{n}{N}\right)] < \infty \tag{14.20}$$

is the **partition function**.

We set

$$\ln \frac{\eta_1(k/N)}{\eta_2(k/N)} = 2\beta \triangle G\left(\frac{k}{N}\right).$$

According to Aoki (1996, 141), we can interpret β with

> **the degree of uncertainty** in the economic environment surrounding agents, or the general level of economic activity.

Then **the equilibrium probability** can be expressed by

$$\Pi(n) = \frac{\exp[-\beta N U\left(\frac{n}{N}\right)]}{Z} \tag{14.21}$$

[4] In a continuous case, we may make

$$\eta_1(x) = \frac{\exp[\beta \triangle \pi(x)]}{\exp[\beta \triangle \pi(x)] + \exp[-\beta \triangle \pi(x)]}.$$

Here β expresses a degree of uncertainty over the concerned system.

Neglecting the items $O(1/N)$, it follows:

$$U\left(\frac{n}{N}\right) = -\frac{2}{N}\sum_{k=1}^{n} \Delta G\left(\frac{k}{N}\right) - \frac{1}{\beta}H\left(\frac{n}{N}\right). \tag{14.22}$$

Hence,[5]

$$U(x) \approx -\int \Delta G(y)\mathrm{d}y - \frac{1}{\beta}H(x) \tag{14.23}$$

$$= -G(x) - \frac{1}{\beta}H(x). \tag{14.24}$$

Taking the relations obtained in the above preliminaries into consideration,

$$\frac{\mathrm{d}U(x)}{\mathrm{d}x} \approx -\Delta G(x) - \frac{1}{2\beta}\ln\frac{1-x}{1+x}. \tag{14.25}$$

In the equilibrium in which the potential never be changed, it holds

$$2\beta\Delta G(x) = \ln\frac{1+x}{1-x}. \tag{14.26}$$

This is just a *Boltzmann-Gibbs distribution* derived from the discrete time formulation. This approach rather demonstrates a *qualitative* prediction in social interaction of heterogeneous agents by use of the concept of **equilibrium distribution** or an ensemble mean.

14.2.4 Choice Under Uncertainty: Cluster Dynamics

Finally, we close this section to take an example employed in Chap. 2 of the textbook Aoki (2003, 17–20). When all the members in this system succeed to maximize their utilities, the system can reach the level of $u(a)$. If some of the members failed to maximize utility, the level of the system could go down to $u(b)$. In other words, the system may be constituted by the two groups, one of which is successful for optimization, the other of which failed optimization. We may construct the average utility by

$$pu_1 + (1-p)u_2,$$

where p is the ratio of the failure subgroup (Fig. 14.3).

[5] If $\Delta G = 0$, it holds the simple birth-and -death process.

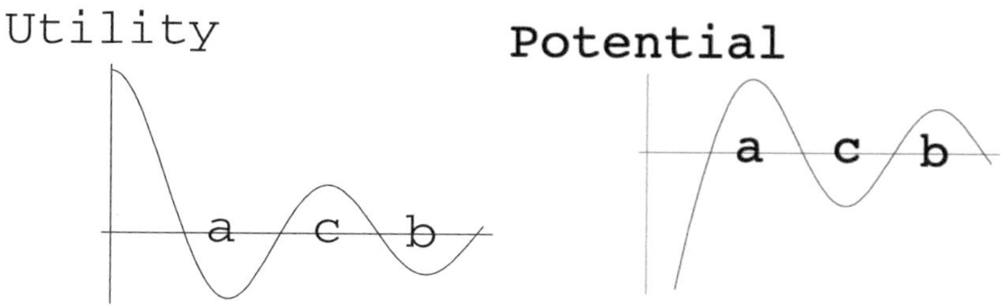

Fig. 14.3 Utility and potential

The state point a and b are the equilibrium points. Between them we imagine a Markov process by employing the transition rates[6]

$$
\begin{aligned}
w_{ab} &= \mathrm{e}^{-\beta(V+v)} \\
w_{ba} &= \mathrm{e}^{-\beta V}, \ \beta > 0.
\end{aligned}
$$

On the side of potential, we assume

$$v = V_b - V_a > 0.$$

It then follows from the Eq. (14.4) that

$$\pi_a = \frac{w_{ba}}{w_{ba} + w_{ab}} = \frac{1}{\mathrm{e}^{\eta v + 1}} \tag{14.27}$$

$$\pi_b = 1 - \pi_a = \frac{\mathrm{e}^{\beta v}}{\mathrm{e}^{\beta v + 1} + 1}. \tag{14.28}$$

If v is taken small enough,

$$\pi_a \approx \pi_b \to \frac{1}{2}.$$

This system then has equally **two local equilibria**. Either of them can equally occur.

First passage times of unstable dynamics

Measured in the levels of potential, the figure suggests an unstable situation of the macroeconomic states. There are three critical points arranged as

$$\phi_a \geq \phi_b \geq \phi_c.$$

Here ϕ is a macroeconomic state. We take ϕ_a the initial state and ϕ_c the final state. The final state may be interpreted an absorbing state (Fig. 14.4).

---

[6] As β changes, the number of equilibrium changes.

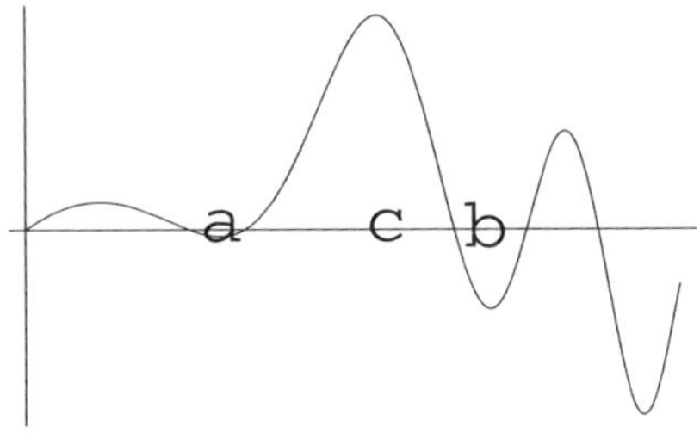

Fig. 14.4 Critical states in terms of potential

van Kampen (1992) and Aoki (1996) showed that a **passage time** τ_{ca} from c to a is given by

$$\tau_{ca} \propto e^{\beta N V(v)}.$$

> **the critical values** of the potential are the critical points of the equilibrium probability distribution $[P_i(n)]$ and are the same as **the critical points** of the macroeconomic dynamics. (Aoki, 1996, 142)

14.3 Preliminaries for the Stochastic Cluster Dynamics in the Case that Types are Unknown

14.3.1 The Elementary Polya Process

Now we turn to illustrate an elementary **Polya Urn Process**, which was just introduced into Economics by Brian Arhtur, **Snata Fe Institute** and also generalized by him and others,[7] which has been applicable to illustrate *a path-dependent process* as well as to confirm an evolutionary end point like industrial locational by spin-off, and a dual autocatalytic chemical reaction, and the like[8] According to Arthur, **Polya Urn Process**, which was formulated by Polya, Eggenbarger (1923), can be illustrated as follows:

> Think of an urn of infinite capacity to which are added balls of two possible colors - red and white, say. Starting with one red and one white ball in the urn, add a ball each time, indefinitely, according to the rule: Choose a ball in the urn at random and replace it: if it is red, add a red; if it is white, add a white. Obviously this process has increments that are path-dependent - at any time the probability that the next ball added is red exactly equals the proportion. We might then ask: does the proportion of red (or white) balls wander indefinitely between zero and one, or does a strong law operate, so that the proportion settles down to a limit, causing a structure to emerge?

[7] Yuri M. Ermoliev and Yuri M. Kaniovski, the Glushkov Institute of Cybernetics, Kiev, Ukraina, originally have proved some generalized theorems.
[8] See Chaps. 3, 7 and 10 in Arthur (1994).

Arthur called a limit **proportion** in such a path dependent stochastic process an asymptotic **structure**. As long as the classical proposition of two balls is considered, we shall be faced with a limit of proportion, *i.e.*, a simple structure, as George Polya proved in Polya (1931). In the classical Polya example, we have a restriction such that the probability of adding a ball of type j exactly equals the proportion of type j. In the following, we will see a generalization of Polya urn process of n different balls (types) which Arthur challenged in cooperation with Ukranian mathematicians, and furthermore a more generalization to **the Ewens distribution** in Ewens (1990).

The original Polya urn model

Suppose k kinds of balls $\alpha_1, \alpha_2, ..., \alpha_k$ in an urn. Here we introduce the stochastic variables $X_1, X_2, ..., X_k$ to regard X_k as the ball colored k. These balls may be distinguished by color, weight, and so on. Take out a ball, check the color of the ball, and add the same colored ball to the urn. Repeat the same procedure n times to take n_j balls. It is then generated $n = n_1 + \cdots + n_k$ in total. Hence there are $\alpha_j + n$ balls in the urn. Thus the probability to take the ball colored j is $\frac{\alpha_j + n_j}{\alpha + n}$. Here it is noted that the emergence of colors is irrelevant to the order of color emergence. This circumstance is relevant to the idea of exchangeability to be illustrated soon later. At this stage, $X_1, X_2, ..., X_n$ are the stochastic variable of exchangeability. In this view, we regard the state vector of the Polya distribution function as follows:

$$n = (n_1, n_2, ..., n_k).$$

Denote the set of color i by S_i. Thus we can represent the probability to take the ball colored j in the following manner:

$$Pr(X_{n+1} \in S_j | n_1, N_2, ..., N_k) = \frac{\alpha_j + n_j}{\alpha + n}. \tag{14.29}$$

Here $\alpha = \sum_{i=1}^{k} \alpha_i$. As for a state vector n and $n' \neq n$, it holds the detailed balance condition:

$$\pi(n)p(n'|n) = \pi(n')p(n|n'). \tag{14.30}$$

Hence we obtain the detailed balance condition in this case:

A derivation of the Polya distribution function

We specify n' as a state where an agent of type j transitions to the agent of type k as follows:

$$n' = n - e_j + e_k.$$

Here e_j is the unit vector where only j-th component is 1 excepting all the others 0. In order to confirm the detailed balance condition on this transition, we can refer to the next probabilities as follows: The probability that an agent of type j leaves by one:

$$P(n - e_j | n) = \frac{n_j}{n}.$$

The probability that an agent of type k enter by one:

$$P(n + e_k|n) = \frac{\alpha_k + n_k}{\alpha + n}.$$

The probability that an agent of type j transitions type k, also an agent of type k enters:

$$P(n - e_j + e_k|n - e_j) = \frac{\alpha_k + n_k}{\alpha + n - 1}. \tag{14.31}$$

Thus, assuming the stationary distribution to be the form of

$$\pi(n) = \pi_1(n_1)\pi_2(n_2)\cdots\pi_k(n_k), \tag{14.32}$$

it follows the next relationship:

$$\pi(n) = \frac{P(n|n')}{P(n'|n)}\pi(n') = \frac{n_k + 1}{n_j}\frac{\alpha_j + n_j - 1}{\alpha_k + n_k}\pi(n'). \tag{14.33}$$

Hence we can assure for $l = 1, \ldots, k$:

$$\pi_l(n_l) = c\frac{\alpha_l + n_l - 1}{n_l}\pi_l(n_l - 1) \tag{14.34}$$

Here c is some constant.[9] By the successive iteration,[10] we found that $\pi_l(n_l)$ would be proportional to $\frac{\alpha_i^{[n_i]}}{n_i!}$., i.e.,

$$\pi(n) = \Pi_{l=1}^k \pi_l(n_l) \propto \Pi_{i=1}^k \frac{\alpha_i^{[n_i]}}{n_i!}. \tag{14.35}$$

Under the condition $\sum_n^k \pi(n) = 1$, it holds:

$$\pi(n) = \frac{n!}{\alpha^{[n]}}\Pi_{i=1}^k \frac{\alpha_i^{[n_i]}}{n!} = \frac{n!}{n_1!\cdots n_k!}\frac{\Pi_{i=1}^n \alpha_i^{[n_i]}}{\alpha^{[n_i]}} \tag{14.36}$$

We then call this expression **the Polya distribution function**.

9

$$\frac{\pi_j(n_j)}{\pi_j(n_j - 1)}\frac{n_j}{\alpha_j + n_j - 1} = \frac{\pi_k(n_k + 1)}{\pi_k(n_k)}\frac{n_{k+1}}{\alpha_k + n_k} = c.$$

10 It is noted that

$$\alpha_l^{[n_l]} = \alpha_l(\alpha_l + 1)\cdots(\alpha_l + n_l - 1).$$

This is called the ascending factorial. Hence it then holds:

$$\frac{1}{n_l!}\alpha_l(\alpha_l + 1)\cdots(\alpha_l + n_l - 1) = \frac{\alpha_l^{[n_l]}}{n_l!}.$$

From the Polya distribution to the Dirichlet distribution

It is quite useful in practice to know the approximation. Let the population of agents to be composed by agent type j whose ratio is allocated by p_j for $\sum_{j=1}^{k} p_j = 1$ for $p_j \geq 0$ which is defined on:

$$\Delta = \left\{ p_i \geq 0, i = 1, ..., k, \sum_{j=1}^{k} p_j = 1 \right\}.$$

Given the types of agent that there are n heterogenous agents, this ratio is then will be represented by **the multinomial distribution** for a partition vector $n = (n_1, ..., n_k)$:

$$\Pr(n) = \frac{n!}{n_1! \cdots n_k!} p_1^{n_1} \cdots p_k^{n_k}.$$

With $K \geq 2$ the probability distribution δ_K with a simple structure is defined on the simplex δ_K by the density

$$\frac{\Gamma\left(\sum_{i=1}^{K} a_i\right)}{\Pi_{i=1}^{K} \Gamma(a_i)} \Pi_{i=1}^{K} p_i^{a_i - 1}$$

where $1 \geq p_i \geq 0, i = 1, 2, ..., K - 1$, and p_k is substituted out by $1 - p_1 - p_2 - \cdots p_{K-1}$, so that the density is defined for $K - 1$ variables, $p_1, p_2, ..., p_{K-1}$. This called the **Dirichlet distribution**. Aoki (2002, 230).

In the case that the the expression of $1 - p_1 - p_2 - \cdots p_{K-1}$ is unchanged for any replacement of indices $1, 2, ..., k$, i.e., types are *exchangeable*, it then holds the *symmetric* Dirichlet distribution $\vartheta(p, \alpha)$ for some parameter $\alpha \geq 0$.

$$\Phi(p_1, p_2, ..., p_k) = \frac{\Gamma(k\alpha)}{\Gamma(\alpha)^k} (p_1, ..., p_k)^{\alpha - 1}. \tag{14.37}$$

In short, according to Aoki, it follows:

Chen (1978) introduced a distribution that a mixure of multinomial distribution where the mixture is a symmetric (exchangeable) Dirichlet distribution, and has shown that his Dirichlet-multinomial distribution reduces to the Bose-Einstein and Maxwell-Bolzmann distributions. Aoki (1996, 13)

In the later section when we deal with the majority voting paradox, we will employ an approximation of the Polya distribution by the Dirichlet continuous distribution if n is a large number.

Among excellent evolutionary models of evolutionary economics, I have learned the Polya urn distribution from Brian Arthur (1994), and also learned the Master equation from Weidlich (2000). These studies have decisively been influential to renovate my way of thinking about the emergence of events in general until I meet the works of Masanao Aoki. In retrospect, the latter works have been different in the standpoint to observe the events, although either works are dealing with the same kinds of nonlinear phenomena. In particular, in the finite discrete domain, Aoki mainly focused on the economic motions of heterogeneous agents whose activities can be be categorized by *type selection*, but those can be *exchangeable*. The latter characteristics may be in line with *Bose-Einstein* form of **the classic occupancy problem**, contrary to the distinguishable *Maxwell-Boltzmann* form.

Definition

Two vectors x and y are called exchangeable if the empirical distribution of the two vectors are the same.

14.3.2 A Flat Prior for Our Stochastic Dynamics

We are interested in studying the evolution allowing the advent of new types, under which circumstances Bayesian approach is invalid. Also in Bayesian approach, if we have no prior information available, a commonly used non-information prior distribution has a uniform distribution as Non-informative, NI it then is called **a flat prior distribution**. Alternatively, we must look for **a specific prior** for our own purpose.

de Finetti representation Aoki (2002, 220–1)

Suppose each of the exchangeable sequences whose frequency vector is the same to be equally probable. It then holds

$$\Pr(X_1, X_2, ..., X_n \mid n) = \frac{n_1!n_2! \cdots n_K!}{n!}$$

where $n = n_1 + n_2 + \cdots + n_K$. The observed frequency counts n_j are called **sufficient statistics.**[11]

We have **the de Finetti representation theorem** for exchangeable sequences: if an infinite sequence of k-valued random variables $X_1, X_2, ...$ is exchangeable, then the infinite limiting frequency

$$Z := \lim_{N\to\infty} \left(\frac{n_1}{N}, \frac{n_2}{N}, \cdots, \frac{n_K}{N}\right),$$

and if $\mu(A) = \Pr(Z \in A)$ denotes the distribution of this limiting frequency, then,

$$\Pr(X_1 = e_1, X_2 = e_2, ..., X_N = e_N)$$
$$= \int_{\Delta_K} p_1^{n_1} p_2^{n_2} \cdots p_K^{n_K} \, d\mu(p_1, p_2, ..., p_{K-1}).$$

[11] These probabilities conditional on the frequency counts depend only on n. They also are independent of the choice of the exchangeable probability P.

Johnson sufficientness postulate

Here we show the derivation of a flat prior for our stochastic dynamics. By virtue of **Johnson sufficientness postulate**, it uniquely determines $d\mu$[12] as a flat prior as follows:

$$\Pr(X_{N+1} = c_i | X_1, X_2, ..., X_N) = \Pr(X_{N+1} = c_i | n) = f(n_i, n), \tag{14.38}$$

if $\Pr(X_1 = c_1, ..., X_N = c_N) > 0$ for all c's.

14.3.3 The Partition Vector and the Transition Rates

The multinomial distribution will not be applied to the case that the types of agents in the economic system are *unknown*. In such a circumstance, it does not hold the Bayesian learning may be valid. Instead of using **the state vector**, we rather use **the partition vector** $a = (a_1, a_2, ..., a_n)$ where its component a_j is the number of boxes in which there are j balls. That is to say, we study the so-called occupancy problem in the case of n indistinguishable balls. In Aoki (2003), it is mentioned several application examples to explain the the partition vector: $a_{50} = 3$ means 3 different rules which 50 traders currently use when traders are dealing with financial commodities. If we take an example of insect collecting, $a_4 = 5$ means 5 subsets in which group there are 4 insects of the same kind each. The subset of these groups may be called the cluster of size i.

It is trivial that

$$a_j = 0 \text{ for } j = 1, ..., n-1; a_n = 1, .$$

if all the agents use the same rule.

$$a_1 = n, a_j = 0 \text{ for } j = 2, ..., n, .$$

if each agent follows each independent rule.

If we assume that agents are not distinguishable even in different categories, that is, exchangeable in the technical terminology of the probability literature then the total number of possible configurations is given by

$$W(N) = \Pi_j \frac{(N_j + g_j - 1)!}{N_j!(g_j - 1)!},$$

where g_j is the number of possible microeconomic states that an agent can assume.[13] Aoki (1996, 13).

12

$$d\mu(p_1, p_2, ..., p_K) = d(p_1, p_2, ..., p_{K-1}).$$

13 Recall that the number of ways n identical balls can be placed in g boxes is given by $(n + g - 1)!/n!(g - 1)!$.

Type i belongs to a subset of size i. This subset is called the cluster. Here,

$$a_i = \#\{n_j = i, j = 1, ..., k\}, i = 1, ..., n..$$

If we introduce the following function

$$\chi_j(i) = \begin{cases} 1, & n_j = i \\ 0, & n_j \neq i \end{cases}.$$

$$a_i = \sum_{j=1}^{K} \chi_j(i).$$

In this context, by the use of transition rate among the clusters, we can derive the stationary equilibrium state distribution. Suppose to be n discrete number of clusters categorized by the finite types among where each agent freely moves. If one quits from the cluster size of j, the size of its cluster a_j will be reduced $a_j - 1$, correspondingly while a_{j-1} will be $a_{j-1} + 1$. If we define

$$u_j = e_j - e_{j-1},^{14}$$

it then holds the conditional[14] transition rate:

$$P(a - u|a) = \frac{ja_j}{n}. \tag{14.39}$$

Conversely, if an agent joins in the crowds of size j, a crowd of size $j + 1$ increases while the crowds of size j will be reduced by one. The transition rate of this event, which means that an agent leaves from the crowd of size j and joins in a crowd of size $i - 1$, will be described as follows:

$$\Pr(a - u_j + u_i|a - u_j).$$

14.3.4 From Negative Binomial Distribution to Ewens Distribution

Now we are ready to derive the equilibrium distribution as an **Ewens distribution**.

[14] e_j is a unit vector where the j-th component is 1 while all the components except for j are zero.

14.3.4.1 Example 1

We firstly assume the transition rates in the next three different manners:

$w(a, a + e_1) = \nu\lambda$:	Agents enter in the system but do not belong to any existing boxes. New agents then form e_1, a subset of size 1.
$w(a, a + u_{j+1} = \lambda j a_j)$:	An agent joins by one in the crowd of size j.
$w(a, a - u_{j+1} = \mu j a_j)$:	An agent exits by one from the crowd of size j.

It hen holds the detailed balance condition:

$$\pi(a)w(a, a + u_{j+1} = \pi(a + u_{j+1})w(a + u_{j+1}, a). \tag{14.40}$$

Thus the equilibrium distribution of this case will be solved as follows:

$$\pi(a) = \left(1 - \frac{\lambda}{\mu}\right) \Pi_{j=1}^{\infty} \frac{\beta_j^{[a_j]}}{a_j!}.^{15} \tag{14.41}$$

Here it is defined:[15]

$$\beta_j = \frac{\nu}{j}\left(\frac{\lambda}{\mu}\right)^j,$$

$$\beta_j^{[a_j]} = \beta_j(\beta_j + 1) \cdots (\beta_j + a_j).$$

14.3.4.2 Example 2

Similarly in the above argument, suppose the transition rate of entry to be

$$w(n, n + e_j) = \frac{h_i + n_i}{h + n}.$$

Here $h = \sum_{i=1}^{K} h_i$, $n = \sum_{i}^{K} n_i$. It then holds the recursive relationship from the detailed balance condition for $j = 1, ..., K, n_j \geq 0$.

$$\pi_j(n_j) = (\frac{c_j}{d_j})\frac{n_j - 1 + h_j}{n_j}\pi_j(n_j - 1) \tag{14.42}$$

[15] By taking into account the next formula,

$$\frac{1}{(1 - x)^{\nu}} = \Pi_{j=1}^{\infty} \exp \frac{\nu x^j}{j},$$

it is easily verified $\sum_a \pi(a) = 1$.

We then confirm the next **negative binomial expression**:

$$\pi_j(n_j) = c_j \binom{-h_j}{n_j} \left(-\frac{c_j}{d_j}\right)^{n_j} \tag{14.43}$$

Thus the stationary distribution of this system will be given:

$$\pi(n) = \binom{-\sum_j h_j}{\sum_j n_j}^{-1} \Pi_{j=1}^{K} \binom{-h_j}{n_j} \tag{14.44}$$

For simplicity, let c_j/d_j to be all common to g for all j. It then holds

$$\pi(n) = \frac{n!}{h^{[n]}} \Pi_{j=1}^{k} \frac{h_j^{[n_j]}}{n_j!}. \tag{14.45}$$

14.3.5 On the Well-Known Probability Distributions Surrounding the Negative Binomial Distribution

The negative binomial expression will be described as follows:

$$\begin{aligned}\binom{-n}{k} &= \frac{(-n)(-n-1)\cdots(-n-k-1)}{k!} \\ &= \frac{(n)(n+1)\cdots(n+k-1)}{k!}(-1)^k \\ &= \binom{n+k-1}{k}\end{aligned}$$

Finally, it may be useful for the reader to discuss the well-known probability distributions surrounding the negative binomial distribution and their relationships below.

The relationships between gemometric, negative binomial, exponential, and gamma distributions are represented in Table 14.1.

The exponential distribution is a distribution representing the interval between random events such as the interval between earthquakes or the life of a light bulb. A random phenomenon follows an exponential distribution if considered in terms of

Table 14.1 The relationships between gemometric, negative binomial, exponential, and gamma distributions

		serialization of k	
conversion	Geometric dist.	$\Longrightarrow$	Negative binomial dist
to continuous	$\Downarrow$		$\Downarrow$
time	Exponential dist	$\Longrightarrow$	Gamma dist

the interval between occurrences, and a Poisson distribution if considered in terms of the number of occurrences. Let μ be averaged over a long period of time.

Find each expected value and each variance of both distributions respectively.

The negative binomial distribution is the distribution followed by the number of times it takes to succeed k times when iterating a trial such that it succeeds with probability p. The expected valu to be $\frac{k}{p}$. Its variance is $\frac{k(1-p)}{p^2}$. Incidentally, Then the times how many failed before succeeding k times is $\frac{k}{p} - 1 = \frac{k(1-p)}{p}$.

The geometric distribution $P(n) = (1-p)^{n-1}p$ is the distribution representing the number of times k until the first success if the same trial is iterated. The expected valu is $\frac{1}{p}$. Its variance is $\frac{1-p}{p^2}$. The times of consecutive failures until a success is attained then is $\frac{1}{p} - 1$.

As mentioned above, the exponential distribution represents the distribution of the time it takes for a random event that occurs about once every period μ to occur once. If $X_1, \ldots, X_n$ follow an exponential distribution with mean μ independently of each other, $Y = X_1 + \cdots + X_n$ follows a gamma distribution wiht mean μ and n. Its variance is $n\mu^2$. It is noted that n need not be an integer. The gamma distribution is represented as follows:

$$f(x) = x^{n-1} \frac{e^{-\frac{x}{\mu}}}{\Gamma(n)\mu^n} (x \geqq 0)$$

Here $\Gamma(n) = (n-1)!$.

14.4 Majority Rule for Voting and the Tree Structure

In social choice theory, it is quite well known the Possibility Theorem proven by Arrow (1951), when one must choose an alternative from a given multiple alternatives. That is to say, the transitivity rule socially generated by the voting aggregation will cause a social contradiction, i.e., a possibility that only one agent may fulfill any social outcome of socially formed ordering by the majority voting. This is a logically inferred deduction. In the context of Prof. Aoki, however, this possibility may be neglected if the number of alternatives is large.[16] Incidentally, this part has not been found either in Aoki (1996; 2002) in this books of the fifth stage. So we then deserve referring to this example.

14.4.1 A Stochastic Assessment on the Majority Voting Rule

According to Aoki (2002, 78–79), it is shown that there may be few emergence of Arrow's contradiction by applying the Polya urn theory. Let K be 3 in the following.

[16] The stream of a probablistic view on Arrow's theorem was initiated by Wiiliamson and Sargent (1967). As for Sen's theorem in view of a probablistic theory, see Li and Saari (2008). Also see Aruka (2015) on an assessment of the standard choice theory in view of imperfect identification.

By the Polya theory, we attach color respectively each ordering of the alternative A, B, C. Suppose to allocate 6 different colors to the next ordering:

$$A \succ B \succ C, A \succ C \succ B, B \succ A \succ C, A \succ C \succ A, C \succ A \succ B, C \succ A \succ B.$$

Suppose also n to be:

$$n = n_1 + n_2 + \cdots + n_6 \text{ for } i = 1, 2, ..., 6$$

Thus it follows the partition vector on the concerned distribution that

$$P(n) = \frac{n!}{n_1! n_2! \cdots n_6!} \frac{a^{[\sigma,n_1]} \ldots a^{[\sigma,n_6]}}{6a^{[\sigma,n_6]}}. \tag{14.46}$$

Here $a^{[\sigma,n]}$ is the ascending factorial:

$$a^{[\sigma,n]} = a(a+\sigma)(a+2\sigma)\cdots(a+(n-1)\sigma).$$

The expression (14.46) means in the Polya urn that there exist a balls in the urn at the beginning, and after identifying the color of taken balls, σ balls of the same colored in return added in the urn. It is then denoted q by a/σ.

$$q = \frac{a}{\sigma}$$

Whilst applying the **Stirling formula** for large factorials to q,[17] it holds:

$$a^{[\sigma,n]} = a(a+\sigma)(a+2\sigma)\cdots(a+(n-1)\sigma) \tag{14.47}$$
$$= \sigma^n q(1+q)(2+q)\cdots(n_{i-1}+q) \tag{14.48}$$
$$\simeq \sigma^n \frac{\Gamma(n_i+q)}{\Gamma(q)}. \tag{14.49}$$

Hence

$$P(n) \sim \sigma^n \frac{\Gamma(6q)}{\Gamma(q)^6} \Pi_{i=1}^6 p_i^{q-1} \tag{14.50}$$

Here

$$p_i = \frac{n_i}{n} \geq 0, \sum_{i=1}^{6} p_i = 1.$$

[17] $\Gamma(n_i+q) \simeq \sqrt{2\pi} e^{-n_i} n_i^{n_i+q-(1/2)}$.

Aoki (2003, 86–87) has shown that the alternative A will be assesed as the majority among the alternatives if the above density function is integrable on the domain that

$$p_1 + p_2 + p_3 \geq \frac{1}{2} \text{ and } p_1 + p_2 + p_5 \geq \frac{1}{2}. \tag{14.51}$$

these conditions naturally imply that

$$A \succ C \text{ and } A \succ B$$

both hold, then always confirm A as the majority. This situation will naturally remove the Arrow paradox.

14.4.2 A Tree Dynamics

On the contrary, it is interestingly to see an ultimate attainment through the transitions among the leaves of alternative orderings, when starting from an initial conditions (14.51). We firstly construct a tree dynamics by applying the ultrametrics to the tree structure represented by Fig. 14.5 to obtain the next master equation system on the transition dynamics among the alternatives. In the case of our tree structure, it is seen that

$$d(1,2) = d(2,1) = d(3,4) = d(4,3) = d(5,6) = d(6,5) = \epsilon_1 = 1$$

As for the other pairs of (i, j),

$$d(i, j) = d(j, i) = \epsilon_2 = 2.$$

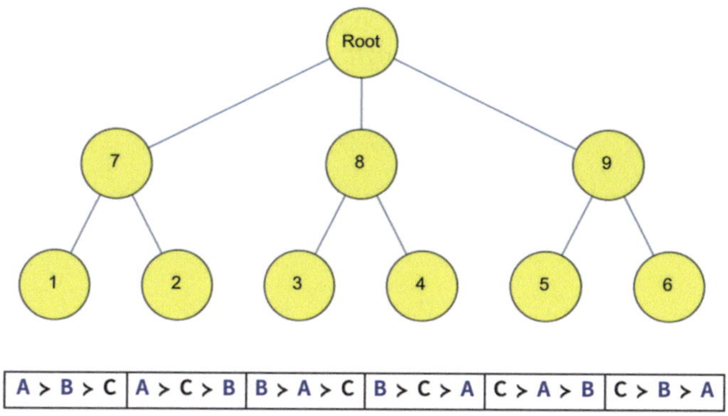

Fig. 14.5 Majority rule and the ultrametrics

Hence we can formulate the transition state equation system on this transition dynamics:

$$
\begin{aligned}
p_1'(t) &= \epsilon_1\left(p_2(t)-p_1(t)\right)+\epsilon_2\left(-4p_1(t)+p_3(t)+p_4(t)+p_5(t)+p_6(t)\right)\\
p_2'(t) &= \epsilon_1\left(p_1(t)-p_2(t)\right)+\epsilon_2\left(-4p_2(t)+p_3(t)+p_4(t)+p_5(t)+p_6(t)\right)\\
p_3'(t) &= \epsilon_1\left(p_4(t)-p_3(t)\right)+\epsilon_2\left(p_1(t)+p_2(t)-4p_3(t)+p_5(t)+p_6(t)\right)\\
p_4'(t) &= \epsilon_1\left(p_3(t)-p_4(t)\right)+\epsilon_2\left(p_1(t)+p_2(t)-4p_4(t)+p_5(t)+p_6(t)\right)\\
P_5'(t) &= \epsilon_1\left(p_6(t)-p_5(t)\right)+\epsilon_2\left(p_1(t)+p_2(t)+p_3(t)+p_4(t)-4p_5(t)\right)\\
p_6'(t) &= \epsilon_1\left(p_5(t)-p_6(t)\right)+\epsilon_2\left(p_1(t)+p_2(t)+p_3(t)+p_4(t)-4p_6(t)\right)
\end{aligned}
\tag{14.52}
$$

We then look for the initial values to satisfy the conditions (14.51). We may then allocate the initial values such that

$$p_1(0)=0.2,\ p_2(0)=0.2,\ p_3(0)=0.2,\ p_4(0)=0.1,\ p_5(0)=0.2,\ p_6(0)=0.2.$$

It then holds that

$$
\begin{aligned}
p_1(t) &= 0.166667e^{-6t\epsilon_2-2t(\epsilon_1+2\epsilon_2)}\left(0.2e^{2t(\epsilon_1+2\epsilon_2)}+1.e^{6t\epsilon_2+2t(\epsilon_1+2\epsilon_2)}\right),\\
p_2(t) &= 0.166667e^{-6t\epsilon_2-2t(\epsilon_1+2\epsilon_2)}\left(0.2e^{2t(\epsilon_1+2\epsilon_2)}+1.e^{6t\epsilon_2+2t(\epsilon_1+2\epsilon_2)}\right),\\
p_3(t) &= 0.166667e^{-6t\epsilon_2-2t(\epsilon_1+2\epsilon_2)}\left(0.3e^{6t\epsilon_2}-0.1e^{2t(\epsilon_1+2\epsilon_2)}+1.e^{6t\epsilon_2+2t(\epsilon_1+2\epsilon_2)}\right),\\
p_4(t) &= 0.166667e^{-6t\epsilon_2-2t(\epsilon_1+2\epsilon_2)}\left(-0.3e^{6t\epsilon_2}-0.1e^{2t(\epsilon_1+2\epsilon_2)}+1.e^{6t\epsilon_2+2t(\epsilon_1+2\epsilon_2)}\right),\\
p_5(t) &= 0.166667e^{-6t\epsilon_2-2t(\epsilon_1+2\epsilon_2)}\left(0.3e^{6t\epsilon_2}-0.1e^{2t(\epsilon_1+2\epsilon_2)}+1.e^{6t\epsilon_2+2t(\epsilon_1+2\epsilon_2)}\right),\\
p_6(t) &= 0.166667e^{-6t\epsilon_2-2t(\epsilon_1+2\epsilon_2)}\left(-0.3e^{6t\epsilon_2}-0.1e^{2t(\epsilon_1+2\epsilon_2)}+1.e^{6t\epsilon_2+2t(\epsilon_1+2\epsilon_2)}\right).
\end{aligned}
\tag{14.53}
$$

Now we may examine how our transition system will eventually evolve into the final situation, according to each initial condition. We focus on the first condition of $p_1(0)=0.2$, $p_2(0)=0.2$, $p_3(0)=0.2$ to how the ratio will be changed by transition among the nodes.

$$p_1+p_2+p_3\to 0.51 \text{ as } t\to\infty.$$

It is interesting to know that $A\succ C$ will still be guaranteed as the majority. As for on the second condition of $p_1(0)=0.2$, $p_2(0)=0.2$, $p_r50)=0.2$, it also then holds:

$$p_1+p_2+p_5\to 0.51 \text{ as } t\to\infty.$$

This suggests that $A\succ B$ will still be guaranteed as the majorityness. In summing up, the majority of A will be eventually guaranteed even through transition among the nodes if we start the initial ratio of $p_1(0)=0.2$, $p_2(0)=0.2$, $p_3(0)=0.2$, $p_4(0)=0.1$, $p_5(0)=0.2$, $p_6(0)=0.1$. Finally, it is noted that Figs 14.6 and 14.7 are formally the same shaped because the particular solutions are the same forms.

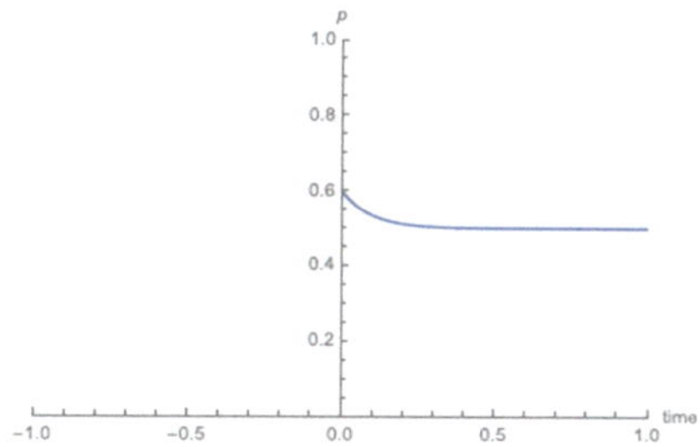

Fig. 14.6 Trajectory of $p_1(t) + p_2(t) + p_3(t)$ given the initial condition $p_1(0) = 0.2$, $p_2(0) = 0.2$, $p_3(0) = 0.2$, $p_4(0) = 0.1$, $p_5(0) = 0.2$, $p_6(0) = 0.1$

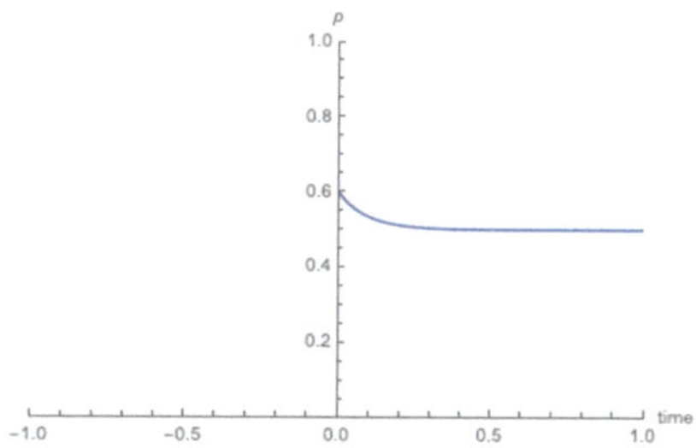

Fig. 14.7 Trajectory of $p_1(t) + p_2(t) + p_5(t)$ given the initial condition $p_1(0) = 0.2$, $p_2(0) = 0.2$, $p_3(0) = 0.2$, $p_4(0) = 0.1$, $p_5(0) = 0.2$, $p_6(0) = 0.1$

Exercises

14.1 Using the simulator by "Cawley J, Meinberg, F. Macroeconomic effects of interest rate cuts" (Cawley & Meinberg, 2011), choose an index and policy enforcement period of your choice and find a "case of conflicting effects," and review why the desired effect did not resulted in the concerned period. Note: Use Wolfram Demonstrations Project: http://demonstrations.wolfram.com/MacroeconomicEffectsOfInterestRateCuts/.

14.2 Money holdings generated from random money transfers presented in Sect. 10.2.1.1 was expressed in a continuous form to formulate a Boltzmann-Gibbs (exponential) distribution. Compare this contiuous form with the Boltzmann-Gibbs distribution in a discrete form.

14.3 In Chap. 9, the Luce-Saari theory of choice was studied. In this framework, we are faced two kinds of problem of voting/ranking profiles and probability profiles. In this cicumstance, the ranking problem is not necessarily uniquely solved. Arrow's paradox will be then eliminated in Saari's construction. On the other hand, another elimination of Arrow's paradox has been suggested in this chapter. Examine behind the scenes of this way above and Saari's way of Chap. 9 on how to remove the paradox, and check both if they are equivalent.

14.4 The choice theory is reconsidered in a form of stochastic process above. Verify to make n bigger to reduce $P(n)$ in the expression (14.50).

14.5 Evaluate the pros and cons of ultrametrics when applied to voting rules.

14.6 Let $S = a, b$ be a Markov system $x(t)$ with state space. The probability that the state variable $X(t)$ takes the value a is

$$P_a(t) = \Pr(X(t) = a).$$

The probability that the state variable X(t) takes the value a is. In this case, the master equation is

$$\frac{dP_a(t)}{dt} = w_{ba}P_b(t) - w_{ab}P_a(t) \tag{14.54}$$

Specify the transition rates as follows:

$$w_{ba} = e^{-\beta V} \tag{14.55}$$
$$w_{ab} = e^{-\beta(V+\tau)} \tag{14.56}$$
$$w_{ba} > w_{ab} \tag{14.57}$$

Verify that the transition from b to a appears with highe probability than the transition from a to b.

14.7 A two-level asymmetric tree with five states is shown in Fig. 14.8. Then specify the transition matrix W as follows:

$$W = \begin{pmatrix} -\epsilon_1 - 3\epsilon_2 & \epsilon_1 & \epsilon_2 & \epsilon_2 & \epsilon_2 \\ \epsilon_1 & -\epsilon_1 - 3\epsilon_2 & \epsilon_2 & \epsilon_2 & \epsilon_2 \\ \epsilon_2 & \epsilon_2 & -2(\epsilon_1 + \epsilon_2) & \epsilon_1 & \epsilon_1 \\ \epsilon_2 & \epsilon_2 & \epsilon_1 & -2(\epsilon_1 + \epsilon_2) & \epsilon_1 \\ \epsilon_2 & \epsilon_2 & \epsilon_1 & \epsilon_1 & -2(\epsilon_1 + \epsilon_2) \end{pmatrix} \tag{14.58}$$

Define the transition dynamics in terms of the differential equation system, and solve it.

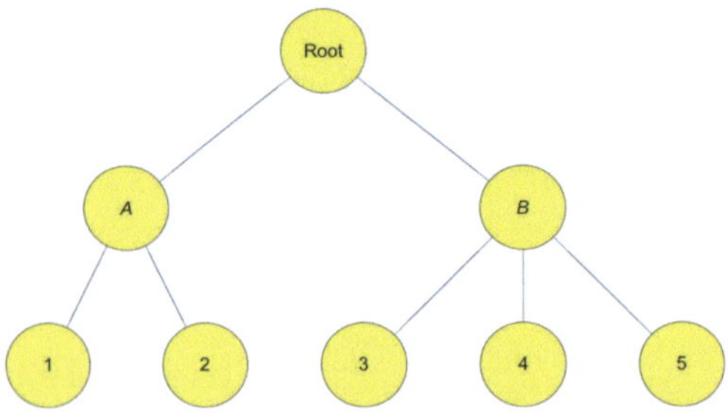

Fig. 14.8 A two-level asymmetric tree with five states. * This figure is adopted from Aoki (2003, 87)

14.8 If the initial conditions are set $p_1(0) = 1, p_2(0) = 0, p_3(0) = 0, p_4(0) = 0, p_5(0) = 0$, the solutions are given as follows.

$$p_1(t) \to \frac{1}{10} e^{-5t\epsilon_2} \left(2e^{5t\epsilon_2} + 5e^{5t\epsilon_2 + t(-2\epsilon_1 - 3\epsilon_2)} + 3 \right), \tag{14.59}$$

$$p_2(t) \to -\frac{1}{10} e^{-5t\epsilon_2} \left(-2e^{5t\epsilon_2} + 5e^{5t\epsilon_2 + t(-2\epsilon_1 - 3\epsilon_2)} - 3 \right), \tag{14.60}$$

$$p_3(t) \to \frac{1}{5} e^{-5t\epsilon_2} \left(e^{5t\epsilon_2} - 1 \right), \tag{14.61}$$

$$p_4(t) \to \frac{1}{5} e^{-5t\epsilon_2} \left(e^{5t\epsilon_2} - 1 \right), \tag{14.62}$$

$$p_5(t) \to \frac{1}{5} e^{-5t\epsilon_2} \left(e^{5t\epsilon_2} - 1 \right) \tag{14.63}$$

Set the initial conditions another way, and examine a new dynamics if any.

14.9 In the same system above, specify the submatrices as follows:

$$W_{11} = \begin{pmatrix} -(\epsilon_1 + 3\epsilon_2) & \epsilon_1 \\ \epsilon_1 & -(1\epsilon_1 + 3\epsilon_2) \end{pmatrix}; W_{22} = \begin{pmatrix} -2(\epsilon_1 + \epsilon_2) & \epsilon_1 & \epsilon_1 \\ \epsilon_1 & -2(\epsilon_1 + \epsilon_2) & \epsilon_1 \\ \epsilon_1 & \epsilon_1 & -2(\epsilon_1 + \epsilon_2) \end{pmatrix} \tag{14.64}$$

Define the transition dynamics of the submatrices W_{11}, W_{22} respectively in terms of the differential equation system, and solve the subsystem dynamics A and B in Fig. 14.8.

14.10 Compare the last two exercise, and invetigate the dynamics between the entire dynamics and the subsystem dynamics A and B in Fig. 14.8.

References

Aoki, M. (1996). *New approaches to macroeconomic modeling: Evolutionary stochastic dynamics, multiple equilibria, and externalities as field effects* (p. 288). Cambridge University Press.

Aoki, M. (2002). *Modeling aggregate behavior and fluctuations in economics: Stochastic views of interacting agents* (p. 263). Cambridge University Press.

Aoki, M. (2003). *Ishitsuteki e-jennto no Kakuritsudougaku nyumon (Introduction to Stochastic Dynamic Approach of Heterogeneous Interacting Agents)* (p. 187). Kyoritisu Publishing Co., Ltd.

Aoki, M., & Yoshikawa, H. (2006). *Reconstructing macroeconomics: A perspective from statistical physics and combinatorial stochastic processes* (p. 333). Cambridge University Press.

Arthur, W. B. (1994). *Increasing returns and path dependence in the economy*, Japanese ed. University of Michigan Press.

Aruka, Y., & Akiyama, E. (2009). Non-self-averaging of a two-person game with only positive spillover: A new formulation of Avatamsaka's dilemma. *Journal of Economic Interaction and Coordination, 4*(2), 135–161.

Aruka, Y. (2015). Hodgson's bibliometric report and the reconstruction plan of economics. *Evolutionary and Institutional Economics Review, 15*(1), 189–202.

Aruka, Y., Gallegati, M., & Yoshikawa, H. (2015). Preface: Special issue in honor of Masanao Aoki. *Journal of Economic Interaction and Coordination, 10*(1), 1–4.

Cawley, J., & Meinberg, F. (2011). Macroeconomic effects of interest rate cuts. Wolfram Demonstrations Project: http://demonstrations.wolfram.com/MacroeconomicEffectsOfInterestRateCuts/

Chen, W.-C. (1978). On Zipf's law. Ph.D. dissertation. University of Michigan.

Ewens, W. J. (1990). Population genetics theory—The past and the future. In S. Lessard (Ed.), *Mathematical and statistical development of evolutionary theory* (pp. 81–104). Kluwer Academic Publishers.

Li, L., & Saari, D. G. (2008). Sen's theorem: Geometric proof, new interpretations. *Social Choice and Welfare, 31*(3), 383–413.

Namba, K. (1951). *Social choice and individual values*. Yale UP.

Polya, G., & Eggenberger, F. (1923). Über die statistik verketteter vorgange. *Zeitschrift für Angewandte Mathematik und Mechanik, 3*, 279–289.

Polya, G. (1931). Sur quelques points de la théorie des probabilités. *Annales de l'Institut Henri Poancaré, 1*, 117–161.

van Kampen, N. G. (1992). *Stochastic process in physics and chemistry*, rev. ed.

Weidlich, W. (2000). *Sociodynamics: A systematic approach to mathematical modeling in the social sciences*. Harwood Academic Publishers.

Williamson, O. E., & Sargent, T. J. (1967). Social choice: A probabilistic approach. *The Economic Journal,77*(308), 797–813.

Index

Y. Aruka, *Evolutionary Economics*, Springer Texts in Business and Economics,
https://doi.org/10.1007/978-981-97-1382-0

MIX
Papier aus verantwortungsvollen Quellen
Paper from responsible sources
FSC® C105338

If you have any concerns about our products,
you can contact us on
ProductSafety@springernature.com

In case Publisher is established outside the EU,
the EU authorized representative is:
Springer Nature Customer Service Center GmbH
Europaplatz 3, 69115 Heidelberg, Germany

Printed by Libri Plureos GmbH
in Hamburg, Germany